A VIEW FROM THE RIDGE ROUTE

VOLUME IV

THE RESOURCES

WRITTEN BY

BONNIE KETTERL KANE

ILLUSTRATED BY

SUSAN SJOBERG

First Edition

 Questions, corrections and purchase information may be directed to:

Bonnie's Books
POB 2035
Frazier Park, CA 93225

SAN 253-391X
Library of Congress Control Number:
091930 (add on)
ISBN: 0-9703992-6-X

Printed & bound in the United States of America
By: Jostens Printing and Publishing
POB 991
Visalia, CA 93279

Front Cover: see page 87

FOREWARD

If you were a member of Jesse James's band of outlaws and people asked you what you were, you wouldn't say, "Well, I'm a desperado." You'd say something like, "I work in banks," or "I've done some railroad work."

Ray Blount, Jr.

As I began this series of books, I often felt as the above quote. I was more comfortable saying that *"well, I collect history"* than that *"I am a writer of history"*. With this fourth book in the series, I now feel comfortable in calling myself a writer, but Volume 4 again shakes my comfort level. To cover the subjects of this book one needs to be a geologist, a mineralogist, a naturalist, a scientist, a hydrologist. I am none of these but have drawn on the expertise of the many who have left valuable clues to the history of the resources of the San Emigdio Mountains. With great appreciation, archival records as well as more contemporary newspaper articles and oral interviews have contributed to the information in this book.

Perhaps more than any of the other books in this series, the past written of in this volume influenced the future of our area. Mining, logging, the National Forest, the Forest Service, aqueducts and reservoirs have made us what we are today. I do believe that to know who we are we must know who we have been. Herein I have attempted to compile all the information that I located on the Resources for your review.

Please be aware that in quoted material well-known words might not be spelled as we know them today and often nouns are not capitalized as we do today.

Bonnie Ketterl Kane

VOLUME IV

TABLE OF CONTENTS

Part One

MINING

Part Two

NATIONAL FOREST

Part Three

WATER

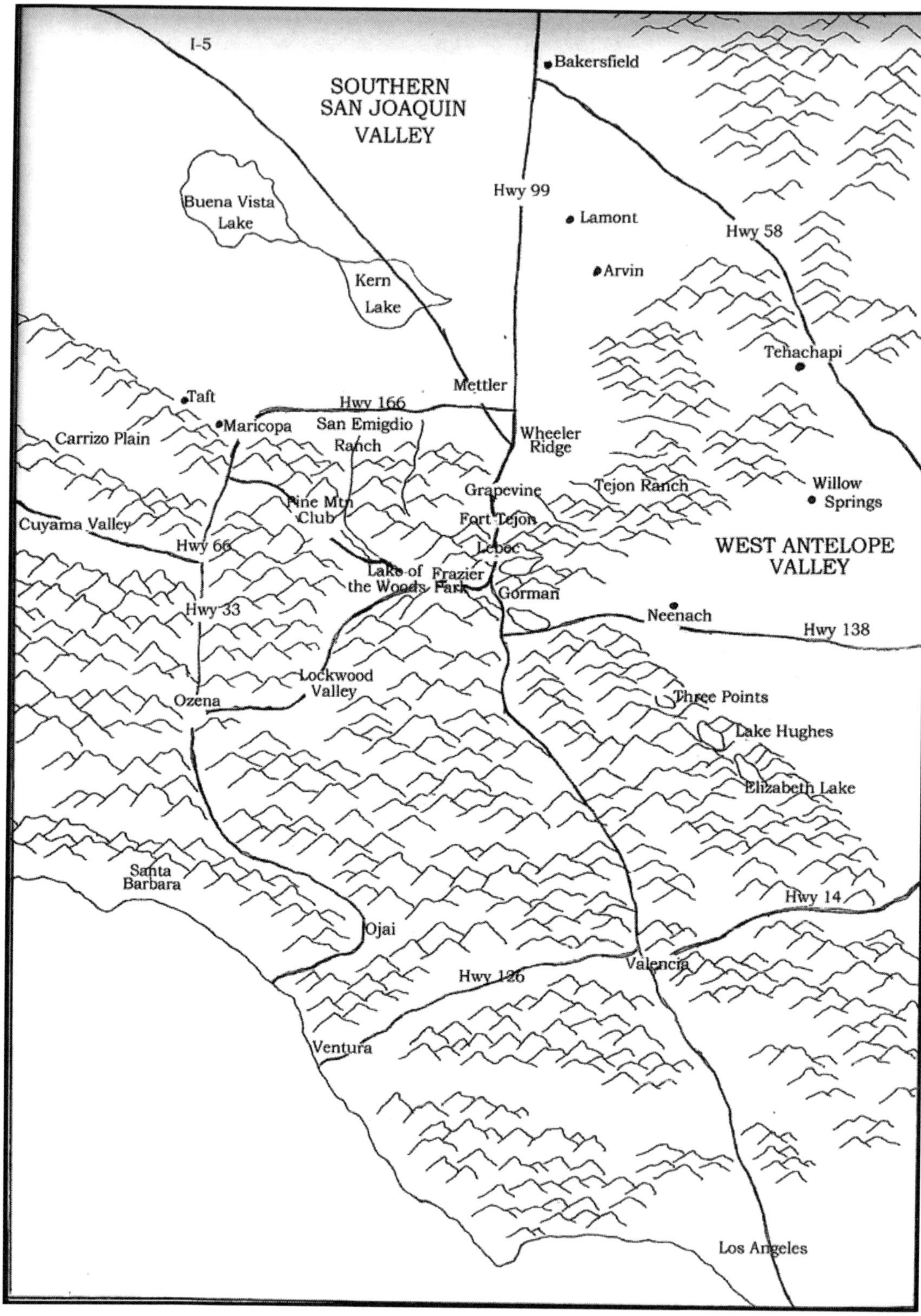

Present day map of reference to locations covered in this book

A VIEW FROM THE RIDGE ROUTE

THE RESOURCES

Part One

MINING

I - THE LOST LOS PADRES MINE

The following information has been gathered and compiled in an attempt to record some of the mining history in the area where Los Angeles, Ventura and Kern Counties meet – the San Emigdio Mountains of Southern California. In the late 1600's and 1700's, *"explorer priests"* from Spain were the first to introduce the desire for gold and mining techniques locally. In the mid-1800's the United States military post of Fort Tejon opened the area to hundreds of newcomers; many of whom stayed and were lured further into the mountains for the riches derived from mining. After the *"Gold Rush"* in Central California lost its luster thousands pursued the search for gold throughout the *"Golden State"* and the local mountains tempted many as well.

The grandest of all local mining legends to come out of these mountains is that of the "*Los Padres Mine*". Information on the earliest mining ventures of the padres is covered in Volume I of this series of books. Little is written about the first missionaries into the present area of Southern California but they were a Catholic order of Jesuits Priests from Spain who had arrived in Mexico in the late 1500's. A powerful and wealthy order of priests it seems they not only came to establish colonies in these lands new to them but also to search for precious metals. It is not known as to exactly when they might have found their way to the San Emigdio Mountains but at some point they did. They had begun using an ancient trail that came from the Southwest through the Antelope Valley, along the north side of the present Frazier Mountain and down through San Emigdio Canyon from where they traveled on to their settlement in Monterey. When the native people were shown the desired metal the explorer-priests were led to the source as the local people had found no use for it.

Mission translations indicated that gold was being taken from these mountains by the late 1600's to early 1700's. With the help of Indian laborers the gold was loaded on mules, taken across the desert, across the Colorado River and on to the Gulf of Mexico where it was shipped back to Spain. Sunken ships laden with bars of gold and other items made from gold and silver, that had probably been acquired from throughout the Southwest, have been located off the South-Eastern Coast of this country. One such ship with such treasure was recently located off the present coast of Key West, Florida and has been determined to have sunk as early as 1622 – just one of many that might have met such a fate.

Gold was also transported west to the Pacific Ocean. A historian of this mountain area in the 1970's, Joyce Campbell, found this bit of information and wrote:

"In 1754 a Spanish Galleon, the San Sebastian, went down in the Santa Barbara Channel with two million in her holds."

Santa Barbara has one of the oldest harbors on the West coast.

When the King of Spain expelled the Jesuits from Alta California the Franciscan Order of priests took their place in the late 1700's. The new priests continued the mining practices, but not as aggressively.

The following tales have been gathered from many sources. All are shared here for the reader to draw your own conclusion about the gold that was taken from the San Emigdio Mountains and about our local *"lost Los Padres Mine"* – as there were supposedly many Los Padres Mines in the Southwest.

Some of the most revealing, and among the earliest recorded accounts of the local Los Padres Mine, come from California mission archives. The following statement about the mine was taken in May of 1860 and was translated as follows:

"I, Jose Raymundo of the Mission San Buenaventura, California, am between 109 to 110 years of age. I was dedicated to the work of tapestry maker in the weaving shop, then a guard at the mission, then a team driver. After this the missionaries took me into their confidence and their secret not to reveal where the natural treasures' of the earth were.

They sent me to Tashlipun (the village at the bottom of San Emigdio Canyon). *I saw the ovens when they sent me to the Mine. I was a team driver of four mules. We would leave the mentioned ovens in a southern direction, climbing extended hills, till we climbed high mountains. About halfway of the pines we turned coming down in direction of the north, along a trail passing through an open road of rock-steps until we came to a plain, where the metal had been piled.*

They loaded my four mules while I went to see the mine. I saw it in the following manner. Standing facing to the north, you can see the direction of the ovens, the ranch, and halfway of Buena Vista Lake, turning around facing the south, you can see the mouth of the mine. To your left, you can see an enormous rock on top of the other rocks. The rock on top, hitting it with a piece of iron or another rock, will sound like the peal of a bell. To the right of the one standing facing the south, you can see a tall rock cliff, a grey color, from its major height water flows. More to your right, you see another spring of water spouting out of the ground, and from the mouth of the mine another flow of water. These form three different springs of water. They are the three flows of water from the mouth of the Mine of San Emigdio. The rock that sounds like a bell, looking up high and to the right of the one standing in front of the mine, you can see a white rock with a green stripe in the center. Look for this place in the mountains of San Emigdio and you will find the silver mine.

The one (mine) *of antemonio* (antimony) *is of the following way. The mine is situated at the east of the ovens, about three leagues more or less. I carried the metal that the missionaries know how to take out of the mine. The direction is the following: standing at the ovens, on your feet, and in the direction of the east, where you can see the mountains to the right, to the south, and in front, to the north, you can see something like a carriage door extended. The climb is very high, the path or road is more to the north. You take said road skirting the mountain that is to the right, until you arrive to el Cerro de Los Borregos* (sheep plains) *or borregos hills. From there you take a pathway until you come to a canyon of blowing winds. Halfway down you see like a hole. From the center of this hole, you count 300 steps in the direction of the most immediate elevated mountain. There is the Mine of Antimonio.*

In the Silver Mine, I myself worked in her, it has 60 steps in depth inside the mountain. We make three ladders out of branches of pine trees. I worked in said mine when the Indians of San Buenaventura, Santa Barbara, and Santa Inez, rebelled and ran away, and ended there with us (1824). *Two representatives were Jose and Blas, who were sent by the P.P.* (?) *missionaries to go and plug the mouth of the Mine of Silver and the Mine of Antimonio. They came up to the ranch of San Emigdio, and from there they returned to the mission. I came with them this time, until now.*

I don't know how many years have passed, but I believe more than forty. I saw at that time the dead ones, assassinated by the Indians of El Tejon (see Volume I). *This is the notice that I give regarding the Mine of Tashlipun; I cannot give more information or signs, because over so many years, I do not remember. Well, that is all. I place my cross and all that I have said is the truth."*

From the files of the BAKERSFIELD CALIFORNIAN of March 1st through the 9th, 1915, W. J. Graham wrote a series of articles, which are included in this chapter. Some additions of material from other writers covering the same stories have been added as well. Note that the spelling of various person and place names varies with writers. The first story is told as follows:

> *"At 3 o'clock in the afternoon of July 28, 1862, a bareheaded, ragged, footsore prospector staggered into Fort Tejon, Kern County, California. He was almost starved, was coatless, and clothed in shirt and overalls which were badly torn. He carried a sack whose contents weighed between twenty-five and thirty pounds, and its burden was almost pure gold. The direction of his entry to the Fort was unusual enough to mark him as a more than interesting traveler for virtually no one ever approached the fort from the rugged Pleito mountains of the West.*
>
> *On the hot July afternoon when the haggard prospector staggered into the Fort there were several vaqueros or cowboys, a few soldiers and some Indians lounging in the shade of the sutler's store. For this store the prospector made his way, staggering under his heavy load, and curiously watched by the crowd until he arrived near enough for them to discover that he was in a serious condition."*

Prospector coming into Fort from the hills to west

Graham mentions soldiers being at the Fort but there are no recorded military units at the Fort at this time unless he has the year wrong. Fort Tejon had been abandoned by the U.S. military in 1861 though a unit of the California Volunteers was there in July of 1863. Of course there could have been soldiers traveling through that would still have made use of the abandoned buildings when this event took place. Graham continues:

> *"The stranger was taken to the post hospital where he was treated, fed and slept ... never letting go of the heavy bag he carried.*
>
> *By early the next afternoon several local men and soldiers had gathered in the shade of a huge oak next to the hospital, waiting to hear the travelers story. When the prospector regained his strength he told of his experiences. He had left Tuolumne country, at that time the richest known gold fields in California, with his pack train of burros and followed the Coast Range mountains southward to a place on the coast where Los Angeles and Ventura counties join. Running short of supplies he turned eastward to find the fort where he knew supplies would be available.*
>
> *He told his story as follows: 'I lost my way and a few days back drove my burros up a long canyon. When I reached the top of a hill at the end of the canyon I found myself in a very bushy country. There was a spring there which seemed to have been made by men for it had been dug out of solid granite. It was four feet wide and three feet deep. The water was perfectly clear and cool, and just a little was running over the top of the wall. I made camp and turned the burros loose, as I generally do, and spread my blankets and went to sleep after cooking supper.*
>
> *The next morning after breakfast, I went out to look for the burros, but could not find them. I camped there for three days, looking for the burros, all the time but unsuccessfully. On the afternoon of the third day, when I was about a mile from the spring in another smaller canyon I came to a clearing in the brush. The ground was perfectly barren for about an acre. In the center of this barren ground, a ledge of rock had cropped out some thirty or forty feet above the surface. It seemed that it had fallen over, perhaps through the action of an earthquake, and the rock was held together with gold.* (This would have been shortly after the massive 1857 earthquake.) *Near where the canyon formed a wall at the end of the clearing was a solitary finger of rock of crumbling quartz held together with virgin gold.' "*

Another writer, Jack Black, in his book, BURIED TREASURES AND LOST MINES OF SOUTHERN CALIFORNIA, said the prospector described the area as such:

> *"He came to small clearing consisting of a tremendous flat rock about one hundred feet square. Near where the canyon formed a wall abruptly ending the clearing was a monolith about forty feet big. As an experienced prospector he could tell even from a distance that the solitary finger of rock was highly mineralized.*

On closer examination he found that the rock was crumbling quartz held together with virgin gold!"

W. J. Graham continues his account:
" *'There was more gold in sight on that acre of ground than had ever been minted in the mints of the world. I went back to camp after a sack and filled it with forty or fifty pounds of gold, as much as I thought I could carry. It was my intention to travel northward on foot and try to find settlement. I knew Fort Tejon was somewhere near where I was. With such a heavy pack of gold, I wasn't able to carry much in the way of provisions and in fact had very little anyway.*

On the second day, my grub gave out, and the tubes in my shotgun got out of working order, so I couldn't shoot any game. Then I began to dump gold out of my sack. Every hour I could feel myself growing hunger and weaker and kept on throwing out chunks until I had got rid of nearly twenty-five pounds by the time I reached here.

There's enough gold there for all of us ... enough to make everyman in this fort have as much as the richest man in the world. It will take about two days and a half to get back there on horseback, but I know the country pretty well and am sure I can make no mistake in finding the place again.' The prospector asked for a canvas and spread it on the ground. To the surprise of everyone, there proved to be more gold than quartz in the sack he carried."

The prospector showing the gold

Graham continues:
"The news spread in the Fort that a prospector had arrived with the richest find in history. Mr. Sam Bishop, also at the Fort that day (he owned the property on which the fort was located), *agreed with the prospector that as soon as he felt like hitting the trail he would finance a detachment of men, soldiers and civilians, to relocate this valuable find.*

The prospector, who never did give his name, was very liberal with his samples and told the boys to help themselves. Everybody grabbed for a chunk, but Mr. Bishop and the commanding officers forbade the men to take any of it, and ordered all who had taken any to return it. The stable sergeant of the troop retained a piece about the size of a man's thumb. Not wishing to be caught with this in his possession, after having been ordered to give it up, he secreted it in a saddle blanket hung up with an extra saddle.

After the prospector had rested three days and regained his strength, he announced that he was ready to go back to the gold ledge. The officers had an extra horse saddled up for him. The soldiers and vaqueros waited on the parade ground until the officers and the prospector were ready. It so happened that the blanket in which the stable sergeant had slipped the stolen sample was put on the horse the prospector was to ride. He was not a skilled rider, and when he mounted the chunk of ore pressed into the horse's withers and caused him to buck. The rider was thrown onto the hard parade ground and his neck was broken, so that he died shortly after without regaining consciousness."

Prospector being thrown from the horse

"The deceased was carried to the room in the fort where the dead were laid out and there he was searched. The soldiers found a $50 slug, the largest piece of gold money made of that kind, and also a few dollars in silver. The only paper found on him was a rough sketch of the country he had traveled over from the mine to the fort. This map gave a fairly good description of how to get to the spring, and from there to the clearing he had described. The following day the unfortunate discoverer of the mine was buried with full military honors and a rifle salute.

On the first morning that Mr. Bishop started out with the small detachment to look for the mine which the prospector had described, an old Indian (Tecuya) *came and attempted to dissuade him from making the journey. This Indian had lived in that part of the country for a long, long time* (as had his family before him). *He was very friendly to Mr. Bishop, who paid no attention, however, to his remonstrance. The Indian's parting words were: 'You will never find the mine, if you do find the mine, and get away alive, you will never live to go back there again.'*

Tecuya warning Sam Bishop not to continue the search for the mine

Several days later Bishop, some officers and six cowboys started out for the gold mine and reached the spring after three day's riding. There they found, as described, the prospector's camp, his pack saddle, his cooking utensils, etc. The burros were not to be found. A diligent hunt was made for the clearing, but it was not found. Sam Bishop had made up his mind to locate the mine, unless it was the creature of the prospector's imagination. It seemed to him that the prospector told the truth; that he had brought with him evidence in the shape of gold, and that he seemed anxious to get back to where he had made his find. For years, Bishop and the men working for him searched the country in the spring's vicinity. As one prospector would tire of the fruit less search, Bishop would engage another and give him a grubstake.

When Bishop returned from the fruitless searches he remembered the Indian's peculiar actions and went to him saying: 'what do you know about this mine? Why did you tell me not to look for it, and that I would not get back if I found it?'

The Indian (Tecuya or Tucoya) *then told his story* (one of the oldest recorded references to the mine). *Robbed of his picturesque idiom, it is not so forceful, but I will repeat his story as I remember his telling it: 'My story is a long one and dates back to before my birth.* (Tecuya was possibly born in the 1790's as he is later referred to as being over 100 in 1898 and would be telling this story in the 1860's.) *This is not the first time that white men lived in this country. Do you not remember the old smelter in San Emedio canyon? That was built before I was born, and I am a very old man. This old crucifix that you see on my neck was given me by a father* (priest) *and when he gave it to me he told me a story, part of which I already knew.*

When my father was a very young man, some men who wore long black coats (Jesuit priests) *came here. Their clothes were all black, but they always wore white collars. Each carried a cross with an image of a man nailed to it. These strings of beads around his neck with a cross fastened to it were so long that when the man stood erect, the end of the beads would touch the ground. They were good men. They came to bring the Indians peace; pour water on their heads and baptized them.*

The priests settled in San Emedio, where the frost never comes more than once in four years, and generally not as often as that. The priests built adobe houses and also the smelter not far from the village. There were many horses, then running wild and all kinds of game, elk, antelope and deer were as plentiful as cattle are now.

Every Spring the priests would start out with thirty or forty men and sometimes a hundred pack animals, the latter having good pack saddles and pack bags. Sometimes they would be gone until late in the Fall, but when they returned their pack animals were loaded with different kinds of ore ... lead, silver and gold. The gold they worked separately into yellow bars. The silver, lead and other ores were melted in the upper smelter and that was run into heavier bars. Once a year, they would load the bars on pack animals and go south.' "

A black robed Padre and men leaving the canyon with a load of gold

"*The Indians always accompanied them south until they came to the big river* (supposedly the Colorado River). *There they would be met by other priests who would ferry the bars across the river and load them on other animals. From there I don't know where the gold and silver went. Sometimes the older priests would go across the river with the gold, and when they did they never came back again. This went on for years and all liked to go on the trips for ores because the men with the long black coats were always good to them and loved them as their children. But the Indians way north of here ... the Piutes ... got on the warpath one Spring and drove back the priests. Two priests were killed, and many of our Indians, leaving but three priests with us.* (See Volume I of this series of books when even these three were killed.)

Nobody came to work the smelter for many years, but my father always said some of the priests would come back some day. When I was a very small child, there came to my father's place one day a white man, white as snow, dressed all in white and riding a white mule (believed to be a Franciscan priest – who wore gray). *He led twelve other mules, each one's head tied to the tail of the mule in front. He had good pack saddles. As he rode up to my father's place he raised up his hand in benediction and was at once recognized as a priest, but not as one of the priests previously known. All others had been dressed in black, and this one wore white.* (There was no word to describe gray in the Indian language.)

He could talk Spanish, as could my father, who had learned it from the other priests, and told my father he had come to get some

of the gold which was in the mountains, a three days' ride from where we were. He said he knew where to get it without trouble and would rest a few days and then go with my father to the place. While he stayed at my father's house, my father sent for the Indians to come and the priest blessed them, pouring water on the young ones' heads and baptizing them. After resting six days he and my father went into the hills, and were gone seven days, returning with as much gold and ore as eleven mules could carry. Of the two other mules, one was ridden and the other was used to carry blankets, cooking utensils, jerked beef and panole.

The priest then rested two days at my father's house and started away with the gold, saying he would return next year. He did, and for eleven consecutive years, each time bringing the same number of mules, except on the last trip, when he told my father he had lost one of his animals at Tres Lomas (in Arizona?). *He told my father it would be his last trip, and asked that I be allowed to accompany him, along with my father on this expedition after gold.' "*

A white robed priest with mules tied *"head to tail"*

"'We went, and we camped at this spring the prospector has told you about. It was my father and this priest who dug that hole. He and my father filled our sacks with the gold and then on the morning when we were to leave he showed me the mine. We went to the clearing in the brush. He told us that he and people far away, besides ourselves, were the only ones who knew about it and that others might come looking for gold and they would take from us whatever they could and that they would be stronger than we; that we would fight them, but they would conquer us; that there would be priests in various parts of the country who

would establish homes for the Indians and when the white men came for us to go where the priests were we should go and we would have peace, but if we stayed and fought we would surely lose. (Information given to them about the establishment of the missions.)

He told us never to tell anyone the location of the mine until he gave me a sign, and that no one who found the mine would ever live to go back to it. If I received the sign I was to tell some relative of the mine's location ... or tell someone who would benefit.

I have never received the sign, and have never told anyone. Mr. Bishop, do not look for the mine, for you will have bad luck. I would not show it to you for anything on earth. Before the white priest left he had my father call all the Indians, and he blessed them. He had my father and me kneel down, and gave me a special blessing. He gave my father this crucifix saying: 'When you are old, which you will be, very old, and cannot ride at the head of your men to the battle or in the hunt, make this boy chief. Keep the crucifix until you die, and then give it to the son. He will live to be old and will always have plenty. If I see him in need, I will give him the sign to get the gold. It will be a sign from the skies that he can understand. If I don't give him the sign he must never tell, the secret I have entrusted to him. If he betrays the trust, he will be cursed, and my curse will follow him to the grave.'

'You see, Mr. Bishop, although I like you better than anyone, and you have done very much for me, I will not betray the confidence the priest put in me anymore than I would betray you if you trusted me with a secret. Never ask me again, for I will never tell you where the mine is without getting the sign. I pray and kiss this crucifix that you will never find the mine, for something terrible will happen to you.'

Bishop laughed and said: 'I will find it!'

The Indian replied: 'Then you do not believe Tucoya, chief of the Diggers? Do you remember how you tried to kill me at Hayway Meadows? Do you remember when I stood on the rock as my men fought yours and that you shot at me many times? A hundred times you have said you cannot explain how I was saved. I knew all the time that I was not to be killed in that battle. Do you remember when you drove me and my few remaining warriors to Owen's Lake? When you and soldiers surrounded us, my men jumped into the water, water that they knew would kill them. Did

I not stand my ground? When Big Fred wanted to kill me, it was you who stepped forward and said: 'Let the old savage live. We have got them all but him.' (These incidents can be matched to events that took place in the 1850's.) *I have loved you always for that, but I love you too much to tell you where the mine is.' "*

Graham ends with:
"Many years have passed since Bishop and Tucoya had that conversation. In 1882 Tucoya was still alive on the ranch, carefully cared for by the ranch people, well fed, and considered the only man alive knowing the location of the Los Padre Mine. The prospector was dead, Tucoya's father with his ancestors, and the priests massacred or driven away. But Tucoya lived on ... and with him, his secret."

Sometime in the mid-1800's a prospector approached a well-known mining investor, Adolph Sutro of Los Angeles, to grubstake him in relocating a Spanish mine he had seen long ago in the mountains to the north. According to his story, the prospector told Sutro that he had stumbled into a wide canyon more that two miles long where much mineralization was in evidence. While prospecting the canyon he was taken prisoner by Indians and then taken to a large mining camp in a nearby, smaller canyon. He counted some two hundred Indians working the mines in addition to the Spanish miners. For some reason the Spanish decided to let the American prospector go and after being blindfolded, he was tied to a horse and led away for several days. When the blindfold was removed he found himself in a Joshua tree desert somewhere north of where the town of Pearblossom is now located.

Blindfolded man tied to horse being led away as Padre looks on

Many mining articles appeared in Southern California newspapers in the 1860's & 70's, many of them with news of the rediscovery of the Los Padres mine. An article published in the VENTURA SIGNAL in 1871 prompted one of Los Angeles' most prominent men, a Mr. Jonathan J. Warner of the Warner's Ranch, to the east of the city, to make his claim of ownership to the mine. Through an editorial in the LOS ANGELES STAR dated September 9th, 1871, he based his claim only on having been at the site some forty years prior. The article read:

> *"Editor Star: I see in the newspapers that the enterprising people of San Buenaventura have recently discovered an old but rich mine, and that the right of discovery is contested by a gentleman of this city* (a Mr. A. or E. J. Weston was claiming rights to the mine). *To prevent the prosecution of groundless claims to the San Emigdio mines, I wish to give notice through the columns of your widely circulated, influential, and valuable paper that I shall contest the right of any living persons to that mine, founded upon priority of discovery. Forty years ago, save one and a few days, that is to say in October 1832, in company with three men all belonging to the party of Captain Ewing Young, who was himself one of the three men, we ascended the San Emigdio water course from the plains where its waters are lost in the sand and drift* (they would have been traveling on the trail called El Camino Viejo) *to its source in the pinon forests of the mountains. That we found in the pinon forests an Indian camp, in which there were Indians, male and female, with many little ones, and pinons in numbers like the sands of the seashore, which no man could count."*

Old maps from 1872 and 1873 indicate that partners, E. J. Weston, F.P.F.Temple and S. Boushey had several mining claims in San Emigdio Canyon at the time Warner writes this.

Men looking over the smelter where two creeks meet in San Emigdio Canyon

Mr. Warner continues:

"While traveling up the brook, and near where the plain swells into the base of the adjoining mountain, we beheld upon the right hand side of the brook a furnace or oven, built of burnt brick, which had been used for the smelting of ores. As we could not, after diligent search, discover any trace of the owners, we took possession of the discovered furnace and the country round about, and filed our claim to all the mineral imbedded in, and hereafter to be found in or upon any and all the lands which shed their waters in the brook of San Emigdio; and the records thereof may be found in the chronicles of the wanderings of the party of Ewing Young, in the year of our Lord One Thousand Eight Hundred and Thirty-two and three. J. J. Warner"

Photo taken by the author in 1972 and thought to be the above described smelter site, though the artifacts may be from more recent use

A letter in the VENTURA SIGNAL of September 30, 1871 responded:

"We are the rightful owners of the mine, and have had possession of the same ever since 1826, and according to the Mexican laws of that date, fulfilled the requirements forbidding, forever, any relocation. If the Los Angeles papers would not pick up such scurrilous articles, as it is a bilk, etc., our situation is such as regards the center of trade that we might in the future afford them a market for their grapes and peanuts!" Signed *"Claimant"*.

As the frenzy of the 1849 Gold Rush faded into history mining articles continued to be a popular item in all newspapers of the late 1800's with each paper trying to outdo the other to capture the interest of those still hoping to find their fortune.

Another old reference to buried treasure or a possible mine site, comes from the Santa Barbara Mission Archives where a translation from one Juan Esteban Pico has been discovered. It is included here as the same man then seems to also go in search of the Los Padres Mine. The translation reads:

> *"In the year 1870, my uncle, Jose Faustino, a native of the Mission of San Fernando, Los Angeles County, California, about the beginning of September of that year committed a murder on the person of a woman that he had in the Rancho Tejon, Kern County, California. Before committing the murder, he and another Indian of Tejon went out together to a mine prospect that is to the south of the above mentioned ranch Tejon. Having committed the murder, and his companion already sick unto death, Faustino fled, fearful of being killed as well. He barely had time to see his companion to tell him that he was leaving Tejon forever. His companion said, 'Are you already leaving here for good? Look at the consequences for me of your action. I am near death. Of our treasure nobody knows about it but you and I. Now, mark the place where it is located.'*
>
> *Faustino did what his dying companion told him, putting over it some branches, stones and earth. Faustino came to El Escorpion, Los Angeles County. Three or four days after his arrival a pursuer arrived looking for him for the murder he had committed, and noting that he was sorrowing for the woman he had killed; in the night he took his horse and a mare and went to Saticoy near Ventura. Three days later the same pursuer arrived. Faustino took his horses again and went to Ventura. Two days later a letter arrived for Faustino telling him to take to the road again immediately.*
>
> *Faustino then stopped at my house since all my family was innocent of the fact that he had committed a crime from which he was fleeing. He took his horse, saddle and bridle to my house where he ate and slept. He spoke to my wife, Maria Dolores de Pico, and told her, 'take care of this mare, I don't have anything else to give you for your kind services. Receive this mare in memory of me because maybe we won't see each other again in this life.' Turning to me he said, 'You, beloved nephew, I live and will always live, thankful for your help and I reveal to you a treasure whose value nobody knows.' "*

Faustino giving Maria his horse and Juan Pico the map

"From this house you go toward Camulos (Rancho Camulos east of the present community of Piru), *from Camulos to Alamar* (possibly in the area of Castaic), *from Alamar to Lake Chico Lopes* (Elizabeth Lake), *from there to the Ranch of the Viuda* (Ranch of the Widow as the future area of Gorman was called around 1850), *from Rancho Viuda to Fort Tejon which is not far from some houses belonging to the government. From there a little farther along you come out to the grape canyon, from there you see at the north a stretch of plain. At the right you have the field of oats that is very high and a little farther, following the same road that leads to Tejon in a northerly direction, and at the foot of a high mountain range, on the side of the sunrise, you see some trees planted along a stream, sometimes dry and sometimes with water. These trees will point out to you the direction you should take which is up stream of the current of said river.*

Upon arriving at the foot of the hills, for up to here you can ride in a carriage, the river flows more or less to the northwest. On the north side of the river is a hill with an elevation of 8 to 10 feet above the level of the flat earth there. Between the river that is at the south and the hill at the north, take the road to the east between an opening in the hills, going until you arrive at a ravine. In that ravine there is a cliff. Almost at the head or beginning of the cliff there is an oak tree that is on the cliff. On the west side of the oak you see a hole. There is the hidden treasure. Take out the overload and you will see the pieces of gold. This is the treasure that I reveal to you so that you can go and get it. I ask God to be my witness that this is true.' "

These directions indicate the gold is in an area east of the old headquarters of Tejon Ranch. Juan Pico no doubt pursued this information from his uncle and while there became intrigued by the rumors of gold throughout the area. The following translation is by a friend of Pico's who accompanied him on one of his explorations but obviously not the one above. These very detailed directions to the possible Los Padres mine come from the Mission San Buenaventura archives. They were given in the Indian language of Mizkanaltan and recorded in Spanish in December of 1871. The translation reads:

> *"I, Carlos Juan Capena, native of the Mission of San Buenaventura, say that I live very grateful to Juan Esteban Pico, and seeing that he is very eager to go in search of mines. In this very year of 1871, the 11th of August we left on an expedition ... Juan E. Pico, Don A. Cuellar, Don Lazaro Arreola, Don Manuel Anzoisola, stonecutter, and Don G. Elvoell who took me in his coach. On the 19th of the same month we entered into arroyo salado* (Salt Creek Canyon) *where we faced a terrible disaster when a stream flooded and nearly caught us.* (They possibly went up Salt Creek Canyon to not be noticed as at this time the entrance to San Emigdio Canyon contained a sizable village and ranching operation.)
>
> *Since it had been more than forty years since I had been to the Mine of Silver the last time, I do not remember well, but I shall say what I remember.*
>
> *After our return of the mentioned expedition, I remember that the road they took, the one coming from El Tejon to the Mine of San Emigdio, was the arroyo salado* (again Salt Creek). *That is to the west of del cajon de las Uvas* (Grapevine). *Entering said arroyo, up to the end, where there is a canada canyon, only one with blowing winds, because there is no other, you see up ahead a hillside with yucca plants. At first sight you see a small plain at the foot of the highest mountain. There is the Mine of Antimonio buried.*
>
> *You leave this mountain to the right and go down a canyon that has water. That is the one that gives water to the rancho viejo of the same name as the mine. This canyon is the one that divides the mountain of Los Borregos* (the sheep) *and the mountains of San Emigdio. Once inside the canyon, having to the right, a pathway that descends from the mountain, you take it against the current of the water until you find at your right hand an opening in direction to the west. You follow this entry leaving the pathway that was before to the east. Now to the left hand side a mud-pit and a spring of water.*

Further ahead you see two creeks, one that comes from the left side south, the other one with much water that comes from the west. You cross the one that comes from the south and you climb up a steep incline to a cliff that is also to the south. On the opposite side, to the north of this pine grove, you will find a cienega with much water and a well. More to the east you see a pasture. At the edge of this potrero, to the west, there is a pinon tree all alone. From this only pine you go in the direction to the west until you reach a small pasture land that is at the feet of the mountain on the north side. You pass some of this pasture on the west side. From there in the direction to the north, you enter a canyon and you start climbing the mountain. A little way you see a pile of rocks, further ahead you'll find a spring of water, you still go up some more until you see some peaks of rock, white as marble. At the foot of this white rock there is a fall of water.

Now in this direction, always to the north, you climb the mountain. You look always to the same direction, to the north. As you commence to descend, you see within the pines three waterfalls almost together, that starts to form in the direction of northwest. Follow the waterfall until you come upon creeks almost close together. One is a geyser, the other drips from a rock that is very high and the third, which is at the east of the other two, which are to the west, is coming out of the mouth of the silver mine of San Emigdio. More to the east of this last stream of water, you can see a rock on top another of great weight. It sounds like the most romantic soft peal of a bell.

These are the directions I give to the one I am very grateful for the numerous favors he has bestowed upon me. From the mouth of the mine water pours forth in abundance. A white rock was placed at one side of the mine. To the east is a small place where the metal was placed to load the mules. This is all I remember, that the mine has sixty paces that one may walk into the mountain and it has ladders. This is the truth, that the mine of pure silver is covered and that it is this place that I have indicated."

Also from the Ventura Mission came this statement taken in September of 1876 – memories from some 50 years earlier. This information also seems to be recorded at the request of Juan Pico and would be, to what is believed to be, the local Los Padres Mine. It reads:

"I, Luis Anasheye, stonecutter, native of the Santa Ines Mission of about 80 years of age, say that because of the urging of my friend, J. E. Pico, to whom I owe many favors, and knowing well all that he ask me, I declare the following: Being about 27 to 30 years old, I always used to go to enjoy myself at Tejon for the

festivities. I already knew a little how to read book and also how to write a little. Being in the Tejon, I was asked to return to my home in Santa Ines. I went soon and found preparations for a war with the Indians of the Missions of Santa Ines, Santa Barbara, San Buenaventura and San Fernando against the Spaniards and Mexicans who maltreated us for no reason at all.

I was frightened at such news, took my son who was with the monks at Santa Ines, and at night left for el Tejon. When I entered the canyon that today is called 'the Rock', I found Blas, Saturio, Mariano, father-in-law of the dead Evon Jose, who were all mayors and some other neophytes of San Buenaventura. My son and I arrived at the ovens, where we found several Indians prepared for war. This was in the time that the Indians of the missions already mentioned made an agreement among themselves to rebel, but I don't remember what year it was (1824). *They told us that they had killed two smelter workers at the smelter and two Indians because they did not want to obey him. The chief was called Macal which means 'bat', who commanded the rebel and he was very brave.*

Of the smelters, before dawn we approached the antimony mine which is at the east of the smelter. We took the river upstream against the current until we came to a little canyon through which you climb up to the mine. As this antimony mine is not of interest, I'll tell my friend Pico but I will not fail to give him a short description of this in case it might be of interest to him, he can find it.

The silver mine there in the middle of the San Emigdio mountains is as follows: You come to the old San Emigdio ranch which is south of lake Buenavista; you take the upstream route about half way from the ranch to the high sierra which is south of the origin of the stream you are following. On the west side, or right hand coming from ranch to the sierra, you see some weeping willows. In these willows are the ovens of the smelters where the silver ore was made into ingots or bars. Once at the ovens, you take the road in a southerly direction going up and down slopes until you arrive at the top of the high sierra. About half way up the climb and from the pines, you see a deep canyon. This canyon starts from the heights of the sierra in a northerly direction. The ridge that is at the east of this canyon you take going downward almost in a northerly direction leaving the greater height of the main body of the sierra in a northerly direction which causes you finally to arrive at the streams of the aforementioned deep canyon and the other which comes and extends from the streams of the acerradero (a lumber mill) *and other tributary streams of the main one, or which form one bed at the exit from the San Emı Ranch."* (a bit confusing)

It's interesting that Luis mentions a lumber mill in the canyon as early as the 1820's. It could be possible the missions had been cutting the tall straight pines from the forest for use in their buildings. The mill would have been located along the Spanish trail – El Camino Viejo – a roadway that had been used through the Canyon for centuries. The first recorded mill in that area was established in the 1850's. Possibly Luis had returned and is indicating the streams he had known of before were then coming from the latter mill.

Senor Anasheye continues:
"As was said, at the east of the canyon you take the ridge and keep going down to a little plateau which has no more downward passes. From there you go straight north, extending your arms, with the right arm you point to the mine opening which is about a hundred or so paces. There are the three falls, one is in a slope, the other drops the water over a stone ledge that is very high ... as high as the front of a church ... and the other fall which is the biggest, comes out of the silver mine opening. All this faces north. At the east of the mine opening you see a stone with a lead stripe and on top of it there is another that if you strike it, it sounds like a bell. I would take a bar and strike the stone which would ring like a church bell. I told this to Padre Juan, but he didn't believe me, but it is the truth and no lie. At one side to the west of the mine and at the height of ten paces you see a stone and a pine in front of the mine opening. This is the description that I gave you, my friend, and I hope this serves to eat heartily (make you rich), *and may you always remember me all the rest of your life. The mine has in its center about sixty paces.*

Dear friend Pico, my not wishing to go and show you the place is because I consider it would take thousands of pesos to work it. Twenty years after the padres had the mine closed up, I went with Joaquin Ahala and we found everything very different (possibly in the 1850's after the 1857 earthquake that centered in the area). *There was a slide of mud over it and everything is covered. According to the description that I have given you and everything I have told you about the mine I write because it is the truth. I put my name and cross as a Christian that I give this saying it is the truth."*

It seems that Juan Pico then locates the site of his uncles buried treasure some twelve years later:
"I, Juan Pico say that on March 22, 1882, I went with my friends Oriol Moraga and Maueil Morroquin from Adobe Station, Kern

> *County,* (south of Bakersfield) *California, toward a place called La Rinconada de la Pastoria* (the entrance to Pastoria Canyon). *From Adobe Station you see the pasture with the trees toward the east and to the south of El Tejon. We went toward the plain which is southeast of Adobe* (18 miles) *from the plain* (4 miles) *to the corner* (entrance). *We arrived at the ravine. I saw the cliff so often described. I saw the oak, the only one on the cliff. Water ran there, and I finally saw the hole which had been covered twelve years before. So that what I have written is true. The fact is that I saw it and my companions saw it. We planned to go back to work it after concluding our present business, but to date we have never gone back."*

Written in 1915, W.J. Graham continues the series of articles he wrote about the Los Padres Mine. He writes:

> *"In the year of 1882, a man named McKinsey* (correct spelling is McKenzie) *and who had formerly been a vaquero for Beale and Bishop of the Tejon ranch, took up a quarter section of land, fenced it, and built houses and lived there with his wife and four children; his eldest son was eighteen years of age at this time. McKinsey and his sons worked the field, while the two girls went to school six miles away at Tejon headquarters.*
>
> *One day in August while the men were cutting the grain, Mrs. McKinsey was startled to see a strange man darting from tree to tree in the heavy timber growing a few hundred yards in the rear of the ranch home. This was about 11 o'clock in the morning. Mrs. McKinsey was a woman not easily frightened, and she contented herself with getting her husband's six-shooter, which she laid on the kitchen table so it would be handy in an emergency. She then continued with her work of preparing the noonday meal.*

Larrisa McKenzie notices the stranger hiding outside their home

"At noon Mr. McKinsey and the boys came into dinner, but the wife delayed telling them about the stranger in the woods, thinking to tell her husband after he had finished his meal. But McKinsey asked her why she was standing in the kitchen instead of eating dinner, and she said: 'I am watching a man who has been acting very strangely up there on the hill.' McKinsey was an old frontier man of the type that investigated anything like that very quickly, and not stopping to finish his dinner he arose from the table and said: 'Hand me my gun. I'll go up and see what he wants.'

He mounted the hill and found a Frenchman standing behind a tree with a sack over his shoulder, and called to him: 'What do you want here? Why are you jumping from tree to tree?' McKinsey then saw that the Frenchman was nearly naked. In broken English the stranger explained that he had been traveling through heavy brush and had had most of his clothing torn off. He had seen the woman at the house, and not wishing to be seen in his almost nude condition, he had tried to keep out of sight until the arrival of the men. In mixed jargon he made it plain that he wished a pair of overalls and a shirt, and that he was almost starved. McKinsey found some clothing for him at the house and after donning it the Frenchman accompanied the rancher to the house, where he eagerly asked for something to eat.

His condition was truly pitiable, but Mrs. McKinsey would not let him sit down at the bountiful table for fear he would fill himself with food after his prolonged fast. She prepared bread and milk for him and fed him this in such small quantities that it could do no harm. The prospector ... for such he proved to be ... was suffering horribly from his feet, which were mutilated and bruised and in a festering condition.

For thirteen months he had been in the hills prospecting and in that time had not met a human being. His shoes had worn out weeks ago and his blood had become so impoverished that every bruise festered. Many blades of foxtail grass had penetrated the flesh and remained imbedded in both his feet and legs, and his moans were pitiful when McKinsey dug these out. For several months he had lived on meat he had shot or trapped, but with exhaustion of his ammunition his fare had been scanty.

The only earthly possession of this strange unfortunate was the bag he had borne over his shoulder and this he guarded carefully at all times, not allowing it to leave his sight. That night McKinsey offered him a bed in the house, but he refused saying the barn would be preferable so he was given some blankets and made himself a sleeping place in the hay. After five days of kind treatment and careful nursing, he had greatly recuperated his strength, and told McKinsey he wished to go to Bakersfield some thirty miles away.

McKinsey contemplated making the trip himself in a few days and told the Frenchman he would be welcome to go along. Three or four days later he hitched up his wagon and told the prospector he was starting for Bakersfield. Then the stranger replied: 'I've changed my mind about going to town. Come into the house, I want to show you something.'

He got his grain sack and emptied it upon the kitchen table. Now McKinsey had been at Fort Tejon on the July day twenty years before when the old prospector had stumbled into the settlement with the sack of rich gold ore on his back and had been given a sample of it; and immediately he recognized it and that of twenty years ago as being identical. McKinsey shouted: 'Oh man, you've found the Lost Padre!' "

The prospector shows McKenzie the gold he found

"The Frenchman was familiar with the legend of this great mine. 'Yes, I've found it', he said, 'and it's bigger and richer than anyone has ever said. There's millions of tons of gold ore and gold on top of the ground. You have treated me kindly and your family has been good to me. I want to divide this find with you. From there to here I have blazed trees and taken the bark from bushes and I can find it again. Now that I am so well rested, I feel I can start anytime.'

'If you are willing,' said the rancher, 'we will start in the morning.' They then talked excitedly for some time, and McKinsey said; 'Of course you have heard that no one who has ever found that mine has lived to go back to it?' 'I have heard,' was the noncommittal reply, 'I believe in religion, too, but we will get back to the mine. I have blazed the way.'

Early the next morning, good Mrs. McKinsey had breakfast ready for the men, and while they were eating, the two boys saddled up their horses for them. The Frenchman was given a little brown pacing mare to ride. The children frequently rode it to school and it was considered unusually gentle and surefooted. After the meal the men set out, each with a saddlebag of provisions tied behind him on his saddle. McKinsey carried a rifle and his son, who was also with them, a shotgun, so they could be assured of game to eat and plenty of fresh meat. McKinsey, having lived for many years on the Tejon ranch, of course knew about Tucoya, the Indian Chief, to be the only man alive knowing the location of the Lost Padre mine, so he thought they would call on Tucoya and inform him he was no longer the sole possessor of the great secret. (McKenzie had come to The Tejon as an Indian Trader in the early 1850's so knew the Indians well.)

The old Digger chief lived in a lonely hut eight miles from the ranch buildings. When they reached his hovel, speaking in Spanish McKinsey told the bent old warrior that the man accompanying him had found the Lost Padre and was then returning to it in company with him and his son. The old Indian smiled and said: 'I am sorry for that man. Neither you nor him will ever see that mine.'

McKinsey and his son both laughed, and told the prospector what the Indian had said. Bidding the old man good-bye, the party rode back to the road. The Frenchman rode a little ahead of the others, as the pacing mare traveled at a faster gait. About half a mile past the Tejon headquarters, a badger had dug a hole in the soft dirt along the side of the road and then tunneled under the highway close to the surface. The little mare broke through with her forefeet and fell throwing the Frenchman off. McKinsey and his son hastened to his assistance and found he had broken his leg at the ankle. They put him on the mare again and returned to the ranch where rough first aid was administered and McKinsey's son rode into Bakersfield to get Doctor Buckman. The latter pronounced it not serious and said the patient would be all right in a short time, but a week went on the bones did not knit and the physician was summoned again.

On the second trip another physician accompanied Dr. Buckman and after an examination and consultation they decided that amputation below the knee would be necessary. The sufferer assented willingly enough and the operation was successfully performed. However, gangrene set in and when the Bakersfield medico was hurriedly summoned a few days later, he stated that amputation of the leg above the knee was the only chance of saving the Frenchman's life.

Before the operation McKinsey and the prospector had a conversation in private. Knowing his life was probably close to its end, the prospector described as exactly as he could the mine and the trail leading back to it. A map was also made, with the directions given so explicit and simple that McKinsey did not doubt his ability to find the mine in short order. A few hours after the second operation the Frenchman died."

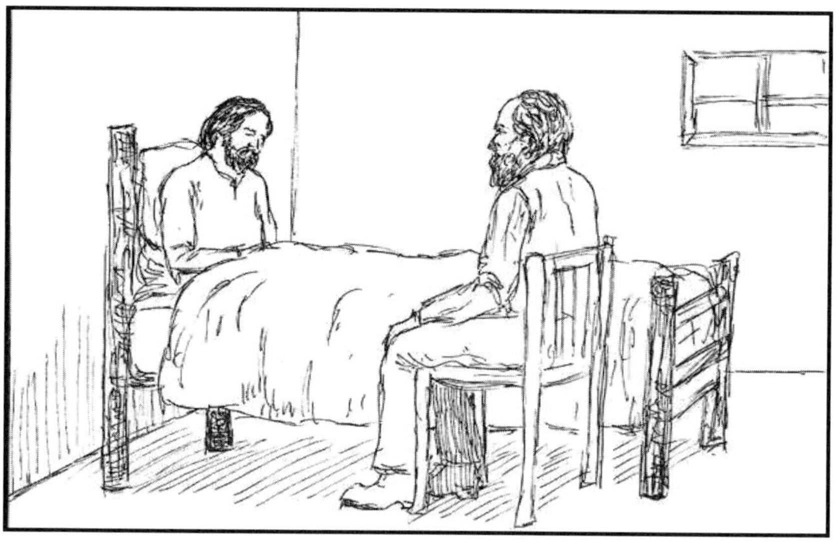

The prospector confides in Mr. McKenzie

"The gold in the sack he had brought with him was sufficient to pay the doctor's bill and still leave McKinsey several hundred dollars. The writer of this story (Graham) *has in his possession one piece of this ore, presented to him by McKinsey. After the burial of the strange adventurer, McKinsey made no secret of the rediscovery of the mine and the news spread like wildfire.*

Prospectors from all quarters of the country set out to find the mine and they were as unsuccessful as was, of course, McKinsey himself, for he and his son had vainly gone over every foot of the country that could possibly be the lodging place of this fabulous deposit of the yellow metal. Storekeepers, bankers, mechanics,

> *and businessmen in all walks of life formed little companies and grubstaked prospectors to go out and look for the Lost Padre Mine. Some hunted for months, and more obstinate ones for years, but eventually all quit. Of course strangers coming into the country and hearing the story would start for the Tejon mountains determined to wrest from them the secret, but the gold remained in Mother Nature's grasp."*

Susan Miller McKenzie, a daughter of Mrs. McKenzie from her first marriage, later often told a different version of this same story. She said that when she was a young woman her step-father, David McKenzie, found the Frenchman by the creek down near the road that ran out in front of their home. After caring for him he showed them the gold he had found and offered to take them to the mine. Her story is that the mule they gave him to ride threw him which broke his neck and killed him. He had described the location of the mine to them as having a spring under an outcropping of white quartz in a vein of blue manganese mud in a canyon on the south side of the Antelope Valley where there was a mountain peak to the southeast. Susan McKenzie said the mine wasn't found for many years because it was not a year-around spring, and some years the spring didn't run at all. The blue manganese mud is again mentioned in information about the Antelope Valley's *"Oh Susanna Mine"* at the end of Chapter 14 in this book.

Members of the McKenzie family lived near a wooded stream in Tejon Canyon, at Fort Tejon and at the Liebre headquarters of Tejon Ranch so it is unclear as to which of these three locations has been described here though Susan seems to indicate it was when they lived at the Liebre in the western end of the Antelope Valley when the Frenchman found them.

An oral story passed down through descendents of this same McKenzie family gives another interesting description of gold mining lore. The family had heard and passed on the story that when the mission system was dissolved padres loaded a buckboard with gold and silver and pushed it into a mine shaft hoping to return for the treasure in future years. Another Lost Los Padres Mine??

From Santa Barbara Mission Archives we read of yet another interesting account of travels to the Los Padres Mine in 1884:

> *"Expedition promoted by Prospero Calli, an Italian, and Maria Ventura, Indian of Tejon. Maria Ventura contracted to reveal the entrance to the old silver mine of San Emigdio. Prospero Calli contracted to pay all the expenses necessary to carry it out. Prospero would send a trustworthy man to take his place. Juan E. Pico was informed* (hired to go) *instead of P. Calli."* (Again Pico continues his quest.)

The following has been translated from Pico's description of this incident:

"Sierra de San Emigdio, Kern County California, April 27, 1884. On April 21st we left Bakersfield on an expedition by order of Don P. Calli accompanied by Maria Ventura, Neophyte, born and brought up in El Tejon, her husband Jose Estanislao, native of the ex-mission of San Fernando. Maria was the one who guided us, having contracted with Mr. Calli to show him the old mine of San Emigdio, the one that the priests of the mission of San Buenaventura worked after the uprising of the native Indians of almost the whole state of California, with exception of San Fernando to the south. This was in about 1824. The mission fathers had the San Emigdio mine closed. Thus, having contracted the already mentioned Prospero Calli and Maria Ventura, that Maria would come with those designated by P. Calli to show them the buried mine. It was my luck to become the one empowered by Calli to go on the expedition and the discovery of the mine. With the guide, Maria Ventura, about 55 years of age, we left, as I said the 21st of April and arrived at the foot of the mountains the 26th of that month.

Before moving from where we were camped, I asked Maria the following questions: 'Aunt Maria, how many years is it since you came to the mine the last time?'

She answered: 'More or less forty years. I was thirteen or fourteen when we came and were near the opening of the mine, and the last time that I came to this place must be about twenty-five years ago. I am going to show you the places we camped and had pinons (ate pinon seeds).'

Her husband asked: 'Any way you could find the fireplaces where you roasted pinons?'

Maria replied: 'I am sure I can find them, for they were near an oak.'

Pico continued: 'Aunt, this lean-to that you speak about, was it near the mine opening?'

Maria: 'Not far. It seems far because of the steep and rocky trail. Coming down you roll and going up you slip, well, all of it is either going up or down. Just look, when you go down it is descent and when you go up it is ascent.'

Pico: 'Aunt, do you remember this trail well enough to go to the mine?'

Maria: 'Yes, I remember, and I will remember better when we have gone into the mountains, then we'll see the signs that we have to look for.'

Pico: 'Yes, we'll look for them and we won't go without finding them.'

Maria: 'I have already said that those marks that we made will show us how to go to the mine and return before midday. You'll see! In all those mountains you will not find one stone on top of another that sounds like a bell except beside the opening to the mine. Those who were with us threw stones at it to hear it ring. At one side is this rock at the other side are two water falls and another comes out of the mine opening, so that there are three falls and the stone on top of another which are the signs that we must look for. The water fall in the middle passes over the top of a rock, the other streams down a slope, and the biggest in the center and to the north, comes out of the mine opening. My father always said when the Reverend Padres sent him to cover up the mine, those who did the work took care to look for stones of silver that came out of the mine and they took care to put them inside. Then they covered it with ordinary stones so that there would be no indication that anything had existed there at all. They also put a little pine in front as a sign, and they left a fallen pine on top of the covered entrance. From this pine they tied ropes to lower the wood for the prop for the mine. In the entry way there is a white stone with very green stripes that you will see tomorrow.'

On the 27th we went up the mountain and made camp. On the 28th we did not go anywhere because Maria was tired. The 29th in the morning, Maria pointed out the fireplaces, in fact there was now indication of their being nearly three feet deep, of the coals and pinons. We left, but not in the direction of the mine, but some other way, the 30th of April. The first and second of May we only went hunting. The 3rd of May one of my companions and I went out. We took the direction that Maria had indicated. We found a cut and we discovered a sort of ancient path made of stones. We continued descending and found a little plateau which must have been used as a resting place because it had been cleared of trees. We continued descending and came down to a canyon in a few steps.

The sun went down behind the pines, and since the evening was upon us, considering that we were far from our camp, we began to go up the mountain again, but not the way we had come down, but directly toward the camp. We had walked a little when we saw a rock like the facade of a church, as Maria had said. At the east we saw the stone on top of another that rings like a bell, the white stone with green stripes, and the three water falls. 'The three water falls discovered!!' we said at the same time. The only stone on top of another that rings like a bell, and all the signs that Maria had told us in Bakersfield on the morning of the 21st.

My companions and I agreed not to say anything to Maria of our discovery so that she might take us herself to the place she had described. So not on the day of our discovery, nor on another, nor the 5th did she take us anywhere, and if we did go out, we never took that direction. So we waited until the morning of the 18th when at last I said to her, 'Aunt, it seems to me that such signs as you have described do not exist, with the exception of the fireplaces. Instead of wasting time here and incurring useless expenses, it would be better to leave.'

Maria replied: 'Tomorrow we will go (to the mine).'

I noticed that she said this as if relieved of having to be careful. The 19th, as a matter of fact, we did go out, and on the road she appeared to be worried as if she were being taken to receive a sentence of punishment. Three times she seemed to change directions; she walked up and down saying, 'This way you can see better to walk.' But my companions and I told her that only by returning could we change directions. She finally decided to go down, and we went down near the three falls, she stopped. Maria, with a profound sigh, pronounced these words, 'Poverty requires sacrifice. Let us go!' "

Maria urging her companions to not continue on to the mine

"I heard those words very well. My companions did not hear them or if they did, they did not understand them, for they did not show that they heard or understood. At last I stepped forward and said to her with a gentle voice, 'Aunt, this is the best road!'

She then went down and ascended to the spring that according to her is the one that comes out of the mine opening. Looking at each other, we realized that we had arrived at the place we had been searching for. Maria sat down, and when she sat, she uttered these words: 'I am sad to return to this place ... to return to see where my dead parents lived. My poor children! Soon they will be orphans!' She stood up and walked toward a pine, she sat down again by us crying inconsolably and spoke no more until we returned to camp. It must have been about 11:00 in the morning when Maria spoke those words and it was a little after 4:00 in the afternoon when we arrived back at the camp. Again she embraced her children and began crying; but she finally spoke. She called me and said; 'Do you know why I have cried so much?'

I answered: 'No, senora.'

Maria continued: 'Because I remember that my father told me not to show anyone that treasure, that this is what the Padres told him ... that anyone who knew of the treasure and told where it was would die. But you discovered it and nobody showed you.' I asked her again if that was the place we were looking for and Maria said, 'The place was discovered by you, but the mine is very much buried and I fear making you work without discovering anything.'

I asked: 'Aunt, then I can write to Mr. Calli to have him send the miners?'

Maria replied: 'This is what upsets me every time I think of the agreement. What have I done to him ... work and more work. But if it doesn't turn out like that, what will Don Calli say? He will say I am a liar ... that I only told him to please him ... but the mine is very rich!'

With these remarks I knew that she denied having showed us the place where the mine is ... that I was the discoverer, so I said, 'Aunt, tomorrow we go back to Bakersfield. I don't expect anything more.'

She replied: 'Tomorrow we'll leave.'

> *The next day we went down from the mountains. The 21st of May we left the foothills and on May 22nd, 1884 we arrived at Bakersfield. The 24th I left Bakersfield for Ventura. The 22nd of June of 1884 I had the sad news that Maria Ventura had died. The 4th of July of the same year of 1884, her husband, Jose Estanislao, died. The 21st of July of 1884, a daughter of Maria Ventura who had been with us in the mountains, age eleven, died. The oldest daughter of Maria Ventura and Jose Estanislao, Sinforiana, after a year and a half, died; also Fermin of the same family, they couldn't find him. He went to the River Tule; there they killed him by beating him with their fists. He was nine years old when he went* (to the mine) *and murdered five years later when he was fourteen. It is known that these five deaths are owed to a heathen captain of the River Tule* (ghost)."

No information was located as to whether Juan Pico attempted to return to the mine or not – or when and how he died.

In the late 1890's a bit of news reached Bakersfield that stirred the gold fever once again. A Mexican by the name of Juan Maccho, a veteran prospector, was found dead out in the great Mojave Desert about twelve miles from Rosamond. He had died of thirst. On his body were found several pieces of rock and gold that greatly resembled other specimens of the Lost Padre Mine, and many believed that Juan had found the mine.

II - TECUYA'S LAST TRIP TO THE MINE

Tecuya was the last of the old tribal leaders remaining on the lands of what had been the Tejon Indian Reservation. It was said that he was the last to hold the secrets of the Los Padres Mine, which had been passed on to him by his father and his grandfather.

The last tale of the mine is again from W. J. Graham's writings, as found in his articles published in the BAKERSFIELD CALIFORNIAN in 1915:

> *"In 1898, a half breed Indian, Skinner by name* (Billy Skinner - raised by Alexis Godey – see Volume 1), *came to me and said, 'I have been up to see Tucoya, I'm his nearest relation living and he tells me he feels death approaching. He also says he has never received the sign from the skies to reveal the Los Padre mine, but he believes this feeling of death may be a sign, and he is willing to show me the mine. I would like to have you go with me.'*
>
> *Needless to say I consented, and next day we* (Skinner & Graham) *drove to Tucoya's hut. The old Indian was unusually talkative. He had known me for many years and we were good friends. 'Tomorrow,' he said, 'we will start from here at daybreak. I have not been a hundred yards away from this cabin in a great many years and my strength is failing, so this will be my last trip. I will show you the mine and then I will come back to die. My time has come.'*
>
> *We wanted to get a saddle horse for the old man, but he would have none of it. He told us he would go farther in a day on foot than we could travel on our horses. Next morning we started. Tucoya came out of his hut bent double, a man wrinkled and old, with feeble step for his somewhere around one hundred years of age. No one would scarcely believe he could travel a mile. He hobbled slowly out to the road and started slowly away, his body swaying from side to side, but he increased his pace until finally he was to a trot. At sundown we had made thirty-seven miles* (about the distance from Tejon Canyon to San Emigdio Canyon).
>
> *After we had made camp and cooked supper, he seemed one hundred per cent fresher then when we had started off that morning. He went a few steps from the campfire and taking his rosary and crucifix from his pocket, prayed for half an hour. To*

Skinner, he couched the request: 'When I die, be sure that this rosary and crucifix are put into the grave with me, the beads on one wrist and the crucifix on the other. Promise me.' And Skinner promised, raising up his hand and swearing by the God in the heaven that the wish would be carried out. Then Tucoya wrapped himself in his blanket, feet towards the fire and with his head covered up, slept peacefully. We talked until a late hour and built many an air castle."

Tecuya praying

"Next morning Tucoya was first up and that day we covered thirty-five miles. (The mileage becomes questionable here. All together they seem to travel well over 75 miles. The distance from Tejon Canyon to San Emigdio Canyon is about 20 miles.) *The old chief was still fresh that evening, devoted half an hour to his prayers as on the previous night and went to sleep. And so it was on the third day late in the afternoon Tucoya said: 'We will take our time tomorrow forenoon and get to the mine before noon. There is no use of being in a hurry, for tomorrow will do.' We did not hesitate to go into camp, for we knew we would not pass the spring anyway. Tucoya said the pile of gold was just three-quarters of a mile away, but that we would have to crawl as the thorny brush was dreadfully thick.*

We dismounted and turned our horses loose to graze. I started the fire while Skinner went out after game and returned with two cottontails and half a dozen mountain quail. The bacon and bread had been fried however, so we ate that and kept the game for the morning. We ate quickly and then spread our blankets, smoking and talking until 9 o'clock. Tucoya was in the best of humor and entertained us with tales of his fights with white men and the massacres he had been in; some of the tales were frightful to listen to.

About 9 o'clock, Skinner lapsed into silence, absorbed in contemplation of the wealth that was soon to be his. Tucoya moved to an old burnt log about thirty steps from the campfire and knelt to say his prayers. We paid no attention to him until suddenly a moan from Tucoya broke the silence. Skinner was on his feet in a second and ran to the old man, asking what was the trouble. Tucoya pointed to the skies: 'There he is! See him!' All the while he moaned and sobbed pitifully. His bent form had straightened ... he was leaning backwards if anything ... and Skinner asked: 'What have you seen?' Tucoya replied: 'The Priest. He has been here. Mea culpa, (I am guilty) *Mea culpa, mea culpa maxima.' Then he went on reciting the Apostle's creed in Spanish and again suddenly cried: 'I must go home, let me go. It is not for you to have the mine. I have been warned from the skies. The priest has appeared to me. Let me go.' Skinner and I tried to calm the old man but he was both frightened and filled with remorse beyond the point of reason. Tucoya begged the two men for permission to return to the ranch and without waiting for their consent took off in the dead of night.*

Skinner and I looked at each other, and as we stood there we could hear his cries growing fainter in the distance. All I could say was, 'This is a hell of a note.' But Skinner was part Indian and accordingly superstitious and murmured, 'I did not see the warning, but I know it came. It was not meant for us to have the mine.'

I said, 'All I wish is that we'd gone on and not made camp here.' Skinner replied, 'It would have ended just the same. We could not find the mine because Tucoya would have received the warning just the same. All we can do is stay here until morning and let the horses rest. Then we'll go back. We never can overtake the old man because he knows all the short cuts and will take them. Besides we can't take those cutoffs with our horses.'

At daylight we made a hasty breakfast not even stopping to cook our game. We had coffee and bacon and fried bread. Then we saddled up without saying a word to one another and headed for the Tejon ranch, striking a Tejon ranch round-up camp at 9 o'clock that night. We slept in the camp and in the morning the vaqueros let us have fresh mounts as the horses they were riding belonged to the ranch. We hit the main buildings at 3 o'clock that afternoon and the stableman asked us what we had been doing to old Tucoya. 'He got in at 9 o'clock this morning,' he told us, 'and they say he's dying.'

We went to the hut and found it surrounded by a crowd of squaws and Mexicans. Some of the squaws were praying and the older ones were putting pitch on their faces for mourning. Inside the hut, Tucoya lay dying on a bed of sheepskins. Under his head was a feather pillow put there by a Mexican woman, a luxury he had never known before."

Tecuya's death

"Skinner and I lifted the old man to a half sitting position. He looked at us and his lips moved as if he were saying something. The crucifix was in his right hand, and the beads were around his left wrist. Skinner put the Crucifix to the old man's lips. There was a slight tremor of the age-worn body and we knew that Tucoya had passed to his happy hunting grounds. Then a great wail went up from the women.

They told us that when Tucoya had reached the ranch that morning, a missionary was there and Tucoya asked him for the last sacrament, which was given. After that the priest went to the rancheria and at Tucoya's death, a young Indian runner went to the house to ask him to officiate at Tucoya's funeral on the morrow. The ranch carpenter constructed a rough coffin of redwood boards covered with black crepe and stretched white cloth on it to make a great cross.

A large crowd of old men, women, children and neighboring ranchmen attended the funeral the next day. Skinner, McKinsey (McKenzie), *Bodfish and myself* (Graham) *were the pallbearers. We filled the grave of the last man living who knew positively where the Lost Padre Mine was located. The Indians and many of the ranch hands always believed that the old man had seen a vision and was punished for his attempt to reveal the location of the Padres' mine."*

Thus ends the writings of W. J. Graham's references to the lost Los Padres Mine.

The Mr. Bodfish, mentioned as a pallbearer, made a fortune in 1872 when he picked up $90,000 in gold nuggets in Arizona at a place called Tres Lomas, between Phoenix and Prescott. This gold was of the exact character and fineness of the old nuggets from the Lost Padre Mine, and he with many others believed this gold to be that lost by the priest on his tenth trip from the mine told about in Chapter 1. There is a community near Kernville named after Mr. Bodfish.

III - LATER LOS PADRES STORIES

Additional stories have continued to surface about the lost Los Padres Mine of the San Emigdio Mountains. Local historian, Joyce Campbell, wrote of an Apache Indian who had worked for the Reyes Ranch in the Ozena area and for whom Apache Canyon was named. Joyce wrote:

> *"The Indian supposedly died rather than tell the secret* (of having found the mine) *saying nothing his attackers could do to him in life would frighten him half as much as the fear for his soul after death, as 'that mine was cursed by the Padre'. True to his word, he accepted hanging rather than to talk. In this version, however, the 'bad guys' had followed him up Apache Canyon from Cuyama Valley, and the mine, Rudolph Reyes said, was supposed to have been 'somewhere on San Emigdio Mesa'. More than that I shall not say."*

In another longer version of the story, which probably took place in sometime about 1870 or 1880, Joyce Campbell told of her interview with Rudolf Reyes in the Summer of 1972 who told the story in more detail as follows:

> *"Apache Saddle just west of Pine Mountain Club, was so designated because it stands at the head of Apache Canyon, which rises up from the desert floor near Highway 33 and the Cuyama River. It appears to have some connection with the cursed Los Padres Mine.* (Apache Canyon is a way of traveling to San Emigdio Canyon from the west) *The legend was told by Rudolf Reyes, descendant of one of the first ranchers in the area. His ancestors arrived in the 1850's, and the Reyes Adobe stands yet today near the junction of Reyes Creek and the Cuyama River adjoining the Scheideck Camp.*
>
> *Somewhere along the line the original Reyes' had picked up an Apache Indian who had come west from the reservation in Arizona and they put him to work as their horse-wrangler on the ranch.*
>
> *Rudolf said he'd take the herd up Apache Canyon to San Emigdio Mesa (or could go over Apache Saddle to Mil Potrero, a well-watered grazing meadow where Pine Mountain Club now stands).*

One time when Rudolf's mother lost a tooth and didn't have the money to pay the dentist for a new gold one, the Apache brought her a small sack with enough gold for the tooth.

On his periodic vacations the Apache would go to Ventura and have a spree, paying for everything with raw, rich nuggets. According to Rudolf, on his way back to the ranch one time, some 'bad fellows' followed him bent on finding the source of his wealth. Once into Apache Canyon he, knowing the rugged land well, eluded them. Consequently the best the bad fellows could do was to wait and ambush the Indian when he came out again.

When they had their chance they trapped him tied him up and, as Rudolf so succinctly put it, 'hung him a little' to show they meant business. When they took him down and revived him, he said he'd never divulge the location of the vein he's been tapping, no matter what they did to him. He told them 'Nothing you may do to me in this life would matter. I fear for my soul in the next life ... that mine is cursed by The Padre.'

Being calloused souls themselves, the bad boys didn't understand how deeply the Apache meant his statement, and as Rudolf said, 'they hung him again, but they hung him too much.'

So having killed their 'goose', the frustrated men hunted the area in vain, finding nothing but sand and rocks.

Thus we hear of another case of the appearance of Los Padres' Mine ... and always, its subsequent disappearance."

Joyce Campbell, also located these additional notes about the mine. She wrote:

"A Bakersfield newspaperman, Fred G. Tredway, continues the story. He reported that J. A. Miklas and C. F. Salazar arrived in Bakersfield in January of 1915 with a map which supposedly came from the padre via one of the two's great-grandmothers. It was bought, reputedly, for $500 by three men; a Mr. Secrest, J. W. Kelly and H. B. Frank. Kelly was one half of the famous Kelly-Rand mine and Secrest ran the Grand Hotel on Chester Avenue in Bakersfield.

Considering the means at hand of the two 'peons' (Miklas and Salazar), *it isn't likely they could have forged and prepared such a convincing specimen; a complicated package containing a parchment map two feet square, yellowed and ancient looking; also a smaller map, a letter, and key to the property ... and they were all enclosed, first in silk, then in buckskin, then a layer of tin which had since oxydized into a state of frailty ... and all then finally wrapped in rawhide!*

The package, they said had been buried (presumably by the great-grandmother) *until the two fellows had dug it up shortly before presenting it for sale.*

This writer (Mrs. Campbell) *is not informed on methods of preservation 150 years ago, but it looks like somebody tried to protect the papers ... and tin can't be rewrapped around anything after it has oxydized to that fragile state.*

Shortly after the sale of the map there were rumors running around Bakersfield that Mr. Secrest had filed papers on a silver mine in Tejon country. When questioned by Tredway, he kept mum, and that's all the farther that story goes. If it was the 'Padre' he filed on, our contention is proved secrecy is the password to nullifying the curse.

Here, now, is another instance where a well-known man attests to the credibility of Tecuya's story. Frank Burton, a Bakersfield police officer at the time Tredway takes over the story, said that in his younger days he had seen with his own eyes twelve crosses made of rough stone indicating the graves of the padres near San Emedio.

If you're thinking of prospecting, however, and believe, as the Frenchman, that the curse of the padres has dwindled, hear this. In 1927 two boys, armed with a map they had received from a 'dying desert rat' reputedly lowered themselves into a blind canyon by ropes, where they found a shelf of ore 'more like bars of gold and silver than like rock'. Around them they could see indications of use and improvements made many years ago.

They returned to Bakersfield to try for a grub-stake, where they got into trouble. One boy disappeared while the other was jailed. The latter departed town also, upon his release from jail, but he left the map with a 17 year old friend named Eddie O'Neill."

There was an O'Neill (O'Neal) family in the future area of Wheeler Ridge in the early 1900's – an area people would travel to when beginning their quest of the Los Padres Mine. There were also O'Neils of one spelling or another in the area of the future Los Padres Estates. Mrs. Campbell wrote:

"O'Neill seems to have been an enterprising sort. He was boarding with the J. C. Cotters in Bakersfield, was just beginning

> *as a professional parachute jumper and was in the process of building his own airplane. He planned to fly over the area indicated on the map and parachute into the canyon just as soon as he finished the plane. Apparently he completed it and publicized that he was getting ready to search for the mine. That very week he was practice-diving over the Kern County Airport. He jumped, and his chute failed to open.* (and as Mrs. Campbell says) *What did you expect!"*

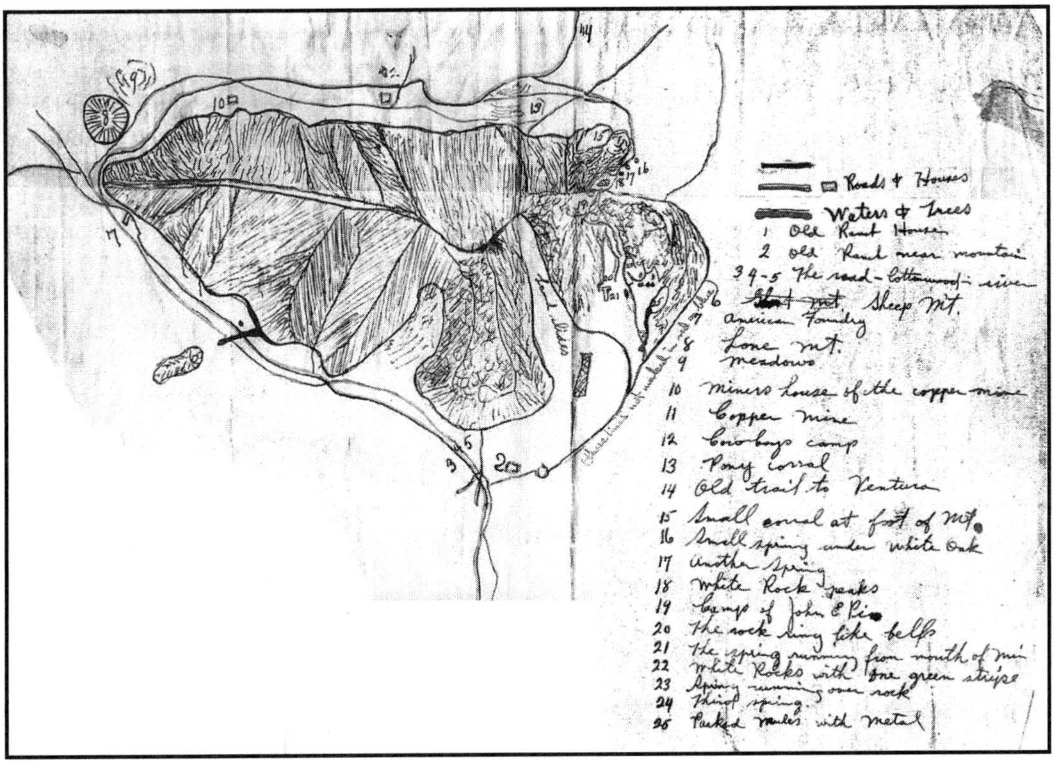

Map given to the author of this book in the 1980's
by a Frazier Park old-timer, Art Novak

Another story Joyce Campbell writes in the early 1970's is as follows:

> *"A few years ago something occurred which may or may not have bearing on the Lost Padre's Mine. A stranger named Ben Clark came into my office and showed me a tarnish-blackened silver ingot about the size of the palm of a hand, which he said was one of 29 he had found in a hollow tree near Lockwood Flat. He would have passed them by, he said, except for a noisy metal detector.*
>
> *He said he took them to the Los Angeles County Museum where he was told there should have been 40 ingots of that type to a pack, and they were probably made before 1790. The ingot he*

showed me had an apparently sand-cast bas-relief form of a lamb carrying a banner with the Jesuit treasure sign of a cross with extensions to each side of the base of the cross on it and this was supposed to indicate the mission or parish for which it was refined.

Concerning other recently found relics, Kenny Cope, 'Mayor of New Cuyama', and the late Bill Owens of the Plunderosa Ranch, found some old Spanish coins while prospecting in Ballinger Canyon one day. Also, the Don Roberts family (he was fire control officer at Chuchupate Ranger Station for years) *found an old sabre, very rusted, in a clump of bushes near the station. Just below the hilt was what I imagine to be a blacksmith's mark: the outline of a shield with a scorpion engraved within. In CORONADO'S CHILDREN, J. Frank Dobie said, 'the best time to enlist the aid of angels in the business of recovering treasure is in the sign of Scorpio, for then, they rule over legacies and riches'."*

Jim *"Sonny"* Gunn with a revolver he found at the site of an old mine in 1977. The gun dated back to 1845. (Joyce Campbell/MOUNTAIN ENTERPRISE photo)

The ore taken from the Los Padres Mine has been described as having the unusual characteristics of chocolate-red quartz, rich in gold. A similar ore has been located throughout the San Emigdio Mountains, in an eleven foot vein in the foothills south of Neenach in the Antelope Valley and on the Sawmill Mountain that is east of Liebre Mountain which might account for the fact that they are all within the San Andreas Fault rift zone. In a 1976 article in the MOUNTAIN ENTERPRISE the interviewee indicates there was also a padres' mine on Frazier Mountain. The Padres were said to, and would have very likely, had mines in numerous locations.

It would seem logical that such earthquakes as happened in 1857, 1906, 1933, 1952, etc. may have had their effects on the site of the Los Padres Mine and especially the springs thereof. The San Emigdio Mountains are not the only possible site of a Los Padres Mine as they are supposedly located throughout the Southwest, all no doubt worked by Catholic priests in their quest to finance and decorate the mission chapels. It is assumed that when the local mines were closed in the early 1800's, attention to it was long diverted by the big rush for gold in Northern California. The remains of smelters, wells and mine shafts that may have been associated with the afore-told mines are now barely discernible in the San Emigdio Mountains.

To review the possible location of the San Emigdio mine, it is supposed to be up a steep rocky trail. Facing the opening there is a large rock on the left with another rock on top of it that when hit with a rock rings like a bell. Somewhere nearby there is a large white rock with green strips. On the right side of the opening there is a waterfall/flow that passes over a large rock. To the right of that another waterfall/flow streams down a slope. A third waterfall/flow, and the largest comes from the opening of the mine. When the mine was closed up a large rock was rolled in front of the opening and a large pine tree felled over on that.

The above is a photo of one such mine located off San Emigdio Canyon by this author in the 1980's, though I do not know how to revisit the site nor judging by the legends would I care to return to it.

In the 1923 Charles Saunders wrote a book entitled the SOUTHERN SIERRAS OF CALIFORNIA and suggested another possible use of the gold in the latter years of the missions. He describes a visit to Mt. Pinos so the desert he refers to below was possibly the Antelope Valley. He wrote:

> *"The desert was just over the hill with its will-o-the-wisp stories of treasure, it is said that there was a popular one about the 'Lost Mine of the Padres'. You may be sure of its essentials without my going much into detail ... such tales are alike the West over. The incidentals in this case, I believe, involved a manse (as the Christianized Indians of the missions were called) of San Fernando stealing in under cover of the night by undivulged trails with a little sack of gold nuggets to replenish the Church funds, which so often ran low under the greedy demands of the secular government; and then, when the blow of secularization fell, and the mansos were scattered and swallowed up in the wild life of the hills again, this secret of the gold's source was lost with them though the tale of it survived and still lingers, to spur prospectors and vagrant treasure hunters to a hopeless quest; for there is slight reason to believe that the Franciscan missionaries had any regard for gold except to fear it and its hateful influences on their labors."*

The last family to occupy and run the old road stop located a mile or so beyond the mouth of Grapevine Canyon was the Rose family – thus the name of the location was known as *"Rose Station"* – later Wheeler Ridge. In the 1950's, the Rose daughter, Annie, wrote the remembrances of her childhood and young adult days there. Among her poems were some two dozen pages about her and her brothers' search for the lost Los Padres Mine that they had heard of as they grew up. The following are excerpts from her writings:

> *"The summer sunshine now is gone, we're starting on our quest,*
> *Of all the seasons in the year, the Fall we like the best.*
> *The reds, the browns, and yellows too, are in a glory bright,*
> *The intruding beauty of the day, will last us through the night.*
>
> *The gold is there, we've seen it shine, a pure and yellow glow,*
> *Free milling, fine and plenty rich, but covered deep and low.*
> *The ore is yellow, red and brown, the colors of the Fall,*
> *And if we cannot pick the best, will try to mine it all.*
>
> *Around the Padre's stamping grounds, are many eerie things,*
> *The Spirits there that walk at night, the sounds where echo clings.*
> *The weird and wistful beauty there, the peace and pathos too,*
> *The memory there of tragic things, that scarcely yet are through.*

The canyon where the padres stood
and watched them hide the gold
The lives they held as valueless, the stories never told.
We only guess the breaking hearts that followed in its trail,
The joy of each discovery, the hurt to see it fail.

The gold they stored so safely there, is still a hidden mass,
The treasure seekers dream of gold, the story of the past.
The Padre stands a guarding well, the gold he tried to mine,
The Indians who worked so freely there, are keeping even time.

The symbols they made can't be burnt, nor can they slide away,
They last a hundred years or more, as perfect as that day,
And yet you'd hardly notice them, so hidden and so clear,
Perhaps the superstitious ones, regarding them with some fear.

A big raised sunburst marks the way, the Padre placed it low,
A bar, a serpent or a mark, all show the way to go.
The cross he marked it for his faith, the meaning had to be,
The crescent, wide and pointing south, nor make it hard to see.

And then you'll them all combined, a meaning all its own,
Don't be sure you have it right, the mystery has grown.
A serpent of a different kind, is laying by the hill,
Best to note it carefully indeed, or you might read it ill.

Up through the big ___ ___ ___, (unreadable)
a weary man goes past,
A brave man and a patient man, how will his courage last.
He climbs up on the farther side, to find his own way through,
Going down on the Northern slope as some prospectors do.

He found his gold on the way down,
much greater than he'd known,
He felt so good, if he'd had wings, he surely could have flown.
But an old man and a tired man, went pleading on his way,
His hopes were high and samples bright
he's coming back some day

Someday someone will find the gold
when they're just wandering by
And most of all the rest of us, will sit right down and cry.
Relief itself will be so big, there's no more use to climb,
We'll all just quit our camping out, and wasting all our time.

We started trenching from the wash,
we worked hard side by side,
We knew the shaft was just ahead, for which so many died.
A mound of rock was standing there, a reaching arm below,
Its bones a-bleaching in the sand, as white as driven snow

It tried to point us out the way, we could not read the sign,
But now we've followed farther back, and found the fabled mine.
How does it seem for thirty years, to know your neighbor's scorn,
To travel on your lonely trail from night till early morn.

We'll try to crowd the envy out, with love and honor by,
We'll pray to those who love us best, to guard us as we try.
For the old shaft was just above, they'd turned the water in,
It took unfounded faith and pride and thirty years to win.

The Chief who took us to the place, and showed the symbols old,
We're sure he thinks it now is time to carry out the gold.
And surely he can venture back and wander round at will,
To show us if he wishes to, the gold upon the hill.

We've worked it out by patient faith, in one man's spoken word,
What matter that for twenty years, his voice we have not heard.
It's twenty years since we last heard, that patient voice explain,
Yet never once have we lost faith or questioned it again.

Eight years ago and twenty men were sure they had it found,
But greed and grasping hands reached out
and all they touched was ground.
And as we glanced along the path, there was a mighty hand,
It swept that mass of gold away from all that maddened band.

The Chief had reached across that day, to save for those he knew,
The gold he'd helped to store away where all those symbols grew.
And then he took us up around and showed a massive vein.
The gold a-shining in the quartz like yellow drops of rain.

It's up to us to take it through, with courage as we may,
And as the Chief would have us do, for he must have the say.
His steady step is strong and proud as he goes back and forth,
At first he's starting down the hill and then he's starting north.

And now our faith is justified, in every sign and hope,
The vein is all uncovered there, along that barren slope.
The little ditch they built by hand, to turn the water there,
Is showing now as plain as day, it's almost like a dare.

In the old shaft the timbers stand, a mass of rotting wood,
While over on the new claim, the ore is getting good.
In the old shaft the water's bad, it's pumps we're needing there,
But over on the new claim, the chances seem so fair.

The old shaft is down so very deep, it's cold and dark as doom,
And over on the new claim, it's like a sunny room.
It's high and dry and perfect there, a glory in its view,
Nor sorrow nor of tragic things, its very thoughts are new.

At the old mine we'll carry through, if God will give us time,
For after all, the new claim is really quite a climb.
We'll let the spirits take a hand, and point us out the ore,
We'll take what they will grant us there, nor ask for any more.

The path it is not ever clear, the price they ask is high,
We'll slip so carefully through the brush, and many times we sigh.
But step by step and foot by foot, we're building history still,
And strength and patience they must hold, as we toil o'er the hill.

Perhaps we'll work it out alone, maybe new help we'll see,
To open up the tunnels old and help build history.
For it's a very famous Mine, and as it opens more,
The romance of a hundred years, we're standing at its door.

And what could show a greater hurt,
than those four murdered men,
Who went down in that darkened hole, and no're came out again.
Is it their ghosts we hear at night, clear up along the trail,
Or is it just the restless flight, of some young mountain quail.

The gold they stored along the point, the padre guards it well,
And even on the darkest night, we see him on the hill.
He's weeping now in deep regret, for sorrow haunts his years,
And all the growth across that point, is salted with his tears.

Six tons of gold and treasure great, they stored it there so well,
And many lives were taken there that none who lived could tell.
And gold that's stained with human blood can only bring us grief,
Unless it's used in some good way, to cause a great relief.

Each cache is marked so very clear, the size almost the same,
Each three feet wide and seven long, you'll find is quite a game.
And every mark will read four ways, you'll have to try them all,
And patience great is needed there, it might be great or small.

And on the trail with breaking heart, the Padre paces slow,
He's wondering as he's walking there
just which way he should go.
And step by step and mile by mile the Chief in patient stride,
To keep the wrong before his heart and punish by his pride.

For after all the gold was his, the land belonged to him,
And but for his own efforts there, the chance to find was slim.
And we who love his mountains so, would surely be his choice,
And as we help dig out the gold, he'll look on and rejoice.

We're starting now to understand the story all the way,
The things that never should have been, haunt it through the day
A score of men who disappeared, just vanished as they went,
And others hunting for those men, until their strength was spent.

On _?_'s rugged Western slope a point stands proud and high,
And as we toil around its foot, it towers to the sky.
It covers well the Padre's vein, the gold is massed below,
And as we follow o'er the top, we're glad that this is so.

Eleven feet and standing straight, just as 'twas said to be,
We find our vein up high and wide and toward the setting sun.
The trails are rough and brush is thick, winter tipped with snow,
We're glad to follow it so far and trace it to and fro.

A promise great it shows us plain, our search is nearly done,
We find our vein up high and wide and toward the setting sun.
The Padre's vein a wondrous thing, fabled for ninety years,
Causing deaths galore, love and hate,
anguish and greed and tears.

The Padre's gold, a yellow mass, it shines a lovely glow,
But seems to call from every man the worst that he may know.
We're trying hard with every breath to hope away the curse,
We're trying hard with all our strength that it may get no worse.

History tells of the Padre Mine, of its great unmatched size,
Its fabled wealth as yet unknown, an untouched Midas' prize.
'Twas closed in silence and closed in stealth,
by fifteen husky men,
'Twas a thorough job and a secret job and no one answers when.

The answer stayed with fifteen men, a mountain hid them well,
And when or where no one could say, or answer what befell.
Time went on and the mine was still, the mountain all a slide,
Perhaps the faithful Indians know, but silent in their pride.

History tells of the Padre Mine, the path of a Man of God,
And all the gentle Chumash tribe, who loved to till the sod.
We followed the trail for forty years and learned the history well,
And when the 20th Century wandered in,
'twas an easy tale to tell.

Times there were such that made us pause,
and wonder can this be,
For here before us a terrible thing, and this we had to see.
We stood and looked across the shaft, maybe eight by ten,
Knowing as we faced each other there, the fate of fifteen men.

I was a girl of the mountain, I'd known no other life,
He was a hard boiled Engineer, used to the world of strife.
We faced each other with startled eyes,
our hearts turned slowly cold,
And know without any spoken word what had been done for gold.

I was just a mountain girl, no church was asked to join,
He was a hardened Engineer, who liked his gold in coin.
We thought of the trail we'd followed, the softened evening glare,
And both of us we raised our hands in one deep heartfelt prayer.

No loving hands had placed them, or thrown the dirt above,
No brother had folded silent hands, no sister offered love.
No loved ones ever had paved the way for fate was far too fast,
So now we all can only hope the hand of God was last.

We followed the trail for many years,
we saw the work they'd done,
Starting out at the break of day to pause at the setting sun.
The word of God as taught by man, does it at all compare,
With the work of the Chumash Tribe as it was shown us there.

They've asked us since to join the church, to travel another road,
To leave the trail we've followed so long
and learn to speak in code.
I'll take what my hills have taught me
nor question God's own word,
In the pictures he has shown me, the voices I have heard.

I've reached the end of the Padre's trail, let others carry through,
I love the early morning there, the smell of the mountain dew.
I love the colors of the Fall, the winter land of snow,
I doubt if any can learn more there, then I already know.

To see the sights I've longed to see, the words I've longed to hear,
A wondrous thing a massive thing, a pleasure and a tear.
To follow yet the Padre's path, whether for work or fun,
To follow it high and going east, right to the morning sun,

For this is what I've wanted to know, to follow and to see,
Is this some strange unknown delight or is this person me?
If those who lead me say I'm through, I give a weary sigh,
And step aside if it is best, to bid my hills goodbye.

And in years I followed this and it was told to me,
The symbols used to make a map, that all men could not see.
No one could read this map they made, unless they had the code,
No one would even notice this, along the Padres road.

Worth sixty million so they say, the gold in masses great,
Can wealth like this in any way, change crooked into straight."

Annie writes of finding the bones of the fifteen men written of above – though she later mentions them as sixteen, *"that had been at rest for 200 years"*. She does indicate that they died in the time of the Jesuits who were supposed to have been in these hills in the late 1600's to early 1700's. She titles one of her writings THE JESUIT PADRE'S SEVEN CACHES OF GOLD. At age fourteen (about 1900), Annie and her brothers, Glen and Dick, were in the hills searching for the gold when she stepped on a rattlesnake – guarding the bones of these men. *"He made no effort to strike but all the vibration from the furious rattling went up the full length of my spine."* Annie also writes of brothers Eddie and Bill.

Annie Rose was also involved with a Los Padres Mine located to the east of the old Ridge Route Road. According to writer, Jack Black, in the 1870's an Indian asked one Dr. D. F. Bragg for some horses in trade for giving him information on the location of this Padre Mine. Bragg located five partners, and the Indian, beginning to regret his actions, led them to a small vein which he claimed would lead them to the richer diggings. Bragg and associates set up a mining operation and tapped into an extremely rich vein of gold supposed to be over ten feet thick.

Among the partners was a somewhat *"unsavory character"* by the name of Bronco Charley Riley. To avoid the law in Los Angeles, Charley built a small cabin near the mine and lived there year around. Some time later, angered by the taunts of his fellow miners about the fact that he had to hid away like that, Bronco Charley shot them all dead. It is said that Doc Bragg helped Charlie drag the bodies into the mine shaft, seal up the entrance and they went their separate ways. It seems two more men prospecting in the area of the mine were later discovered shot to death. Not long after that Bronco Charlie was found shot to death in his cabin. Doc Bragg never returned to his mine and before his death, some thirty years later, he told his friend, William Blackburn Rose, the father of Annie Rose about the mine. It wasn't until the 1920's that Annie was able to locate the canyon described to them as east of the Ridge Route somewhere between Sawmill and Sawtooth mountains. She filed about twenty mining claims though little is recorded of her success or failure there. Relics and artifacts have been found in the area that prove Spanish miners once worked in those hills.

It seems after Annie, a brother and her husband, an engineer, found the mine, her brother lost his mind and had to be institutionalized. Annie's husband, Adrian Briggs, wanted to bring the gold out but as Annie was so superstitious she wouldn't allow it. The dispute was thought to have caused his early death. Annie took the secret of both mines and the gold to her grave.

As a teenager, David Wasdahl of San Diego worked the *"Los Padres Mine"* north of Castaic with Annie and Adrian Briggs and said that Mrs. Briggs told him a similar story about the mine. The Wasdahl family lived up the canyon from the Briggs so he would join them as they traveled north to the mine site. He said that you could also reach the mine by driving the Ridge Route to Kelly's Ranch and hiking in a little over a mile or so.

The Los Angeles Times of October 3, 1927 carried a version of this same story:

> *"About 1840 (1740?) an Indian hunting for his horse started up Bear Creek. When he stooped over to drink from the creek he discerned through the rippling water a rock ledge rich with gold. He reported his find to a padre who organized the Indians for the job at hand. They turned the creek from its bed and began a mining operation. Legend has it that they took about a million dollars in gold from this mine in three years.*
>
> *But one day in the third summer the tunnel caved in, burying fifteen Indians. The rest of the Indians refused to go into the mine thereafter and the padres were forced to seal the entrance.*
>
> *The mine was 'lost' until 1876 when Dr. B. F. Bragg came to California from Kentucky with some fine horses. An Indian admiring the horses but having no money told the doctor that he would tell him where gold could be found if he would give him some horses. Bragg took him up and the Indian led him to the old Padre mine.*

> *The doctor and his associates went to work and it is reported that the operation took out some $800,000 in gold in two years. The venture was cut short when his Irish foreman ran amuck and killed four men, one of them being the Indian who had showed Dr. Bragg where the mine was."*

Years later, Annie Rose, apparently not married yet, begins her search for the mine. A Mexican fellow told her that the entrance was in the old creek bed. In the year this newspaper article was written, 1927, Miss Rose located someone to develop her mining claims. B. E. Miller had a trench dug up and down the dry creek bed until they came to a few large buried boulders running at right angles across the creek. In excavating the area they soon found evidence of the rock being blasted out and visible gold. They expected to be in the original old Padres tunnel within six months. . . .

Possibly the poem Annie Briggs wrote above could be a combination of information from both of the mine sites?

In a recent October 2004 issue of LOST TREASURE magazine, Tom Vance writes of circumstances that might be related to the San Emigdio lost Padres Mine. They are:

> *"During the 1850's, near Wheeler's Ridge, a skeleton was found along with several pieces of mining equipment and a pair of saddle bags holding several thousand dollars in gold nuggets, giving rise to the speculation that a rich deposit of gold may lie somewhere near there.*
>
> *Some years later a cowboy riding a trail through Mt. Pinos following a heavy rainstorm found two powder horns that contained $1,500 in gold nuggets.*
>
> *At the time of his mysterious death in 1963, well-known treasure hunter, Frank Fish, was in the process of searching for a rich Spanish gold mine he thought to be located in San Emidio Canyon. He had just come back from a trip into the canyon where he had found relics he felt substantiated his belief that the Old Spanish mine had once been active there. He was found dead of mysterious circumstances and never got a chance to continue his long-time search for treasure in the San Emidio Canyon area."*

Thus ends the collection of miscellaneous stories that seem to relate to the local Los Padres Mines.

IV - THE SAN EMIGDIO DISTRICT

As you drive Mil Potrero Highway, to and from Pine Mountain Club, one gets a fantastic view of San Emigdio Canyon to the north, with San Emigdio Mountain to the left and Antimony Peak to the right. This canyon holds some of the area's oldest known non-Indian history. The old Spanish Trail – El Camino Viejo – first an Indian trail, comes from the east and winds its way down the canyon. The Spanish explorer-padres and soldados (soldiers) who traveled this inland route between Northern and Southern California were quite aware of the precious metals to be found in this canyon. What those early miners might not have been aware of, or interested in, was the abundance of antimony in the region, though their precious silver and gold was found within the antimony. Antimony is a dense, brittle, silvery-white metal with a bright metallic luster. It is used especially in alloys. The California Division of Mines and Geology's 1962 report indicates that the native people may have used the antimony as a source of pigment in their pictographs of that area.

Geological records from the mid-1800's give the first reports of smelting of antimony in San Emigdio Canyon. Geologist and Mineralogist, William F. Blake, after visiting the site in the 1850's and again at a later date wrote of it, *"I believe the antimony is of sufficient importance to pay for transportation to San Pedro on mules, a distance of over one hundred miles"* – the nearest seaport.

Old maps from 1872 and 1873 indicate that S. Boushey and his partners, E. J. Weston from Ventura, and F.P.F. Temple – a name well-known in Los Angeles, had several mines and a mill site in San Emigdio Canyon in what was called the *"San Emigdio Mining District"*. Among the interesting names of their mines were the *"Clara Luisa"*, *"Templito Silver"*, and *"Summit"* all listed as quartz mines. Others nearby were the *"Whale Q"* and *"Padre Juan's"*.

An 1880 map shows the Boushey house, a smelting furnace and smith shop where the creek coming from the *"Mil Potrero"* (presently Pine Mountain Club) enters into San Emigdio creek – along the El Camino Viejo. Mr. Boushey also built more refined buildings and a smelter further down the canyon.

In the 1888 report of the State Mineralogist Steven (or Stephen) Bowers, gives this excellent description of the mine. He wrote:

"July 31, 1888 – Started down the San Emido canon. Thermometer this morning was 27 degrees. Owing to a cloud burst the canon was badly washed and almost impassable. The antimony mines are extensive and if worked with capitol would be very profitable. A London company once offered a million dollars for these mines (interesting). *They are now owned by Mr. Stephen Boushey. He has works for reducing and smelting tin ore. The ore is rich in gold, silver and antimony. Mr. Boushey gave me a specimen of magnetic iron ore, grit rock, marble and fire proof sandstone he has found here.*

The San Emidio Antimony Mine was located by its present owners in 1872. It is claimed that this ledge was known to the Jesuit fathers at an early day and was worked under their direction. I learned that there is a record to this effect in some of the old missions and that implements have been found here and elsewhere in this portion of the country indicating their use in these mines many years ago.

Professor William R. Blake, who visited this locality in 1853, as geologist and mineralogist of the expedition surveying a route for the Pacific Railroad, refers to this deposit of antimony, and says that in one place he found the remains of some old smelting works. Mr. Blake revisited this locality some years afterward, being much impressed with the character of its mineral deposits. The ore is principally sulphuret of antimony. The vein crops out on the summit of San Emidio Range, and is from thirty to one hundred feet in width. The hanging and foot-walls are composed of granite. The ore is carried on donkeys over a trail two and one half miles to smelting works in the canyon, which is 2500 feet below the vein at the place where it is being mined. Here is a pulverizer and three concentrators, with other machinery, run by steam power.

Messrs. Boushey & Co., the owners of this mine, are preparing to erect a tramway or slide from the mine to the works, which will be about one and one half miles in length. There is an abundance of pine timber growing near by that may be utilized for the purpose, while in the canon, where the smelting works are located, is a never failing stream of water. The ore averages from 30 to 35 percent antimony. It is also stated that it contains from $4 to $16 per ton in gold, and from $10 to $14 in silver. Owing to a combination of circumstances, but principally from the want of capital, these works have been idle for some time past; but at the time of my visit they were ready to start again. I observed that the machinery was in good order, and that the mineral brought down from the mine was of excellent character."

The Boushey smelting furnace, blacksmith shop, home and gardens
lower San Emigdio Canyon – late 1800's
(Kern County Museum photo)

"The mountain west of this ledge is capped with metamorphic sandstone, which Mr. Boushey has tested for lining the furnaces of his smelting works, and pronounces it equal to the best imported firebricks. He showed me some of this stone that had been subject to frequent intense heat in his furnaces, and it was apparently uninjured.

We left the mine and as we proceeded down this canon we found vast quantities of syenite and gneiss on the right side or north. A mile below the mine the mt. is covered with metamorphic sandstone. Here we went into camp.

August 1, 1888 – Continued down the San Emidio canon. About a mile below our camp found fossil beds in the sand rock mostly bivalves. It is very picturesque. The sandstone capping continues for some distance down the canon and much of it is grit rock. Thousands of tons have fallen as talus. Reached San Emidio ranch house about 10 a.m. Mr. Miller, the sup't supplied us with melons, tomatoes, berries, etc. which were very acceptable."

In the 1890 State Mineralogist report, Myron Angel reported on the Antimony mine as follows:

"The vein is apparently eleven feet wide, running north and south through a high ridge. Four claims have been located on the vein and United States patents obtained. The claims were located on what appears to have been a break from the vein, following a curved line around the east side of the hill. Two tunnels, called the 'Two Brothers', have been run on the north end, and two, called the 'Two Sisters', on the south end of the mine. Another is in 230 feet and has struck a body of ore one foot in thickness.

The metal is hauled to Bakersfield, forty miles, at a cost of $8 to $10 per ton, and transshipped to San Francisco, 314 miles, by the Southern Pacific Railroad, at $8 per ton in carload lots. The ore is said to carry from $4 to $16 in silver per ton. The cost of producing the pure antimony at the mine and works is 8 or 9 cents a pound. San Emigdio Creek is a stream of four hundred inches flow, and with a rapid fall may be utilized as a great power.

Throughout the coast region there are legends of ancient mines which gave fabulous wealth to the padres under the Spanish regime, and the San Emigdio is thought to have been one of them. This is thought to be proven by the discovery of an old shaft by the workmen running a tunnel, from which came a strong current of air. This shaft, however, did not come under the observation of any of the owners of the mine, or other intelligent person, and was filled by the workmen with timber and mining waste. This, however, will soon be removed and possibly the first padre mine will be rediscovered."

Mr. Angel also writes:

"Three miles south of the San Emigdio is a vast amount of magnetic iron. A great ledge is there found, three thousand feet long."

A miscellaneous mining news item found in the KERN COUNTY ECHO about this time reported on a miner from somewhere in the area:

"In our rambles we happened to stumble into camp on a queer character in the shape of a prospector and miner but found him rather hard to get anything out of concerning the country. In order to render our host more communicative we proposed a bumper to the mining interests. It had the desired effect and forthwith he produced from under the bed some rare specimens. Among them was a silver spike weighing about a pound, evidently an old Jesuit spike smelted long ago. We were afterwards shown the spot where the old smelter stood."

The 1894 State Mineralogist, J. J. Crawford wrote:

"The Padre Mine is situated on the east side of Tail-hold Canon, (a trail so steep one would hold on to the tail of the mule for help to climb it) *which leads to Pleyto Canon. The lode appears to have the same general strike as that on which the Boushey mines are situated. The workings consist of a 25 foot tunnel, which cuts a body of antimony-bearing matter 15 feet in width. The wall rock is granite. In 1893 there were about three tons of high-grade antimony ore (stibnite) on the dump. The mine is reached by a rough trail, but a road could be made without great difficulty to the Pleyto Ranch.*

The San Emidio Mines have veins outcropping on the sides and over the summit of a rugged granite peak rising over 6,000 feet. It is almost perpendicular on its eastern side, where the position and character of the deposits are well shown. The ore appears in places over a vertical distance of 1,000 feet or more. Where the ore is not found the line of the fissure is marked by a red stain and the decomposed condition of the granite. On the summit of the mountain the ore bodies are not confined to a single fissure, but occur over an area 2,000 feet wide. The property consists of five patented and four unpatented claims. The ore averages 40 per cent antimony. In places it is rich in silver, with the occasional appearance of iron and arsenical pyrites. A tunnel from the San Emidio Canon 1300 feet long would cut the veins at a depth of 2000 feet. At present the mines are reached only by a steep and narrow trail, down which all the ore had to be packed to the reduction works. Nothing but assessment work has been done for some time."

Antimony Peak or Mountain, is also sometimes referred to as San Emidio or Emigdio Mountain because of the mining activity in the canyon below. The mountain is the site of the oldest recorded mineral exploration and mining in Kern County. In 1940-41 the United States Bureau of Mines prospected the top and south slope of this peak with a number of trenches. The work disclosed a shear zone of quartz running along a northwest angle but no continuous ore chute was found.

It seems that after the Kern County Land Company purchased the land at the base of the mountain in 1892, mining activity diminished. The Mines & Geology Report did indicate some mining claims were issued in the early 1900's. The BAKERSFIELD CALIFORNIAN of October 5, 1937 once again touted that *"Frazier Center of Mining Boom"*. The article read:

"An active mining boom has started in this section with many mines in operation and a large mill nearing completion. In answer

to the increasing demands of miners, a 100-ton mill has been constructed at Big Tree. The mill will be in operation in several days and is equipped to handle all the production in the mining district. (Big Tree is thought to be the huge big cone spruce in Pleito Canyon written about in chapter XXIII of this book.)

The Lone Star mine in Nieson canyon (near Nieson Flat to the north of Tecuya Ridge), *one of the several mining claims leased by Charles Cuddy is in operation and is producing large quantities of antimony. Silver is expected at a deeper level. The value of antimony has been steadily increasing in the past two years. The chief use of the element is as a constituent of alloys to which it imparts hardness and the property of expanding on solidification. It has a metallic appearance but is actually a hard, brittle, crystalline structure of a tin-white color."*

In 1941, Charles B. Fife, postmaster and storekeeper in Frazier Park, must have gained a lease as it was recorded that he shipped five tons of ore from a mine on Antimony Peak which at that time was reported to contain 35 percent antimony.

Visitors to the San Emigdio Canyon antimony smelter site in the 1960's and 1970's found remains of the old smelter still standing with hand-hewn logs and square nails about. Local writer, Grace Bradley, hiked to the site with others and reported in the BAKERSFIELD CALIFORNIAN of March 28, 1961:

> *"An old furnace made of sandstone slabs and adobe mud mixed with ashes still stood with many burnt clinkers or slag in evidence in and around the ore bin. Here was also a mystery as hundreds of balls of tin were found at the ore bin. These balls about the size of a large head of lettuce, were composed of scrap tin, some in long narrow strips about one-eighth inch width and others which look like the tops and bottoms of tin cans had been cut from the tin. All the scraps were wound into round balls of the same size."*

Local Historian, Joyce Campbell, led a group to the antimony smelter in 1973. As the Pine Mountain Club recreation director at the time, this author joined the group with my three young sons. In the September 28th, 1973 issue of the MOUNTAIN ENTERPRISE Mrs. Campbell wrote of the adventure. Excerpts from that article are as follows:

> *"For this trek we had to back-pack our lunches and canteens and cameras, as the terrain down the canyon forbade the use of any kind of vehicle. The very wet winter last year had caused deep cuts in the creekbed we followed, and it was hard to picture the*

fact that this had been in the last two centuries, a heavily traveled route.

On the steep canyon wall nearby is the remnant of a 'Tailholt Trail' which led in precarious fashion to an antimony mine on Antimony Peak. Bill Meukow, one of our companions, said the name comes, of course, from its steepness which forced a prospector to 'grab a-holt-a my mule's tail' and be pulled along." (Bill Meukow was a long-time resident of the hills to the east of the canyon.)

Mrs. Campbell continued:
"Climbing back up the canyon made me feel as old as the ruins we had seen...most aptly expressed by another fellow traveler, the artist and sculptor, Dick Nickerson of Frazier Park, in his poem inspired by the canyon:

'Gone the weary traveler,
long from this rocky canyon floor,
he struggléd as I, upon this slope
and stumbled what I stumble o'er.
he stopped where I stop to rest his tired limb;
if he was as sore as I am sore,
Lord! I feel for him.' "

The balls of tin – about the size of a soccer ball – were not so prevalent in the 1970's as Mrs. Bradley described in the 1960's. The tin was no doubt used in the smelting process.

Remains at antimony smelter – 1973

Remains at antimony smelter - 1973

The most recent story from the San Emigdio Mining District was located in a MOUNTAIN ENTERPRISE of June 15, 1987. The mine, *"The Silverville Mine"*, was located at the top of San Emigdio Canyon. From the article we learn:

> *"Mr. William Sagerman greets you when you come up to the location of the Silverville Mine. June 1st marked the fifth anniversary ince Mr. Sagerman began extraction of the ore which contains platinum, rhodium, palladium, iron group minerals, etc. He mentioned platinum being recovered in the amount of $800 a ton. Gold and silver are not present in significant quantities.*
>
> *After taking the ore from the mine shaft with hammer, chisel, pick and shovel, it is ground to a very fine grey powder in a gasoline powered ball mill on the site. Sagerman, who is the sole owner and operator of the mine, then packs the grey powder into five gallon tins which are placed in crates and shipped to Ohio for processing. He is currently awaiting results from recent assays and says that the ore is becoming richer as the shaft is sunk deeper into the canyon wall.*
>
> *The 60 year old Sagerman enjoys showing and talking about his Silverville Mine and the beautiful mountain paradise in which he makes his home. He lives alone with some 16 cats, all named, and a ten year old chicken, not named. Ohio is his home state and his mining interest stems from his childhood association with coal mines."*

The Silverville Mine at the top of San Emigdio Canyon

V - THE PIRU DISTRICT

The area south of Frazier Mountain, north of Alamo Mountain, from Lockwood Valley to Hungry Valley – along the Piru Creek – was referred to as the *"Piru District"*. One of the first recorded gold discoveries in California was reported to have come from the *"Piru Watershed"* just south of the Piru District as early as 1841. The discovery was in Santa Feliciana Canyon to the south of what is now the Pyramid Dam. The VENTURA SIGNAL of 1879 told of prospectors bringing gold to Ventura from the northeast corner of the county as early as 1850.

An old book or report entitled STOKES MEMORIAL AND BIOGRAPHICAL HISTORY stated that a director of the mint in Philadelphia reported one million(!) in gold had been sent out from the placers (alluvial deposits containing valuable minerals) of the southern Piru area in the year 1841 by an Andreas Castillero. This information was also given in a 1932 report by the State mineralogist based on information from HITTELL'S HISTORY OF CALIFORNIA. The gold probably did come from the Piru Placer as its location was given as north of San Fernando by six leagues (18 miles) and north of Los Angeles by fifteen leagues (45 miles) at a locality that has been worked more or less during the first half of that century.

Mineralogists reported the gold of the lower Piru Placer had no doubt occurred in fissure veins in the mountains to the north and in gravel in drainage basins probably deposited by a Pliocene River. Underneath the gold-bearing gravel is a deposit barren of gold belonging to the Miocene Period.

The first newspaper article located about mining in the Piru came from an 1873 copy of the VENTURA SIGNAL. A Tom Newby wrote a letter dated May 7th to the newspaper from the mining town of "*Centerville*", *"Piru Mines"*, in the *"Lockwood District"*. The Lockwood District was next to and basically a part of the Piru District. The article gives an excellent look at the mining activity in that locality in the early 1870's. Mr. Newby wrote:

> *"Ventura county can now boast of another city of importance, or so, at least in the estimation of some that are interested in the new enterprise. Since my last we have had quite a deputation of new comers from different parts of the country; San Francisco, Santa Barbara, Venturans and Colonians* (from back east?) *have made their appearance among us. All seem well pleased with the*

appearance of things in general. Some have been quite successful in discovering very good mines. Others are busily engaged prospecting with the hope of accomplishing the desired object.

We are now feeling glib over the prospect of a mill, as we have been promised one by a San Francisco company in a few months. I believe it is to be a ten-stamp custom mill. If it was in running order now it would have steady employment, as the mines generally have more or less rock ready for crushing.

The 'Smith & Hunter mine' is in full blast again under the superintendence of Colonel Reed; a fine lot of rock of good quality is already put, and a fine body of ore of still better quality in sight. The 'Moraga mine' is making excellent progress, the tunnel is in about 180 feet, striking the ledge formation which prospects well; a few feet more, it is thought, will strike the ledge proper. A shaft is also being sunk to intersect the tunnel as a ventilator. The same parties are busily engaged on other mines of their own discovery.

Noah Stanton and Charles Swift are working their mines, the rock showing and prospecting well. Don Juan Kays has fine cuts in all his ledges, which number six in all, the rock working $21.50 per ton by mill process. Warren Frazier has just discovered a ledge or spur of about one and a half feet in width of exceeding richness in gold, silver and chrome of lead; the ledge proper, it is thought, has not been found as yet, but prospecting for it is steadily going on. William Warriner has also discovered one similar to the Frazier, and in the immediate vicinity. These ledges are near the placer mines, which were worked some two years by one Lockwood, and worked the past winter by Warriner and Frazier. The 'Chase & Shepherd mine' has a fine cut in it with a good lot of rock on the dump and a fine body in sight. The 'San Jose mine' has a fine cut and a lot of rich rock on the dump ready for the mill, with plenty of a very good quality in sight.

The newly discovered 'Flora mine' is worthy of mention as it is very rich in galena (lead) *and yellow oxide of silver; a large dump has been made and quite a lot of fine ore is ready for the mill. The 'Preble mine' is a large ledge with a splendid body of quartz, highly sprinkled with galena, also carrying gold and silver. It is an extension of the San Jose ledge. The 'Mountain View' and 'Mountain View Extension' are two very rich mines in gold, chloride of silver and galena; considerable work has been done on the two mines and there is a considerable lot of rock on their dumps. The 'Pride of the Mountains' makes the best showing of any mine here in the way of minerals; many samples have been taken to Ventura and other places for purposes of exhibition. There are many other ledges here that are being worked and many more that will have to be worked soon or the claimants will forfeit their rights. I believe that there are about one hundred entries made on the register for mines and mill sites.*

The placer boys are making about $4 per day to the man hauling their dirt some four hundred yards to water. A ditch has been surveyed and work commenced on it, that is to bring the water to the tops of the mountains for mining purposes. The health and mining prospects of the mines are good.

Born ... In Piru mines; April 23rd to the wife of Jesus Romero, a son. And still the world moves on. We are much in need of a store here. Send one of your small establishments out this way. We have a saloon, but the article of food furnished will not keep soul and body together. We are in need of many other necessary improvements for the advancement of the country, which would be liberally patronized, such as a blacksmith shop, hay yard, etc."

Articles such as these sent rumors of gold through the coastal communities, and prospectors continued to fill the hills and canyons with miners – many short term – some longer, and a few stayed.

Housing for the early miners, and their families if they chose to follow, was very crude. Tents were used and possibly a cabin achieved. Cabins were typically of logs with a door and sometimes a window. The roof, often of tin, had a hole in it for the flue vent of a stove; a sink was a wooden box lined with galvanized sheet metal with a pipe leading to it for running water, if they should be so lucky to have it, and several small shelves nailed to the wall nearby created a kitchen. Yucca stalks were often split and put up on the interior walls to help keep the wind out as needed. It was not unusual to see a healthy garden growing nearby with a dog to keep the deer and rabbits away. The deer and rabbit also provided a good diet of meat.

A typical miner's cabin with garden nearby

In *"The Lockwood"* there were forty to fifty white miners scattered about in groups of one and two and about twice as many Chinese. Most of the Chinese were working for the Sespe & Piru Mining Company and mining on their own as well. The Ventura newspaper of March 28, 1874 had reported, *"the Chinamen are washing out 5 to 12 1/2 cents to the pan and are delighted with the prospects"*. The white miners were not taking kindly to the Chinese mining *"their American gold"* and managed to harass them enough to drive them off from the area known as Leopold Flats.

> About 1950 Grace Bradley wrote of this incident as follows:
> *"Family records found here and there tell that in the old days many miners were working around Piru and Lockwood Creeks mining for gold. One record tells there were many Chinese miners in the area. The few white miners resented the Chinese being there. The white miners borrowed two guns and two guns were all they had. These resentful miners rode close to the Chinese camp and one by one they rode to the top of the hill in plain sight of the Chinese. Each rider as he reached the top of the hill could be seen with gun in hand outlined against the sky. He would then ride down the hill and pass on the gun to the next rider. To show their strength and numbers, each rider in turn rode over the hill and down on the other side to join the rear end of the line of miners. This went on for hours. They hoped their little war-like party would frighten the Chinese and cause them to believe there was a large army of white miners. The miners decided to wait a few days to see if their bluff worked. In a few days the Chinese did load up their donkeys and move out of Lockwood Valley."*

One of the great difficulties in mining the area was the lack of water. The LOS ANGELES EXPRESS of April 1876 reported:

> *"Mines at the edge of Ventura county where it joins Los Angeles county have been worked off and on for the past forty years* (this is an interesting statement as it dates mining in these mountains to the 1830's – following the mission era) *and a great deal of gold has been extracted from them. The entire region is auriferous* (has gold in the soil) *and a good placer may be found almost anywhere. The great difficulty to successful mining has been the paucity* (lack) *of water. A number of schemes have been inaugurated at intervals to bring water from Elizabeth Lake and two years ago very extensive work was done on a large ditch from that point, but the enterprise was either abandoned or left in abeyance for we have heard but little of it lately."* (that would have been a noble feat!)

The Snowy Mining District was organized in 1877 and included the Frazier and Castac Mines. The Castac or Castaic Mine was at the southern base of Bear Mountain near Piru Creek, seven or eight miles downstream from Lockwood Creek. The Castac and Frazier mines were two of the most successful producers in the area. The Alamo Mining District – west of Alamo Mountain – was created in 1879.

In the Spring of 1877 the VENTURA FREE PRESS reported the Chinamen were once again returning to the mines, *"equipped with mining tools, a rocker, etc. carrying their provisions in baskets on the ends of long poles."* A rocker is a piece of mining equipment that is rocked back and forth to remove the unwanted material.

Chinese miners arriving in *"the Lockwood"*

On May 26, 1877 the VENTURA FREE PRESS noted:
"Snowy Mining District has been organized in the northeastern part of the county. The Fraser quartz mine is very promising. (Because of the spelling this could possibly be Alexander Fraser's mine in Hungry Valley though Ventura County did extend to Frazier Mountain and near the Frazier mine) *From the amount of placer gold extracted during the past thirty years, there can be no doubt of the existence of good ledges."* (again a reference to very early mining locally)

In 1882, Dr. Steven (Stephen) Bowers, then referred to as the Director of the United States Mint, wrote of the Piru:
"The Piru District takes its name from the Piru Creek which runs through it in a southerly direction, carrying, according to season, from one hundred to one thousand inches of water, and has

placer diggings in its banks that have been profitably worked. It is about fifty miles in length by twenty five in width and is a strongly marked mineral belt having mineral veins of almost every kind, such as gold, silver, copper, tin, iron, bismuth, and antimony. It seems never to have attracted the attention of that class of men who get up booms in mining camps. Those who frequent it are poor men, who go there to make a raise, working the rich gold quartz they find in arrastras. The district is in Ventura County a distance of fifty-five miles from Bakersfield."

It was just four years later, about 1886, that *"that class of man"* mentioned above, did make an effort to create a mining boom town on Lockwood Creek – in fact Stephen Bowers was one of those investors. Colonel Alonzo Winfield Scott Smith encouraged forty to fifty white miners to take up mining claims at that location. Smith was a land promoter out to make a buck in the real estate boom of the 1880's. He convinced miners that he had located the *"Lost Los Padres Mine"* and gained a following of investors from the Santa Maria area. It was the Colonel's dream to begin a town called Lexington after the well-known community in Massachusetts. A crude trail joined Lexington to the Fillmore area but generally investors would reach Lexington from the south by traveling to Castaic, then up San Francisquito Canyon to Elizabeth Lake, to Gorman and twenty miles further west to the mining town. The nearest railroad stop was some sixty miles east at Lancaster.

The VENTURA FREE PRESS of January 19, 1887 tempted its readers with the following:

"Colonel Smith would not sell any of his valuable mining claims in spite of the fact that miners are rapidly filling up that section and we predict one of the richest discoveries ever made in the state."

The February 11th issue of the VENTURA FREE PRESS reported: *"Col. A. W. Smith, the discoverer of the rich mines in this county has caused the town of Lexington to be laid off by a competent surveyor, at the junction of the Lockwood and Piru creeks. The location is a very pretty one for a town site ... on a flat almost hemmed in by mountains. The whole covers an area of 560 acres and has been divided into blocks and lots. The blocks are 300 X 162 feet, lots 25 X 75 feet; alleys 12 feet wide, streets 60 feet wide. The survey commences at the corners common to sections 16, 17, 20 and 21, township 7, north range 19 west, SBM.*

The Colonel's idea is to have a company formed to be divided into twelve shares, and draft rules and regulations to be adopted by the company. Several shares have been purchased and the full number will doubtless be completed shortly. Different parties contemplate establishing business houses in Lexington and in a little while miners from far and wide will pour into the camp and things will be exceedingly lively in that section of the county."

The Colonel was able to claim the land under the Townsites Act of 1864. The settlement was located at the junction of the two creeks, (mostly along the Piru) a remote, wild, yet beautiful site. A plat map was filed with Ventura County. The main street of the village was called *"Center Street"* with some of the other streets given such names as *"Piru"*, *"Lockwood"*, *"Granite"*, *"Wallace"*, *"Ruby"*, *"Placer"*, *"Emerald"*, *"Gold"*, *"Silver"*, *"Carbonite"*, *"Prince"* and *"Yellow Jacket"*.

There were a hundred and fifty men in the camp/community in February of 1887. Many pine trees were cut and brought down from Alamo Mountain south of the settlement. A few cabins, a post office and an arrastra were built but most of the miners lived in tents or just camped out while there. Colonel Smith was everywhere, giving orders for the development of the mining camp.

Suggested view of the settlement of Lexington

Heavy snows in February of 1887 pretty much shut down all mining operations and a March issue of the VENTURA FREE PRESS reported a snow slide/avalanche had carried away most of the cabins at the Frazier Mine with Superintendent J. G. Babb fortunate enough to have been in the small portion left behind – though he suffered badly frozen feet. Also in March of that year, the correspondent from

Lexington reported that a grocery store was being constructed with logs, a blacksmith shop was to be started soon, San Francisco investors were negotiating for a claim for the price of $50,000 and *"Lexington has a complete system of water works. A fine stream of water flows through the town"*. That same Spring, William Aram, who had been in the area since 1881, described the mining district as a mineral belt that extended from the Castac Mine in Piru to Mt. Pinos being several miles in width.

The next newspaper article located, in April of the same year indicated there was some disillusionment with Col Smith's land promotion. It was no doubt written by a friend of Smith's as it read:

> *"The citizens of Ventura are scarcely alive as yet to the possibilities of the mining camp of Lexington in this county. Some say there is nothing there, without knowing anything about it. No one should express that opinion unless he is a mining expert and has been on the grounds. The Ventura people cannot realize what a rich mineral belt there is in the northeastern portion of this county as the mines do not receive much support from them."*

According to Jason Marmor's article: *"Lexington: Ventura County's Forgotten Mining Camp"*, and following Col Smith's efforts to create a community, the Piru Mining District was officially organized at the cabin of a former school teacher of the area, Wm Aram, in May of 1887. The District ranged from Sespe Creek on the south to the Kern County line on the north, from the west side of Mt Pinos to Los Angeles County line on the east – a sizeable area. Officers were appointed such as a judge, inspectors, and a recorder of claims. A dollar was collected from each miner residing in the district to pay for the necessary recording books and advertising.

In May 17, 1887, the LOS ANGELES TIMES carried an informative letter from a miner at the Champion Mine, again in the Piru Mining District of Ventura County. It read:

> *"I write this letter for several reasons ... to fulfill my promise to answer, through your paper, the many letters I am receiving from old prospecting and mining men all over this coast, and to tell the facts just as they are.*
>
> *Having been prospecting in the Piru mining district for three years. I believe it is a good mineral-bearing district; that there will be millions of dollars of the precious metals taken out of the many quartz lodes that crop out for miles in every direction. In over thirty years prospecting I have not found any mining camp that shows better surface indications than can be found here, yet there are no mills to work the ores. If there were a small custom mill here, so that those who have good pay ore on the surface could*

get it worked, it would be a good thing for us miners. We then could get money to open up our prospects, which, I believe, well prove to be good paying mines. I think, from what I can learn, that such a mill will be built this summer.

To my many mining friends I will say: If you want to prospect, or buy a prospect, come up here; but if you want work, don't come here yet. There is no one here able to hire men, and there are no mines being worked, expect by the owners, who are too poor to hire help. There is no new mining camp in the Pine (Piru?) *district, and all the flowing down by florid writers only hurts the camp, and those who come up here and go down to what they call Lexiton get so disgusted that they leave the next day. The new mines are not new, however, having been found years ago, and owned by other parties. There are few good prospectors here. The most of the men we have are bean-pullers and pumpkin-rollers* (farmers).

I read in the Los Angeles Times that there were 250 men in this district last winter, when the fact is there were not twenty all told. I also read that this is on the Calico belt, when it is not, and has no more to do with the Calico mines than the great Comstock of Nevada. Neither is the Cedar mining district north of this, but southeast, and fifty or sixty miles away. Your correspondent 'B.' had better go and look over his geography again.

This mining camp is fifteen miles west of Gorman's Station and on the west side of the Torazier Mountain. (Could this be a combination of the old name for the mountain of Toshololo and the new name then of Frazier??) *Gorman's Station is our post office. The mail comes but once a week, leaving Lancaster from the Southern Pacific Railroad every Saturday morning, and arrives at Gorman's Station the following Sunday at 4 p.m. From there you have to hire a team or walk. Through the kindness of Mr. Cuddy, who is an old-timer in this district, we get our mails every Sunday evening at his rancho, as he sends some of his sons to Gorman's Station every Sunday, which is a great accommodation to us miners.*

There is a store at the junction of Lockwood and Piru creeks, where Mr. Flores has provisions and wines (at Lexington). *There are several other things I would like to mention, but as this letter is altogether too long I will save them for another time.*

Yours truly, Isaac Haylock"

In October of 1887 an issue of MINING & SCIENTIFIC PRESS, a publication out of San Francisco, reported:

"Lexington is dead; not a man in it. Bar-room mining has also stopped. There is some show of something being done here in the way of opening up our mines, as there are several parties who are doing actual work and not making any noise about it ... men who are working for what is in the ore, and have sense enough to know that the days of booming up 'wildcats' have passed and gone."

Within two years time, having not discovered the fabled Los Padres mine in that area, the Colonel and his men seemed to be gone. The *"town"* of Lexington stood deserted. The Ventura County voting records of 1912 listed a William Alphonso Smith living near the site of Lexington. He was said to be age 84 and a miner from England, *"a citizen by virtue of naturalization of father"*. Back when Lexington was founded in 1886 this Smith would have been 58 years of age. Could this be the Colonel with a bit of a change in name, or a relative?

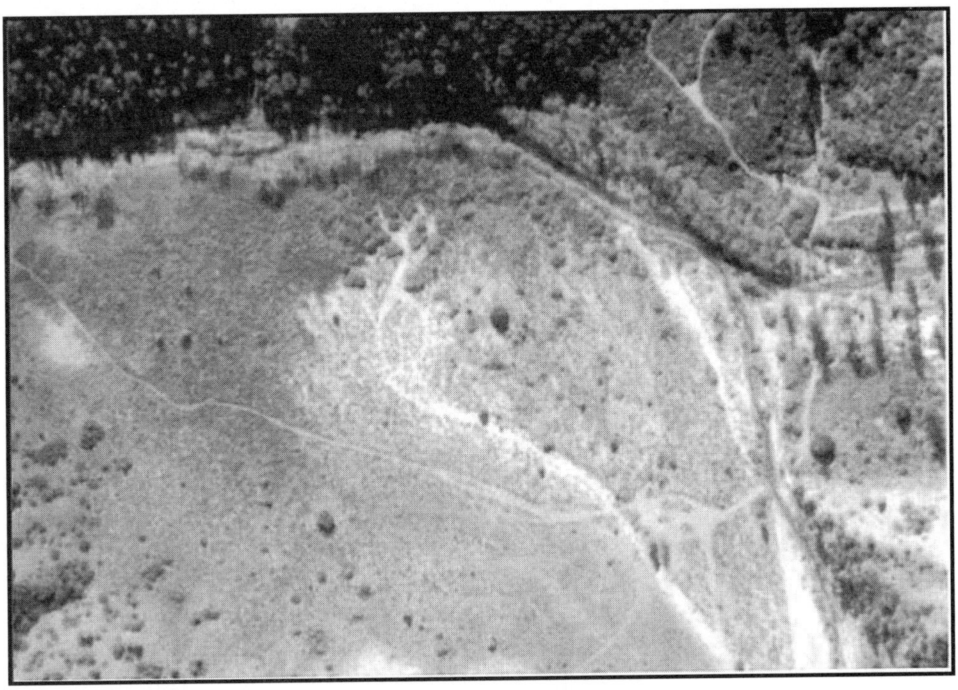

Google Earth photo of the Lexington site – Piru Creek in the lower area of the image is joined by Lockwood Creek coming from the north

Also from the Piru-Lockwood area, the State Mineralogist, Steven Bowers, has left an interesting and factual review of local mining activity in 1888:

"July 13 – We drove to Sneddens where we went into camp. We found a deserted miners cabin near the Snedden residence on which we constructed a roof of boughs of willows. It is on the Lockwood creek which empties into the Piru about four miles

below. Near our camp is an old arrastra and another a few hundred yards down the creek. The thermometer at noon ... 88 degrees. The Lockwood and Cuddy canons are full of massive granite variegated with blotches of crystalized feldsparic.

July 14 – We started for the 'Brown Mine' which is located on the west side of Brown Mountain, one mile south of Lockwood Creek at an altitude of 5740'. The country rock, as elsewhere in this district, in principally granite and syenite. The former contains large crystals of rose-colored feldspar. The vein matter of this claim is about 300 feet wide, with granite walls on either side, the strike being east and west. Gold bearing quartz is found between these walls, while near the center is a rich streak of ore from fifteen to eighteen inches in width which is said to assay far up into the hundreds. On each side of this streak is pay ore, making a width altogether of four feet, with hanging and foot-walls of talcose slate. Some clay and tale are found mingled with the ore.

This is a true fissure vein, standing nearly vertical, dipping slightly to the south. A tunnel has been run into the mountain on the vein for a distance of one hundred and ten feet at an altitude of 5700 feet, and a shaft has been sunk on the vein to a depth of eighty feet. At the bottom of the latter the vein matter widens to six feet. This mine yields free milling ore averaging from $10 to $70 per ton. A slide or tramway could easily be constructed to the Lockwood Creek, one mile distant, a stream which affords abundance of water the entire year for running a large stamp mill or other machinery required for the reduction of the ore. Pine timber is found in sufficient quantity on the sides and top of the mountain to construct a tramway and for all other purposes necessary in working the mine. This mine is owned by Messrs. D. M. Menzies and Wilhoit. Several other ledges of good-looking quartz occur on this mountain, two of which run parallel with the vein of the Brown Mine.

July 15 (Sunday) *– The mercury fell to 40 degrees last night and to 94 degrees during the day. I read the 34th Psalm and Romans 5 to the camp and commented upon the same. Mr. Menzies visited our camp and took dinner with us. Horses got away and I went for them."*

The next day the Bowers party continued to the next mine site and Dave Menzies, a fellow of local legend, seems to join them as a guide. Bowers recorded:

"July 16 – We started early this a.m. for a dry-wash on the south side of Frazier's Mt. and for the White Mule mine. The latter we reached about four miles from our camp in Lockwood. We

> *ascended the mountain to the White Mule Mine, altitude 6,500'. There is an incline about 110' showing a rich load. We got specimens and ascended to the cabin which is at 6800' where we took dinner. There are four fine springs here.*
>
> *July 17 – Went up to the Silver Queen mine today. The ledge carries gold, silver, galena ore copper sulphates. The main vein runs north and south with branches coming into it. It is about three feet wide and promises well. The outcrop being of the upper ledge is at an altitude of 6500'. Killed a rattle snake.*
>
> *Mr. Menzies and myself started for Fitzgerald mt. to examine some claims and mines. Found the altitude to be 6750'. From two claims or mines belonging to the Fitzgerald heirs we found apparently rich diggings but at present nothing is being done as Mr. Fitzgerald recently died and his heirs are doing nothing with the property as to working them. They are high up on the south side of the mountain north of the Piru creek and would be difficult to work for the prospector. The trip today involved about 10 miles of travel. In the evening we had trout for dinner."*

After several days of exploration on Mt. Pinos (see Chapter XX) the Bowers party is back in camp.

> *"July 22 – This is Sunday and I remained in camp writing and resting. The mercury reached 91 degrees in the shade. Two rattlesnakes were seen near camp yesterday. DeMoss went down to Lexington today."*

Though just founded in 1886 Lexington was little more than a ghost town by 1888. The only comment Bowers makes about Lexington is:

> *"Near Lexington is a boulder of white quartz about 18' long to 15' wide. It is nearly pure white silica and wavy and may have capped a rich mine somewhere."* (no comments as to whether or not anyone is living in Lexington)

Bowers then moves the camp two miles down the creek so that they can record the mining operations in that area of the Piru District:

> *"We moved our camp down the creek nearly two miles on a flat where there is feed for the horses. Our camp is under cottonwood trees and if it does not rain we will be quite comfortable, I think. I went up with Menzies and examined the Agosy claim. It was dark when we got there ... 6200 feet above sea level.*
>
> *July 25 – Mercury fell to about 50 degrees. It is cold and windy. I started early for Campbell and Foley's mine on the side of Frazier Mt. The ascent is through Long Daves canon. We entered a*

beautiful grassy valley about a mile wide by 1½ miles long at the top of the canyon. Reaching the cabin of Foley and Campbell I found a vegetable garden with cabbage, corn and beans doing well at an altitude of 6450 feet above sea level." (Mr. Foley also, or later, had a place in Tejon Pass near Gorman Station.)

Long Dave or Long Dave's Canyon runs east from Lockwood Creek and up along the south face of Frazier Mountain. The valley at the top has been referred to as Long Dave's Valley. Whoever Dave was, he might have been tall, and rumor has it that he was hiding from the law in that area in the mid-1800's. Could the guide, Dave Menzies, have been *"Long Dave"* – though there was no doubt more than one Dave in the area in the early days.

This same Dave Menzie or Menzies did have a place near where the County Road presently crosses over Cuddy Creek as you head west from the freeway to Frazier Park. This was long known as *"Menzie's Crossing"*. Writer, Grace Bradley, wrote of Menzie:

> *"When he wasn't working at his mine of Frazier Mountain he tended his pear orchard just to the rear of his house. He was well known for this pear orchard and for his bad disposition."*

A Google Earth view of Long Dave Canyon

Mr. Bowers continues:
"Then I met Mr. Campbell ('Three Fingered Bob') and Happy Jack Wardell and I went to the mine and examined it. I went into the tunnel and shaft and brought away specimens. Happy Jack came to California 1849 and Three Fingered Bob in 1859. Both

are characters, Jack is full 6 feet tall and 59 years old and has been a man of unusual strength. His Indian wars travel is interesting. He has been variously engaged, is full of incidents and likes to relate them. Much that he has seen and experienced should be rescued from oblivion. After dinner I returned to our camp down Long Dave canon. It is wild and picturesque.

July 28 – Started down the Lockwood at 5:15 a.m. this morning to make the ascent of Alamo mt. reached Henderson's on the Piru 8 miles by 8 o'clock. We began the ascent and was accompanied by J. L. Henderson. Mr. Henderson insisted on walking up the mt. though 67 years old. The distance traveled from his cabin must have been near 4 miles yet he rested but once, I believe, and refused to ride until near the top of the mt. At 7100' we reached the first sheep camp. The sheep herded here eat every green thing, even sage brush. The highest point of 8175' was reached about noon. At the summit the view is grand.

I concluded to ride along the longer axis of the mt. westward and came down the western side of the junction of the Piru and Lockwood. It proved to be 4 or 5 miles and descent was not too impossible for man or horses. The ground is thickly shaded with a specie of scrub oak scarcely higher than a man's head buthaving stiff crooked barbs which is very destructive to clothing. A horse can get through it with difficulty and is very loathe to go forward. The last two miles taking at best one and a half hours.

Reached camp at 3 o'clock having traveled nearly 20 miles. DeMoss returned in the evening having killed a deer which he hung up in a tree.

July 29 – I arose at 5 a.m. and after a tasty breakfast went up the Lockwood a mile to Millikens camp with letters for the post office 20 miles distant.

July 30 – Rose early this morning and went to the Brown mine and the Argosy claim, also the 'Junie'. Menzies returned with me and took dinner. We then loaded up, broke camp and drove to Cuddy's 8 miles distant. I received a letter from home calling me there at once (to Ventura)."

From the Cuddy place, Mr. Bowers then travels northwest, down San Emigdio Canyon to report on the antimony mine there (Chapter IV), through the lower San Joaquin Valley, up Grapevine Canyon, to Gorman, through the Antelope Valley, to Lake Elizabeth, down San Francisquito Canyon, through the Santa Clara Valley and arrived at his home in Ventura by midnight on August 4th.

On February 11, 1893, the LOS ANGELES TIMES carried this article gained from the Piru Mining District. It reads:

> *"A practical miner recently from that section gives the following interesting details.*
>
> *The principle new claims that are being developed are about sixteen miles west from Gorman's station where a rig or horse can be hired to take the traveler to the mines, or after staying all night at Gorman's, where good lodging and meals can be had for a moderate charge, the traveler can easily walk to the mines in time to dine at 12 o'clock.*
>
> *Messrs, Harbell, Hazlett & Bergoren have just completed putting up a three and one-half foot Huntington mill on the White Mule mine, and next week are going to start up and run night and day. Their mill will be lighted by electricity and a gang of men put at work in the mine sufficient to keep the mill supplies with rock. They have about one hundred tons of ore on the dump, which averages about $12 to the ton, free gold, and the concentrates from $70 to $80 per ton.*
>
> *Messrs. George Reed and Isaac Haylock* (see his letter on page 72)*, owners of the Fairview mining claim, have several hundred feet of tunnel run in their mine, and it prospects good. They intend to keep on prospecting their claim, and show it up in good shape before offering it on the market or getting capitalists interested in putting up machinery on it.*
>
> *Messrs. George Haylock and W. H. Carpenter are owners of the Bunker Hill mine, situated further up the mountain above the White Mule and Fairview. The ledge in the Bunker Hill mine averages about seventy-five feet wide, and has gold from the top of the ground down. The Haylock brothers have been in this camp several years, and, as they are both old miners, they know what they are doing. By next autumn, it is considered by those who are well posted, this will be one of the liveliest camps on the coast."*

One of the last of the old stories located from the Piru District comes from an unnamed January 1894 newspaper article when the reporter comments on the Snedden mine:

> *"Samuel Snedden, who has for many years lived in the Piru district, located a mine twenty years ago. He ran a tunnel 250 feet and has a 25-foot ledge of nearly solid sulphuret, but on account of the mills not being able to separate the gold from the iron, has not done much with it. Recently he took some of the ore that has*

lain exposed to the weather for twenty years and had it assayed by the new process and it ran $75.24 to the ton in gold. He at once went to work again."

A more recent story from the old Piru District was found in the MOUNTAIN ENTERPRISE dated March 23, 1967. Entitled *"Gold Strike in Lockwood"*. From this article we learn:

"The ancient allure of the most exotic of all metals has triggered another find, as Earl Woody and Ross Russell have reported that they have made a sizable gold and silver discovery in the westerly portion of Lockwood Valley. They have some 23 claims in the area and have located eight different veins. The news will come as no great surprise to many old timers of The Hill, who have often told this reporter of the mineral wealth of the area.

According to Mr. Woody, assays made on ore taken from the 'RW Mine' in Lockwood indicate values running at about $1,500 a ton. Mining engineers estimate that there are some one million tons of the gold and silver ore in this mine. Woody reports that the main sill is some 2000 to 3000 feet in length and varies between 5 and 75 feet in width.

The two prospectors, who own the R & W Rock Shop in Palmdale, are no greenhorns, having been in the mining business since 1950. They first discovered the deposit while flying over the region, prospecting from an airplane, three years ago. They report that this method gave them maximum opportunity to view the geological formation and the vivid colors of the earth in the area.

The locality of the mine is one of natural beauty, complete with numerous water falls, shear vertical rock cliffs and a pine forest. Lucky Stevens of Lebec has his earth moving equipment on the site and is clearing the area and cutting access roads. Lucky will also supply the necessary mining equipment."

In June of 1967 the same newspaper carried additional information about the R W Mine. It reads:

"Earl Woody and Ross Russell report that they have completed development work on their claims in Lockwood Valley. The Lucky (Stevens) *Mining Company is now constructing a Mill which will crush and concentrate ore. Deliveries of the ore from the R W Mine to the Mill are expected to start within the next 60 days.*

The two men have worked from sunup to sundown and then some, for many months developing their find. Sample ores, sometimes as much as a ton in a day, have been packed out by the prospectors. Then they drive to their Rock Shop in Palmdale to perform assay work before returning to the mine the next day. This they do seven days a week, week in and week out. The Mining Corporation also includes other mines in other places but Ross and Woody feel that their strike in Lockwood is 'the big one'.

Mr. Woody states that a search for the Lost Padres Mine originally brought them into the area."

VI - THE FRAZIER MINE

In the 1860's the sacred mountain of *"Toshololo"*, to the southeast of the Cuddy Homestead, had become known as *"Cuddy Peak"*. By the 1880's the mountain became more commonly known as *"Fraser's Mountain"*. Some references give the date of 1867 as to when the Frazier brothers, Warren, Edgar and William, made claim to the most important mining location on the mountain. But it wasn't until in the early 1900's that references to the mountain were spelled Frazier instead of Fraser. There was a miner living in Lockwood Valley by the name of Fraser in the mid-1800's and a homesteader named Alexander Fraser (possibly the same person) in Hungry Valley in the early 1900's though no other information could be located on these men.

Our first introduction to the Frazier mine was written by a Robert Adams Maddux who worked with and wrote about Warren Frazier. Because what he later wrote is significant to the Frazier Mountain area as well, some of Mr. Maddux's other interesting experiences in the area in the 1870's are also shared here. Bob Maddux wrote:

> *"In the early seventies my folks settled northeast of Bakersfield near the town of Glenville* (the family had come first to Northern California from Arkansas in the 1850's). *Bakersfield at that time was just a small village and had more fever and ague* (chills) *than anything else ... even the dogs shook with it ... and while there I contracted a case of the malarial fever and was sick for some time as well* (Valley Fever?). *I had a fine team and wagon and used to team about the country and in that way saw a good deal of California. I had become interested in the mining game and spent quite a lot of time prospecting between jobs and learned a great deal about different methods of mining.*
>
> *I became acquainted with a man named Bob Thompson who owned a cattle ranch not far from the foot of what is now Frazier Mountain. Bob was a big good-natured fellow about six feet six inches tall and I had a standing invitation to come out and batch with him which I did on several occasions. On my frequent trips out to his ranch I became acquainted with a Mexican family by the name of Olivera who had a ranch about two miles from the Thompson place. They had a few head of cattle and a garden and were making a good living and they were mighty nice people. The old lady cooked some swell Mexican dishes of which I was*

very fond and they had a grown daughter, a beautiful girl and very bright ... another attraction for me. I enjoyed many a pleasant evening at their place playing a card game called 'cen kin' when I would be up at Thompson's ranch.

One evening on my way back to Bob's I turned a point in the canyon when not far ahead of me was a grizzly bear and two cubs paddling along down the trail. I was proud of my horse and wasn't a bit afraid so I thought I'll give the old lady a good scare and have a race with her. I fetched a yell and touched 'Selim' with the spurs. The old bear ran all right, but she ran the wrong way and Selim and I were the scared ones. I gave her the full right-of-way of the trail and took to the sagebrush, the old bear giving us a good run for our lives. When I got back to the ranch I found old Bob sitting up reading ... he never went to bed before midnight. When I told him what happened he roared and roared some more and made fun of it for days to come."

Bob Maddux out races the grizzly

"Now Bob had a beautiful meadow of clover and grass all fenced in where he used to cut hay and which he prized very highly. There was an old long-horned brindle (a striped coloring) *cow belonging to old Pio Pico that used to roam around there and to whom the meadow looked mighty good. That cow made it her*

special business to break thru Bob's fence and as soon as he'd fix it she'd do it again. Finally he decided to give her a good scare and chase her away. He went after her with a yell and like my grizzly bear she ran, but she also ran the wrong way and turned on him with a vengeance. He didn't climb over the fence, he took a dive over it and she wasn't ten feet behind him. When he caught his breath he headed for his old Henry rifle and shot her dead. He never made fun of my grizzly episode again."

Bob Thompson escaping from the angry cow

"There was another experience that I had on one of my trips to Bob Thompson's ranch that was somewhat of a thriller. When we had the carcass of a deer for meat we would tie a rope to it after it was dressed and throw the rope up over the limb of a big oak tree that stood near the house, and pull the meat up off the ground in the shade of the tree to keep cool for our use as we needed it. One morning I was coming out of the ranch-house door and happened to look up in the tree and there to my surprise was a large mountain lion crouched on a limb over our meat getting ready to make a spring for it. I was a pretty good shot in those days, so I rushed back in the cabin and got my rifle and caught that old fellow right between the eyes, and incidentally got $28 for the head and ears. Bob had an old bull-dog that when the lion fell he ran over and acted as if he were claiming credit for the kill and that we should show our appreciation of what he had done."

Mountain lion after the deer carcass

"On one of my trips up to Bob Thompson's I became acquainted with Warren Frazier for whom Frazier Mountain was named. I had known his brothers in Bakersfield and they had told me so much about him that I had a great desire to know him because I felt that we would be sort of kindred spirits ... we both loved the out-of-doors and the freedom that went with such a life. Bob told me how to find Frazier's camp so one day I took my trusty rifle, started out on foot, found his camp and made myself known to him. We became great friends and he seemed glad to have me for company. His camp was in wild country and miles from any habitation, but that was the kind of life that Warren Frazier loved. His capital stock consisted of his rifle and two little pack mules and outfit. He was a great hunter and hunted for meat and not for the mere pleasure of killing. Deer were very plentiful in those mountains and when he would have the urge to go into Bakersfield he would kill three or four bucks, load them on his pack mules and travel after night fell because he could keep the meat fresher. He sold his game to the butchers. That was his business and he loved that kind of life.

After we visited awhile he took me not far from his camp to the croppings of a quartz vein and I broke some off and could see gold in it. He asked if I had experience in mining and if I had this, what would I do. I suggested he build an arrasta, which he knew nothing about, so I helped him build it. We could, with the help of *one of the mules, grind about three hundred pounds of rock a day, which ran about a hundred dollars to the ton. It was hard work and slow but we were getting a great kick out of it. After we had worked a couple of months, we 'cleaned up'... that is we drained off all of the tailings and scooped up all the amalgam that was left in the crevices in the bottom of the arrasta. Then it had to be retorted, but of course we had no mining equipment for doing that so we would heat it up in an old pot to save the quick-silver. The heat would vaporize the quick-silver and it would go off in the air and leave the gold on an old shovel or sheet-iron that we used, without wasting any. It was crude, but as near as I can remember in our first clean-up, we got something over $300. We worked on a fifty/fifty basis, Warren appreciated my teaching him how to build the arrasta and we were both pleased with the way it worked out.*

We worked faithfully for two or three months, then Warren felt that he must have a vacation. I didn't want any vacation, but he was crazy to go to Los Angeles to cash his gold and I knew that meant spending it for booze. For the fine fellow that he was he just seemed to have to go on a spree about every so often and I didn't intend to spend my hard worked for earnings in that way. I didn't want go with him but loaned him my horse and saddle that was down at Thompson's. From there he took the much used trail to Los Angeles which went down thru Gorman Stage Station, then cut off down by Elizabeth Lake and on in to Los Angeles. I vacationed helping old Bob shear his sheep."

Warren Frazier heading for town

"Warren came back within a week and had spent most of his money as I had expected he would. We went back up to his camp and the mine and set to work building a log cabin to live in and another at the mine about a half a mile away. I knew we had a gold mine and a chance to make some money. I was pretty husky and understood the work and enjoyed it for a time.

One time while I was staying with Warren a bunch of Bakersfield fellows came up for a deer hunt. They brot their packs and plenty to eat and drink. Warren would not hunt around the cabin but he took them over to Alamo Mountain a few miles from there for two reasons, we didn't want the deer scared around our camp, and there was better hunting over there. Alamo Mountain for about a half mile up the side was covered with brush and there were hundreds of deer up on the slopes. Those Bakersfield fellows just about went crazy. Some had pistols and some had shotguns and they didn't know much more about hunting deer than I would know about a printing press.

Warren knew that the deer would rush for the brush, so he stood still near there and let the other fellows 'hunt'. Every few minutes an old buck would come and Warren would down him. After the hunt was over those Bakersfield fellows had one small deer and Warren had six bucks. I didn't kill deer just for the sport so I stayed behind and cooked a meal for them of deer ribs and three or four batches of biscuits in the Dutch oven. The way they ate was a compliment to any cook. They went back into Bakersfield claiming all the glory for the deer killed.

Warren continued to spend his money for booze but I took care of the mine. After a time the news of our find began to be noised around and a fellow from San Francisco heard about it and came up to see Frazier about forming a company and putting in a mill. I could see that he was a shrewd conniver, much too shrewd for poor old Warren. He wanted him to go down to Bakersfield and fix up some papers and then they would put in the mill and do great things. I felt pretty sure that if he succeeded in getting him to go to Bakersfield that he would get to drinking and that would be the finish for Warren. I pled with him not to go, for I knew his weakness too well but his fellow prevailed upon him so hard and made it look so rosy that he decided to go. Warren promised me faithfully that he wouldn't touch a drop, but it went just as I feared.

That was the end of the arrasta mining for Frazier and me. The last time I saw old Warren Frazier he was down and out in Bakersfield and he told me with tears in his eyes how he wished he had listened to me. I always felt bad about it for I thought a great deal of him and we had had so many happy times together."

The new mill must have been quickly added as in October 1875 the Kern County Gazette reported:

"the 10 stamp mill on Frazier Mountain, during a recent two-week period, produced a thousand dollars in gold values."

The BAKERSFIELD COURIER CALIFORNIAN of August 17, 1876 picked up on the Frazier Mine about where Bob Maddux left off. The newspaper reported on the Piru District in general and uses the spelling of *"Frazer"* in reference to the Frazier Brother's mine. The article reads as follows:

"Although gold in paying quantities had been long known to exist, yet, strange to say, nothing has yet been done in the way of developing what must be acknowledged as a rich mineral bearing district. The placers, it is true, have been worked for the last twenty years, more or less. That is, the ground has been scratched over by stragglers every year for a few weeks during which the snows lasted and furnished water for washing, but no attempt has been made to bring water to the placers that they might be worked to advantage.

The principal quartz mine or the one by which the District is best known is the Frazer mine. It was discovered and located originally by Warren Frazer in June 1870. Soon afterwards Mr. Frazer associated with himself the Treadwells of San Francisco under the hope they could further develop the mine. These people however, by a system of sharp practices not unfrequently associated with mining enterprise, succeeded in gaining a major portion of the shares. Mr. Frazer, however has, we are glad to say, stayed with them during the six years that have elapsed. At present the ore is brought down on sleds a distance of some three miles from the mine to the arastas where it is reduced. The arastas are of the most primitive style but about five hundred pounds of good milling ore is produced daily.

The Frazer lead, in the croppings where it was discovered, was but six inches wide, but was considered rich. It has been proven now for a distance of some seventy feet from the surface, and it now shows a true feasure (fissure) *vein averaging four feet in width. It has been prospected for a distance of twelve hundred feet longitudinally with the most satisfactory and gratifying results. The quartz is of the very finest for milling purpose. It is red and rotten with rust in most places, and but little blasting is required in excavating. It is very porous and brittle, and in a small pile that was waiting to be crushed we saw many pieces that showed free gold. The rusty porous rock in which nothing could be discerned, however, was considered the best. As soon as the mill is erected, we are confident that we shall hear of good returns from the Frazer mine.*

Several other locations have been made in the vicinity of the Frazer mine of them by some of our Bakersfield people, but they do not seem disposed to develop them at present, if they have not abandoned them. About eight miles southeast of the Frazer and in the same range, some other valuable ledges have been discovered, but they too fell early into the Treadwell clutches, and of course no one has received any benefit yet."

In 1882 the Director of the United State Mint said this of the Frazier Mine using the spelling of *"Fraser"*:

"The Principal lode in the Piru District is called the Fraser Mine. During the time it was worked, a period of eight years, until operations ceased October 31, 1879, because from litigation arising from disputed ownership, it is believed to have yielded about $1 million in gold. The difficulty is now said to be on the eve of settlement and it will be worked by improved methods and on a larger scale than heretofore. The vein varies from two to sixteen feet width and will average eight feet in depth. The ore contains iron and other sulphurets that assay from $500 to $3,500 per ton. They are all saved, but there is no means of treating them at the mine."

During his visit to the San Emigdio Mountain area in 1888 the State Mineralogist, Dr. Stephen Bowers, wrote his Eighth Annual Report:

"The Fraser Mine is located on a mountain of the same name. Work was begun here about twenty years ago, since which it has had a varied history. The early reduction works were arrastas, and it is said to have yielded much wealth. But owing to the fact that it has been in litigation, and from other causes, its later showing is hardly equal to the first. The altitude of the mines is six thousand five hundred feet above the sea level. The vein from which the ore is obtained runs southeast and northwest, and is nearly vertical. Seven tunnels have been excavated, varying in length from forty to five hundred feet. The vertical depth reached from the surface is four hundred and twenty-nine feet. The ore yields gold, silver and copper.

The company owns a ten-stamp mill (each stamp a heavy pestle raised by water or steam power for crushing ore), *but during the litigation referred to, it has fallen in disuse and needs repairing.*

Happily the matter is now settled and a responsible company controls the mine and we learn that work on the mine will be pushed forward at once. The company has constructed six miles of road."

Example of the ten-stamp mill used at the Frazier Mine site

The December 30, 1893 issue of THE CALIFORNIAN, a Bakersfield newspaper, reported:

"At the Frazier mine, seven miles west of Gorman's Station, a very rich strike has recently been made by Bicknell & Co., of Los Angeles, who purchased the mine from the Frazier brothers, its former owners. (It would seem the Frazier Brothers won the litigation and again owned the claim.) *The old workings were eighty feet in depth, but a tunnel has just been completed which strikes the ledge 130 feet from the surface, that is fifty feet below the old explorations. Here the vein is found to be six feet wide and it mills about $30 a ton in gold, besides the sulphurets, which are found to be very rich. There is a twenty-stamp mill at the mine and the present owners think they have ore enough exploited to keep it running steadily for two years to come. On Alamo mountain, the other side of the slope from the Frazier mine,*

> *Frazier & Co. are running their five-stamp mill on high grade gold quartz and are making it pay handsomely."*

Having profited from the sale of their old claim, the Frazier Brothers must have gone on to a new location.

A Ventura newspaper dated January 19, 1894 gave this account:

> *"I visited some of the tunnels of the 'Reliable Fraser' and found over one hundred feet of rich ore being in sight. This mine is working six men at present and they are getting out from ten to twenty tons of ore a day, that assays $97.43 to the ton. A portion of this mine contains richer ore than they are getting out at present. Their ten-stamp mill could not begin to crush one-fourth the ore in sight in two years, running day and night. E. P. Chilson, an expert miner, is foreman and manager of the mine. He has been working very hard for the past year to get the mine in good shape, so that the ore can be handled to the best advantage. At the present time they are getting out a good deal of ore. This winter they expect to make a new wagon road from the mine to the valley, but by early Spring they will push the work. The 'Red Rose' mine, a north extension of the Fraser, has four tunnels in from 40 to 250 feet ... this is owned by S. Beach. He expects to put up a mill in the Spring, but at present is running an arrasta."*

In August of the same year THE CALIFORNIAN reported:

> *"Last Friday night the mill at the Frazier gold mine burned near Gorman station. Everything was so dry that it went up very quickly. It is supposed to have caught fire near the engine, perhaps by a spark from the ashes. Much of the machinery and bunk houses were saved. The ore at this mill is worked by a cyanide process that has proven very successful and put the mine on a solid paying basis. Manager Chilson has few equals as a practical miner and mill man. It is unfortunate that the accident should have happened just at this time when the company was pushing the mining so successfully."*

From the Thirteenth Annual State Mineralogist's Report of 1896 we read:

> *"The Frazer Mine is on the southern slope of Frazer Mountain six miles west of Gorman, at about 7000' altitude. The workings consist of 2,200' of tunneling, and since our last report more systematic mining has been carried on. The old mill burned in August 1894, has been replaced by a ten-stamp mill and a three and one half foot Huntington mill. Pine timber is abundant. There is only enough water to run the mill half-time during summer. The ore is said to average 8% sulphurete, which are worked by the cyanide process. Eighteen men are employed."*

As to the Frazier brothers, family members remember that two of the brothers had come to California from Ohio while working on bringing the railroad across the country. The brothers were in Utah in 1869 for the occasion of the driving of the golden spike when the east coast track met that coming from the west. That job completed they came on to California to prospect for gold.

The voter registration records of 1877 list Warren Spencer Frazier as being 31 years old, born in Mississippi with an occupation as a miner. Frank Latta, in the BAKERSFIELD CALIFORNIAN of June 1951, wrote that Warren was a market hunter, shooting ducks and geese on Kern and Buena Vista Lakes during the winter, and deer and bear in the mountains during the summer – no doubt while he was working the mine – for sale to the markets in Bakersfield and surrounding areas. The article continued:

> *"His summer camp, and later permanent residence, were in the valley which now bears his name and where many Kern county residents have summer homes."* (the present Frazier Park area)

Warren died at his daughter's home in Compton, California about 1920, so it would seem he had married.

Warren Frazier from old newspaper clipping

Property records indicate that a William T. Frazier, Warren's brother, owned property at the northeast end of the present Frazier Park in the 1880's. Possibly Warren lived on his brother's property when he wasn't up on the mountain. Warren did have a cabin over the hills from the mine in a beautiful mountain meadow complete with a generous spring nearby.

A photo of Warren Frazier's cabin with ladies picnicking nearby

The descendents of the William T. Frazier, believed to be the William Frazier of Frazier Mountain fame, did remember that he had lived at San Emigdio Canyon where obituaries state he died in 1918 while working for the Kern County Land Company as a *"pumper"*. William T. was thought to have been about 65 when he died which would have him born in the early 1850's and a newspaper article about his death stated that he was known to have come to Kern County at the age of 17, which might have been about 1870. He left his family in Bakersfield in the late 1890's to follow the Klondike gold fever of that time, prospecting in Alaska and taking part in an U.S. Zoological Institute expedition *"almost to the North Pole"*. It is believed that he did not return until about 1902. One of his brothers went with him to Alaska. It is thought this was Edgar and that he was killed there when being robbed of some gold dust.

A descendent of William T. Frazier lived in the Frazier Park community until his death in 2001. One of William's son's, Frank, had one child named Harold before he died. Little Harold's mother remarried and her new husband adopted the boy who was then known as Harold *"Shorty"* Wells. William also had two other sons, Charlie and

Tom and a daughter, Alta. Alta Frazier Blain's daughter, Betty Treaster, of Visalia was helpful in providing information on the family.

There seem to have been half a dozen William Fraziers in Kern County in the late 1800. This information on a William W. Frazier also seems to possibly fit the William Frazier of Frazier Mountain. He was educated at the Citadel Military Academy at Charleston, North Carolina, worked for Union Pacific until after the golden spike was driven then came to California teaching school in a number of locations from Stockton to South Fork in the Kern River Canyon. He was listed as a teacher at the San Emigdio Canyon School in 1877, the same year that Warren is working the mine. William turned from teaching to farming when he married Francis J. Gardner in about 1883.

No information could be located on Edgar *"Doc"* Frazier who supposedly had worked the mine with Warren. It is thought that the brother who died in Alaska would have been Edgar as no record of his death has been located. In a 1923 newspaper article, mention is made of a location at the east end of Frazier Mountain know as *"Doc Flat"*. Possibly it was named for Doc Frazier as it might have been the location of his cabin, campsite, mine – or perhaps he's buried there. . .

Mrs. William Frazier

Mrs. Edgar Frazier

No pictures have been located of William and Edgar Frazier but fortunately these pictures of their wives were found in the Cuddy Family collection of old photos. It seems that in the late 1800's a popular thing to do was to exchange photos with your good friends and neighbors.

In 1964 an early resident of the area, Fred W. Sprung, answered a request from the President of the Kern County Historical Society, Jack Dowty, for information about the Fraziers. From his letter we read:

> *"I first came into the Frazier Mt. area in 1914. Here is what I learned about the Frazier gold mine on Frazier Mountain.*
>
> *The three Frazier brothers, Warren, Doc and William were camped at Arrastra flat on the southeast side of the mountain (at the headwaters of the Maxey Creek watershed). They were out of meat and Warren took his rifle to find and kill a deer. He shot a deer but did not knock it down; so he followed the trail of blood that the deer left. The deer went over the outcrop of gold ore that became the famous Frazier gold mine. That is the way the Frazier gold mine was found. William Frazier, the youngest of the three Frazier brothers told me this himself. They built an arrastra at Arrastra Flat and milled the first gold ore from the mine there. I think Arrastra Flat got its name from this arrastra. I have seen the remains of it. There was both water and feed for pack stock on this flat. All of the old timers claimed the Frazier gold mine had produced a million dollars in gold. Gold was $20.67 an ounce at that time.*
>
> *The three Frazier brothers were a bit wild and they eventually lost the mine. I think it was the next owner that put in the ten-stamp mill with steam boilers and steam engine to operate the ten-stamps. The road up the west side of Frazier Mountain to the Frazier mine was very steep and rough. Horses could not haul in the boilers to the Frazier mine. At the time, Joe Harris, the youngest brother of Tom and Dick Harris had a sawmill in Mil Potrero and was logging with ox teams. They got Joe Harris to haul the boilers up to the Frazier mine with his ox team as horses could not do it. Most of the supplies for the Frazier gold mine were hauled in from either Lancaster or Bakersfield.*
>
> *It was in 1914 that I first saw the Frazier gold mine. Only one small house and the metal parts of the ten-stamp mill remained. It looked like to me that the mine had been idle for at least ten years. In the last few years I understand a cloudburst washed away the stamp mill tailings and part of the mine dump.*
>
> *This has nothing to do with the Frazier mine but William Frazier was one of the first guards of the buffalo herd in the Yellowstone Park area."*

By the 1920's the Frazier Mine was still in the Bicknell (or Bicknel) family and was registered to three sisters, Nannie Bicknell,

Edna Bicknell Bagg and Mary Bicknell Cates. In 1932 the Frazier Mine workings consisted of 3000 feet in seven tunnels driven on the vein at different elevations. Well-known Frazier Mountain miner of the 1970's & 80's, Max Schmeling, located a report on the Frazier Mine from which a good deal of information has been gained. It was written by L. M. Kellogg, *"an examining engineer"* in 1927, shortly after the Frazier Mountain Park subdivision was established. Portions of the report read:

> *"The mine is positioned near the summit of Frazier Mtn., and on its easterly side. It may be reached by a road running south from the Lockwood Valley road at a point near the Cuddy Ranch at the top of Cuddy Canyon. This main road connects with the Ridge Route at Chandler's Station. The road up over the north side of the mountain part of which is under construction, is at present impassable to auto for the last three miles. Another road branching off from the Ridge Route near Gorman, passes around the eastern spur of the mountain on the southern side. This road ends at the Wallace Maxey Ranch from which point a good pack trail connects with the mine which is at an elevation of about 7,400 feet above sea level. The total distance by trail is approximately four miles.*
>
> *For the past ten years Mr. R. C. Beck of Los Angeles, a man of wide experience in mining and milling practices throughout the West has been compiling data relating to this property. In this work he has interviewed a number of old miners, who, at different times, worked in and on this property, and whom are for the most part now dead. Old underground maps and assay sheets of the mine were studied along with other data of interest and some dating as far back as the early nineties. Further than this he has opened up and entered some of the old workings, taken assays from the inside of the old works, and from the old dumps, also milled several hundred tons of ore from various openings, all of which appears to check favorably with the old assay sheets and other like information.*
>
> *Mr. Beck reports that the mine was discovered in 1867 by two brothers after whom the mountain was named ... Frazier Mountain. The Frazier brothers worked the mine for about thirty years thereafter. They built three mills at different times on the property and it is reported that they took out something over $200,000 in gold. In those early days only the free gold ores were amenable to the methods of treatment of that period, therefore, the Frazier Bros. worked only the oxidized ores from the upper levels of the mine leaving the sulphide ores standing. Reference may be had to a reprint of an old map of the old underground workings, but it is here stated that for the most part*

it and the assay values indicated thereon were all copied from other old maps now nonexistent except those assays shown in dotted circles which were taken more recently by Mr. Beck and his associates.

The Frazier Bros. made their money easily and spent it all to freely for the good of the property. They borrowed money from a Los Angeles Bank by mortgaging the mine which they finally were forced to turn over to the bank for the debt, and at a time when they were very old men.

Following the ownership of the Fraziers, Mr. J. D. Bicknel, then an officer of the bank, took the mine off the bank's hands with a view to reopening it and developing the sulphide ore below the old Frazier workings. Mr. Bicknel spent $30,000 driving the lower (chilson) tunnel, stopes, and other workings marked on the map B-- B. About the time he had good tonnage blocked out and was getting estimates for a new mill, Mr. Bicknel died thus throwing the property into an estate in which it remained submerged for a number of years. The estate was finally cleared up releasing the property into the hands of the heirs. Outside of the work done by Mr. Beck and his associates there has been nothing done with the property since, save the yearly assessment work.

The ore bodies in this property consist mainly of four closely associated veins carried within a true fissure having a width of approximately forty feet. The fissure is formed in a contact between diorite on the hanging wall side and quartzite on the foot. The fissure shows considerable movement and carries a large amount of crushed material aligned between the veins. The fissure has a strike of 20 degrees east of north and an easterly dip of 75 degrees. This great fissure can be traced for several miles along the surface and on the two Frazier Claims can be seen in elevations differing by 1,000 feet. By reason of the great distance the fissure can be traced along the surface and be seen in elevations so widely varying, and also because of the heavy movement in evidence between the fissure walls, it is believed that the fissure and very probably the ore bodies also will extend to great depths."

The report continues with five more pages of the *"Geology and Structure of the Ore Bodies"*. This report may be read in the Ridge Route Communities Museum files. Kellogg ends with:

"Historically speaking, the property passed from the Fraziers to Bicknel, and from the Bicknel Estate to Beck and his associates. Following the death of two of Beck's associates, he was without resources to carry on the work and the property passed back

again to the Bicknel Estate. What I wish to point out is that the property has been a success so far in that it has produced something for those who endeavored to work it and has not been peddled around nor failed under operation at any time. While looking at this proposition with conservativeness it is hardly to be expected that such a heavy ore body exists as is indicated by the old maps, assay sheets, and etc., yet if the indicated values of the ore amount to only one fourth of those stated it is still represents a handsome mining proposition.

Taking into consideration its natural advantages of position, water, timber, accessibility, its strong geological structure, and that the exploitation of the mine has scarcely been begun, the amount of ore ready for almost immediate milling, and also the small amount of capital required to bring the property to a state of production, makes the Frazier Mine in investment which is safe and clean-cut as a business proposition. And one that is certain to repay with remarkable returns many, many times more than the amount of the investment."

Mr. Kellogg referred to one of the tunnels in the mine as the Bouchet tunnel – possibly Mr. Boushey of San Emigdio Canyon had worked at this mine at an earlier time. A mining article in a U.S. Borax magazine of 1963 made the following reference to the Frazier Mine at some time in it's past: *"Judge McKinley's old Frazier Mine and stamp mill paid off and continued to operate in a modest sort of way for twenty years"* – possibly in the 1930's and 40's and he could have been working for or with the Bicknells??. After many years of having been closed, *"Edco Mining"* hired Max Schmeling to reopen the Frazier mine in 1981 only to find that it had been thoroughly mined out. The tunnels have since been blasted shut to avoid dangerous cave-ins.

Max Schmeling at the Frazier Mine – early 1980's (Schmeling Family photo)

Brad Thessen and Mike Schmeling in the Frazier Mine – early 1980's
(Schmeling Family Photo)

Joe Matori in the Frazier Mine – early 1980's
(Schmeling Family photo)

Rick Schipper bringing diesel to the Frazier Mine in the snow – early 1980's
(Schmeling Family photo)

VII - THE HARRIS BROTHERS

Reference is made to the Harris brothers living and mining hereabouts in other chapters of this book but as Tom, Ed, Dick and Joe Harris did become quite a legend in their day in the San Emigdio Mountains, they warrant a chapter of their own.

The first information located on the brothers comes from the Bakersfield MORNING ECHO of August 1902. The newspaper reported on the Harris Mine as follows:

> *"T. J. Harris of Griffin, Ventura county,* (a small mining community in Lockwood Valley near the Snedden Place) *was in town yesterday with some bullion for shipment to the mint. It came from the Contract mine; a property located near the Kern-Ventura line and is owned by the Harris Brothers. A clean-up was recently made at the mine and as a result about $8000 in gold was gathered up. The property has not been developed to any great extent but it shows up splendidly and the owners are confident that the lower levels will yield richer ore than has yet been taken out. They are now down 180 feet and it is from this level that the recent clean-up was made. The property is now under option for thirty days and the consideration named is $20,000. If the rock continues to hold out the deal will no doubt be closed up in that time.*
>
> *Mr. Harris says there is a lively interest in the development of the mines of that locality. The deposits consist not only of gold and lead, but there are immense beds of iron that will some day be opened and furnish the material for supplying big smelters and mills."*

The article gives some additional information about a railroad being considered from Lockwood Valley – which obviously didn't happen:

> *"The residents of that section are much interested in the construction of a railroad from this valley to the coast and even at the present day would furnish no small quantity of freight."*

Early area resident, Fred Sprung, came to the Frazier Mtn area in 1914. In an early interview he shared some remembrances of the Harris Brothers of that time:

"There were four Harris brothers, Tom, Ed, Dick and Joe. The three youngest were born on the Mono Indian Reservation back of Madera. Their father had a trading post there and all three could speak the Mono Indian language. They were some of the best mountain men I ever seen. Tom and Dick helped kill the last grizzly bear in the east fork of San Emidio canyon (one of the brothers had a cabin in the Pleito Creek area). *I think this grizzly was called 'Old Baldface'. They killed him with black powder rifles and they said he was one tough bear.*

Tom and Dick had the Harris mine on the head of Dry Creek on the south side of Frazier Mt. It is just east of Long Dave Valley and they had their log cabin and two stamp mills at the lower end of Long Dave Valley. They took out a worthwhile amount of gold ore there."

It seems Tom Harris took his own life in 1928. According to the local Forest Ranger J. D. Reyes:

"Tom Harris was despondent because his health had failed. He came up into the forest and brought a thirty-pound box of blasting powder along. He was considerate enough to pick a place up the canyon from here where he would not set fire to anything. Then he apparently sat on the box, touching a match to a short fuse, and waited for results. All we found was a big hole in the ground and a few scraps of clothing."

Joyce Cuddy Tifft, the granddaughter of the original Cuddy couple to settle in the area, later wrote of this incident as follows:

"The Harris brothers, Tom and Dick, used to come out to Stauffer (in Lockwood Valley) *to get their mail twice a week. They were old and sickly, and had an agreement that someone would come to check on them if they didn't appear when expected.*

One time when Tom didn't come out from the Long Dave Mine, an expedition went up to check on him. They found a note indicating suicide, which said the dogs and horses had been fed and asked that someone take care of them.

He obviously used dynamite to end his life, as all they found was a hole in the ground made by the dynamite, and Tom's hat."

A final description of the unusual death has been found in the November 16, 1928 issue of the LOS ANGELES TIMES. The brief news report read:

"Despondent and ill, Thomas J. Harris, 64-year-old pioneer homesteader and miner of Northern Ventura county, ended his life by igniting the fuse to a heavy charge of dynamite, then sitting on

> *the container. Inside the house was found an undated note which read: 'I have suffered all night. Can't stand it any longer. I'm going to end it all with a box of powder. Goodbye, everybody.' "*

The Harris brothers were said to be from a family of twenty children. Tom became a legendary figure in these mountains who supposedly got his mining experience on the old Frazier mine. A young man who would assist Mr. Harris in the summers, Jack Willett, later said of Tom:

> *"Everybody liked him. He was a man cheerful and loud, heavy and never so happy as when people were around his camp and he could get up in the morning to cook breakfast. He would ask nobody to do the dishes, he would do them himself."*

Born in the 1860's, he and his brothers must have come to these mountains as young men as Willett said Tom worked his claim for 35 - 40 years.

Tom Harris about 1918
(Willet Family Photo)

The Harris brothers camp near their mine in Long Dave Canyon
(Culbertson Family photo)

In 1923 Lockwood homesteader, Bill deLancey wrote of Tom Harris:

> *"He was one of the almost legendary figures of the Far West – one of the most colorful men of his time. He still worked his one-man gold mine on Frazier Mtn. and wore two modest-sized pearl handled revolvers, often using one as a pointer."*

Some oldtimers of the area – 1922: George Willett, Tom Harris, Richard Harris and Doc Coolidge – at Mr. Willett's cabin on the Sespe (Willett Family Photo)

The old Harris Gold Mine made the news again in 1979 when three men became trapped inside. The men had entered the mine to look into the possibility of reopening it when the cave-in occurred. A companion hiked down to the Snedden place where she gained a ride to the Ventura County Sheriff's Substation to ask for help. They brought local mining expert, Max Schmeling to the site by helicopter and after being trapped for twenty-two hours the men were successfully freed. The Bureau of Mines offices in San Bernardino and Arizona had crews ready in the event that they were needed but Mr. Schmeling and his assistant, Ray Bramlet, were able to accomplish the rescue. Max Schmeling, the son of a Pennsylvania miner, had been in mining all his life. Schmeling attempted to reopen the Harris mine in 1985 but found it mined out.

Mike and Max Schmeling at the Harris Mine about 1980
(Schmeling Family Photo)

VIII - MISCELLANEOUS MINING MEMORABILIA

The names of the mines on Frazier Mountain over the years are numerous, whether they changed ownership often or whether there where that many is uncertain. Some of these colorful names are: *"Fair View"*, *"Bunker Hill"*, *"Spotted Fawn"*, *"Red Jacket"*, *"Big Four"*, *"Gnarled Oak"*, *"Hidden Value"*, *"Hornet"*, *"Lookout"*, *"Arastra"* and *"Max B"*, most located on the southern slope of the mountain. The latter two of these were owned by a D. W. Maxey of Gorman. A. F. Maxey and Charles Maxey, also of Gorman, owned the *"Oro Fino"* and *"Golden Era"*. The Maxey Ranch is still well known in the Hungry Valley area. The *"Blue Bell"*, *"Red Bell"*, *"Silver Bell"* and *"Yellow Bell"* were owned by a C. H. Crandall and Dr. W. R. Colbert of Gorman and were located on the western slope, as were the *"Golden Bloom"*, *"Lead Bloom"* and *"Crooked S."* owned by R. H. Colbert of Gorman. When it is said that these men were from Gorman – that is where they got their mail anyway. They probably lived within five or ten miles of that settlement.

Also located on the west side of Frazier Mountain was the *"White Mule Mine"*, at an altitude of six thousand five hundred feet. It was the claim of David Menzie, mentioned in earlier chapters of this book, but later owned by men named Reed, Hazelton, Haylock and Lockwood. About ten miles south of Gorman there was the *"Castac Mine"* owned by a corporation out of the Pasadena area. W. P. Meacham of Gorman was the superintendent of the Castac Mine as well as owning eight other claims jointly with G. L. Bergman of Los Angeles on or about the present Gold Hill area. William Snyder of Gorman owned the *"Red Rock"* and *"Oak"* mines. The *"Sibert Mine"*, owned by a Bessie Sibert of Los Angeles, and the *"Gold Bug"* mine as well as the *"Frazier Mine #1 & #2"* and others, were still known on the mountain in the mid-1900's.

It is apparent that the area surrounding Gorman would have been a thriving mining community in the late 1800's – early 1900's. On her way to live at Rose Station (at the bottom of Grapevine Canyon) a young writer, Mary Hunter (Austin), made a stopover with her family in Gorman in 1888 and left this very descriptive account of the visit. She wrote:

> *"On the next to the last day of our journey we took dinner at 'Hell', a supply station and hostelry, known sometimes as 'Gorman's', situated just at the head of the valley. Bob McCord, from Nova Scotia, familiarly known locally as 'Old Three-Finger', one of the*

habitués of the place, a miner, a veritable 'forty-niner', looking as if he had just stepped out of one of Bret Harte's stories, was there on a periodical 'drunk'. He was very urgent in his entreaties for the man of our family (her brother) *to 'come take one more drink and then swear off'!"*

A 1920's homesteader from Lockwood Valley, Bill deLancey, later wrote of the Frazier Mountain mines:

"Several gold camps, in an abandoned or semi-abandoned condition, could be found here and there along the pine-clad flanks of Frazier Mt. This made the mountain rising across the east end of the valley (Lockwood Valley) *very interesting to explore. Occasionally I would roam through the forests there, snooping along the faded trails of old-time miners.*

One day I came upon a most surprising sight, all by itself among the yellow pines on the side of the mountain. A giant wooden paddle wheel, fully 15 feet in diameter, poised above what had once been a ditch. No doubt water had been diverted from somewhere higher up, its power turning the wheel to run a mill, perhaps to crush ore.

Impressive about this silent wheel was the amount of labor involved in merely hewing out the individual paddles, which were three or four feet wide; and the massive framing, also fashioned by hand. All this patient work had been done in the long ago, on a lonesome but beautiful mountain, many, many miles from any civilized comforts. There were no trails to this unexpected scene, and when I tried to find it a year or two later, couldn't locate it again.

Then there were the many buildings of the White Mule Mine, whose shafts were worked spasmodically by the people who bought it after its heyday. This gold mine had been the most extensive on the mountain, which was of unusual formation.

Andy Johnson (an old-time prospector who also homestead in Lockwood Valley – with his two sisters) *once described Frazier as a 'mountain of mud, with a thin cap of rock on top'. This condition could explain why its ledges of gold and other metals 'ran out' unexpectedly, though some pockets were rich. I've heard that it had a greater variety of precious metals, including more platinum than any other mountain in the world.*

Most famous, long enduring and uncertain of the gold mines on Frazier was the Esperanza. Early Padres from the missions of San Fernando and Los Angeles were said to have taken

> *thousands of dollars from the small, perpendicular hole that looked like anybody's water well. Above it stood its original hand-operated windlass.*
>
> *The padres apparently worked it out, but deeper digging was revived in various generations. A story around the Lockwood had it that a hired man on a cattle ranch got fed up with the boss's failure to pay his wages, and finally made threatening remarks. The boss was then the owner of the Esperanza, which at the moment wasn't showing any colors. So he snarled, 'Well, you ---, go up on the mountain and dig your pay out of the --- mine'. The cowboy did, immediately hitting a pocket that paid him $1,500. With this he happily went over the hill."*

Mr. deLancey also wrote of a confrontation with a timber rattler at the site:

> *"The snake lay hidden under a corner of the old Spanish windlass of the Esperanza Mine, staking out his own claim on the famed round hole ... the guardian of the old Spanish treasure trove."*

According to early mining records, the Esperanza was purchased in 1887 by R. B. Harper, *"an experienced mining expert"*, from E. J. Tobin who an area of Cuddy Valley called *"the Tobin"* may have been named for. At the time of that exchange of ownership the ore was assayed at $65-75 a ton. Mr. Harper named his venture the *"Espranza Gold & Silver Mining & Milling Company"*. Edward Tobin, from Ireland, was listed in the Ventura County voter registration of 1882 as a *"stock raiser"* in the Lockwood area. Margaret Gale Cuddy's sister, Mary Gale, married a W. H. Tobin but it is not yet know if the two men might have been related.

Another reported unusual mine was a mica mine on Alamo Mountain. Donkeys carried the mica down the steep mountain to the mine headquarters of *"Alamo Mountain Mica & Milling"* on Piru or Alamo Creek – as it is written both ways. Here there was also a cook house and bunk house. Annie Hollenbeck and her son *"Bub"*, from Lebec, had the contract to haul supplies to the mine from Bakersfield. Annie was the postmistress of Lebec and so possibly brought the supplies with the mail as many who carried the mail did in those days – late 1800's. Mrs. Hollenbeck was the mother of Florence Hollenbeck who married Joseph Cuddy of that well-known family. Mica was used for insulation and the glass in lanterns as it could withstand a lot of heat. It can be found throughout the San Emigdio Mountains.

Another possible mica mine in the same area is further mention in an unusual incident that took place about the same time. It was recorded later in a book written by Lester G. Loomis about his experience there and shared by his great grandson, Norman Ross. Mr. Loomis was on his annual hunting trip with friends from the Los Angeles area to Alamo Mountain in the Fall of the year and writes:

> *"We left Los Angeles in my camp wagon, which I had built for me, according to my special needs and ideas. After some days, one more beautiful than the other, we reached Mt. Alamo where we went into permanent camp.*
>
> *Whenever I went on such a hunting trip, I made it a point to prospect for minerals. This was just as natural to me as it was for my companions to rest in camp after the hunt. I got up into the upper reaches of the Piru Creek and ran on to two people, man and wife, who were living in a hut built of old logs, brush and twigs; a very desolate looking shack, resembling a wicki-up as we call the brush teepees of our Indians out here. When I explained my prospecting, he informed me that he had located a very promising mica prospect and that he had started a small mine.*
>
> *At that time mica was quite in some demand, so I became interested and asked him to show it to me. After looking it over carefully, I offered to buy the mine from him and we agreed on the purchase price of $1,500. I was to pay $500 down and the remainder within a year's time. As I had explained to him that I was on a hunting trip, he agreed to wait four weeks with the down-payment so as to give me enough time to finish my vacation, return to town and then to come back with the money for the sum agreed upon.*
>
> *At the end of the month we returned to Los Angeles well pleased with the results of the hunt and the fine peaceful days spent in the open. I looked up matters pertaining to the value of mica and the demand for it, got my $500 and began the trip back to Piru Creek. I boarded a train as far as Lancaster. There I took a stage to Gorman Station. On the way we were caught in a very severe snowstorm that had come up suddenly. I was glad that I had brought a heavy overcoat and warm clothing. Of luggage I had just a small satchel containing some fresh underwear, towels, a bottle of whiskey and a box of cigars. I had intended to push through to the shack of the miner that same day, but since it had gotten quite late by the time we reached Gorman Station, I decided to stay overnight.*
>
> *I was sitting on the porch of the small hotel waiting for supper time when an old timer, and old prospector, dripped into the chair next to mine and it wasn't very long before we started to talk about mines. I told him I had come up to look at the nearby mica mine and to make my down payment on it. Then I told him how*

and when I had met Mr. Rob, the owner and his wife. When I finished with my story the old prospector asked me 'Are you going to pay him cash'? I replied in the affirmative. The old man shook his head, thought a while, and then replied, 'Now see here young man, let me give you a little advice. I know that man and I don't like him. You better turn around, don't see him at all, or you will wish you had. That man is bad all through. He has never been convicted of any crime, but he ought to be.'

I told the old timer that I would see it through and that I knew how to handle that kind of a man. No more was said by either of us. The supper bell sounded just then and I went into the dining room hoping that I would get a good meal. I was very hungry after the long trip. I slept sound that night, got up early on the following morning, after eating a hearty breakfast, hired a horse to make the twelve mile trip up to Piru Creek.

The traveling through the deep snow was slow work and it was late that afternoon before I sighted the miner's shack. The man stepped out of the house to greet me. Not wanting to waste time I said to him 'Well, I am ready to do business, all you need do is to sign the contract that I had drawn up'."

It seems the fellow had changed his mind and wanted more money. Loomis called the deal off and asked if there was some place he could stay for the night before he headed back to Gorman. They couple shared their supper with him, gave him a ragged old blanket and let him sleep in an old shack nearby. He slept until he heard crunching in the snow and saw the couple was approaching with a light, a shotgun and an axe. Loomis yelled at them that he had a gun and to go back and not come out again.

Not sleeping another wink, at the early morning light he saddled his horse and rode to the door of the shack with his six-shooter handy and called out for his satchel. The man brought it out. Loomis rode out of sight and then opened his satchel for a swig of whiskey. He found the satchel had been cut up by the lock as the couple no doubt looked for his money, the whiskey had been replaced with tea and his cigars were gone. He realized that when they did not find the money they probably came out to kill him.

Lester Loomis continues:

"When I finally got back to Gorman Station, I met the old prospector again. He asked me at once what had happened so I told him of my adventure of the night. He shook his head and remarked, 'Boy you are sure lucky if that's all they done to you'. Again we sat on the porch waiting for the supper bell."

A few years later, Lester recognized Mrs. Rob at a train station and when he confronted her she confessed how much she feared her husband and had left him. She said Mr. Rob had killed another man at the mine under very similar circumstances and had been put in prison.

* * * *

In 1976, area historian, Grace Bradley Toenjes, wrote of the status of the Frazier Mountain mines in an article in the MOUNTAIN ENTERPRISE. The article was based on her visit to several of the mines some years before and an interview with the owners of the claims at that time, Mr. & Mrs. Baggett. Mrs. Toenjes wrote:

> *"In the 1940's, V. F. Baggett decided to look over some of the abandoned mines of the early days. He told us that he talked to the late Mr. Tucker of the Bureau of Mines in Los Angeles, who encouraged him to go to the west end of Frazier Mountain where legend tells that Indians, under Spanish Padres supervision, mined fabulous amounts of gold.*
>
> *The gold had to be brought out of the mountains in baskets made by the Indians and carried over the narrow trails through the Mutah Flats country and down into Fillmore, through Ventura and Santa Barbara, where it was loaded onto ships.*
>
> *Following up a few clues Baggett found a man living in Ventura who told him that years ago the young teen age boys of the area, on seeing the Indians stalking into Ventura, each laden with a basket of ore, would form gangs and declare they would follow the Indians on their way homeward and find out the source of their gold. Time and time again the boys were able to follow the Indians to where they would start to climb over the mountains. At this point, the Indians would camp for the night ... so would the boys. In the morning the Indians would be gone, leaving not a trace. Not too long ago, a cave was found in that vicinity containing Indian baskets in which traces of gold dust were found.*
>
> *After several prospecting trips, Mr. & Mrs. Baggett moved into an old cabin in the Summer of 1947. Legend tells that this cabin had been built by the Spanish Padres, who were searching for gold in the early 1800's. The cabin rests on a fairly level shelf of Frazier Mountain at an altitude of 7,000 feet. The 12 X 14 foot room is constructed of pine logs ranging from 20 inches in diameter at the bottom to sixteen inches at the top. The logs are put together by laying one on top of the other, notching them at the corners and using adobe mud to fill the cracks. Ten inch poles formed the*

ridge and rafters and hand hewn shakes covered the roof. The dirt floor was about four inches above the door sill. The door opening was only four feet five inches in height and the door itself was a strong, sturdy affair made of hand cut logs. This construction was for defense against the bears and the cold, so the story goes.

Mrs. Baggett soon caused many drastic changes to be made in the old domicile. The old shakes were covered with roofing paper. Two windows were cut in the wall and a wooden floor laid, then came a bedroom and a lean-to that housed a bathtub with running water which was heated by the good old sun shining on a storage tank. The primitive old room also contained a sink, butane stove and a gas refrigerator along with some modern pieces of furniture.

Being pioneers of 1947/48, the Baggetts purchased a large truck, a Fordson tractor, which Baggett made into a caterpillar type tractor with a hydraulic blade for grading the road. They made a brief promise of a road, beginning at the county highway and taking out over the mountain to their cabin.

Having already found the remains of an old dump, Baggett started working in the vicinity trying to locate tunnels of old mines. Using a skip-loader fashioned to fit the Fordson, the two miners dug and scraped for three months before they found the portal to what they thought was the 'Penn State Mine'. All the portal of this tunnel had caved in and pine trees and bushes had grown over it. When they first opened this entrance of the tunnel, they found an old shovel leaning against the side. A few hours later the blade of the shovel was completely disintegrated. Just the handle and a pile of rust remained. The large slightly curved handle had been fastened onto the blade by means of wooden pegs."

One of the mines the Baggetts re-opened (Photographed by Grace Bradley – 1953)

"Several tests of the ore found in this portal and the reports caused the Baggetts to decide to continue the work. Knowing that only the high grade ore had been taken out by the Indians, the next step was to build a mill. Having plenty of timber at hand, a saw mill was also built that sawed the lumber for the process mill.

Following an old Jack (donkey) *trail farther up the mountain, two more mines were found that show evidence of once producing much gold. These were called the 'Dark Horse Mine' and the 'White Mule Mine'. In the center of the dump of the White Mule Mine a pine tree was found growing which measured twenty inches in diameter and was estimated to be 150 feet high. Using the time it takes a pine tree to grow, this was mute witness to the fact the mine had been worked many years ago.*

About two and a half miles down the mountain from the Penn State Mine, in a shallow basin near a small creek another mill in the form of an old Spanish arrastra was found. Although it testified to later re-construction, some of the hand forged bolts and nuts could be seen. The square, hand made nails could be picked out of the decaying wood. The axle of the arrastra was hand hewn as were the mortices through which ran the poles that turned the arrastra. The rock basin that held the ore to be ground was probably six feet in diameter and saucer-shaped. The little check-dams in the creek with their rocks worn smooth and hollow by the passing of the water washing the sand out of the gold ore, mutely tells the story of gold mining in the early days."

The arrastra found by the Baggetts near one of the mines on the West side of Frazier Mountain – 1953. (Grace Bradley photo)

> *"Due to several cave-ins in the old tunnels as the mining operations continued, the Baggetts decided to sell the claim and move out. Then along came the Forest Service and as a fire prevention measure and a policy to eliminate 'attractive nuisances', burned the old cabins and buildings."*

This author's husband, Jim Kane, remembered that Mr. Baggett died in the late 1970's on the *"76 Curve"* – near the first bridge as one drives west to Frazier Park. Baggett's truck rolled over on him and pinned him under it.

Jim Kane also remembered that in the 1950's he and his friend, Sid Fredholm, found old dynamite in the old Sibert or Gold Bug Mine and hauled it out in their jeep – a very dangerous (and foolish) venture down those very bumpy mountain roads. They took it to Sid's dad to use at his mine along Lockwood Creek.

By the 1970's the Forest Service had realized that the abandoned mining shacks throughout the mountains presented a fire risk to the forests. Most all structures were then removed through controlled burns. After one such burn, Frazier Park resident, Art Longbottom, bought a metal detector at the local hardware store and went up on the mountain to check out some of those sites. One of the items he found was a can with gold and silver melted in it that had no doubt been in the floor or wall of that particular structure.

It is not often that a detailed story about a miner is located but author, Mary Hunter Austin, wrote about one of the miners she got to know well. She may have met this man when she lived below Grapevine Canyon at Rose Station in the late 1800's or when she lived at Lone Pine some years later. Never-the-less he could have well lived in the foothills of the San Emigdio Mountains. She refers to him as a *"pocket hunter"* which was a term given to the miner in search of that elusive pocket of gold. Mrs. Austin left us with this excellent description of a miner of that time in her book LAND OF LITTLE RAIN. Mary wrote:

> *"I remember very well when I first met him. Walking in the evening glow to spy the marriages of the white gilias, I sniffed the unmistakable order of burning sage. It is a smell that carries far and indicates usually the nearness of a campoodie, but on the level mesa nothing taller showed than Diana's sage. Over the tops of it, beginning to dusk under a young white moon, trailed a savering ghost of smoke, and at the end of it I came upon the 'Pocket Hunter' making a dry camp in the friendly scrub. He sat tailorwise in the sand, with his coffee-pot on the coals, his supper ready to hand in the frying-pan, and himself in a mood for talk.*

His pack burros in hobbles strayed off to hunt for a wetter mouthful than the sage afforded, and gave him no concern.

We came upon him often after that, threading the windy passes, or by water holes in the desert hills, and got to know much of his way of life. He was a small, bowed man, with a face and manner and speech of no character at all, as if he had that faculty of small hunted things of taking on the protective color of his surroundings. His clothes were of no fashion that I could remember, except that they bore liberal markings of pot black, and he had a curious fashion of going about with his mouth open, which gave him a vacant look until you came near enough to perceive him busy about an endless hummed, wordless tune.

He traveled far and took a long time to it, but the simplicity of his kitchen arrangements was elemental. A pot for beans, a coffee-pot, a frying-pan, a tin to mix bread in ... he fed the burros in this when there was need ... with these he had been half round our western world and back. He explained to me very early in our acquaintance what was good to take to the hills for food: nothing sticky, for that 'dirtied the pots'; nothing with juice to it, for that would not pack to advantage; and nothing likely to ferment. He used no gun, but he would set snares by the water-holes for quail and doves, and in the trout country he carried a line. Burros he kept, one or two according to his pack, for this chief excellence, that they would eat potato parings and firewood. He had owned a horse in the foothill country, but when he came to the desert with no forage but mesquite, he found himself under the necessity of picking the beans from the briers, a labor that drove him to the use of pack animals to whom thorns were a relish.

I suppose no man becomes a pocket hunter by first intention. He must be born with the faculty, and along come the occasion, like the tap on the test tube that induces crystallization. My friend had been several things of no moment until he struck a thousand-dollar pocket and came into his vocation. A pocket, you must know, is a small body of rich ore occurring by itself, or in a vein of poorer stuff. Nearly every mineral ledge contains such, if only one has the luck to hit upon them without too much labor. The sensible thing for a man to do who has found a good pocket is to buy himself into business and keep away from the hills. The logical thing is to set out looking for another one.

My friend the Pocket Hunter had been looking twenty years. His working outfit was a shovel, a pick, a gold pan which he kept cleaner than his plate, and a pocket magnifier. When he came to a watercourse he would pan out the gravel of its bed for 'colors', and under the glass determine if they had come from far or near, and so spying he would work up the stream until he found where the drift on the gold-bearing outcrop fanned out into the creek; then up the side of the canon till he came to the proper vein. I think he said the best indication of small pockets was an iron stain, but I could never get the run of miner's talk enough to feel instructed for pocket hunting. He had another method in the waterless hills, where he would work in and out of blind gullies and all windings of the manifold strata that appeared not to have cooled since they had been heaved up.

There are many strange sorts of humans bred in a mining country, each sort despising the queernesses of the other, but of them all I found the Pocket Hunter most acceptable for his clean, companionable talk. There was more color to his reminiscences than the faded sandy old miners 'kyoteing', that is, tunneling like a coyote ... kyote in the vernacular ... in the core of a lonesome hill. Such a one had found, perhaps, a body of tolerable ore in a poor lead ... remember that I can never be depended on to get the terms right ... and followed it into the heart of country rock to no profit, hoping, burrowing, and hoping.

These men go harmlessly mad in time, believing themselves just behind the wall of fortune...mostly likable and simple men, for whom it is well to do any kindly thing that occurs to you except lend them money. I have known 'grub stakers' too, those persuasive sinners to whom you make allowances of flour and pork and coffee in consideration of the ledges they are about to find; but none of these proved so much worth-while as the Pocket Hunter. He wanted nothing of you and maintained a cheerful preference for his own way of life. It was an excellent way if you had the constitution for it.

He was a perfect gossip of the woods, this Pocket Hunter, and when I could get him away from 'leads' and 'strikes' and 'contacts', he was full of fascinating small talk about the ebb and flood of creeks, the pinon crop and wolves. I suppose he never knew how much he depended, for the necessary sense of home and companionship, on the beasts and trees, meeting and finding them in their wonted places.

About the opening of winter, when one looks for sudden big storms, Pocket Hunter became trapped in thick, blinding, knee-deep snow. According to his account, he knew where he was, but couldn't exactly say. He was able to take shelter with a flock of wild sheep under wind-tilted cedars. Accepted by them, he snuggled in the warmth of the packed fleeces and slept. If the flock stirred in the night he stirred drowsily to keep close and let the storm go by. When morning came the very soul of him shook to see the wild sheep of God stand up about him nodding their great horns beneath the cedar roof, looking out on the wonder of the snow.

The Pocket Hunter had gotten to that point where he knew no bad weather, and all places were equally happy so long as they were out of doors. I do not know just how long it takes to become saturated with the elements so that one takes no account of them. Myself can never get past the glow and exhilaration of a storm, the wrestle of long dust-heavy winds, the play of live thunder on the rocks, nor past the keen fret of fatigue when the storm outlasts physical endurance. But prospectors and Indians get a kind of a weather shell that remains on the body until death.

The Pocket Hunter had seen destruction by the violence of nature and the violence of men, and felt himself in the grip of an All-wisdom that killed men or spared them as seemed for their good; but of death by sickness he knew nothing except that he believed he should never suffer it. He had been in Grape-vine Canon the year of storms that changed the whole front of the mountain. All day he had come down under the wing of the storm, hoping to win past it, but finding it traveling with him until night. It kept on after that, he supposed, a steady downpour, but could not with certainty say, being securely deep in sleep.

But the weather instinct does not sleep. In the night the heavens behind the hill dissolved in rain, and the roar of the storm was borne in and mixed with his dreaming, so that it moved him, still asleep, to get up and out of the path of it. What finally woke him was the crash of pine longs as they went down before the unbridled flood, and the swirl of foam that lashed him where he clung in the tangle of shrub while the wall of water went by. It went against the cabin of Bill Gerry and laid Bill stripped and broken on a sand bar at the mouth of the Grape-vine, seven miles away. There, when the sun was up and the wrath of the rain spent, the Pocket Hunter found and buried him; but he never laid his own escape at any door but the unintelligible favor of the Powers."

Pocket Hunter buries Bill Gerry

Mrs. Austin concludes her story about the Pocket Hunter as follows:

> *"It was no news to me then, two or three years after, to learn that he had taken ten thousand dollars from an abandoned claim, just the sort of luck to have pleased him, and gone to London to spend it. The land seemed not to miss him any more than it had minded him, but I missed him and could not forget the trick of expecting him in least likely situations. Therefore it was with a pricking sense of the familiar that I followed a twilight trail of smoke, a year or two later, to the swale of a dripping spring, and came upon a man by the fire with a coffee-pot and frying-pan. I was not surprised to find it was Pocket Hunter. No man can be stronger than his destiny."*

Annie Rose Briggs, who wrote of her quest for the Los Padres Mine in San Emigdio Canyon in Chapter III, also wrote a poem entitled *"The Doodle Bug"* in tribute to the other miners later working claims near them in Castaic Creek Canyon south of Liebre Mountain, where another Los Padres Mine was supposed to have been located. It would seem that the doodle bug is the name of an old vehicle that might have been driven to the mine and engine of same used to run equipment. Written about mining in the early to mid-1900's, a portion of that poem reads:

"The weary Miner goes his way, he's found a piece of ore,
He is wearing out his very heart, he hopes to find some more.
Along comes quite a friendly man,
his words are smooth and smug,
And he can promptly put his right, with his little doodle-bug.

Across the way another man has worked it just as hard,
It always seems it's just too much, he really needs a pard.
In spite of all he can do, it goes so very slow,
A stranger comes across the hill and his is radio.

Up on the hill a third man works, and his goes down so deep,
It's hard to know if it is wise to follow down so steep.
But some decision must be made; he feels the time is ripe,
Some strange invention tempts him sure, the geo-physic type.

And we are working just as hard to make our own success,
And bring things there to such a head, they bring us happiness.
Some one is coming down the hill, with very secret mean,
He knows that he can solve the game
and shows a queer machine.

And friends are working to the north; they're having quite a time.
They hope that they can beat us yet, to get a working mine.
Of course this is a silent hope, they're working out the thing,
Along must come the strangest quest, perhaps a psychic King.

And all of these are truthful things, their knowledge can't be beat,
And if the miner don't believe, he's crazy with the heat.
Or else he's lacking sense to see that these things cannot lie,
It's sad to be misunderstood, the doodle-bug will sigh.

You did not listen hard enough, that wail meant something more,
It yelps another angry howl
and bounces on the floor. (the engine)
You screw the pieces on again, you feel it must be you,
It waves around in wicked glee and starts on something new.

We know the fault must be our own, maybe we're just too dumb,
I guess we'll have to work it out and let the neighbor's hum.
We know the gold is on the hill, we almost see it shine,
The doodle-bug says surely no, it's down there in the mine."

One such "doodle bug" at Bill Meukow's mine in Black Bob Canyon

Mrs. Briggs goes on to write about those working in the hills near where she and her husband mined in a poem entitled *"Our Neighbors"*. It reads:

"And now the strangers wander in, the story travels fast,
They hunt the gold, so they say, and reach our camp at last.
No doubt they speak the simple truth, the day's find was great,
And traveling far across the hills, they reach our cabin late.

They must be tired and so they stay, they study all our ore,
They've brought their food, these kindly men,
they have been there before
We're glad to see them once again, they're meaning us no harm,
And all enjoy the evening there, afar from town and farm.

And these are men who wish us luck, as they start on their way,
And we think all their stories o'er as we work through the day.
For often in their simple words, a thing is shown so clear,
And what we thought was far away is standing very near.

Our neighbors working to the south, 'tis Bob and Eunice there,
They drill with hope as great as ours, alike hard work they share.
Their ore is white as winter snow, the yellow gleaming through,
They work as late as we at night, and beat the morning dew.

To all of those we're wishing luck, as they must come and go,
A toiling in the summer sun or up there in the snow.
Their hearts are gold and courage great, as they all carry through,
We know the best is none too good, if they all get their due."

A last miscellaneous mining item comes from Ozena in the Cuyama District. The news comes from the LOS ANGELES TIMES of November 11, 1915 and reads:

> *"A placer gold strike, which is said to have uncovered a rich territory, has been made in the Cuyama, four miles east of Ozena.* (the Scheideck area) *R. H. Thompson and S. V. Perry, the original locaters, have filed on a number of claims and others are joining the activity, indicating that in the district ranch men generally are stampeding for the scene.*
>
> *According to reports, the ground is perhaps rich as any discovered in this part of the State in a very long time. The range links in with that in which the Frazer mine is located further south, and between the two points placer gold has been found in several canyons. Several prospectors have left here for the scene, and if their investigations prove the ground nearly as rich as claimed, it is expected there will be a general rush from this county and Ventura."*

IX - BURIED TREASURES

In his series of books, author Arnold Rojas collected volumes of stories from old vaqueros, cowboys and Indians as well as stories about the bandits and the gold they left behind. One such great story reads in part:

"The talk around the fire then turned to the bandits who had buried gold along old trails in California that lead from Sonoma to far away Sonora and of old Avelino Martinez who, some said had been a bandit or had been in league with them. Men who really knew said that Avelino had herded sheep in order to keep a large stock of provisions on hand to feed the fugitives/bandits without arousing suspicion when they were in hiding near his camp. He was also to see the bandits who kept watch on the peaks pass on, and only he remained to sit by the fire and tell stories of another age.

One morning several men rode up. After grave salutations, one of the riders asked Avelino if they could have meat. He told them to slaughter as many lambs as they needed. After the lambs had been killed and quartered, the spokesman for the band, in return for Avelino's courtesy and in payment for the sheep, said, 'On the other side of this mountain you will find a mesa where three pines stand apart from the other trees and make a triangle. One is blazed (marked by removing the bark in some shape). *Dig on the side that is blazed and you will find gold. Take what you need.' Avelino never took advantage of the offer. Though he knew or had been told where a number of 'entierros', treasures, were to be found, he never searched for them. He worked for a living and died a poor man. Perhaps, like all 'paisanos', he thought that buried money will be found only by men who have no greed in their hearts and are destined to be rich."*

Blazed trees or *"witness trees"* mentioned above were used through these mountains. Some can still be seen today. They gave directions, indicated a message in some form, or that something, or someone, was buried at the base of the tree or nearby.

The Rojas story continues about a Tejon Ranch hand:

"But once, when a vaquero's wife had been ill for a long time and he was desperately in need of money, Avelino heard of his distress and rode to his friend. Being a blunt man, after a brief

greeting and without ceremony he said, 'Vale, I have learned of your bad luck. I am going to tell you where you can get money but you must not be afraid.' He pointed toward the south and continued, 'On the side of that mountain is an oak tree which has a branch that curves out and upward like a bent elbow. If you will dig where the point of the elbow aims at the ground you will find a box with money in it; not much but enough for your needs.'"

Oak tree with an *"elbow"*

"The vaquero rode away and found the oak with the branch bent like an elbow. Then he rode back to the ranch store and bought a demijohn of vinegar. Carrying the demijohn and a shovel he rode back to the tree where he dug up a box. He pried the lid off and holding his breath, he poured the vinegar over the money in the box. He did this because buried gold creates a gas which is fatal when breathed, but vinegar counteracts the poisonous fumes. The contents of the box did not exceed a thousand dollars. Much of it was apparently loot from some gambling table or merchandise store, as it was in small coins. It was sufficient for the vaquero's needs as the old man had promised and it was the only 'entierros' found on Tejon Ranch of the many that legend says were buried there in the old days."

In another story on Tejon Ranch, Rojas writes:
"The Treasure of Tunas Canyon has never been found though the gold pieces, which filled two buckskin bags and made a load for a pack horse, lies deep in a fissure of a cliff at the mouth of a 'barranca' (ravine) *beside the trail traveled by many men for a century or more.*

Once the red men had lived here in abundance and drove great herds of elk up the canyon to be killed by hunters hidden in the hills to provide meat for many days of feasting. But lean days had come to the Indian and hunger stalked the camp in Tunas when the bandit, the girl he was supposed to have kidnapped and the pack horse load of gold he had stolen, came riding up the creek. The man was on his way south with his loot when he entered Alamos Creek near Comanche Point. He was captured by the young men of the tribe and brought before the chief who spared his life because he had the girl with him and warriors do not war on women. They were held all night. The next morning the Indians returned the saddle horses. The bandit rode away with his companion, unharmed, but the pack horse was relieved of his burden only to be killed for food.

In those days chiefs had power and authority and their orders were obeyed without question. Knowing full well that the misery and wretchedness which was the Indians' lot was caused by lust for gold, the chief ordered the bandit's loot to be buried deep under ground so that the clean earth would cover the glitter which lit the fires of greed and cupidity (excessive desire) *the heart of the white man and brought suffering, outrage and death to the redman. They took the gold up Tunas Canyon and poured it into a deep fissure of a cliff.*

This 'cuento' (tale) *was one of the buried treasure stories known to the viejos, old ones, on Tejon who are sure the gold has not been found yet because every now and then some old vaquero caught out on the plains after dark would come in and tell of seeing a greenish light glowing off toward El Canon de Las Tunas."*

In still another story Rojas recorded:
"Numerous bandit tales told by the viejos (old people) all agree on two points, the robber was a great lover and a champion pick and shovel man. How he and his confederates found enough night in the short period they were active here, to bury all the gold that is said to be in every locality in the state where Spanish speaking people settled, is a mystery ... though the bandits naturally must have used as much secrecy as possible in their nocturnal operations. The 'entiero', buried treasures, seem to have become common knowledge to the paisanos.

This inconsistency can by made clear, however, by asking any old vaquero to explain it. Buried gold, the vaquero will say, gives off a heat which breaks into a flame above ground, over the entiero and if it is your destiny to be rich and your heart is free of greed and avarice (excessive desire), *you will not be afraid to seek the location of the gold when on certain nights ... depending on the phase of the moon ... you will see a greenish light glowing over the treasure, it is to lead you to wealth. But if your intentions are evil in respect to the future use of the money, you may see the light but it will move away from the entiero and lead you into quick sand, over a cliff, or into some other dangerous situation.*

Buried gold that is minted money, he (the old-timer) *will further elucidate* (explain), *has a means of revealing its proximity by making noises in the night such as the sound of groans, the sound of rattling chains or deep rumblings. Kern county has its share of buried treasure. Old-timers say strange noises are heard at night on most of the old Spanish ranches here. Tecuya Mountain is known for the sounds of phantom footsteps so regular in their occurrence that the people living there moved outside the house in order to sleep. Of late years the footsteps have ceased since a Spaniard herding sheep there found the treasure, or so they say. Pleito Mountain has its peculiar noise, the sounds there are like the rattling of chains."*

About treasure in the Carrizo Plain, Rojas writes:
"Far to the southwest of Bakersfield, across the valley and over the Tremblor Range, lie the Carrizo Plains. Over looking this plateau and standing on an eminence in solitary grandeur is the Painted Rock (Piedra Pintada). It is called so because at some distant age the artists of a long gone race, migrating from the frozen North, left their indelible paintings in the shallow caves of the rock.

The Piedra Pintada seems to be a crater of a long extinct volcano which has been covered with earth until only the top remains above the level of the plain, making a hollow circle. There is a narrow opening into the crater.

The early Spaniards found it very useful as a corral when they ran the wild mustangs that abounded on the plains. It was a hiding place for the gangs of Murrieta and in later years for Vasquez and Chavez, so legends says.

A short distance away is a spring of bad but useable water in an otherwise thirsty land. Because of this vaqueros have used the rock as a camping place since it was first discovered.

Over the years there have persisted stories of strange lights seen there by the campers who told of having heard the rumbling of phantom bands of horses and the crack of the ramal as goblin vaqueros struck their chap legs to urge on their charges.

There is a story told of a young cattleman named Jesus who rode the range constantly on the look for lepes, motherless calves, which he would catch to add to his meager herd.

One day there came into a Bakersfield a gringo who spoke fluent Spanish. A close observer would have noticed that this man had learned the tongue in Sonora for his mannerisms of speech were those common in that part of Mexico. This gringo was even a shade more inquisitive than the general run of them. He asked many questions and learned of the vaquero, Jesus, who knew the Carrizo Plains so thoroughly and had camped at the rock many times. The gringo hired Jesus to go with him to Painted Rock.

They set out in a buckboard and on the second day made camp in the old crater. The next morning the gringo said, 'Jesus, find me a spot in the opening there where there are rocks of the same color', which Jesus did. Then the gringo said, 'Now find some rocks which resemble sheep. They should be north of the opening into the crater'. Jesus, knowing where to look, pointed them out. The gringo paced out a distance from each point and said, 'Now find the figure of a serpent in the paintings', Jesus went and stood by the figure. Then measuring his angles from rock to figure, the gringo pointed to a crevice and said, 'Jesus, there is a crucifix in that crevice. Get it'. The vaquero found the article under a well-fitted slip of rock and gave it to his employer who said, 'You may think this is gold, but it is not'. He twisted the crucifix apart and revealed a paper folded to fit into the shaft of the cross.

The paper was a yellowed chart or map which broke into pieces when he tried to unfold it. The man had come prepared, and all through the day he sat and pasted the pieces of the map on a large cardboard and traced out the faded words and drawings. It was late afternoon when, with a satisfied look on his face he put the map away and helped Jesus prepare supper. But that was as far as the gringo was to go. Perhaps it was the nervous tension or the vile water which made him ill. That night the boy was awakened by his employer moaning in pain. Seeing he was violently ill, Jesus broke camp and in a forced drive took him back to Bakersfield and a hospital.

Jesus waited in Bakersfield but the gringo never contacted him again so he went back to riding the range. After a time he began buying large numbers of cattle and lo he was a rich man. But there seems to be a curse on buried treasure and a rule that he who finds it never can keep it. The gringo, after all his labor of searching out the people in Sonora who knew of the treasure and his efforts here, never profited for his pains. And Jesus, who found the gold in time, lost all his cattle and ended his life as he had begun it, as a poor man."

In another story Arnold Rojas records:
"There is an old belief still current among paisanos to the effect that no man can come into possession of buried treasure without the will of fate and old men tell numerous tales to prove the truth of this saying.

There is an old trail that comes over the mountains from Santa Barbara to the San Joaquin Valley. It was used by the first padres when they turned toward the heathen tribes that peopled the great valley. The many fugitives from the mission knew and followed its many twists and turns to a refuge in the tulares. Toribio Cordova was born at the foot of this trail in the little pueblo below San Emidio Ranch house and in time became famous as a jinete (skilled in the old style of riding) *in a day when expert riders were commonplace. When I* (Mr. Rojas) *came to know him he was an old man* (early 1900's), *soft-voiced and mild mannered. At the time he was caporal on Tejon Ranch.*

One day we were campiando on the plains near Rose Station. Since Don Toribio was an interesting talker, I searched the landscape for some object to remark upon and thus start the flow of reminiscences. I pointed to a line leading down over the hills from mil potreros, thousand pastures, and said, 'That must be the trail from Santa Barbara.'

The caporal answered, 'There is an old trail to Santa Barbara down San Emigdio Canyon but the one you see leads to Pleito Rancho (coming from Salt Creek Canyon). *I know it well because I found and lost a great fortune on that trail. I learned to ride on San Emidio and one day while yet a boy and riding with an older companion we came to a place up Pleito Canyon where there was a circle of adobe bricks. The circle was too small and too far away from the ranch building to have been a corral. It stood on a shelf that jutted out from a side of a mountain and lay in a sort of depression. It could not be seen unless a person stood over it. Cattle had died there on the shelf and the grass had grown thick and tall as it does wherever dead bodies enrich the soil.*

The circle of adobes could be seen from a distance in winter when the ground was bare and clear of grass. My companion said that surely there must be something buried there and we decided to return to the spot the next day and dig, but manana never comes. The next day we were sent in another direction and when we returned to that vicinity some days later we forgot to take a shovel and left the place without digging.

I was a young man before I saw the place again. A friend and I rode up to it one cold day and as we did years before, my companion and I decided to return later and dig. But holes cannot be dug from horseback and the shovel was left in the shed at the ranch when we rode away the next day and we never went back to the circle of adobes.

More years passed. It was rodeo time (the gathering of the cattle) *in the San Joaquin and the vaqueros were camped at Pleito. One night when the crew was lounging about on the ground, a light appeared up on the hillside. I immediately thought of the circle of adobes and buried treasure. I knew deep grass covered the spot at that time of the year so I got an old Winchester rifle and using a wheel as a prop, I sighted the rifle on the light, tied it to the reach and went to bed. In the morning we were sent out on a long circle and when we got back the boss said we could rest and shoe our horses the next day.*

The cook hadn't bothered to remove the rifle and so the next day a vaquero rode up the hill to the circle of adobes while I directed him by sighting with the rifle. When he had located the spot he motioned for me to go up to where he waited. When I got there he pointed to an empty hole within the circle of adobes. Parts of a chest lay scattered about. The boards were of a hard black wood and were covered with strange marking or symbols. The chest had been placed in the hole and boulders packed around it, forming a solid wall in the empty hole.'

I said to Don Toribio, 'You were close to riches, why didn't you dig sooner?'

He replied, 'One can never have treasure which is not intended for him no matter how close he may come it, and that was surely not intended for me.'

I asked him what he thought the symbols or markings meant and he answered, 'Pues, quien sabe, well who knows. Hay algunos cuentos, there are some tales of Chilenos coming over this trail from a ship at Santa Barbara. The chest may have come from across the seas from some strange land.' "

In the last of the quotes from Arnold Rojas he states:
"Ghosts are always associated with buried treasure. The sound of groans, moans and appearance of a light, indicate buried gold. Many years ago in 'Horcasitas', a ghetto district inhabited by paisanos, in what became the town of Kern, on certain nights there would appear a light which no one could explain, and which the paisanso came to call La Lumbrita (little light). A woman owned a house in the settlement, but could not live in it because she was disturbed by the sound of moaning and groaning, heard throughout the night. She rented it to a young couple who were also disturbed by the noises, but instead of moving out, they dug up the entire foundation until they came on a treasure. Instead of sharing it with the owner of the house, they bought a house of their own and left the woman's house untenanted."

There were many such instances of treasure being found beneath the floor or foundations of a structure. Native American legend speaks of the strange glow of light and unusual sounds seen and heard at night in the hills. Soldiers from Fort Tejon once camped in the area of Cuddy Valley also reported such sights and sounds.

In just one more treasure story, former Frazier Park resident, Gene Weigel, once met the treasure hunter and author, Frank Fish, who said he had found an old cooking pot or *"Dutch Oven"* full of gold coins out in the area of one of the Lockwood Mining camps

X - THE LOCKWOOD BORAX MINES

In more contemporary local mining, colemanite, used as a source of borax, was discovered in the foothills of Mt. Pinos in 1898, about a year after the discovery of borax in the United States in 1897. A prospector named McLaren was said to have made the discovery of calcite, as he called it, while searching for gold on the southwest slopes of Mt. Pinos. He and a friend quickly filed claims which set off *"hundreds"* of prospectors filing claims along the six and a half miles of the formation. There must have been quite a settlement in that corner of Lockwood Valley for a while.

According to the book HERE ROAMED THE ANTELOPE, published by the Kern Antelope Historical Society, McLaren found two or three well exposed sedimentary strata's of the rock and sent samples of it to the analyzing laboratories to see if it contained gold. This book written in 1912-13 spells his name McClaren but the U.S. Borax & Chemical Corporation records spell it McLaren. The excerpt from the book reads:

> *"These samples were returned with the report that they contained no gold, but nothing was said of the valuable mineral of which they were composed. But McClaren, when in Los Angeles for supplies, found out that his specimen was rich in borax and sent word to his partner, Joe Comer, to stake out two claims. McClaren later sold his claim to Comer's cousin and part of it was jumped by a man named Kelly. At about this time the Calm Brothers sent out an agent from New York, who located the present National Mine under the name of the Columbus Borax Mine. The first mine to be developed was the McClaren/Comer claim and was named the Frazier Borax Mine for the nearby mountain. Nearly all the mines have government timber grants, the timber from which can only be used in the construction work for the mines."*

The Colemanite crystals were often referred to as *"white gold"*. With so many prospectors flocking to the area, the VENTURA FREE PRESS of August 24th, 1900 exclaimed:

> *"The Frazier Borax mines are among the richest and most productive in the United States."*

Most of these men soon abandoned their claims but three sites were developed into borax mines of importance. The Frazier Borax

Mine, McLaren's discovery, was opened in 1898 and the Columbus Borax Mine, in 1899 by a B. F. Stevens. The Columbus mine was in Seymour Canyon about a mile to the northeast of the Frazier Borax Mine. There was also the Russell Mine – midway between the Frazier and the Columbus, said to have been discovered by John Kelley (mentioned above) and also developed by the Calm Brothers of Chicago (or possibly New York as written above). The Russell Mine may have been called something else before W. H. Russell of Ventura, bought it in 1906 and in partnership with his son, Scott Russell, they operated the Russell Borate Mining Company.

In an article written by Harry Gower, for the U. S. Borax Corporation magazine, Gower stated that at one time or another each of the mines had calcining plants in an effort to reduce freight charges. Mr. Gower was a former chief engineer for Pacific Coast Borax Company.

McLaren sold his share of the Frazier Borax Mine to Gale Borden, a manufacturer of food products in which borax was used, at that time, as a preservative. Borden further developed the mining operation. John Stauffer, of the famous Stauffer Chemical Company, and Thomas Thorkildsen (or Thorkelson), another *"Borax King"*, purchased the site from Mr. Borden and operated the Columbus Mine and the Frazier Borate Mine under the name of the Stauffer Chemical Company. The Columbus Mine had some very high-grade material called needle colemanite because of its peculiar fibrous crystals.

The Frazier Borax Mine about 1912 (U.S. Borax & Chemical Corp photo)

The Columbus Borax Mine about 1911
(U.S. Borax & Chemical Corp photo)

The Russell Borax Mine about 1911
(U.S. Borax & Chemical Corp photo)

Possibly a better description of the Lockwood Borax mines, their owners and other good information comes from an undated article printed in the LOS ANGELES TIMES in those early years. From *"The Times Resident Correspondent"*, thought to be from Nordhoff – later called Ojai, the news item reads:

> *"The borax fever has successfully attacked every mining and oil expert prospector and speculator in this city. George Russel came to town yesterday with rich samples of borax from his mine in Lockwood Valley in the northeast end of this county.*
>
> *In this valley there is an abundance of borax, which is very valuable. It sells for from $20 to $60 per ton. W. H. Russel and W. P. McGonigle are also interested in this mine. Each holds a one-third interest. George Russel has been prospecting in this territory for the past year and he has now uncovered a large ledge of the borax. He made a special trip to town especially to report to his partners the discovery. Russel will return tomorrow morning accompanied by four men. The work will be rushed for the present. They have forty acres, which adjoins the territory of the Fraser Borax Mining Company. Gale Borden, the condensed milk magnate of the East, is largely interested in this Fraser company. It is an Eastern syndicate.*
>
> *Calm Bros. of Los Angeles have an eighty-acre tract. They have been working their claim for some time, and they are now preparing to install machinery to reduce or refine the stuff. The Frazier company has filed on several thousand acres. H. Kelly has eighty acres of very valuable property. This tract is now in litigation between Kelly and the Fraser company. A short time ago Kelly had a deal under way, whereby he was to receive $50,000 for his mine.*
>
> *The Fraser concern has been in this section for the past three years, during which time they have shipped thousands of tons of borax to Chicago and Alameda. It is shipped via Bakersfield, which is sixty miles from the mine. It is hauled in wagons to which are attached ten horses or mules. The rate for transportation is $10 per ton. This big incorporation is employing about sixty miners.*
>
> *The news of Russel's good luck spread rapidly over the city last night, and there will probably be a rush into this valley. Heretofore all operations have been kept as quiet as possible. The Fraser people desire to control the territory. McGonigle and others are now endeavoring to secure possession of other lands in this vicinity.*

Boatic acid is made from the borax, and this acid is utilized for condensing purposes. This explains why Borden, the condensed milk magnate, is so largely interested in borax mining.

A peculiar face connected with this borax is that old settlers in the valley never knew what the borax was until it was too late. Sam Snedden drove cattle over the stuff an innumerable number of times. He was not aware of the value of the borax. Even the Russels traveled over it for some ten years.

The output of borax has been steadily increasing, and with more ledges opened up the output will be greatly increased within a year."

The above would indicate the Russells had been in the local area since the late 1800's.

The office and management of the Stauffer Mine – early 1900's – no doubt with some of the men mentioned above. There is a remote possibility that the man with a mustache could be William Cuddy, the 7th child of John & Margaret Cuddy, as he was known to have been involved with the mine in some capacity. (Kern Co Museum photo)

According to an early Kern County historian, Eugene Burmeister, two major problems faced the borax mine operators – lack of lumber and a road. In the mid-1900's he wrote:

"A sawmill, installed in Seymour Valley north of the mine, proved inadequate and a larger one was built at the 7,000-foot level on Mount Pinos. Not only did his sawmill provide lumber for the

mine, but lumber was sold to the ranchers for miles around. Roads were improved, mainly at the cost of the mine operators."

Because of the delays to grade roads and cut lumber for buildings and the shafts, the first mine didn't get into full operation until 1901.

Men at the entrance of the Stauffer mine – early 1900's
(Kern Co Museum photo)

Borax miners poise for a photo holding water/lunch pails and candles
(Kern Co Museum photo)

Along Seymour Creek a mining town, called Stauffer, grew in the valley below the steep mountainside on the Russell property. The village included housing, office, calcining plant, stables, shops, post office and a school. The arsenic-filled stream flowed from the long mine tunnel. It was said that at one time between five and six hundred men worked at the mines. Most of the men lived in and around the town, many of whom had families there as well. The superintendent lived in a big house on the mountainside near the lower level mine entrance and could look down a street of houses, all painted green, which ended at a great barn and corrals. Thomas H. Larkin served as the Stauffer Mine superintendent from 1904 until it closed in 1908. The post office was not officially established at Stauffer until 1905 with Mr. Larkin as the first postmaster.

A view of the settlement of Stauffer looking to the southeast – 1906
(Sprague Family photo)

Recent view of where the settlement of Stauffer was once located

Street scene in Stauffer - early 1900's (Plush Family photo)

Lockwood Valley homesteader of the 1920's, Bill deLancey, later wrote about the Stauffer Post Office:

> *"Twice a week our mail was brought by wagon, twenty miles up through the mountains from Lebec. Mr. Kingsbury, the postmaster from Lebec, would arrive around noon and nobody in the whole countryside would willingly miss the occasion."*

Mr. deLancey also gives us this excellent description of the harnessing of mules to those borax wagons, as told to him by the caretaker of the site in the 1920's. He wrote:

> *"Fred Smith looked after the interests of the closed-down Frazier Borax Mine, keeping this Sterling Borax Co. holding on a stand-by basis. On his own initiative, Fred took me down to explore the vast barn for the 20-mule teams, and particularly the very stoutly built corral. This area was equipped with intricate fences and passageways that funneled a lone mule into an immensely strong harnessing chute made of beams a foot square. The chute finally let out through a gate that was separated from the main corral. Outside waited the great high-wheeled wagons of song and story.*
>
> *Fred explained the harnessing routine: 'Young mules were always being brought into the teams as replacements. They were untrained in any way, and too tough to harness without chutes. The men could stand inside their safety lanes, then reach through*

hand holes between the beams to fasten the harness that was dropped down from above. Of course an animal as wild as that would have no idea of pulling or doing anything, except to get away. But once he was dragged out into the middle of a long team, he couldn't go anywhere the bunch didn't go. That's how they broke 'em in'."

Mr. deLancey continued:
"As I later heard from two steady-going old timers, it was the 'pole team' with the wagon shaft between them, that was the wise, highly-trained pair that steered the gigantic, tall ... wheeled wagons, safely around the sharp corners in mountain roads.

These smart beasts were spoken to by name, and at command, the one on the outside of the band would spring over the pole to his teammate's side, helping him bring the front wheels around on course. If this story was true, and I had no reason to doubt it, it was a tricky business that called for great skill on the part of both the pole team and driver.

Hitched behind the main ore wagon was another, smaller wagon, carrying a tank for the water supply. This tank trailer was vital, for whether the teams operated from the Lockwood or from Death Valley, much water was needed over the great distances. It was, for instance, 65 miles from the Frazier Borax Mine to Bakersfield, below sea level in the central San Joaquin Valley. The road was all down grade except the section around Shirttail Bend and above Schoolhouse Hill (both at the east end of Lockwood Valley).

By 1920, nothing remained of the ore wagons of the mine except a couple of whopping big neat wheels. But one of the water wagons was still around, and this I later bought for the homestead. It could well have been the last of its kind outside a museum and I used it steadily for several years."

Smaller eight to twelve mule teams, with two wheel-horses – the two next to the wagon, were used to haul the heavily loaded wagons of borax down the steep, rough, crooked trails to Lebec where the company had another large barn for a change of teams. The road from the mine was referred to as the *"Lebec-Stauffer Road"*, at least from 1898 to 1908.

From Lebec the teams traveled to Bakersfield or Lancaster. A 1907 reference to the borax teams indicated that borax from the Frazier mine was hauled to Bakersfield and from the Columbia Mine to Lancaster. A long team would be used for the Antelope Valley route and a smaller team to negotiate the sharp curves and narrow roads in

Grapevine Canyon. More mules would be added to the Grapevine team at Rose Station as needed – and left there before the return trip up the Grapevine. The traditional sixteen to twenty mule teams were used through the soft desert sand or especially when the adobe clay on the way to Bakersfield was wet. At Lebec the Lancaster team would pick up a combination tank and feed wagon needed for the two overnight stops that would be made. For the Bakersfield run the tank and feed wagons would be added or left at Rose Station. Not more then fifteen miles a day was covered along either route.

Frank Duntley of Neenach with his mules, Tom & Jack – the *"wheelers"*, Mike & Pat – the *"pointers"*, Betty & Suzzie, Jeff & Mat, Ned & Dick, Maude & Pete, Maggie & Jerry *"leaders"*. The three wagons of supplies would have been followed by a two wheel trailer hauling food and bedrolls. (Duntley Family photo)

From an early interview that Eugene Burmeister did with Florence Cuddy of Lake of the Woods, she said, and he wrote:

> *"The first hauling was done by Johnny Morris, a rancher living five miles south of Bakersfield on Union Avenue who used a string of three 10-mule teams. As production increased other teamsters began hauling ore until some 150 head of stock were being used. A three-wheel Holt steam-driven farm tractor with a 16-ton iron wheel wagon was tried but after one trip to Bakersfield and one to Lancaster, this project was given up. Each trip with the tractor took one month. The tractor was banned from county roads and had to break its own way as it went, and grades were too steep in many places and the front end would rise in the air and turn the machine around and downhill!"*

Early Lockwood Valley resident, Earl Tifft, explained the name of one of the first hills the teams traversed as they left the Valley. *"Drunkards Hill"*, as it was called, received it's name because the mule drivers believed that they needed to be *"good & drunk"* to attempt it. As Earl said:

> *"The only time a 'long-line skinner' ever tipped over on the hill he was sober!"*

The huge ore wagons were often double wagon units with seven-foot high rear wheels, five-foot high front wheels that pulled the tank and feed wagon or trailer behind them. Each empty wagon weighed almost 7,800 pounds and loaded with borax it could weigh 31,800 pounds. Two loaded wagons plus the tank wagon could make a load of 73,000 pounds. Added to that was a small feed and chuck wagon. The round trip would take six to eight days depending on weather conditions. Freight and goods for the residents up in the mountains were often brought back on the return trip. Goods and supplies could also be purchased at a general store in Lebec.

Wagon and team being loaded at the Stauffer borax mine
(Kern Co Museum photo)

A *"teamster"* had the job of inspecting each piece of harness as he hooked-up the animals. He rode on the high wheeler and handled the brake of the lead wagon. Each driver was assisted by a swamper who had many duties. He rode on the rear wagon and took care of the brake on the downhill grades. He also had charge of setting up the camp, gathering the fuel for fire, cooking and washing the dishes. Not the least of his duties was keeping a supply of rocks on hand to throw at the mules to keep them moving on the upgrades. These men had to be skilled in driving these teams, harness repair, shoeing the mules and care for sick or injured animals.

In June of 1905 Estella Simmers was traveling with her family through the Antelope Valley and she wrote the following good description of a mule team and it's driver recently printed in the Santa Clarita Valley Historical Society newsletter:

> *"Here we saw a mule team ... from 18-24 mules to a wagon ... hauling ore from the mines across the desert. The driver rides on the horse next to the wagon with a single line, which is attached to the lead mule on the left side. It takes lots of cuss words and rocks to make them work ... but most of the drivers are equal to the occasion."*

A KERN ANTELOPE HISTORICAL SOCIETY publication entitled, *"Bears, Borax and Gold"* gives a wonderful explanation the role of each of the mules or horses of the team and of the driver of the wagon as follows:

> *"A jerk-line team consisted of eight mules or horses. They were well trained to the jerk-line, each knowing his place and what to do at all times. After the horses were harnessed and turned loose, each team would take his exact place ... the wheelers on either side of the wagon tongue; the pointers at the end of the tongue; the swing between the pointers and leaders; and the leaders out in front. An iron bar secured to the hames of the left leader and snapped to the bit of the right leader. On a few short jerks the leaders would move to the right; while at a steady pull they would move to the left.*
>
> *The mule-skinner, as the driver was known, rode the near wheeler, with the single jerk-line tied to the horn of the saddle. On a sharp turn the driver would stop the team, tap one pointer on the side of the head with the line, and he would move away from the chain; then the other pointer would jump the chain and stand by the side of his mate. In a left turn the pointers would pull at right angles to the others so as to point the tongue of the wagon out in order to make the curve. A set of bells were on the leaders, to warn anyone coming around a curve to pull to one side to let the freight team and wagons pass. Some of the curves were so*

short the teamster couldn't see the leaders, he could only hear the bells."

This view of a team and wagons shows the men actively involved in moving the borax

An article in the August 2, 1907 issue of the Bakersfield MORNING ECHO reported the change from the use of mule teams to horses at the Frazier Borax mine. It read:

> *"Within the next few days a large number of new borax teaming outfits will be placed in service. A. J. Cote has secured a contract from the Frazier borax mines to put in commission 150 horses and he has already begun the delivering of the new wagons and teams* (purchased from military surplus). *A big camp has been established at the 'County Well' about eleven miles on this side of Rose Station where the main camp of the outfit will be placed.* (Rose Station was just north of Grapevine Canyon and the camp would have been north of that.) *A blacksmith tent and a large quantity of bedding feed and other necessities are now being hauled to County Well.* (Kern County no doubt had a number of water wells dug at locations along roadways for the convenience of travelers and teamsters – a practice that continued with the automobile as well.)
>
> *It is Cote's intention to haul with six and eight horse teams and he plans to be able to haul a ton to a horse. Many doubt the feasibility of using horses successfully and especially in six and eight horse teams. It is claimed the mules stand the rough work much better and handier than horses. If his plans carry out alright at least eighteen or twenty new teams will be put into the*

> *borax traffic and over a score of men will be required to look after the teams. Delivery of the borax will be made at the Wible switch loading dock several miles south of the city. Here arrangements have been made with the railroad to have means provided for loading the valuable mineral onto the cars* (by hand and shovel!).*"*

In her book, HEAP OF LIVIN', Dolores Gentry mentions one of the teamsters as being Dave Menzie, mentioned earlier in this book. He would make the haul to Mojave and was known to stay overnight at the Gorman Inn.

In an obituary notice located for one Anselmos Compass, it indicated that in 1906 he had been a driver for Bill (Wm) Cuddy hauling borax from the Frazier Borax Mine until the mine closed a short time later. The obituary read:

> *"He drove twelve mules with a jerk line and was acclaimed as the best mule driver in the country. The mules pulled two wagon loads of ore and a trailer wagon that contained their feed, as it required four days to make the trip from the mine to Bakersfield ... or eight days in all for the round trip."*

This is one of the few items located that mentioned William Cuddy, the seventh child of John and Margaret Cuddy.

The Frazier Mountain Borax Mine closed after a short eight year operation due to the small veins of ore found there, the wet and treacherous mountainside and difficult transportation. Some 25,000 tons of crude ore valued at approximately one million dollars had been taken from the site during the mining venture. Another reason for the closing was that more extensive and easily mined borax beds were being developed to the east in Death Valley, the Calico Mountains and at Boron where the world's largest borax deposit is situated.

> The MORNING ECHO of January 5, 1908 read:
> *"It is reported that the Frazier mountain borax mines will be closed down shortly and may not be operated again before Spring. The Columbia borax mines, which ship their product via Lancaster, have been closed for the past two months. Superintendent Larkins of the Frazier mines is now in the city* (Bakersfield) *and will return to the mines this week. He has already given orders for the teamsters to cease work and will keep only a few men at the mines during the winter. The shut-down will result in at least fifty miners and teamsters thrown out of work for several months."*

> In an article in April of the same year reported:
> *"The Frazier mountain borax mines which have been closed down for five months will remain closed during the present year. Mr.*

Thos. H. Larkins said the price of borax is too low at present to justify the company in putting it on the market. The Frazier mine and the American of Daggett in San Bernardino county have combined and are now known as the Sterling Borax Company."

In the article written about the mines by Harry Gower he also wrote about Jack Wheeler, a former miner at the Columbus, and his bout with a bear. Jack had stayed on after the mines closed as a watchman. He lived alone in a cabin and after a heavy snow decided to make the trip to Lebec for supplies and the mail for all in the valley. Upon his return he found his door open and stumbled over a sleepy, hibernating bear. Both equally surprised they ran circles around the house not knowing who was chasing who *"until the bear went out of orbit and off through the pine trees"*.

The BAKERSFIELD CALIFORNIAN of September 11, 1912 reported a resurgence in the Frazier District. It read:

"The Frazier Mountain borax industry on the Kern Ventura line is booming. The Russell Borate Company is active there employing more than 10 men and has orders for many thousands of tons of borax to be delivered at San Francisco.

The major part of the shipments will be made from Bakersfield and W. S. Russell, superintendent of the company is now in Bakersfield seeking to secure eight or ten horse or mule teams for the purpose. The work will be steady and the more teams engaged the heavier will be the output of borax sent from the local shipping stations.

The round trip from Stauffer, which is the borate mines post office, requires seven days, the haul being 59 miles. Three days are required for the trip to Bakersfield and a load of borax is measured by a ton for each animal. The teamsters take one day lay over here and make the return journey in three days.

According to Superintendent Russell, the company will give employment to many paying out $8000 to $10,000 monthly (total payroll) *for teaming alone. The company also buys heavily of supplies in this city. Recently the borax has been hauled to Lancaster in the Antelope valley, 61 miles, but Russell says that the roads are not kept in good shape for the Lancaster trip and he believes the Bakersfield shipping point is more desirable. Russell states that his company has contracts for more borax than the old company which hauled borax from Frazier mountain to this city for many years* (actually from Lockwood Valley)."

In 1906 W. H. Russell, in partnership with his son Scott, had sold stock in their mine and developed it with a 250-foot vertical shaft. Their total production before closing down in 1913 was about 8,000 tons.

These mines were finally abandoned, much as though the workers just dropped everything and left, no doubt in hopes the supplies would be needed again. There were tools and the small steel rail carts that were used in the mines of the area scattered around the hills until they slowly disappeared into the yards of residents throughout these mountains over the years.

Stauffer Mine site – 1988

The headline of a May 2, 1926 article in the LOS ANGELES TIMES, written by M. C. Borland, declared *"Deserted Borax Mine, Once Hive of Activity, Now Silent"*. In part, the article read:

> *"Hidden in the tangle of hills that lie just seaward of the Ridge Route is a scarred canyon that once echoed to the dull thunder of exploding dynamite; to the clank of steel on steel; to the creak of*

overburdened wagons; to the clatter of machinery and to the shouts, laughter and curses of a mining camp.

From this canyon more than $1,000,000 worth of ore has been taken ... not glittering gold nor even dull lead, but unromantic, unsung borax. For the past nineteen years, however, the shaft has been innocent of activity, the board shacks which housed the miners deserted and the machinery idle

Only a watchman remains on the property to guard what was once one of the richest claims in the State. He does a specified amount of work on the mine each year to maintain the company's patent rights, but this amounts to little more than pushing a wheelbarrow load of rock from the shaft to the loading chutes and dumping it ... a mere gesture.

At the mine proper there were many interesting finds. An old box of dynamite, with two or three sticks of explosive still in it was one of them. Rubber boots, hats, coats, working implements and all manner of truck were lying about exactly as though the whistle had blown, the men had quit for the day and never returned. In the crumbling stable were twenty stalls. Most of the machinery seemed to be in a fair state of repair. Huge boilers in which the borax was cooked before being loaded in the big mule-drawn wagons, stand beside a narrow gauge track that once carried cars of ore from the shaft to the boilers and thence in the loading chutes. Years of exposure to the elements seem to have done very little damage to them and, strangest of all, one finds no conglomeration of chalked initials indicating the visit of idle tourists."

A final item about the mines, located in the January 30, 1928 issue of the same newspaper reported:

"Up in the valley are some borax mines of untold richness, the borax coming out so pure that very little refining is necessary. It is said the mines are now owned by a well-known borax company, which is holding them as a reserve supply."

XI – LOCKWOOD'S AGGREGATE MINE

The mountains surrounding Lockwood Valley had long been occupied by many gold miners but it wasn't until one of those miner's cabins at the eastern end of the valley burned that the value of the clay deposit there was realized. According to Don Cuddy, who has worked at the plant known locally as *"Ridgelite"* since 1977, below the remains of the burned cabin a ceramic type product was noticed and through the years numerous uses for the baked clay have been found. The extensive clay deposit was laid down by an ancient volcano and may cover a ten square mile area to an unknown depth.

The Los Angeles company, Ridgelite Products Inc., set up operation in the mid-1950's. The raw material is a Bentonite clay which is manufactured into a porous lightweight stone through fusion change. As of 1961, the company had invested some $750,000 in the plant and equipment.

Forest Service records indicate that Cuddy family members, in the area since 1855, made claim to the deposit in the early 1920's. The first recorded use of the clay was as *"rotary mud"* for drilling in the oil fields in the southern San Joaquin Valley. A Forest Service report records that in 1925-26 a light kiln was operating in the clay pit in which the clay was heated and transformed into an aggregate used for drilling muds as well as producing cement. Don Cuddy remembered hearing that a man by the name of Hartman was getting clay from a location to the east of the plant possibly in the 1930's or so. He had an old steam shovel that he removed the clay from the ground with and then would hauled it to a plant of sorts at Lebec where it was ground fine. Also at Lebec there were storage hoppers or silos – also referred to as wooden bunkers – where trucks from the oil fields would pick up loads of the dry clay to be used as rotary mud.

A September 1939 issue of the local newspaper, the RIDGE ROUTE RAMBLER, carried the following interesting news from the plant – then called the Ingalls Mud Plant. It read:

> *"A recent gasoline explosion and fire threatened to destroy the Ingalls Mud Plant and resulted in serious second and third degree burns for Superintendent Carl McDowell. Only heroic action on the part of "Buster" Clark saved McDowell from probable fatal burns. At the time of the accident, McDowell was adjusting one of the large motors*

and was showered with flaming gasoline. Quick thinking by Clark in covering McDowell with the plant product (rotary mud gravel) *no doubt saved his life. With a state police escort; McDowell was rushed to the Mercy Hospital in Bakersfield by Jack Grafton where he was given emergency treatment. Last reports were that McDowell is resting easy but is in a very critical condition."*

In July of 1953 Grace Bradley wrote of the expanding mining operation, then under another name. The article read:

"The White Ridge Mining Company is installing a $50,000 rotary kiln seven and a half miles west of Frazier Park. The kiln is for the manufacture of concrete light weight aggregate to be used in the making of light weight concrete blocks. Fred W. Nelson is president of the company and W. L. Hoeppner is vice president and general manager. Their headquarters will be in Frazier Park.

The site for the kiln, the first of its kind in the area, was placed in Lockwood Valley to be near the clay pits and finished product will be hauled from there. This clay contains a certain impurity that gasifies when heated, causing the clay to bloat and form small balls. This material is strong yet very light in weight, weighing less than half as much as sand or gravel.

According to Hoeppner, only one kiln will be installed at this time. It will run 24 hours a day and 7 days a week. Twelve men will be employed to run the machinery. The kiln which is 5 feet by 50 feet will handle 60 tons of clay in 24 hours and this will produce 100 cubic yards of aggregate, which will be screened into four different sizes."

Cuddy family descendent, Norman Ellis, went to work for Ridgelite in 1955 and worked there for fourteen years. Mr. Ellis remembered that the company was owned by *"Chamko Block"* at that time and they had purchased the property from Don and Florence Cuddy. They did not operate year around when he first started with them but they soon did. Norm worked heavy equipment and remembered that when he started they just had a stake-side truck that they would load with a crane.

In 1963 Mrs. Bradley wrote of the new high 66,000 volt power line that was being run from the area of Highway 99 (now Interstate 5) to the *"Ridgelite Products, Inc."* plant for expansions at the facility. The line was also to benefit the residents of Frazier Park, Lake of the Woods and Lockwood Valley. The article stated:

"The company is one of the largest companies manufacturing light weight aggregate and the only company in the entire United States using the extruder machine for the grinding of the clay for

the different types and sizes of aggregate. H. W. Todd, plant manager, states there are 14,000 acres included in the plant and quarries. After the top soil is removed practically one hundred percent of the clay is usable, even the dust.

Three types of sizes of aggregate are produced, a light-weight sand, a five sixteenth inch for concrete blocks and gunite work, and three quarter inch for slab work and roofing. The clay is brought to the plant, ground to almost sand, then mixed with water and run through the extruder machine where it is sized and comes out looking like spaghetti or like meat coming from a sausage grinder. By conveyor belts it is carried to the kilns which are heated by oil and maintained at a heat of 2000 degrees. By means of more conveyor belts, the baked clay, or aggregate now, is carried to the storage tanks. All this is powered by electricity.

The future plans, some of them now in process of installation, call for another two hundred horse power extruder with automatic moisture control, the fifth 125 foot long kiln and a $42,000 dust eradicator machine and electric blower. A new automatic lubrication system is now being installed.

The plant works on a twenty four hour schedule and a seven day week. There are forty seven employees. In the twenty four hours 11,000 yards of aggregate are produced."

The Ridgelite Plant – 1978 (Bakersfield Californian photo)

The MOUNTAIN ENTERPRISE of July 25, 1968 reported on a fire at the plant:

> *"A fire of undetermined origin completely destroyed the weigh station at Ridgelite Products at 1:10 a.m. Wednesday morning. Destroyed with the building were the remote counter and the weigh-out equipment. The loss may exceed $10,000, according to Keith Nelson, plant superintendent. Responding to the call were personnel from the Forest Service at Chuchupate Ranger Station."*

Ownership of the plant changed numerous times over the years. In 1971 the MOUNTAIN ENTERPRISE reported the sale of the *"Liteweight Processing Company"*, which included Ridgelite Products, to Hale Brothers and Associates a widely diversified firm with large interests in the Broadway-Hale Department Stores and Bank of America. The plant superintendent at this time was Keith Nelson. It was then purchased by *"Rocklite"* a division of the Richfield Oil Company. In 1983-84 Joe Bard purchased the plant and it was known as *"Lightweight Processing"*. In 1988 Fred Schmidt Hinie bought the plant and it became *"Pacific Lightweight Processing"*. In 1996, Texas Industries bought all the Pacific Lightweight plants and the local plant became known as *"Custom Materials, Inc."*.

An article in the January 16, 1978 issue of the BAKERSFIELD CALIFORNIAN was written by the local resident and correspondent to that paper, Gloria Cobb. She reported:

> *"Wally Cook, general manager, explained the area the facility occupies is approximately one acre but the raw material, monolithic clay,* (volcanic deposit) *encompasses about a ten square mile area. According to Cook, an employee of Ridgelite for fifteen years, 'I believe this is the only monolithic clay deposit in the United States. If there is another one I am not aware of it, but I do know this is the only one in the West. The mining process has been going on since the 1920's, when it was originated by the Cuddy family, and we haven't even scratched the surface yet. The deeper we go the better it gets. It seems there is enough clay to go on forever.' The land was originally owned by the U.S. Forest Service and deeded to the Cuddy family in the 1920's. The Cuddy operation supplied the rotary mud used in the oil fields of Taft.*
>
> *The raw material is bulldozed in 40-ton complements which take approximately five minutes to make the loop from quarry to the processing plant. It is then extruded and sized into storage bunkers awaiting the trip to the kilns. The kilns fire at 2,000 degrees Fahrenheit reducing the clay to a lightweight ceramic aggregate, screened into seven or eight varieties of sand, gravel and rock.*

Concerned with air pollution, the management spent more than $2 million perfecting a dust collector called 'Sputnik'. It was given its name because it resembles a space ship getting ready to lift off. It keeps the pollution factor far below that allowed by the Air Pollution Control District.

In addition to concern for the ecology of the surrounding area, Ridgelite management has created a natural reserve for wild life. 'As the clay is cleared, we have to scalp about six feet of overburden, roots, rocks, etc., and with this overburden, a waste product, we have made dams. This has created lakes', Cook advised, 'where catfish are found, as well as mallard ducks and blue herons.' Deer previously came down to the plant itself but now frequent a lake. The U. S. Forest Service can utilize the lakes if necessary as an auxiliary supply of water in case of a fire."

The porous material, mostly brown in color, is referred to as *"ridgelite"*. It is used in high rise building, lightweight concrete block, bridge and ship building.

As Cook indicated, Cuddy family members have worked at the plant since it began. Charlie Cuddy, the son of Robert Cuddy who had the earliest lease on the claim, began working there in the 1950's. Charlie's son, Cleve Cuddy worked there from 1960 until his death in 1993 and Cleve's son, Don Cuddy has worked at the plant since 1977. Other Cuddy family descendents have worked there as well.

A clay pit from which the ancient ash is dug so as to make aggregate
(Cuddy Family photo)

A recent view of the Ridgelite Plant

XII - OIL IN BRIEF

Very little information has surfaced about oil in the San Emigdio Mountains – though one of this nation's largest oil fields is located close by at the southern end of the San Joaquin Valley.

Oil from the coastal and San Joaquin *"seeps"* was a valuable trade item for the native people locally. It was used as a glue to waterproof baskets and in some cases medicinally. The earliest use by the new inhabitants of the area was to crudely refine the seepage oil and use the product to light lanterns as early as the mid-1800's. By the late 1800's oil wells were being dug in the valley's below these mountains and by the early 1900's an oil pipeline carried the product through these mountains from the oil fields of Taft and Maricopa, via Grapevine Canyon and on to the harbor in San Pedro. Information on the pipeline and the oil pumping plants will be covered in Volume 6 of this series of books.

The following photograph shows that a well was dug in Lockwood Valley in the late 1920's. Plush family descendent, Louella Plush Lee, the little girl in the photo, said that the well was driven on the homestead of her grandfather, William Plush, a fourth of a mile east of the homestead of her father, Lewis Plush, though no oil was located.

Friends of the Plush family at the oil well in Lockwood (Plush Family Photo)

The brief information that has been located on local oil comes from the MOUNTAIN ENTERPRISE. In November of 1966 the newspaper reported:

> *"Comet Oil Company has capped their well in Lockwood Valley after drilling to a depth of 2500 feet. Because of promising signs indicating the presence of oil and natural gas, there will probably be further exploration. Intex Oil Company plans to drill in the Mutau Flats area to a depth of 9500 feet."*

In February 1967 the newspaper reported:

> *"Madar, Arp and Fields are preparing to deepen their well, Madar #1, in Lockwood Valley area. Intex well USL 1-35, which is being drilled by Clyde Hall Drilling Company, was reported to be at a depth of over 6000 feet at the end of January."*

Later in February an article read:

> *"Intex Oil Co. has stopped drilling their well in the Mutau Flats area. It has been classified by Intex as a 'dry hole' and they have no further plans at the present time. The well reached a total depth of 8,247 feet."*

XIII - LAKE OF THE WOODS' LIME MINE

The next mineral mined in these mountains was limestone. A local correspondent for the BAKERSFIELD CALIFORNIAN of Tuesday, July 29, 1930 reported:

> *"During a trip to the Lebec section I visited the high hills back of Fraser valley park and found high mountains of lime running in the range for miles. There was no change in the entire length of the vast deposits, deposits that can be opened from the road levels and extracted at a little cost.* (the northern ridge between Frazier Park and Lake of the Woods) *Thomas O'Brien of Lebec* (of Lebec Hotel fame) *and associates have located several sections of the lime bearing deposit. The holdings can be easily driven to.*
>
> *More interest in mining, and more prospectors than in years are finding their way into the rough hills, three and four miles from the paved highways. Gold, copper and silver have been mined in the Tejon country in the long ago. George Barton, an old time miner of the Randsberg area, now at Quail Lake, is another well posted resident who can give a prospector much needed information and direction of the back hills."*

This mineral deposit between Frazier Park and Lake of the Woods was also referred to as *"dolomite"* which is a limestone or marble rich in magnesium carbonate. Area historian, Grace Bradley wrote about this particular lime deposit in the November 24, 1950 issue of the BAKERSFIELD CALIFORNIAN and later repeated much of the same article in the March 18, 1977 issue of the MOUNTAIN ENTERPRISE when she was then Grace Bradley Toenjes. She wrote:

> *"In October of 1950, S. Scott Russell of Frazier Park and Los Angeles reported the sale of his properties directly west of Frazier Park which had proven to contain valuable lime deposits. The sale was made to an eastern cement company who planned to build a half million dollar mill complete with dust collector.*
>
> *The first test holes were drilled by the company and it was found that the lime deposits run the full length of Tecuya Ridge from Cuddy Valley to Lebec and contain countless thousands of tons of limestone of high grade.*
>
> *It was estimated that 300 employees would be on the payroll which would average $80,000 per week. After this report was*

published the main topic of conversation among residents of Frazier Park was 'are you for, or agin' the proposed cement mill to be located some two or three miles west of Frazier Park'.

The difference of opinions seemed fairly well divided with those in favor of the development in the lead. But the ones looking with disfavor on the project talked long and loud. Everyone heard a petition was being circulated against the idea, but no one could find anyone who had seen the petition.

There was no question, but that drastic changes would take place in this small unincorporated mountain village of some 600 to 800 inhabitants if that population was doubled. (Lake of the Woods undoubtedly had the same concerns but was a much smaller community at this time.)

Some of the old timers said they had lived in the park for 25 years without industry and they could live another 25 years without it. The pensioners and retired folks said 'we came to Frazier Park to spend our last days in peace and quiet and because our doctor said this was an exceptionally healthy place.'

Dr. L. J. Price, local physician at that time, told of the many people both old and young, who came to the Park who were subjected to asthma and San Joaquin fever, as well as many other respiratory ailments. He fully agreed with an article published in the Reader's Digest quite some time ago, that stated, Frazier Park was one of the healthiest spots in the United States. Regardless of the promise made regarding the dust proof mill, many residents believed the health angle of Frazier Park would be ruined and the water supply would be contaminated by the lime deposits that would accumulate in the streams.

The younger set of residents took a different view. They wanted the mill to start immediately as they figured it would raise the value of property and in that way make better schools possible, better roads and parks and they were even hopeful of having telephones and gas installed in the area. All this besides providing work for a great number of young men."

In another 1950 article Mrs. Bradley addressed the issue of the noise that such a plant would make. She wrote:

"The acoustics of the Park are such that on a clear, cold night or early morning, a loaded truck grinding up the hill on its way to Cuddy Valley sometimes sounds like it is directly under a bedroom window. With the rumors circulating that the new mill would have a capacity of 10,000 sacks of cement each 24 hours

and that 20 ton trucks and trailers would run 24 hours each day, there was room for complaint. (This was before the present highway by-pass when the only road to the proposed mill site would have passed directly through the main part of Frazier Park, up the hill past the rock houses and on to Lake of the Woods.)

One very old timer shrugged his shoulders when asked what he thought about the new mill and said, 'I've heard this story of a cement mill in the area for the past fifty years and my father heard the story before that. I'll believe it when I see it'."

(probably a Cuddy family member)

The mine was established in 1959 and an article in the BAKERSFIELD CALIFORNIAN in November of that year, written by Mrs. Bradley as well, reported:

"The limestone plant, located three miles west of Frazier Park, started operations in May of this year. It produces around 125 tons of white limestone granules per day which, at the present time are being used for roofing material. The mining and milling of the limestone is still in the experimental stage, although according to M. E. Redhead, the chief engineer of the operation, $30,000 has been spent on developing roads on Tecuya Ridge.

The property owned by the Mineral Materials Co., is all within the Los Padres National Forest. The company has constructed several landing areas for helicopters in case of forest fires or other emergencies.

At the present time the limestone is brought down in trucks from the top of Tecuya Ridge, a distance of two miles, to the plant. The perennial report that a cement plant is to be constructed at this site in the very near future is causing much concern among residents of both Frazier Park and Lake of the Woods for fear of the destructive dust from such a plant. According to the chief engineer, no cement plant is planned for the immediate future. Later, after core drilling the entire Tecuya Ridge and if results warrant the production of cement, a new modern, dustless plant may be constructed, he said.

More suction fans and pumps, to eliminate the limestone dust now escaping from the plant, are being installed and now are to be installed as the plant develops. The plant is checked weekly by the Kern County inspectors as well as state inspectors."

Limestone mining operation at Lake of the Woods – 1950's

XIV - WEST ANTELOPE VALLEY MINES

Carl Hawkins of Frazier Park provided much of the information for the history of the lime-stone mine and cement plant near Quail Lake. Aware of the lime deposits in the foothills to the north, at the western end of the Antelope Valley, a company called Pacific Western Industries acquired a lease from Tejon Ranch to do exploratory work there. Three men of the newly formed company, John Kanard, Dave Johnson and Dave Honey began exploration in 1965. (Of interest is that they stayed at the old Lebec Hotel while doing so.)

Ken McCain, a chemist, and Carl Hawkins, a lab assistant, were hired from the Monolith Cement Plant in Tehachapi. The company rented the two old General Petroleum houses that were located at the corner of Hwy 138 and the old Ridge Route Road and the two men lived in two small sheep herder trailers at the site. A lab was set up in one of the houses where Carl did his lab analysis work, testing core samples brought down from the proposed mine site. The men would travel up an old dirt cowboy road or trail to get to the lime deposits. All the minerals needed to make cement were found in the hills – lime, silica, aluminum and iron. The immense quantities of limestone that were found would have been the result of the prehistoric lake that once covered the valley. These deposits would have been heaved upward in the continuous earthquake activity of the area. The iron came from a tin mine to the east of the lime deposits.

The need for such a plant at that time was urgent as the Feather River aqueduct project was coming through Tejon Ranch and the Antelope Valley, and the eight-lane Interstate 5 was being built through the San Emigdio Mountains. A January 25th, 1966 article in the BAKERSFIELD CALIFORNIAN quoted Pacific Western officials as saying:

> *"We hope our product will be used in part of the aqueduct leading from Kern County to Los Angeles as well as for industrial and residential building, highways and bridges."*

Future new road stops, housing developments and industrial complexes were projected for along the new Interstate as well.

The plant was opened in February of 1967 and the MOUNTAIN ENTERPRISE reported:

"Pacific Western Industries new Lebec Cement Plant on the Tejon Ranch about eight miles east of Gorman began operation last week with the first deliveries of bulk cement. The $17 million cement plant is located adjacent to one of the largest limestone deposits in the State.

Mr. Hawkins said that when the plant began production, the holes that the core samples had been gathered from were used to put dynamite in to *"blast off a bench"* – the mining operation is a series of benches along the hillside. The mining process is that huge end-loaders load 100 ton dump trucks with the blasted material. This is then run through crushing and grinding units that reduce it to a fine powder. The material is stored in silos. Next the material is fed into the kiln and baked or calcined to 2300 degrees with the correct ratio of materials added to create cement, which when sand, gravel and water is added, becomes concrete.

In 1971 Pacific Western sold to General Portland which had ten plants throughout the United States. In 1982, Lafarge, a Canadian company, then bought the plant and in 1987 it became part of National Cement which has plants all over the world.

Kiln at the cement plant – 1993 (Mtn Enterprise photo)

Tejon Ranch cowboys (unnamed) at the east end of the plant
(National Cement Magazine – 1980's)

National Cement Plant - 2004

From an un-named Kern County publication we learn of the tin mine to the east of the cement plant. It was listed as North America's only active tin mine at the time the article was written, probably early in 1966. From the article we read:

> *"Tin was discovered in the area in 1940 by Willard Mallery near the headwaters of Los Alamos Creek in the southeastern Tehachapi Mountains. The largest deposits of tin were found at what was then known as the Meeke iron prospect. 'The Meeke deposit', according to the California Division of Mines and Geology, 'consists of two cassiterite-bearing, iron-rich bodies 100 feet apart in bleached limestone. The cassiterite (tin-oxide) is in dark brown grains, some as much as an inch in diameter; but most are very small and are obscured by a coating of oxides. Aggregates of cassiterite grains are in veins and pods, some of which contain as much as 50 percent tin by assay, but generally are at most only a few inches in maximum dimensions.'*
>
> *This mine, on Tejon Ranch, has yielded as much as two and one-half tons of concentrate within a 30-day period. George Warsaw, mine operator, said that 'from the mine's reactivation in 1963 through Aug. 15, 1964, it yielded 45 tons of cassiterite concentrate valued at approximately $75,000. Before the activity at this mine the total California tin production had been about 117 long tons.'*
>
> *The mill, which was assembled under Warsaw's direction, was moved to the Tejon Ranch lease from Wilmington, his former base of operations. Until recently, the raw tin ore was shipped to Wilmington where it was concentrated. The resulting product (it takes 15 tons of ore to produce 300 pounds of cassiterite-concentrate) was then shipped to England for smelting into pure tin.*
>
> *The cassiterite is still sent to England for the final step but an obvious savings has been affected by processing the ore in concentrate prior to making the trip from the mine to the Southern California shipping port.*
>
> *'We can't predict production at the mine,' Warwaw stated. 'We're still on a speculative basis as far as future reserves are concerned. The ore is very pockety, meaning that veins are not continuous. It could turn into a big thing and on the other hand, it might not,' he explained, 'with this unique business in Kern County, we're hoping for continued success.' "*

This same tin mine was written about in an article in the April 6, 1967 issue of THE MOUNTAIN ENTERPRISE. It reads:

"Some eight miles east of Gorman, nestled in the foothills of the Tehachapi Mountains, is a unique mine, the only prime producing tin mine in the United States. The American Tin Corporation operates the open pit mine and to date has extracted approximately $100,000 in tin. High grade magnetite is also produced in sizable amounts.

The Corporation has on the site, mills for crushing and processing the tin and iron ores. They also have a bunkhouse and commissary. A total of six men are employed in the operation and one D8 Caterpillar, three dump trucks and a four yard shovel are used to work the mine.

The American Tin Corporation has an immediate expansion program underway to greatly increase their production."

Carl Hawkins reported that when he first saw this mine site in the mid-1960's there were also a number of mining holes along the ridge that he had heard dated back to the Spanish padres doing exploration for gold and silver and that some very old mining items were still about.

* * * *

A brief reference to copper mining was mentioned in an 1897 issue of the LOS ANGELES TIMES. The newspaper stated that copper had been found in the Liebre Mountains south of Antelope Valley and that the mine was said to have been first opened by the early Spanish Explorers. The article said that owners of the mine were waiting for the railroad to come through the Valley to make the mine profitable.

* * * *

Along the southern foothills of the West Antelope Valley earthquake and volcanic activity seems to have created valuable minerals in the form of gold and silver that extends from that Valley to beyond Frazier Mountain. One of the mines information has been made available on was the *"Rinky Dink"* mine south of Neenach. It seems there were several holes dug in the canyon where this mine was located but the main tunnel was sizeable. Nancy Steiger of Frazier Park, who had previously married into the Tibbet family, provided information on this mine. Nancy did not know how much gold was taken from the mine. In the very early 1900's, Bill Rogers and Burt

Tibbet were partners in the mining operation. Burt's brother, Ed, ran the general store and bar in the little community of *"Hinkley"* located below the mine, which was known to be a popular gathering spot for the locals of that day. It seems the mine was closed when it filled with water. It was below the sag ponds of the San Andreas Fault of Tweedy Lake and Gookins Lake. Another well-known Antelope Valley resident, Bert Riveria, was also involved with this mine and settlement. Mr. Riveria was a member of the Lopez family that settled in the Elizabeth Lake area in the mid-1800's and a nephew of J.J. Lopez of Tejon Ranch fame.

Ed Tibbet and Bert Riveria at the mining settlement of Hinkley
(Tibbet Family Photo)

Ed Tibbet with great nephew and nieces, Donald, Gloria and Margiann Tibbet along the side of the bar (Tibbet Family photo)

Recent photo of the Rinky-Dink Mine

The Tibbet family had an early day cabin in the area of Frazier Park, improved property that the family still owns. Burt Tibbet was known for his interest in mining throughout Kern County and probably did some prospecting on Frazier Mountain as well. Tibbet and his wife are mentioned elsewhere in this book as having a place at *"Buckhorn Station"*, in the present location of the Frazier Park exit from Interstate 5. Tibbet's parents, Edward and Rebecca Tibbet, arrived in the future area of Bakersfield in 1864 and were among the first settlers on Kern Island where they purchased an eighty acre farm from the area's founder, Col. Baker.

Burt Tibbet was also a legend in Kern County. When the last of the notorious western gun fights took place in Bakersfield in 1903, Tibbet, a deputy sheriff, shot the outlaw, Jim McKinney. McKinney had killed a number of men in California and Arizona. Burt's brother, Will Tibbet, also a deputy sheriff, was killed in the shootout as was the town marshal. Burt Tibbet then became the marshal. After that position he did security work on Tejon Ranch.

It seems that after the Rinky Dink Mine closed, Bill Rogers discovered, or already knew of, the same valuable ore in a canyon to the west. Rogers then went into partnership with Tom Gentry and in

1928 they opened the *"Oh Susannah Mine"*, not far from the Rinky Dink Mine. This mine was located just below and north of Tweedy Lake. There was a spring above the mine that flowed when Tweedy Lake was full.

William Thomas *"Tom"* Gentry had grown up in the Antelope Valley area. His father had the first saloon in Lancaster and a wheat farm at Neenach. Tom was a caretaker at the Fairmont Reservoir when the Los Angeles Aqueduct came through the Valley. Additional information on this mine can be found in the book HEAP OF LIVIN' by Dolores McKenzie Atmore Gentry. Dolores married Tom Gentry and Bill Rogers married Dolores' mother, Susan. The men and their crew worked the mine until 1938 when Rogers & Gentry lost the claim. Dolores' only grandson, Bucky Alzola, remembered living at the mine as a small boy. He also remembered filling his toy truck with pieces of gold when playing on a hill across from the mine causing the men to open a new *"glory hole"*. Bucky said that the mine produced some seven million dollars in gold over the years that it was open, much of which was lost to lawsuits as to the legal owners of the claim.

A newspaper clipping from 1934 indicated that the two men had entered into a *"grub stake contract"* with Harry Holland of the Frazier Park area. Holland was suing them for breach of contract in not properly sharing in the profits though he lost the case. The article indicated that the mine had produced about $300,000 in gold from 1933 to 1934.

Tom Gentry – standing and Bill Rogers – sitting, panning out gold at the *"Oh Susanna Mine"* (Atmore Family photo)

Oh Susanna Mine tunnel – 1930's
(Atmore Family photo)

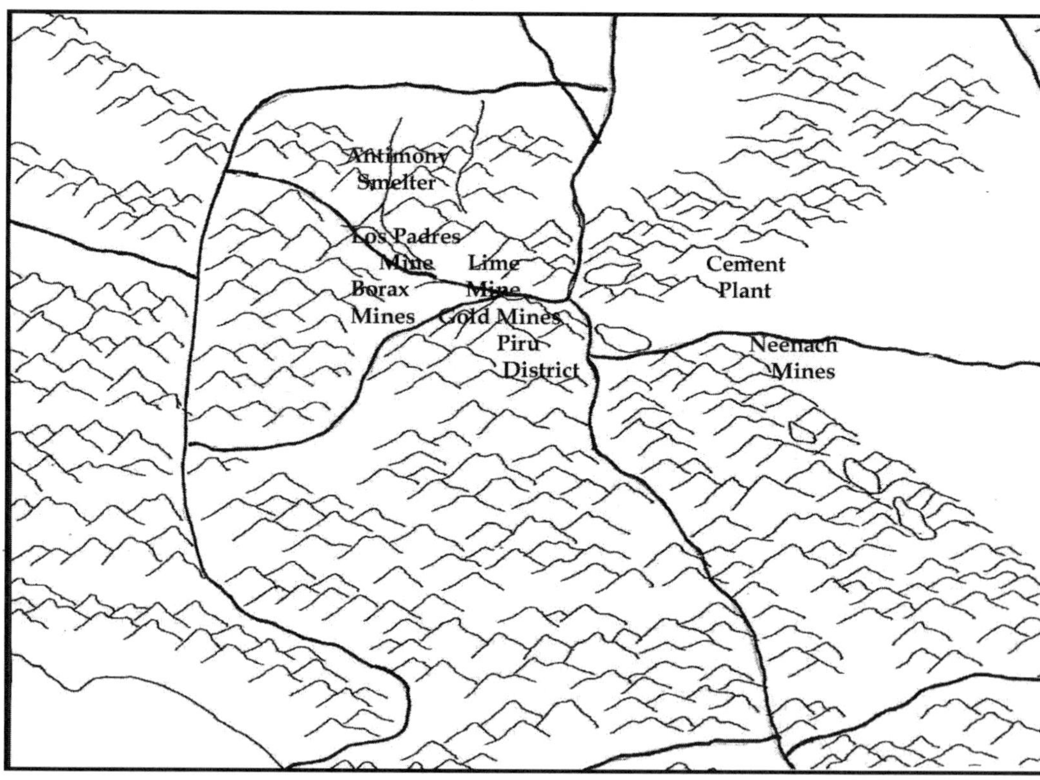

Map reviewing the locations of the various mining ventures in this portion of the book

Part Two

NATIONAL FOREST

XV - FORESTS PRESERVED

There is no greater dominating feature or influence on this mountain area than that of the National Forest which surrounds each of the local communities. The beauty of these forests, mountains, meadows, and the clear air, has through all time lured many to want to settle here.

In the mid-1800's steps were taken that led to the founding of the National Forests. An early forerunner of the government protected forests was the *"General Land Office"* which was created to oversee the distribution of this country's lands to the railroads, land speculators, for logging and to individual homesteaders. The first concern for the use of the lands came from the logging industry which recognized the need to restore, and even to preserve some of the wooded lands. A member of one of those logging families, Gifford Pinchot, created the Society of American Foresters in the late 1800's. At the same time, those claiming public lands for homesteading recognized the need for help in controlling wildfires, and as well there were those throughout the country who were realizing a need to preserve portions of the American frontier in its natural state.

The Forest Reserve Act was passed in March of 1891, which put some lands into public ownership for the future and gave the President of the United States the power to create reserves covered with timber and undergrowth primarily for the purpose of protecting watershed and preventing fires. In President Benjamin Harrison's term, fifteen forest reserves were created and by the time Grover Cleveland left office in 1897 there were about forty reserves.

Locally, William McKinley's presidential proclamation of March 1, 1898, made the Mt. Pinos/Frazier Mountain areas a part of the *"Pine Mountain Forest Reserve"*. The Reserve was named for a mountain over towards the coast. In the December 1903 proclamation of President Theodore Roosevelt, the neighboring Zaca Lake and Santa Ynez Reserves were combined with the Pine Mt. Reserve and the three units became the Santa Barbara Forest Reserve, with the area then renamed the Santa Barbara National Forest in 1908.

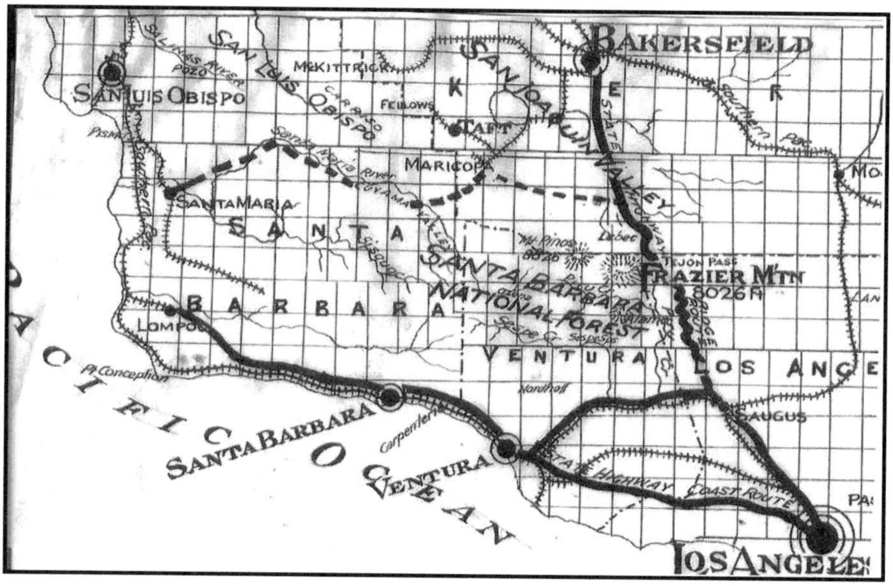

An old undefined Map of the Reserve (Bill Friend collection)

When Teddy Roosevelt, a dedicated conservationist, became President, the United States Forest Service was created in 1905 and placed within the U. S. Department of Agriculture. Named as the first *"chief forester"* was Cifford Pinchot, the founder of the Society of American Foresters. Pinchot shaped the initial ideas of environmental conservation in this country. Under Roosevelt the Forest Reserves became National Forests and soon the designation between National Forests and National Parks was further defined. It has been found, and still seems to hold true, that more people visit the National Forests than the National Parks.

When the National Forests were created there were no boundaries, no roads, no services, no ranger stations, etc. The need for men to establish the boundaries and patrol the preserves was soon realized. Wanted were men known and respected in their immediate area. The *"Forester"* was over the *"Forest Guard"*. It was said that in the vast virgin forests the Forester rarely saw his men. A quote from one early guard's journals read: *"I saw the Forest Supervisor four times this year – he saw me twice"*.

In the early 1900's the Santa Barbara and Monterey National Forests were divided into twenty-five ranger districts with the responsibility of approximately 80,000 acres each or a radius of about fifteen miles, the distance one could cover in a day's horseback ride. These areas were to be patrolled by one forest guard or ranger who was to see that the new rules and regulations governing the forest were enforced and whenever possible that fire was suppressed. Area newspapers ran the following *"Men Wanted"* ad:

> *"The National Forests needs more men. For those who like a hard active life in the open the work is ideal. They must thoroughly know the country, its conditions, and its people. The Ranger must be able to take care of himself and his horses under very trying conditions; build trails and cabins; ride all day and all night; pack, shoot, and fight fire without losing his head. He must ... about the timber ... be familiar with lumbering and the sawmill business, the handling of livestock, mining, and the land laws. All this requires a very rigorous constitution."* (to say the least!!)

New forest rangers were given an exam to measure their proficiency in the use of a rifle, pistol and axe – as well as stock handling and tying a diamond hitch. Once hired, a ranger was given a bucket, rake, axe, map and a badge and set out to be the lone steward of thousands of acres of public land.

Salaries ranged from $50-$75 a month. The Ranger supplied his own horses, mules, gear, place to live and work out of, and uniform which consisted of boots, levis, a white shirt and white cowboy style hat. The cost of equipment needed for the job often exceeded the salary earned. It was said that the heavy Forest Service badge the Ranger was first supplied with was so large that it could be seen from a mile away.

A large part of the ranger's time was taken up in the growing of feed for his animals, traveling about his unit and going to town for mail, messages and supplies. He was to keep a daily journal that would be reviewed by the supervising Ranger or Forester from Nordhoff (Ojai) when he would come on his annual inspection trip. Good pack animals were equal partners to the early forest guards. Mules were the pack animal of choice because on their intelligence, agility and stamina. Pack strings of mules were the lifelines of the early crews.

Even before the Ranger Districts were established two local residents did become Rangers for the area that surrounded their ranchos. They certainly matched all the requirements having been born and raised in the San Emigdio Mountains. Joseph *"Don"* Cuddy, the ninth child of John and Margaret Cuddy, was born and raised just west of the present community of Lake of the Woods where his father homesteaded in the late 1850's. He began his seasonal duties as the first ranger of this forest in 1897 at the age of 24, even before the official creation of the reserve. He worked out of his residence, the old family homestead located in the valley just across the road from the present Chuchupate Ranger Station. He served in what was then called the *"Tejon Ranger District"* until 1910. Don Cuddy's wife, Florence, later recalled how the rangers often camped over-night *"wherever the night caught up with them"* and that there was many a time the other rangers or forest guards would stay at their home or in the barn.

Ranger Cuddy at one of his remote guard camps (Cuddy Family Collection)

The other local man to long serve in the Santa Barbara National Forest was Jacinto Damien Reyes, the first born of Rafael and Maria Reyes. J. D., as he was known, had grown up in the Ozena area west of Lockwood Valley where his family had established a homestead, also in the 1850's. He was twenty-nine years of age when he accepted the position of a Ranger in 1900, the first Spaniard to be appointed as a permanent U. S. Forest Service employee. He was placed in charge of the Cuyama District, a wilderness area of some 400,000 acres. William Brown in his HISTORY OF THE LOS PADRES FOREST described Reyes as:

> *"A man of powerful physique, who never knew when to quit. He was often known to start out on a mule-back trip at six in the evening, riding rough trails until he made camp at midnight, resuming his trip when daylight came."*

Reyes was an outstanding rider and as a young man he once rode fifty miles for medical supplies in just six hours – over mountain trails and crossing flooding streams. In 1910, Ranger Reyes almost single-handedly planted 163 acres with Jeffrey pines in the

Lockwood, Ozena and Piru areas hauling the planting stock by wagon from the railhead at Ventura then packing the small tree starts in by mule. Regrettably, after all that work, his experiment was, for the most part, a failure.

Ranger Reyes surveying his District (Los Padres Nat'l Forest photo)

Both Cuddy and Reyes had proudly told of being among those serving as members of the honor guard for President McKinley, the Secretary of the Interior and the Secretary of Agriculture when they visited Ventura in 1901 and again when President Theodore Roosevelt visited in Santa Barbara in 1905. The Ranger dress uniform was a double-breasted, blue flannel shirt, corduroy trousers, canvas leggings and wide-brimmed Stetson hats. They would all be mounted on black horses and were sporting the handlebar mustaches of the day. J. D. was even more honored when he was assigned to ride at the right hand of the President Roosevelt's carriage. A display of horsemanship by the rangers was presented in honor of President Roosevelt. Mrs. Cuddy remembered how hard her husband and Reyes worked to clean and polish their saddles, horses, and themselves for this occasion, only to then ride for a day and a half over dusty mountain trails to get to the event.

Reyes maintained his first Ranger headquarters at the family homestead at Ozena in the Upper Cuyama Valley, on Reyes Creek at the base of Pine Mountain. In 1915 he built a home for himself and his bride, Glendora Butke, near the home he grew up in. From 1909 until Reyes' retirement in 1932 the Ozena Ranger Station was located approximately where the Lockwood Ozena Station is today.

Much could have been learned from the daily journals kept by these men but as Reyes' daughter and only child, Gloria Juanita Reyes, later said, he was told by his superiors to just burn them when he retired – and he did!

The Reyes family home at Ozena (Reyes Family photo)

Ranger Reyes conferring with one of his forest guards in his home office about 1910 (Reyes Family photo)

Reyes was honored with an extensive interview in the July 1930 issue of the Automobile Club's magazine TOURING TOPICS. In his own words, Ranger Jacinto Damien Reyes shared some wisdom about his experience in those early days of the Forest Service. Portions of the article read:

> *"During my youth I worked on the range as a vaquero among my father's cattle, and it was at this work that I gained a lot of experience that has been valuable since I came into the Forestry Service in 1900. My first appointment in the service was on a temporary basis, and for a period of three months. I was assured, however, that if my work was satisfactory and funds were available, my appointment would be made permanent. This permanent appointment was received and I have been continuously on duty as the ranger in charge of this district ever since. On the whole my district is pretty much the same as it was in the early days, except for being reduced by 50,000 acres in 1928. I still have 400,000 acres, and that's a pretty big back yard.*
>
> *Adventures, in my opinion, are mostly mishaps, and a forest ranger doesn't go around looking for them. He tries to avoid them, but in spite of all efforts he's bound to connect up with them occasionally. A forest ranger is primarily the policeman of the forest, but his job is a lot more than that. He must forever be on guard to protect the forest from its worst enemy, and that enemy is fire. He has many other duties. At times he is a game warden, fish warden, adjuster of rowes between sheep men and cattle men, coroner, detective, court witness, Red Cross nurse, fireman, policeman, and what not. It is almost impossible to say exactly what a ranger's duties are. There are routine duties, of course, but after all, the real test of a good forest ranger is how good a man he is at meeting unexpected situations and doing the right thing at the right time according to the circumstances.*
>
> *During the entire time I've been in the Forestry Service I've only been off duty three weeks on account of sickness or injury. That was in 1908 when I was returning from a fire, almost dead from lack of sleep, and my mule bucked me off. I think I must have gone to sleep. Otherwise the mule wouldn't have unloaded me. I came to my senses to find that I was pretty badly hurt about the right hip and thigh. The injury laid me up for three weeks and I was several months before I was fully recovered.*

There are only a few officers who have been in the United States Forestry Service for as much as thirty years, and I believe I am the only ranger who has the record of thirty years on one district. I've lived in the Santa Barbara National Forest all my life, and more than half my life has been that of a ranger in this, the Cuyama District."

Jacinto Reyes about 1930 (Reyes Family photo)

Florence Cuddy later told that her husband's paycheck would arrive monthly on a freight wagon that came to Lebec. A mail carrier by the name of Skinner (Billy Skinner, who then lived in Gorman) would deliver the check to Cuddy as he passed that ranch on his way to deliver the mail at the Stauffer Mine in Lockwood.

Some years after his death Florence Hollenbeck Cuddy wrote this beautiful tribute to her forest ranger husband. You can certainly feel her love for him and these mountains in this, one of the many poems she wrote.

SONG OF SUMMER

Come back to me, ye Forest Ranger,
That did take my heart away;
Come back across the years to me,
That we may know another day.

The mountain's quail is piping now
Unto his mate upon the hill;
There's a luring trail awinding
Through the forest, deep and still,

To a sunny mountain meadow,
Ringed around with balsam firs;
Where the yellow pollen drifting
Through the mellow sunshine stirs.

There the blue, wild iris blooms;
Ethereal, fairy ranks apart.
O, come back, ye Forest Ranger;
Bring me back my heart.

We'll ride upon the morning slopes
To find the spotted fawn at play;
And on into the afternoon
To heed the call of the friendly jay.

We'll ride again beneath the pines;
Now the western breezes call
At the spring beneath the cliff
Where the cold sweet waters fall

Anent the dewy columbine,
I will cup my hands for thee.
Come again, ye Forest Ranger,
Bringing back my heart to me.

Then we shall have the days of summer,
Happy time of love and joy,
To remember ever after;
Golden days without alloy.

Then whatever hap thereafter;
Whate'er the gods mete out to me,
I shall have this golden summer,
Love and joy forever be.

Mine forever joy and laughter,
Love, forever sweet and fine.
O, come back, my Forest Ranger,
Come to me, dear heart of mine.

Ranger Joseph *"Don"* Cuddy (Cuddy Family photo)

J. D. Reyes and Don Cuddy were the first of many dedicated men and women who have served to preserve our local forests. Other Cuddy family members have worked for the Forest Service through the years, the most recent Larry Darling and Loreigh Tubbs Brannan. To-date, both have, or had, worked at the Chuchupate Station for some thirty years.

Favorable reactions to the new government reserves were recorded by an early Forest Supervisor as follows:

> *"Being acquainted with a great many settlers throughout the reserve, I made it a point to call on them and inquire of them about the rangers and whether they thought the reservation was beneficial. They all seemed interested in the work and believed the reserve a good thing and in nearly every case spoke well of the rangers in charge as seeing them quite often when patrolling. Every day I heard remarks as follows from settlers from within and without the reserves: 'We can't look out every day and see from one to half a dozen fires as we used to before the reserve was set aside, so you fellows are of some benefit.' "*

Impacted negatively by the creation of the Forest Reserves was the sheep industry that was flourishing in the local mountains in the late 1800's. In the 1890's local author, Mary Hunter Austin, wrote that among the herders:

> *"Forest Rangers are a fruitful topic, and bring a stream of invective words that fall away, as does all talk out of doors, to a note of humorous large content."*

Mrs. Austin continued:

> *"Many places were mapped by the viewless line of the Forest Reserve, drawn about the best of the watershed greatly reducing the grazing lands. The sheepmen had always the advantage in superior knowledge of the country, of feeding grounds inaccessible to mounted men, remote and undiscovered by any but the sheep. The most rangers could do against them was to scatter and harry the flock so as to make the gathering up difficult and expensive. The business was also hindered by the inadequacy of the ranger force. Every man had more territory than he could well ride over and his pay was much below the price of the fittest men."*

Mrs. Austin addressed the harm done to the watersheds due to overgrazing and fires willfully set to clear more grazing lands:

> *"When the thick chaparral made difficult passage, the good shepherd set the fire to rip out a path and the next year found tender, sappy browse springing from the undying roots. The flock came to the meadows; they fed close then the foreplanning herder turned the creek from its course to water it anew and the rainbow trout died gasping on the sod.*
>
> *A shepherd is not a forester, nor is he the only sort of man ignorant and scornful of the advantage of covered watersheds though unrestricted devotion of the pine belt to the sheep has done us damage."*

Of course there were others with their objections to the growing government control over the former open ranges as well. John Foley, an Irish miner whose place in the Tejon Pass was known as Foley's Grove because of his orchards, was recorded as *"a tough hombre"*, stubborn and inflexible. He filed a patent claim for 160 acres of land in Tejon Pass and built a home and barn in 1903. Somehow it was thought that Foley had located on, or was using, a portion of land designated as public lands, as were Section 16 & 36 of each township.

In about 1918 the Tejon Ranger Station was located in Section 16 in the Tejon Pass, where the north entrance to the Hungry Valley State Recreational Vehicle Park is today. This 320 acre site was what is called an *"administrative site"* – land outside but adjacent to the Forest. Foley continued to maintain that the Forest Service had located on his property and caused the local forest officers considerable trouble. He continued to fence off the lands for his own purposes, even building a fence across the public road the Rangers had created.

The Forest Service finally realized they were, to some extent, wrong. For some reason there were three major fires near the Ranger Station in 1926, 27 & 28 – possibly Foley's effort to encourage the Forest Service to move their facility. Most of the buildings were lost in the fire of 1927.

Tejon Ranger Station at Tejon Pass at the present north entrance to Hungry Valley State Recreational Vehicle Park near Gorman

In 1930 a new Ranger office was built to the west of the present community of Lake of the Woods – across the road from the first ranger, Don Cuddy's home. The new location was named for a spring further up the mountain called Chuchupate Spring. The legendary *"Chuchupate"* was known to be a great medicine woman among the earliest people of this area. It is said that she tirelessly ministered to her tribe during a winter of famine and illness. As a result of her commitment, she herself became sick and died. Her saddened people were amazed the following Spring to see the ground become carpeted with bright yellow flowers which they believed to be the spirit of their beloved Chuchupate. The plant was credited with having many medicinal qualities.

The new building at the Chuchupate site served both as an office and a home for the ranger until additional buildings were added. Ervin Lyda, the first district Ranger at the new Chuchupate

Station, reported that in 1930 he had a crew of two men the year around and an additional two men during the summer season.

The first building at Chuchupate Ranger Station (Mt. Pinos District photo)

Additional buildings are added at Chuchupate (Mt. Pinos District photo)

In September of 1925, President Calvin Coolidge eliminated over four thousand acres of the Santa Barbara National Forest and for smoother administration approved the transferred of 265,538 acres of the southeastern portion to the neighboring Angeles National Forest.

By the 1930's public opinion instigated the change of the forest's name so as to not be so identified with one geographic location. As the forest then reached into the areas of San Luis Obispo, Kern, Monterey, Ventura and Santa Barbara counties a name was agreed on that all those counties shared a common history in. It was decided that the heritage of the nine missions located adjacent to the forest were a strong influence in all the counties, therefore, in December of 1936, President Franklin D. Roosevelt authorized the change of name to the *"Los Padres National Forest"*, or *"The Forest of the Fathers"*, in honor of the men who had served at the missions and who were the first non-Indians to create trails throughout the area.

It would seem that the small portion of the forest located in Kern County did not have a mission history, as none of the missions were located within its future boundaries. But with the recorded information of the Catholic Padres mining in this, the southwestern corner of Kern County, a mission outpost or asistencia in San Emigdio Canyon, which is in Kern County, and the use of lumber from these mountains of southwestern Kern County for the building of the missions, mission history was found in this county as well. Mission work crews had traveled far and wide to find just the right trees to be used for the rafters and to frame the doors and windows of those early adobe buildings. Oak, willow, sycamore and cottonwood trees growing in the vicinity of the missions did not produce the long straight beams needed but the Ponderosa and Jeffery pines of the higher elevations did. Thirty to forty Indians to a crew, with the help of mules, would travel long distances, further opening the forest trails as they went, to obtain and travel back with the pine beams. Timbers from the mountain areas between here and the coast were even shipped as far as San Diego.

It was December of 1936 when the name of the Tejon District was changed to the Mt. Pinos District to better reflect the area served. The other six Districts of the Forest were the Monterey, San Luis, Santa Maria, Santa Barbara, Cuyama and Ojai. In 1972 the districts were reduced to the present five when the Cuyama District was joined with the Mt. Pinos and San Luis and Santa Maria became the Santa Lucia District. The Mt. Pinos District initially included some 285,000 acres and is now at approximately 500,000 acres reaching into three counties, the largest district in the Los Padres National Forest. The entire Forest consists of two million acres.

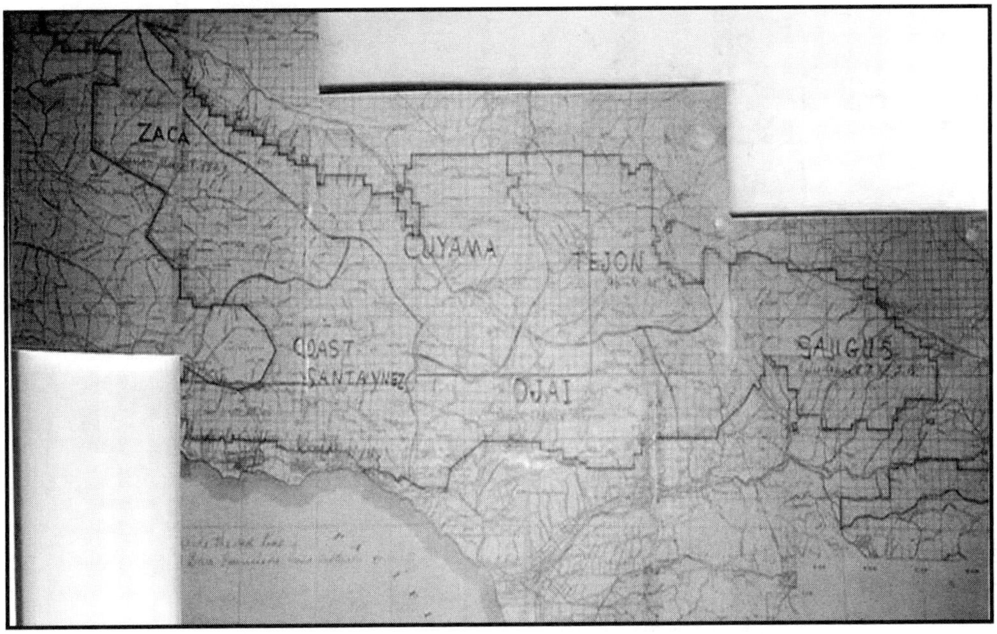

Map of the early Ranger Districts
(Bill Friend collection)

A 1949 Forest Service report describes the growing facilities at the Chuchupate Ranger Station as follows:

> *"There is a small white neat office building where matters such as fire permits, maps and traveling information are obtained. Mrs. Sally Stevens, the wife of the foreman of the fire crew is not only the clerk of the office but the radio operator, telephone operator and weather observer. Other buildings were two residences for the Ranger and the fire control officer, a weather observation tower, a warehouse, bunkhouses, the barn and a corral. In the corral were four to six horses and mules for patrol duty and packing in equipment during fires. Among these is a twenty year old mule called 'Pink Lady'. She has served the Forest Service faithfully for ten years. The warehouse houses two tankers for fire fighting, one of which is equipped with a two-way radio."*

Forest Service employee Harry Thompson in front of the new barracks - 1950
(Harry Thompson photo)

District Ranger Weisgerber & family about 1950 – (Harry Thompson photo)

In 2005 the U. S. Forest Service celebrated its Centennial. Some interesting statistics from it's beginnings to the present are as follows:

1905	2005
83 Forest Reserves	155 National Forests
63 million acres	192 million acres
$400,000 budget	$4 billion budget
270 employees	37,648 employees
76 million U. S residents	298 million U.S. residents

We could not be more fortunate that this forest reserve was created and that it exists for the present and the future. The forest is the reason most of us have chosen to live between these sacred mountains. It would not be so except for the men and women who have worked with and for the U. S. Forest Service as caretakers of the forest lands over the last one hundred plus years.

The following is a list of the Rangers who have been in charge of the Tejon-Mount Pinos District of the Los Padres National Forest with the years that they began working here:

Don Joseph Cuddy	1898
Frank Dunne	1921
Virgil DeLapp	1922
Erwin Lyda	1928
Fletcher Hayward	1933
Crawford Buell	1934
Houghton Durbrow	1935
Garth Flint	1938
Walter Puhn	1939
William C. Meyer	1940
Al Weisgerber	1949
Robert C. Janes	1958
Jack Williams	1960
Gary Plisco	1964
Doug Hayden	1966
Ted Zrelak	1972
David Hammond	1974
David Alexander	1978
Don Ostby	1981
Trinidad Juarez	1985
Mark Bethke	1993
Tom Kuekes	2001

Sign at the entrance to Chuchupate Ranger Station – 1950
(Harry Thompson photo)

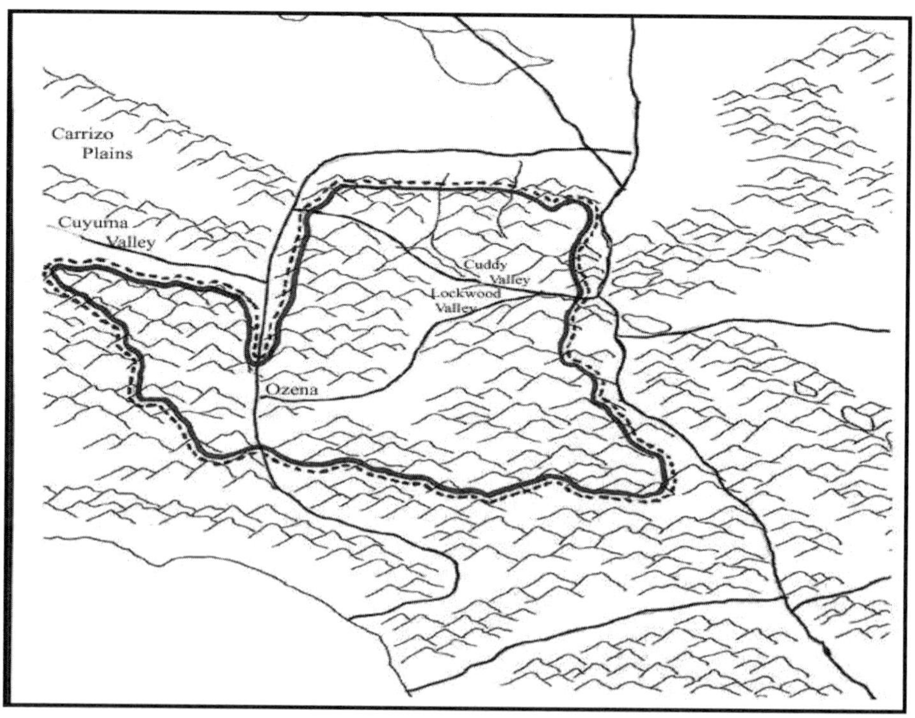

Map showing the approximate boundaries of the Mt. Pinos Ranger District
(map is somewhat distorted)

XVI - FRAZIER MOUNTAIN NATIONAL PARK

The early forest rangers had little more than ancient animal and Indian trails, with a few scattered mining and logging roads, to travel as they patrolled their unit. By the 1920's the public use of this forest reserve had greatly increased with hunting and recreation needs added to the mining and milling already going on. Within the Tejon Ranger District the two new subdivisions of Frazier Mountain Park and Lake of the Woods were bringing many people here as well.

In 1921 there was a movement among Bakersfield residents to create a National Park and Highway that would open to the growing motoring public, *"a scenic route to Frazier Mountain, an area that is of unexcelled beauty"*. The headlines in the BAKERSFIELD CALIFORNIAN read: *"Wonderland at Door of Bakersfield Found Ideal"* and the article extolled the virtues of the cool temperatures, flora, fauna, fishing and a *"hot springs flowing 8000 gallons a minute of boiling pure water and which often equal the famous Arkansas Hot Springs"* (this would no doubt be the Sespe Hot Springs some distance west of Frazier Mountain). The proposal was presented to U. S. Senator Samuel Shortridge suggesting the area be called *"Frazier Mountain Summer Recreation Grounds"*. It further stated:

> *"The opportunities for governmental activities in floriculture, viticulture and botanical work in the proposed park are unlimited. Another consideration which has entered into the proposal is the fact that Yosemite National park is becoming overcrowded and other national parks which have been established for years are experiencing a similar annual rush which gives rise to the demand for new fields which will prove equally attractive to the touring public. The government now is making additional expenditures on its national parks in the West, particularly in California and it is the firm belief of those connected with the movement for the Frazier mountain park that a portion of these funds could not be put to better utilization than for enhancing the area embraced in the newly proposed park."*

The newspaper continued to carry articles throughout the year about the proposed park, repeatedly telling of the area's beauty. In the Fall of that year lines from articles read:

"Visitor after visitor who has gone through this part of Southern California has come away sounding its praises with no uncertain voice, and almost inevitably wondering why no movement has been started to set aside some portion of it as a nation-wide playground and scenic gallery of outdoor wonders."

"Modern life requires every year the safety valve of rest and recreation and no spot in the universe will be more adapted to the restoring of strength and the beneficial tonic of pure air and health-giving qualities than this park." (Still the reason many move here.)

"There is no other mountain park area lying so near the largest populous center that presents such large inviting areas sufficient for thousands in future assemblages."

"In Cuddy and Lockwood valley the novel experience to California of sleighing and winter sports can be added local attractions." (and still are!)

The May 26th, 1922 issue of the BAKERSFIELD CALIFORNIAN reported:

"Mr. East, engineer for the Automobile Club of Southern California, who recently spent three days going through the Frazier mountain country on horseback, met with the civic association directors today in connection with the park and road project report. East is enthusiastic over the possibilities of developing the Frasier mountain area into a recreational center of easy accessibility that would prove an incalculable asset to the state. East emphasized the necessity of developing new recreational grounds in California to continue to attract tourists, who, he declared, are ever in search of 'a new place' to visit."

Mr. East was quoted as saying:

"It is providential that one of the most attractive, diversified and suitable national forest areas in the United States lies between the coast and San Joaquin valley known as the Santa Barbara National forest and also that through this forest, and necessary for its development for the use of practically one-third of the population of California living near, is the location of the proposed highway above suggested. The scenes along the Piru, Alamo, Mutah, Little Mutah and along the Sespe on Mount Pinos, Frazier and Alamo mountain in their silence and grandeur are nature's perfect pictures. For all things considered, location and climatic advantages, a blending

> *between the coastal and interior, I do not know where they can be surpassed in California."*

The proposed road that is mentioned was to be called the *"Matillija Highway ... for the profusion of white Matillija poppies that grow along the area of the roadway".* It was written that it would go:

> *"from the state highway* (the old Ridge Route Road), *one and three fourths miles southwesterly from Lebec, and thence follow upon the north side of the narrow valley of Cuddy creek westerly to and over the Cuddy valley* (the area of the present Frazier Park) *to the slight divide between Cuddy and Lockwood valleys and on to Sheddings"* (Sneddens).

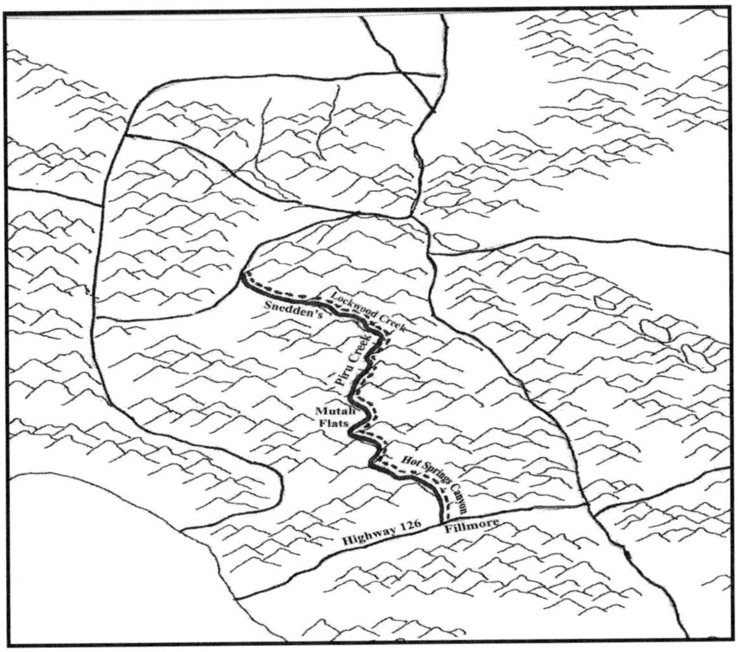

The proposed Matillija Highway

From there it was to go down the Piru, Hot Springs and Sespe Canyons to meet up with Highway 126 at Fillmore. The Cuddy Canyon Road about this time was described by another writer as:

> *"sage brush closing in on a dirt track. One would cross the dry creek bottom by bumping over rocks along the best route for the crankcase to clear."*

A few days later, an editorial in support of the road stated:

> *"It is practically a virgin land that with a quarter of a million investment in road construction may be made to give pleasure to thousands. The forested areas have never been denuded. The streams are filled with fish, the woods with game. The*

elevation runs from 5000 to 8000 feet, and superb scenery is unfolded from every point of vantage."

In July of 1922 a group *"interested in Santa Barbara national park as a summer vacation center"* (different name than that used in last year's article) headed for Frazier Mountain. They reported in the Bakersfield newspaper:

> *"Leaving the city in the early morning, the trip to Lebec and to the famous Cuddy ranch, beautifully located in a valley of the same name* (as the area west of Lake of the Woods was then called), *was reached by automobile. After a rest period at the picturesque home, the party started for the mountain on horseback. We were joined by Don Cuddy* (formally the Ranger of the area), *a resident of the section since boyhood, and Clint Shaddock, long a fisherman, hunter and guide in the mountains. As the climb was in progress the thought was ever prevalent that when the proposed Matillija highway is complete and the mountain accessible to motor travel, unlimited numbers will take advantage of the cool heights and build summer homes among the trees and natural springs of ice cold water."*

The writer of this article, Marjorie Ross, reported:

> *"Clusters of yellow flowers resembling a single rose provide a wealth of color and when mingled with blue and white lupin, brilliant red lavender and cream mariposa lilies and red wild honeysuckle, the colors blend into a delightful picture. The branches of the pine trees are covered in many instances with moss of brighter green than the foliage of the boughs."*

Mrs. Ross continues:

> *"Our trusty steeds seeming to realize the pleasure we were getting out of the trip made the climb to the top of the mountain with all the ambition of a good horse. Long before we reached the top the forest ranger's station was in sight* (probably an early guard shack) *and a salute of greeting was passed. In one place we came upon several little summer houses. In a small enclosure we found a spring and the pleasure of drinking out of that pool of cold water can never be duplicated* (Chuchupate Springs). *From the guide we learned the place was the summer home of Albert Scherer of Los Angeles.*
>
> *When we again reached the Cuddy home, after hours of riding in the mountains, we related our experiences to the charming hostess of the ranch* (Florence Cuddy) *and stretched out in the grass for a rest. The return to Lebec was made in the cool hours of the evening where we visited the forest rangers'*

> *station* (at Tejon Pass between Lebec and Gorman where V. C. DeLapp was the ranger at this time). *Here the young man in charge explained the rules and regulations connected with camping in the mountains saying a 'special use' application was granted that could be renewed annually. With the opening of the forest reserve to the public for camp sites, logs of varying sizes will be sold to those desiring to build rustic homes. It is required that the abode fit harmoniously with the natural background of the forest.*
>
> *As we rode from Lebec to the Grapevine and started across the stretch of highway into the city, the hot winds came as from a furnace* (July!). *The comparison of the fresh, cool mountain breeze with the air of the valley was conducive of the strongest desire to return to Frazier mountain, with all its charm, and build a little summer home far up among the pine trees."*

In the article, Mrs. Ross also indicated another advantage of the *"Matillija Highway"* would be that it will link with the national *"park to park highway"*, a system of highways the government was proposing to link together the National Parks.

No other significant information was located on the Frazier Mountain area becoming a National Park. All the counties involved in the effort had endorsed the proposed road and a resolution was drafted by each county to be sent to the governor, though it seems only the Kern County portion was ever completed. By early 1923 the National Park effort seems to have died.

The notion of a Sespe Canyon Road, or Matillija Highway did continue and in the October 5, 1928 issue of the LOS ANGELES TIMES it was reported:

> *"The proposed Sespe Canyon route from Los Angeles to Bakersfield, via Lockwood Valley and San Emidio Canyon, is feasible and opportune and materially will benefit traffic conditions between the two cities. Wm J. Fox, chief engineer of Los Angeles County stated: 'this project will be thoroughly diagnosed so that this glorious country may be opened to the people of Southern California that they may have the opportunity to enjoy it and to do so conveniently'."*

No doubt delayed by the Depression of 1929, the June 14, 1931 issue of the TIMES then reported:

> *"This project to materialize a long-considered plan of extensive economic and scenic value involves some ninety-seven miles of road building. In addition to its significance as a*

supplementary traffic artery for the Golden State Highway and the Ridge Route, about eighteen miles to the east of Sespe Canyon, other features of importance are it would bring travelers to the Sespe Hot Springs, the road would traverses much territory of importance as a forest reserve and it will provide a direct outlet to Los Angeles Harbor for the government's naval oil reserves in Western Kern County. As an initial step, an automobile road is suggested from Fillmore to the confluence of Lockwood and Piru creeks, a distance of about thirty-six miles."

Possibly World War II further delayed the building of the road and in the 1960's the area was designated as the Sespe Wilderness in which no roads were allowed.

XVII - TRAILS BECOME ROADS

A wagon road had run from the state highway near Lebec back to Lockwood Valley and beyond for almost 100 years but an article by Thelma Bernard in the May 14th, 1923 issue of the BAKERSFIELD CALIFORNIAN indicated that the road from the highway had been improved at some time as far as the Cuddy place and was at that time being completed up Frazier Mountain to the *"Bakersfield camp site"* or Chuchupate Springs and Campground – *"now occupied by Mr. & Mrs. Babcock"* (more on the Bakersfield campground and the Babcocks in the next two chapters of this book).

A group from Bakersfield, including Miss Bernard, had come to the Mountain to inspect the camp site and the new roadway. They secured horses at Sam Young Meadow (the present area southeast of Frazier Park) and were guided by Cliff Shattuck – *"a veteran woodman, trapper and hunter"*, and Tom O'Brien – the builder of the Lebec Hotel who the writer says is *"Lebec's oldest and most prominent citizen"* – he was also well known in Bakersfield. They rode up Frazier Mountain to the Lookout Tower and then down to the proposed Chuchupate Spring campground where they lunched.

The article reported:
> *"The party remounted to follow the trail on down to the Shearer* (Scherer) *Place, the first camp above the motor road. There the riders paused to view the beautiful meadow at the Cuddy ranch where the crew constructing the motor road to Chuchupate was camped. The road is staked out as far as Shearer's camp."*

The party then left the well-worn wagon trail to descend to the construction crew camp along what would be the new road and Miss Bernard wrote:
> *"The trip proved to be rather hair-raising, though as tender feet may follow with impunity wherever an old campaigner may lead, the riders concealed their heart-qualms and followed Mr. O'Brien, riding straight across the face of cliffs where the horses slid and plunged, or picked their way amid jagged rock, with never so much as a shelf to cling to. The new road will yield many glorious views, but only those who scrambled along*

the ragged place where it will be, will ever realize its possibility for real thrills."

The July 6th issue of the same newspaper reported:
"A Southern California Automobile club sign-post marks the road pointing to 'Lockwood Meadows' by which name the road is known. In a very few weeks other signs will be in place but the road is easily seen to be new."

The increased demands of the public brought about the improvement of many trails to roads that vehicles could better traverse. A one-way nine foot wide unpaved road was cut into Mt. Pinos in 1925. The road, known as the *"Up Road"*, later Seymour Creek Canyon Road, permitted access to near the top of that mountain. Another one-way road, known appropriately as the *"Down Road"* or Mill Creek Canyon Road, permitted an exit for lumber trucks and visitors off the mountain. Both roads began or ended off the road to Lockwood Valley at *"School House Hill"*, the ridge between Lockwood Valley and the Chuchupate Valley area west of Lake of the Woods. The newspapers continued:
"Upon the completion of the Mt. Pinos road, government road building crews will be transferred to the completion of a road from Chuchupate to the top of Frazier Mountain."

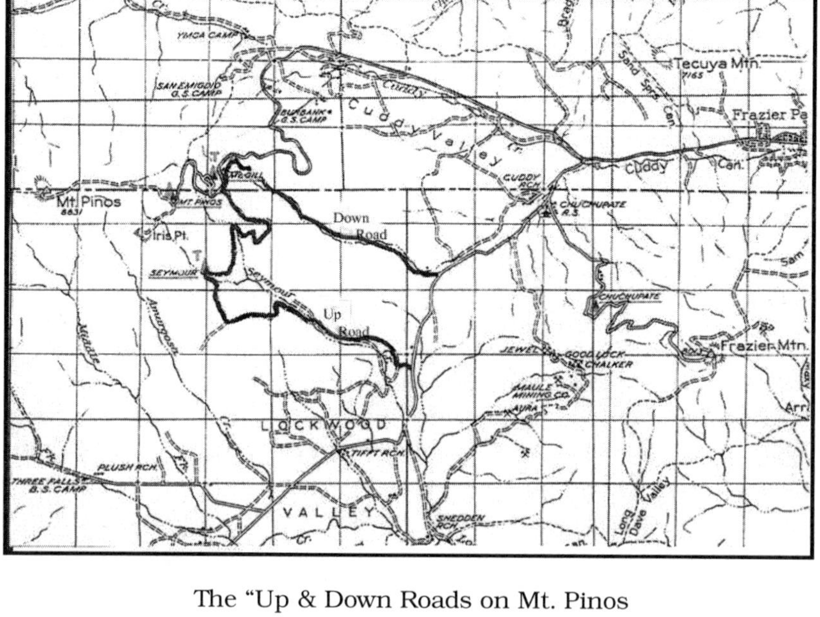

The "Up & Down Roads on Mt. Pinos

The June 26, 1925 issue of the BAKERSFIELD CALIFORNIAN carried a large feature article entitled, *"Mount Pinos Government Road to Open Scenic Wonders for Motorists".* The news feature was complete with six wonderful photos and an excellent illustration of the road traveled by the *"Dodge Trail Blazer".* They traveled from the Ridge Route Road up through Cuddy Canyon, through the Chuchupate Meadow in front of the Cuddy Ranch and on to School House Hill, the entrance to the Lockwood Valley area, which the writer referred to as *"the great divide between the San Joaquin valley and the Ventura river".* This would indicate that from this ridge all streams on one side run to the northeast and on the other side to the southwest.

The writer continued:
"A mile or so up Seymour creek the party began to ascend rapidly. The sturdy Dodge special touring car mastered the steep grades, never faltering or showing the effects of the heat of the day. The forest reserve road camp, situated in Bear Trap canyon at the 6400 foot level, was made the next stopping place. Here a cool clear mountain stream trickled down past the camp offering all the conveniences for the camper under the stately pines.

Dodge Trail Blazer tests newly improved road on Mt. Pinos

The distance of 5.7 miles from Bear Trap Canyon to the summit was especially delightful as the atmosphere was noticeably cooler as we neared the big sawmill at the top of Mt. Pinos. Here we left the car, as the road ended, to inspect the ruins of the old sawmill, drink from the cool sparkling stream and enjoy one of the most magnificent views in California. It is contemplated, according to District Ranger V. C. DeLapp, to clear away all the debris from the sawmill and turn the heaven-like spot into a camp ground to be known as Chula Vista. Applications are now being taken for cabin sites as a few lots have already been laid out."

The Chula Vista Home Tract is further explained in Chapter Nineteen. The Seymour Canyon Road ended at the site of the old McGill Sawmill and the area was later referred to as the McGill campground with the Chula Vista name given to the present area at the top of Mt. Pinos.

The driving tour article continued:
"The return trip was made in three hours from the summit to Bakersfield, with several stops. The party spoke highly of the Dodge car's performance and the balloon tires gave ample traction and real riding comfort throughout the trip."

One of the stops the party made before leaving the mountain area was as follows:
"The next stop was at Stauffer post office (down into Lockwood Valley) *where pictures of an ice laden tree were taken* (in June? – the writer mentions the *"heat of the day"* in the first paragraph!) *and the old borax mines inspected"*.

Such improvements as roads had been slow in coming as the country struggled through the Great Depression of the 1930's, but when President Franklin Roosevelt established the *"Emergency Conservation Work"* program (ECW) 1933, to put unemployed young men to work, a great deal was accomplished throughout the country. The Forest Service was teamed up with the U.S. Army which had the means and knowledge to organize large work projects using the numbers of manpower available. The War Department coordinated the logistics of providing food, clothing, shelter, transportation, education and religious services for the masses of men that joined this peacetime army. The Forest Service provided the guidance and expertise needed to engage in effective resource conservation. For the first time the Forest Service had the manpower to handle large projects and enrollees learned valuable forestry skills which provided many future employees.

This program became the *"Civilian Conservation Corp"* (CCC) in 1937. Young men were paid $30 a month with $25 of that sent home to their families. Between 1933 and 1942, three million young men participated in the CCC. They were stationed in over 4,000 camps throughout the country. Projects included the construction of the camps the men lived in, fire breaks, fire lookout towers, ranger stations, remote guard stations, erosion-control dams, the installation of telephone poles and line, and improvements to trails, roads and campgrounds. These teams of men are credited with replenishing our forests by planting an estimated three billion trees.

The CCC was often referred to as *"Roosevelt's Tree Army"* as it was of a great benefit to the Forests.

Two important roads to this area were constructed by the CCC. One is the fine paved road from the Apache Saddle at the base of Cerro Noreste along the ridges to the north all the way to the Taft and Maricopa communities. The other more major road accomplished by the CCC was the new Highway #33 that joined Ojai (originally called Nordhoff) with Ozena, Lockwood Valley and the Cuyama Valley.

With some twenty CCC camps established in the Los Padres Forest, Forest Service personnel finally had adequate fire-fighting manpower. The July of 1939 issue the local newspaper, the RIDGE ROUTE RAMBLER, mentioned that the fellows from the Piedro Blanco Camp (location unknown) were at the Chuchupate *"Spike"* Camp, at the Chuchupate Ranger Station. The men were at the temporary camp for the purpose of putting in the first section of the San Emigdio water system, which when completed was to bring water to the San Emigdio Campground, thought to be another name for McGill Campground on Mt. Pinos, and Girl Scout Camp in the area presently long known as the *"Y"* at the base of Mt. Pinos. Another CCC camp, used only in the summer, was located in Seymour Canyon on the southern slope of Mt. Pinos and could well have been the Piedro Blanco Camp named for the borax mines not far from the camp. Some local young men were hired to work at these camps, among them Earl Tifft of Lockwood Valley. There was also a CCC camp by the Fire Station in Lebec in the 1930's

A Civilian Conservation Corp camp elsewhere in the National Forest
(Forest Service photo)

Despite the great benefit to America's conservation program during those years, the following phrase developed about that time. It read:

> *"We, the unwilling, led by the unqualified, have been doing the unbelievable for so long with so little, we now attempt the impossible with nothing. . . ."*
>
> Courtesy of Bill Friend

Fence posts being brought to a CCC work site – location unknown
(Forest Service photo)

The CCC program was greatly reduced when the men that oversaw it, and were a part of the program, were needed for military service in World War II. The government continued the program on a smaller scale with veterans and conscientious objectors assigned to what were then called *"Citizens' Public Service Camps"*. Many former CCC camps were used for military related purposes.

Improvements to the roadways did continue and in the 1940's, Cuddy Valley resident, Florence Schaefer remembered that Cuddy Valley Road was paved for the first time to the *"Y"* – *"by a bunch of 'Southern Boys' who lived off the land while there ... hunting for their food"*. Turkeys and eggs were offered from the Schaefer Turkey Ranch in appreciation for the improvements to the road that they also used.

In 1967, approval of the scenic Mil Potrero Highway was announced by the U.S. Bureau of Public Roads. Its primarily purpose was as part of the improvements made by the Tenneco

Corporation when they established the community of Pine Mountain Club but it would also join the road to the top of Mt. Abel with the road to the top of Mt. Pinos. Prior to this the two mountains had been joined only by an ancient dirt trail from the top of one mountain to the other. A project office for this road was established in Lake of the Woods and survey parties laid out the center line for construction of the two lane paved road.

An early road sign near the Frazier Park exit off Highway 99.
(Grace Bradley collection)

In 1958 this sign was installed at the corner of Cuddy Valley and Lockwood Valley Roads, where the California State Game Wardens would set up their check station during hunting season. It was constructed of redwood and large white pine log and intended to be sturdy enough to last a lifetime (Grace Bradley collection)

XVIII - CAMPGROUNDS & CAMPS

By the late 1800's and early 1900's it was quite popular to experience camping adventures in the local mountains.

Above and below are copies of some very old photos of early campers believed to be enjoying an outing in the Upper San Emigdio Canyon area in the late 1800's (Kern County museum photos)

The forest lands were intended to serve as many purposes as could be compatible with the preservation of the watersheds and wildlife but about 1900 there were few forest restrictions. You could camp anywhere and family units would often make claim to a favorite spot, returning to it annually so that it even took on that family's name. Some of these private camping/hunting areas were upgraded during the CCC program of the 1930's and became the public campgrounds of today with, in some cases, them being named for the family that so long used it.

In an effort to further encourage the public in the care of the National Forest, some camp ground areas were dedicated to communities of the surrounding area for their extensive use. With this privilege came the responsibility to care for that camp ground. To the south, in the Angeles National Forest, the Oak Flat Campground in Violin Canyon to the west of the present Interstate 5 was set aside as a playground for the citizens of Los Angeles. To the west of Pine Mountain Club was the West Side Campground and later Camp Condor for the communities of the Taft area which is still being taken care of by that community.

The BAKERSFIELD CALIFORNIAN of May 14, 1923 mentioned that the Frazier/Pinos area *"will soon be thrown open to Southern Californians as sites for permanent camps"*. The article continued:

> *"At Chuchupate Springs a slightly acreage has been marked off as a desirable campsite for Bakersfield, and it is now proposed to ask that this area by turned over to the city for free camping grounds. The municipality, in turn for this right, would be under the obligation of developing and properly maintaining the site."*

In the heat of the summer, August 1924, the same newspaper announced the opening of a campground designated for the use of Bakersfield residents called *"Chuchupate Park"*. One article reported:

> *"All material necessary to establish the Bakersfield camp site on Frazier mountain will be hauled to the recreation center Thursday morning. One thousand feet of pipe, a large tank and 1000 feet of lumber will be transported by the Kern County Land company. V. C. De Lapp, forest ranger in charge of the Tejon station for Santa Barbara national park in which the camp is to be situated will receive the material and with the aid of his assistants, install the pipe and tank that are to convey and conserve the waters of the springs, also build the tables and benches to be used by the picnickers who will frequent the grounds."*

Another article later that month read:
"With a temperature between 70 and 75 degrees and with an elevation of 6500 feet, the new Chuchupate Park Kern County recreation center on Frazier Mountain is ready for formal presentation to the public tomorrow, when large numbers of residents from Bakersfield, the West Side (the Taft/Maricopa area), *and other sections of the county will motor to the site to pass the day in picnic fashion.*

Awaiting the arrival of the visitors and providing for their comfort and convenience is an adequate supply of spring water, conserved and controlled by means of a newly installed tank and pipe system: tables and benches for the serving of lunch, and cement fireplaces in which to prepare coffee. The camp site is located in a beautifully wooded section of Frazier mountain. Tall pines and sturdy oak trees shade the park and the surrounding area is covered with foliage that adds to the attractiveness of the location.

The park was provided for the free use of Bakersfield and Kern County residents through the courtesy of the United States Forest Department, once it was determined that the local people displayed sufficient interest to take the initial step toward preparing the place for use and supplying the equipment. The ground has been formally set aside and dedicated by the government as the Bakersfield camp site and as its use becomes more popular and added interest is shown, the forest department will enlarge it and provide more improvements."

The present day Chuchupate Campground

The article went on to review how money for the project had been raised from civic groups and organizations and that the Boy Scouts had cleared the underbrush and shrubs from the area.

The newspaper continued:
"To reach the camp site motorists should follow the Los Angeles highway to a point one mile south of Lebec, and then turn west and travel thirteen miles along the Lockwood Valley Road to the sign designating Frazier Mountain (across from the Cuddy homestead). *A turn to the south at this point and a ride of three miles upward will bring the visitors directly to Chuchupate park. The campsite was given the name Chuchupate because of the character portrayed in a beautiful Indian legend in which Chuchupate, an Indian girl, was the protector of the flowers. During the Spring and Summer seasons wild flowers blossom in glorious profusion on Frazier Mountain and particularly near the scene of the new park.*

Those who have been instrumental in perfecting the plans for the opening of the campsite and providing the conveniences for the visitors urge a large attendance of local residents at the picnic tomorrow that they may see for themselves the beautiful ideally located and easily accessible recreation center."

In a December of 1924 issue of the BAKERSFIELD CALIFORNIAN, Ranger De Lapp was quoted as saying:
"The government has made a survey for a road to go from the Chuchupate Campground to within a short distance of the summit of Frazier mountain and that this road will be constructed in the near future. Also recreational engineers are making surveys for four more campsites to be offered to Camp Fire Girls, Girl Scouts and Boy Scouts for their care and use."

The popularity of the Chuchupate Campground continued despite the fires that burned around the area in 1941, 47 & 48. In 1949 it was reported that 150 campers spent the Fourth of July holiday at Chuchupate.

Most of the campgrounds were outfitted with *"ice can stoves"* – the molds that had been used to make blocks of ice. Each camp had an approximately 6'x6'x4' trash pit that had a cover of wood which was covered with tin. These were put in by the Civilian Conservation Corp as most of the campgrounds had been used by the CCC initially and were later dedicated to the use as public campgrounds. The trash pits were to keep the trash away from forest critters and were cleaned out periodically by Forest Service personal.

A visitor to the newly rehabilitated McGill Campground – 1962. Part of the improvements included a hiking trail from the campground down to the snowgate. (Grace Bradley photo)

Organizational camps on private and public lands sprouted up throughout the mountains in the 1930's to 1960's. The first was established by the Boy Scouts. The Ventura County Council of the Boy Scouts had operated a camp to the west of Lockwood Valley at Wheeler Gorge in the early 1930's but the camp was taken for the construction of Highway 33. Knowing of the need for a new camp location, former Boy Scout, Lewis Plush, donated 10 acres of his ranch in Lockwood Valley to the Ventura Council. The first camping program was offered there in 1933 at a rustic location named *"Camp Three Falls"* for the water falls nearby. Lou Plush dug an open trench piping system all the way from the North Falls to a reservoir in the camp where rowing, canoeing and swimming were offered. Other programs at the new tent camp were rifle shooting, archery, studies of the Native people and horseback riding. It is said that ten rattlesnakes were caught (killed?) that first year.

Boy Scouts in front of the Plush home in the 1930's
(Plush Family Photo)

Sailboat races on the Camp Three Falls reservoir
(Plush Family photo)

By the next year, a lodge was completed as well as twenty-seven cabin sites. Soon a 40' x 90' pool was built where the reservoir had been, a kitchen and dining hall were built and many trees were planted. Eventually additional acreage was leased from the Forest Service and more land was purchased from Lewis Plush's daughter and son-in-law Bert & Louella Lee. Bert Lee had been a scout at the new camp as early as 1934 and went on to become a counselor and then the camp *"Range Officer"*. During his time at the camp he got to know and eventually married the Plush daughter, Louella.

Front L-R: *"Smitty"*, Tom/Bob Carr, Val French – Camp Director, Elwood Greist – Ventura Camping Council
Back L-R: Joe Bradford, Audie Calloway, Louella Plush, Bert Lee
(Plush Family photos)

Ready for a campout with pack mules

The next camp to be established, in the mid-1930's, was located below the *"Y"* at the top of Cuddy Valley. It had been in the hands of several different organizations until 1946 when the Ventura YMCA took over the 13 acre site and named it *"Pine Valley Camp"*. Y.M.C.A. organizations from Ventura, Los Angeles and Kern Counties made use of the facility year around and it was very popular for its winter sports activities. The early facility consisted of a dining hall, four cabins with 16 bunk beds in each, a director's cabin, headquarters, caretaker and staff cabins. Their *"slightly heated"* swimming pool was used by several of the camps in the Upper Cuddy Valley area.

The original dining hall burned down in November of 1951 and a new *"fireproof"* one was built in 1952. A fireplace of native rock divided and heated both the dining hall and a large recreation room. The dedication of *"Cline Lodge"* was held on Sunday, July 27th, 1952 with 150 people present. A local writer, Grace Bradley wrote:

> *"Jack Cline, chairman of the camp development committee gave a few remarks concerning the building of the lodge stating that by the cooperation of the many friends of the YMCA a $30,000 building was built for $12,000. Mr. Cline also told of camping at this location in 1912."*

In 1953 girls of the YWCA were first allowed to use the camp as well. The camp averaged some 5000 visitors annually the 1950's and through the years has been used by many different organizations.

Recent photo of Cline Lodge at the Y.M.C.A. Camp

"Camp Condor", at the base of the north slope of Mt. Abel, was opened in 1938. It was created by oil & oil supply companies, lodges, civic clubs and individuals of the Taft and Maricopa areas so that the children from that portion of the San Joaquin Valley might escape the summer heat, smells and noise of the oil field settlements. Camp Condor was created under the name of the *"West Side Children's Camp Association"*. The Forest Supervisor at that time, Nash Boulden, was instrumental in assisting in the establishment of the camp. It is presently owned by Kern County Parks & Recreation and managed by the Westside Recreation District of Taft.

A forest fire burned to near the boundaries of Camp Condor in 1956 and 95 acres were blackened. The Camp then undertook a project of tree planting in what was called the Camp Condor Plantation. The fire was used as learning opportunity on the damage and destruction that one careless person can do. The plans were, with the help of Forest Service personnel, to plant 1,000 trees each year with each group at Camp Condor planting 250 trees during their stay. Pails of water were carried by campers to the thirsty trees.

2002 aerial photo of Camp Condor looking down the mountain

Camp Condor is made up of three areas. The upper area is the Children's Camp where there is a swimming pool and a fishing pond, which fills from the overflow from their spring fed water tank. Unique to the *"mess hall"* is a comic mural of a condor, the camp mascot, that was painted by a Disney Studio's animator in the

1960's or so. The center area is the *"Happy Gulch Campground"* and the lower area, the ski hut and lodge for snow play. At one time the Ski Lodge at the top of Mt Abel and in the lower area of Camp Condor were run by the same organization.

One of several "quonset huts" from the World War II Taft military base that were moved to Camp Condor

World War II slowed the camping activity but the 1950's saw a spurt of organizational camps throughout the mountains. The area of the Upper Cuddy Valley ended up with the greatest number of campgrounds – eight all totaled.

In 1949 the *"Burbank Girl Scout Council"* purchased forty acres of land from Fred and Florence Schaefer. It was located in the pines on the south and uphill side of the Schaefer Turkey Ranch in the Upper Cuddy Valley. The first buildings were the kitchen and *"messing facility"*, a three ward infirmary, staff headquarters, an administration building with a trading post, outdoor theatre, campfire circle and a large swimming pool. The well there produced 100 gallon of water a minute.

Dedication of the camp took place in June 1954 with a crowd of 400 in attendance. The newspaper article by Grace Bradley reported that the camp had hot water and electricity and also stated:

> *"The American flag was raised for the first time on the new flag pole stationed in front of the main auditorium. Five girl scouts acted as color guard and led the Pledge of Allegiance. The planting of a tree highlighted the ceremony. A chorus, representing members from thirty troops, sang several numbers. Five different groups of 100 girls each will enjoy two week stays during this session."*

Dedication ceremony at the Burbank Girl Scout Camp (RRCM files)

The main building at the Burbank Camp (RRCM files)

In 1951 Grace Bradley wrote that a group called, *"The Christian Churches of California"*, were building on a ten acre *"Conference Grounds"* nine miles west and north of Frazier Park. This is believed to be a site of the present *"Bethany Pines Camp"*. Mrs. Bradley wrote:

> *"The site is a beautiful saucer-shaped dell among the tall ponderosa pine trees over-looking Cuddy Valley. Plans are for a dining hall, administration building with assembly room, stage, fireplace and classrooms. Five dormitories are to be erected, two guest cottages, a chapel and a caretakers cottage. A large swimming pool will be constructed very near the center of the site and the several natural ski runs will be developed for the winter sports."*

In 1952 the Santa Barbara Girl Scout Council established the *"San Emigdio Girl Scout Camp"* at the extreme top of the San Emigdio Canyon – above the *"Y"*. This camp opened around the first of July and closed at the beginning of the hunting season, August 1st. Here the girls took part in archery, handcrafts using mostly natural materials, swimming (down at the YMCA Camp), riding and hiking.

In 1954 another camp was begun on property that had belonged to, and was below or east of, the Schaefer Turkey Ranch. The Pentecostal Church of God began building a large building to house 200 young people and their leaders. The 18 acre tract offered a wide view of the valley below. The large horseshoe shaped structure (still being used) was to include the dormitories, a dining hall, kitchen – with electricity, office and small infirmary.

In 1956, The Ventura Girls Scouts leased Forest Service property below the San Emigdio Girl Scout Camp and began the *"Tecuya Girl Scout Camp"*. That Fall twenty-five Navy CB's (Construction Battalion) from Port Hueneme used their three day furlough to help construct new buildings at the camp and to get a little hunting in on the side.

It seems that by 1961 the Santa Barbara Girl Scout Council sold 16 acres of the lower portion of their lease to the El Camino Conference of the American Lutheran Church. One of the churches of the conference was in Santa Barbara and knew of the Scouts desire to sell that portion of their lease. In September of that year the first building was nearing completion on the *"El Camino Pines Conference Campgrounds"*. The architectural styling of all the buildings was to be of the Alpine *"A-frame"* type for snow load and the mountain experience. The El Camino Pines Camp later purchased the Girl Scouts camp above them and now refers to that camping area as *"Frontier Pines"*.

One of the Alpine style building being constructed at El Camino Pines Camp

In 1963 another special use Forest Service lease was issued in what was then called the *"San Emigdio Organization Tract of the Mt. Pinos Recreation Area"* to the St. Nicholas Orthodox Church of Los Angeles for a camp to be located directly across the road from Camp Tecuya. Two main buildings and five small cabins were completed on the twelve acre tract of *"Camp St Nicholas"* that year. The Forest Service works closely with these *"special use"* permittees during construction and makes annual inspections.

Construction of many buildings at Camp St. Nicholas

The immediate area of Frazier Park had two camps. The first was only a small cabin purchased or deeded in 1943 to the Boy Scouts of Taft, though it was used by local scouts as well. It was said to be located two blocks south of Lake Number One at the Park, which would make it a distance up Pine Canyon Road. It had a full basement in which eight double bunks were located.

Pictured from left to right are local boys Ronnie Willis, Ted Van Amstel, David Dean, Ronnie Frey and Billy Curtis at the Frazier Park Boy Scout cabin

There was also a large private campground located at the north-eastern side of Frazier Park in the Monte Vista Subdivision, an area not a part of the original subdivision of Frazier Park. In June of 1950, newspaper reporter, Grace Bradley, wrote:

> *"Some five hundred people are attending the conference and camp meeting of the Western District of the United Pentecostal Church at their camp grounds in the Monte Vista subdivision just east of Frazier Park. Attendees have arrived from throughout the United States, Canada, South Africa, India and other mission countries. Business meetings are being held at the Frazier Park Club House. The eight acre camp site is just in its infancy. The future plans call for a large tabernacle that will seat 800 people to be built among the pine trees of the area, the completion of the two-story ladies dormitory, the building of a men's dormitory, kitchens and dining rooms and 40 to 50 cabins for the pastors of the district. A camp for boys and girls followed the conference meetings."*

In 1953, although the tabernacle was not completed, the site was usable for the 800 who attended the annual conference there. In 1956, three thousand people were expected to attend the event! The camping programs at this facility operated from April through September.

The tabernacle or main building of the United Pentecostal Conference Center in the Monte Vista Subdivision on the east side of Frazier Park

Not to be left out, four additional camps were developed in the late 20th Century: Vision Valley Camp and Camp AREV to the west of Pinon Pines, a Baptist Camp on Mt. Pinos not far from the snow gate, and the Seventh Day Adventist Campground in the *"Chuchupate Meadows"* west of Lake of the Woods.

XIX - SANCTUARY OF THE PINES

Back to the 1920's . . . . In order to further accommodate the public and to encourage more careful use of the forest, besides the designated campgrounds, tracts of land were set aside for summer homes. Two such residential tracts were set aside on Frazier Mountain called Chuchupate and Sierra Vista, with Chula Vista Summer Home Tract so designated on Mt. Pinos. No residences were built on the Sierra Vista or Chula Vista Tracts but there are still seven homes on Forest Service leases in the Chuchupate Tract between the Chuchupate Campground and the Chuchupate Ranger station. There were originally thirteen homes but six have been lost to forest fires, fallen trees and heavy snow loads.

Sixteen quarter acre lots were laid out in the 90 acre Chula Vista tract which adjoined the ten acre Chula Vista Public Camp Ground on Pinos. A 1926 Forest Service report by Ranger V. C. DeLapp described the area as always having cool nights in the summer, and as to the winter he wrote:

> *"When the snow melts at lower elevations, parties can drive the 'Up Road' to Beartrap Canyon and then hike up into the snow. The forest is of Jeffery Pine and White Fir with no under brush, giving it a decided park like appearance, whose cover is not too dense for recreation. The area has been logged in spots and reproduction is decidedly lacking on account of heavy sheeping."*

Water from Mina Spring was a primary factor in governing the lay-out of the tract but as DeLapp stated: *"there were apparently more lot sites than water supply".*

The tract was further described as having:

> *"an open type of cover and rolling topography that lends itself to hikes and saddle trips at will over the mountain. It is only a day's saddle trip to the Sespe River where trout fishing is enjoyed. All of the lots are so located that an unobstructed view is had from each lot and neighbor's back door scenes do not obstruct the view. No flush toilets will be allowed and refuse burn will be required, in a suitable incinerator. The architecture will be approved by the Forest Service as well as the actual location of the buildings. A harmonizing paint job will be required and no oriental color schemes allowed. Strict*

adherence to fire proofing houses must be enforced and no livestock will be allowed."

By 1938, with the apparent lack of or difficulty in developing water sources, and no doubt other issues, it was decided lots would no longer be issued as home sites on any of the established tracts and they were instead developed into public campgrounds. It seems the Chula Vista Campground was then later named McGill Campground after the owner of an old lumber mill that had been located near there.

The earliest residents of the Chuchupate tract may have been there long before the tract was established. Possibly they had located on a mining claim. The local newspaper, the RIDGE ROUTE RAMBLER of Sept 1939 reported:

"Mr. & Mrs. Jordan, who have lived on Chuchupate for over thirty years, recently sold their home. They purchased a house and lot from the Mandevilles and are moving in to Frazier Park."

(This would mean that they built their cabin at Chuchupate in 1909!)

It is not certain as to exactly when the Chuchupate Tract was established but a few names of other early residents there have been located. A Bakersfield newspaper article of 1922 mentioned the summer home of Albert Scherer of Los Angeles. The Kern County librarian, Julia G. Babcock and her husband, Arthur, visited Chuchupate in 1921 and made claim to an old miner's cabin near there as a summer home, possibly before the tract was laid out. Arthur had an interest in mining but Julia soon had her own dreams to pursue. She made a decision to establish a summer library and gardens of native plants in the forest near their cabin site for the use of the citizens from the five surrounding counties of Kern, Los Angeles, Ventura, Santa Barbara and San Luis Obispo that so closely bordered and still border the mountain area. Deciding that the mountain-side library and garden retreat should be for all to enjoy, Julia sold her idea to librarians in each of the surrounding counties. They were very supportive so went forth to procure the backing of area Garden Clubs, Women's Groups, colleges and universities through out California.

As the effort gained momentum an avid supporter of the project, Harry W. McCray, wrote:

"With the profusion of California perennial wild flowers, some majestic pines, favorable topographical soil, water and climatic conditions there, it suggests that a suitable area be set apart on which to establish an arboretum of California's flowering plants, shrubs and trees suitable to these conditions around the

library building. It is my judgment that no other park area on the coast can compare in presenting California's superior floral offerings to the world. The big trees and other members of the pine family will appreciate the deep soil and climate too.

A short distance above the library location the attractive pines together with quite a large slightly modulating area suggest that this part be set apart for educational purposes. We read of but were too far away this year for the grand lectures in Yosemite (suggesting that such lectures could be held in this new setting). *This area will present a wonderful diversity, greatly adding to the park features of California."*

Mrs. Babcock named the proposed gardens the *"Sanctuary of the Pines"*. Advertising brought groups from far and wide to plant trees there. The Bakersfield Women's Club sent to Syria for Cedar of Lebanon trees and had them planted. Mrs. Luther Burbank and members of the Santa Rosa Flower Lovers Club, from Santa Rosa in Northern California, where the Burbank's lived, motored down to plant a memorial grove of trees and place a bronze tablet at the site in memory of Luther Burbank on May 1, 1927. Priscilla Willard Spencer recalled attending the placing of the Burbank plaque with her Camp Fire Girls troop from Bakersfield and shared a copy of this memorable picture.

Mrs. Luther Burbank is seated in the center back with Priscilla Willard to the left of Mrs. Burbank and Priscilla's sister, Marjorie, on the right (Willard Family photo)

It would seem that since activists for the creation of a National Park on Frazier Mountain were not successful, this more modest effort was pursued.

A 1927 issue of the FRAZIER NEWS reported a plan to erect a great stone cross above the Sanctuary that would be visible *"almost the entire trip from Los Angeles to Bakersfield"*. It was to be 50–75 feet above the summit and would serve as a beacon to aviators as it was thought that *"electricity could be obtained at no great expense to illumine the land-mark"!* The FRAZIER NEWS was a short term publication done by the developers of the Frazier Mountain Park community. In a 1928 issue the same newspaper made mention of the Sanctuary of the Pines being *"on the very top of Frazier Mountain"* but no other information indicates that or that the cross was ever erected..

Though she easily found the backing for the project, and those wanting to come and plant trees, Julia did not easily find those who would come to water *"until the young trees could get a hold in their new environment"*. She appealed for funds for a caretaker but it was usually she and her son who would travel to the site as often as possible to carry hundreds of pails of water to the trees. Occasionally she was able to enlist the aid of a troop of Camp Fire Girls and Boy or Girl Scouts to help out.

The July 13, 1928 issue of the LOS ANGELES EVENING HERALD carried an article and the following poem by Everett Hollingsworth about the Sanctuary:

THE SANCTUARY

The Sanctuary of the Pines,
foregathered from all lands
Upon the wooded slopes
of famous Frazier Mountain stands.
The mingled fronds are earnest
of the peace and harmony
Which all the warring tribes of man
in future days will see.

A sentry at the crossroads,
where the caravans of trade
Pass eastward, westward, northward,
southward...endless cavalcade...
The tow'ring heights of Frazier Mount
look down upon the scene,
From grassy base to rocky summit,
with the trees between.

From every land come pilgrims
to the spot where nature blends
The growths of other habitats,
assembled here as friends.
Distinct in dress and customs,
and diversified in speech,
Kaleidoscopic scenes like this
important lessons teach.

Oh, Sanctuary of the Pines!
Oh, Frazier Mountain, high!
Breathe out your gladsome message
as caravans go by!
If soulless beasts and birds and trees
in amity can dwell,
Shall spirit-nurtured man
appear the only infidel?

Efforts were also made to have the area declared a State Park or possibly a State Game Reserve. Mrs. Babcock wrote to The Joint Parks Committee:

> *"Mrs. Florence Cuddy, who has lived in Cuddy Valley most of her life is trying to have a very large tract reserved* (placed under Reserve status), *including Frazier Mountain, Mount Pinos, and a large tract which belongs to the Kern County Land Co.* (the future area of Pine Mountain Club). *This would be all right if it is not too ambitious a program, which may defeat its purpose. She is genuinely interested, because during all these years she has observed the ruthless slaughter of the deer and other animals of the mountains. Mrs. Cuddy states: The tract about which I am specially anxious is National Forest, but hunting is permitted now, and is not in harmony with the idea of a Sanctuary for trees or birds or animals. The Forest Service is in sympathy with our ideas."*

Mrs. Babcock also found the need to defend the effort as not being a part of the new real estate *"schemes"* going on at the base of the mountain. The developers of the new communities of Frazier Mountain Park and Lake of the Woods were including the *"Sanctuary of the Pines"* in their advertising brochures as another appealing feature to interest buyers. Don and Florence Cuddy were the developers of Lake of the Woods and Mrs. Cuddy was appealing for the surrounding area to be put into a reserve as well so she was, of course, very supportive of the *"Sanctuary"* project.

The 32,300 acres in and around the area were declared the Frazier Mountain State Game Refuge in 1929 and Mrs. Babcock wrote:

> *"I feel that the best thing which has been accomplished as yet, is the passage of the bill protecting the game on Frazier Mountain. That is something which I have longed to see brought to pass ever since I first went up there and found the old miner's cabin which we have adopted and upon which many hours of hard labor have been expended, with a great deal of pleasure, nevertheless. If the gun as a toy could be wholly eliminated, bird life as well as human life would be much safer. My slogan for years has been 'hunt with a camera'."*

The Woman's Club of Bakersfield submitted a proposal for Federal aid in 1931 with some very informative descriptions of the unique eco-system of this mountain environment. It read:

> *"It is an isolated mountain, elliptical in form where the zones of plant life from the north and from the south meet on its summit, as evidenced by the outposts of the pines from the far north in beautiful pine forests on its north face, while on its south face are the Mojave forms of plant life. On its eastern base are the large white oak trees, and black oaks, and some Joshua trees at its southeast base, while intermingling over the mountain an exceptional range of California wild flowers and shrubs are thrifty. Also this line westerly in the Pacific Ocean divides the fishes of the northern and southern waters. Its structure is granitic, with the same general characteristics as the Sierra Nevada, excepting that it is entirely covered with a deep soil without deep serrations or large areas of rock outcroppings.*
>
> *As the outposts of many of the pines of the Pacific coast have already selected their homes there, we are advised by plant life authorities that suitable locations can be found on this mountain, with its varying elevations, moisture and angles to the sun, to grow practically all of the pine trees of the world there, of over six hundred varieties, and it is also suitable for the protection as well of the fauna and flora. What a fortunate location for our Secretary of Agriculture to use for experimental purposes. Hence, with the cooperation of the many women's clubs and other organizations, we hope to establish there one of the great shrines of the world in the Sanctuary of the Pines.*
>
> *The women's clubs of the entire San Joaquin Valley, the State Audubon Society, and the Southern Audubon societies have*

endorsed it, as well as several women's organizations in the South (Los Angeles). *Our local Ministerial Union and Catholic Churches have also endorsed it, the State Fish and Game Commission are co-operating, foreseeing that it can help the friendly farmer and forest birds in maintaining nature's balance."*

Within the Sanctuary of the Pines, religious groups proposed to reproduce the area of Mount Hebron with its famous Cedars of Lebanon from the Holy Lands. Reverend A. S. Donat of Bakersfield wrote:

"I have traveled to the top of Frazier Mountain, and I have also traveled around its southern base and southward to the Mojave climatic conditions. I have studied in the Holy Land and believe that the soil, moisture, climatic and topographical conditions of the area south of Mount Hebron are strikingly similar. On the south slope the vine fig and olive and the lower plant life of the desert parts can find new homes."

On October 25, 1931 the LOS ANGELES TIMES announced the dedication ceremony would be held:

"Days when Frazier Mountain was a happy hunting ground for Indian tribes, will be recalled tomorrow at the dedication ceremony at the Sanctuary of the Pines as the Tejon Indian tribe will be represented by Chief Juan Rafael Lozada and the children of the Tejon Indian School. Among the descendants of the Tejon Indian tribe who will be present are Mary Garcia, Piestonna Garcia, Pelodonia Garcia, Caroline Duran, Louise Cordero, Magdalena Cordero, Elydia Vasquez and Carmel Encinas. Mrs. Anna B. Knowles, teacher at the school, will escort the Indians to the dedication grounds."

The newspaper also reported that the California Federation of Women's Clubs would be planting a rare nutmeg tree and the Southern California Audubon Society would release a covey of quail.

On October 26, 1931 a dedication of the Sanctuary of the Pines and the Frazier Mountain State Game Refuge was finally held near the Chuchupate Campground. The BAKERSFIELD CALIFORNIAN reported:

"Two hundred nature lovers from all parts of the state assembled for a ceremony in which the tree-clad range was claimed forever as a retreat for lovers of the out-of-doors. The ceremonies were opened with a bugle call by the Boy Scout Troop No. 7, followed by a flag-raising ceremony and flag salute led by the Sea Scouts. The audience sang 'The Star-Spangled Banner' and 'I Love You, California' and a women's two part

chorus accompanied by an organ, furnished other music. A lovely pantomime was presented by a group of Camp Fire girls and an Indian legend of Chuchupate was read by pretty Elydia Vaquez of the Tejon Indian tribe. Chief Juan Losada was one of the guests of honor of the day. Baritone Ralph Patrick sang 'Trees' at the conclusion of the dedication."

The LOS ANGELES TIMES of October 26th also reported on the event, adding:

"The Vineland P.T.A. served box lunches at noon, and most of those motoring to the dedication from Bakersfield made the day's outing a picnic occasion as well. Forest rangers and officers of the California State Highway Patrol helped to direct traffic from the Kern County line to the Chuchupate Meadow, where the dedication was held."

Juan Losado at the event. He was said to be the last of the chiefs of the Indians of the Sebastian Reservation in Tejon Canyon (Bakersfield Californian photo)

Another unidentified newspaper reported that the President of the California Federation of Women's Clubs, with other prominent women from around the state, attended the event. This newspaper also indicated that through the efforts of the American Audubon Society this State Game & Bird Refuge had been expanded to 50,000 acres. The Bakersfield Woman's Club hosted the dedication. The article read:

> *"The ceremonial was held at Chuchupate Park amid the pines on the north slope of the mountain. Frazier Mountain is the most notable natural botanical garden in the world. The speakers asserted that its attraction for Nature lovers will be further enhanced as a sanctuary for birds and wild game."*

An article in a January 1933 issue of the BAKERSFIELD CALIFORNIAN reported:

> *"A report from Washington D.C. confirms that the Sanctuary will be placed under the care of the United States Forest Service, under the Department of Agriculture."*

It would seem that all the years of effort were lost as little or nothing remains of Frazier Mountain's *"Sanctuary of the Pines"* – most of it having been lost to the fire on that side of the mountain in the 1940's. The site of the original Sanctuary has not yet been determined.

Back to the Chuchupate housing tract . . . A 1950 article written by Grace Bradley, told about an early resident of one of the cabins at Chuchupate:

> *"Returning to her summer home in the Chuchupate area, after a year's absence, Miss Elsa Pehrson, a Swedish reporter, living in Los Angeles, discovered a family of foxes had established squatters rights to her cabin and refused to move. All the persuasion that Miss Pehrson could use, such as nailing up and rocking up their entrance to the den under the cabin just resulted in another hole being dug under the foundation of the cabin and each time the foxes would dig their den just a little deeper.*
>
> *Maybe Miss Pehrson wouldn't have objected too much to the fox family occupying the basement apartment if they had shown any cooperation in their playtime, but no ..., they would stay hidden all day and just when nice people are supposed to be fast asleep in their beds, four little foxes would begin to play under the cabin floor. They must have been sturdy little rebels judging from the barking, snapping and growling that went on. And every so often one little fox member would hit the floor hard enough to cause the rocking chairs to sway back and forth in protest. Finally the mother fox was captured. This caused the father to dig the den still deeper and dig another way into the den. He had to loose two pups before he would gather up the remaining two and move out, leaving the premises to Miss Pehrson and her guests."*

A stone cabin in the Chuchupate Tract

Another cozy cabin in the Chuchupate housing tract

XX - FROM THE MOUNTAIN TOPS

The prominent mountains of the Mt. Pinos District in the Los Padres National Forest, beginning to the north (from east to west) are, Tecuya Mtn., Antimony Peak, San Emigdio Mtn. and Brush Mtn. – all at or over 7,000 feet. To the west there is McPherson Peak, Fox Mtn. and Cuyama Peak – all in the 5,000 to 6,000 foot range. In the southern portion of the Mt. Pinos Ranger District (from west to east) are Reyes Peak on Pine Mtn., Thorn Point, San Guillermo Mtn., San Rafael Peak and Alamo Mtn. – all near or over 7,000 feet, and on the east Frazier Mtn. is over 8000 feet. Encircled by these mountain peaks is the highest point of the entire Los Padres Forest, Mount Pinos, reaching almost 9,000 feet above sea level. To the west of Pinos are Sawmill Mtn. and Mt. Abel both at over 8,000 feet. All are in or adjacent to the San Emigdio Mountain Range except McPherson, Fox, Cuyama and Reyes which are on the west side of the Cuyama River in the Sierra Madre Mountains.

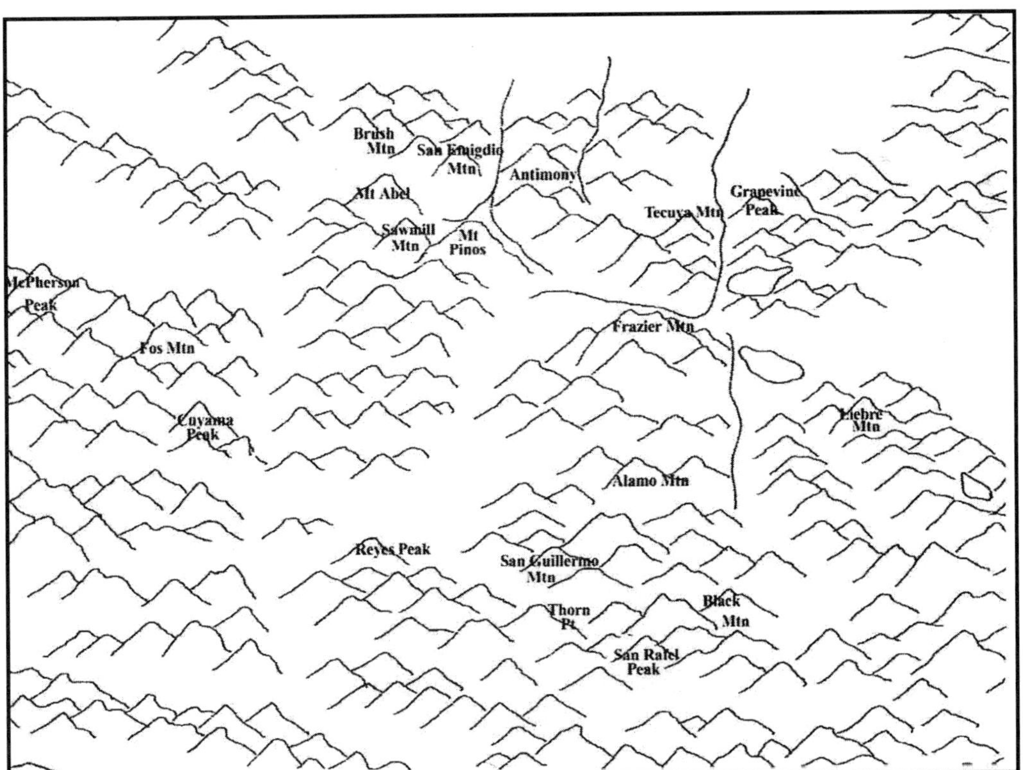

Mountain Top locations

From the peaks of **Mt. Pinos**, on a clear day, one can enjoy views of the San Joaquin Valley, the Sierra Nevada Mountains, and on over numerous mountain ranges to the Pacific Ocean and the Channel Islands – one of the reasons the earliest people held this mountain so sacred. Mt. Pinos was called *"Iwihinmu"* by the Chumash people. It was said that only the shaman were to walk upon it and then only at certain times of the year, and those who approached Mt. Pinos were to do so in silence. At the summit of Pinos, among the wind-tortured trees, there was for some time a radio relay station which connected Edwards Air Force Base with Vandenberg Air Force Base.

Mt. Pinos is the highest peak in the California coast range. Star and comet watchers have gathered at the top of the mountain since earliest man for the phenomenal views of the universe that can be had from there. In more recent times the mountain has become a popular place for the observation of the huge condors, for hiking and for snow play in the winter months. One of the largest land exchanges in these parts, in which forest reserve was gained while giving up some land for private land holdings, was negotiated with the Kern County Land and Cattle Company in 1940 when the Forest Service secured 3,500 acres of extremely valuable timbered slopes of Mt. Pinos.

Mt. Pinos was later referred to as McGill Peak for a sawmill that was operated there by John McGill in the 1870's. The mill was located below the site of the present McGill campground. McGill was also one of the many partners in the San Emigdio Ranch operations of the late 1800's.

This is a picture of Walter McGill found in the Cuddy Family Collection. He may have been a son of John McGill or one of John's names could have been Walter.

George Wheeler of the U.S. Corp of Engineers and his party explored these mountains in 1875 doing topographic, geological, zoological, and ethnic studies. In July of that year he described Pinos as:

"This mountain is called McGill's Peak, after the owner of a saw-mill, below the steepest declivity of the slope, where government lands, as in many another instance noted in various parts of the West, were being despoiled by a non-owner, and naturally in a wasteful manner. The local markets for timber were Tejon Ranch and the vicinities of Bakersfield and Caliente, on the Southern Pacific Railroad."

Logging operations were a common site and sound on these mountains from the 1850's to the early 1900's providing lumber for much of the surrounding area.

In 1888 the State Mineralogist, Stephen Bowers was in the area to record mining activity. From his journal we have this wonderful description of Mt. Pinos in that year. Mr. Bowers writes:

"July 18 – Started up Mt. Pinos this morning about 10 a.m.. A thunder shower began on the mountain reaching down to the foothills about 11 o'clock. We found shelter for ourselves and team under a pine tree. The thunder continued for about three hours and was continuous. Our road lay up Saw Mill canon. There were several grizzly bears here and learning that five had visited the herders camp we decided to camp on the side of the mountain where his camp is and watch for bear. The herders are Hagen & Carr's men, later Kern Co Land Company, who seem to have monopolized this mountain with their sheep. The altitude is 6825'.

We ascended the mountain to an altitude of 7200' and searched for bear but returned to our camp without any. We watched in our wagon which we moved to a convenient place, until midnight. The moon was going down and it being too dark to shoot we brought our blankets down to camp. But about an hour afterward we were aroused by the stampede of the sheep. Jumping up and running to the brow of the hill we could distinctly hear the bears but could not see them for the darkness. They had killed a sheep and ate it. It's mangled carcass being found by us in the morning. Having again laid down to rest we were awakened in an hour by other bears coming from another direction for carrion, but it was to dark too see or shoot. Altogether there must have been four or five bears visited the camp. The track of one measured about 11 inches in length. She was followed by one or two cubs.

July 19 – Early this morning we ascended the mountain. In about four miles we came to the old sawmill erected years ago. This mill then supplied a large district of country. We staked our horses here and continued the ascent of the mountain on foot. It is one of the most lovely mountains I have ever seen. The southeast side which we ascended is a succession of rolling hills with an immense forest of pine in which nearly or quite half a dozen species and included fir. From one of the millions of trees here many are sufficiently large for sawyers and from 80–150 feet high. The ground under these trees is covered with cones. These immense timbers could come to millions of dollars if utilized, I judge. Many granite uplifts into conical and picturesque peaks. Granite, gneiss suynectile, mica schist, quartz and feldspar are the principal rocks. The ground is clean and one can see for a long distance through the pines. Flowers still spring up and bloom on this mountain in considerable variety. Fremontia californicii (gold drops) is in full bloom on Mt. Pinos.

Many birds are found, one kind of huge blue crested jay is most common. One is impressed with the vast numbers of humming birds that live and thrive here. As far as I can ascertain there may be but one or two species, though there may be several. Mountain Quail are also found here and gray squirrels. I saw three valley ground squirrels over 8000' up on the mountain and the festive grasshopper is found on the top. The mountain seems covered with chipmunks.

During the evening we returned to the herders camp where we erected a scaffold nearly ten feet high by tying poles to three trees and securing them in the shape of a triangle with boards we brought from the sawmill. The poles were securely tied with ropes to the trees and one man took a position on the scaffold at each corner ... DeMoss, Menzies and myself. We watched all night but bears did not put in an appearance.

July 20 – Started early this morning for our camp in Lockwood. The rain had swelled all the streams leading from Mt. Pinos making travel difficult. This portion of the country is subject to cloud bursts and water spouts. The sides of the mountains are frequently washed down destroying roads and trails ... a drawback to this region."

In 1923, Charles F. Saunders wrote in his book, THE SOUTHERN SIERRAS OF CALIFORNIA, of the beauty and view from Mt. Pinos. On his journey to the mountain he had camped with the family of caretakers of the old Stauffer Borax Mine in Lockwood Valley, at the southeastern base of Pinos. Mr. Saunders wrote:

> *"One morning ... a bright, dewless morning of July ... I set out for the top of Mount Pinos, following an old wood road that led from the borax mine over a ridge down into a sagey flat where the plant life of the mountains mingled with that of the desert ... manzanita, wild heliotrope, and blazing star cheek by jowl with the fiery red mariposa tulip of the Mojave. Dainty navarretias bloomed delicately in lavender and blue in the shadow of the sagebrush. The air fairly sparkled in the early sunlight, and birds and bees filled it with the melody of their choiring. Now and then a horned toad scuttled for dear life from under my feet or a jack-rabbit bounded into sight, and once the shadow of a buzzard hunting fell athwart the path. The road, brush-grown and dim, by and by entered a thin forest of low pines down the midst of which a musical brooklet flowed cantily, and then after a stiff climb the tracks came to a dead stop at a deserted lumber camp. The sagging cabins and gaping sawmill overhanging the brook might have served to lodge another party of Silverado squatters. The only sign of contemporary life was a forest ranger's neat cabin, and even that was vacant.*
>
> *I was now at the end of all trails, nor was my summit in sight. All I had to guide me was my host's instructions to continue bearing northwest through the woods, pursuing always the highest ridge in view. It was an interesting exercise, that guessing the highest rise ahead among the many that kept swarming up as I climbed ... modified version of Excelsior, where, instead of the snow and ice and the avalanches that beset the aspiring youth of the famous ballad, I had sunshine, resinous odors, and bird chat, and the companionship of noble pines in a parklike forest clear of underbrush.*
>
> *The gently ascending crests of the ridges which I pursued upwards were sylvan boulevards, bathed in light and bordered by dappled shadows. The top of one attained, it would fall away by a gentle descent to a green, open flat carpeted with wild flowers ... with lupines blue and white, scarlet penstemons, Indian paintbrush, golden eriophyllum, mariposa tulips in mauve and lavender. Sometimes the crimson spikes of the snow-plant flamed about my feet; but most charming of all the flowery fellowship were the wild iris gardens that crowded down the sunny swales and up the slopes to the wood's edge like a Lilliputian army with banners, their lovely pale blue petals blowing and rippling under the driving of the passing breeze. A cool breeze it was, even on that midsummer day (the*

snow may fall on Pinos in August, they say), and it hummed a pleasant tune in the pine-tops to the accompaniment of the rat-a-tat-tat of Senor Sarpintero, the woodpecker. I am as poor an ornithologist as Juliet Capulet, who knew not lark from nightingale, but I believe I am sure of a woodpecker.

For a couple of hours, every height though it seemed the ultimate one when viewed from below, proved only a stepping-stone to others ahead still greater; but a last the trees crouched lower and farther apart, and I came out upon the summit, a square mile or so of undulating, grassy sedgy heath, rock-strewn, wind-swept, and dotted with occasional tattered pines and silver firs, 8820 feet above the sea. Endearing little sub-alpine flowers clung to the mountain's breast, among them a prostrate lupine whose miniature spikes of blue and white rose only an inch above the ground, and a little bladder-odor loco-weed, whose crimson, bladder-like pods, mottled with white and lying flat on the ground, strikingly suggested a nest full of birds' eggs. Even more curious I found the pods of another astragalus, also a prostrate plant. They are noticeably beaked and covered completely with a close, white down, and if you do not see them as so many tiny, fluffy chicks you have no imagination at all.

Once you are on the broad summit of Mount Pinos, the whole of the Santa Barbara National Forest country comes surging about your feet; and if the condition of the atmosphere is ideally clear ... it rarely is ... you may see the ocean gleaming in one direction and the desert in the other. Scraps of ancient history floated on the current of my thoughts as I ate my solitary luncheon in the lee of a great boulder, and made it less solitary. The sun had gone into hiding as I sat. Lowering clouds, a chill wind, and some dashes of rain sent me downward in mid-afternoon, and twilight was gathering as I turned the corner of the old borax mine."

A group of Boy Scouts receive instructions from Ranger Sloan near the lookout station on Mt.. Pinos about 1920. One of the boys is Rollin Brown from Lockwood Valley (Brown Family Photo)

As a youngster, Del Black recalled that in the early 1940's his family would drive up to Mt. Pinos from Bakersfield. They would enjoy the day and also spend much of the time filling gunnysacks with oak-leaf mold for the garden. The decomposed oak leaves under the oak trees were several feet deep in those days

Beautiful flower-filled meadow at the top of Pinos
where the Chumash people held a blessing of the mountain in 1996

Sawmill Mountain, just west of Mt. Pinos, was so named for the logging done at the base of the mountain in the 1850's. It is the second highest of three peaks in that range, at 8,800 feet. According to John Kelly of the U.S. Forest Service, the largest block of Jeffery pines, that have existed without much change or logging, is on Sawmill Mtn.

The summit of **Mt. Abel**, sometimes called *"Cerro Noroeste"* (meaning *"hill to the northwest"* – of Sawmill Mtn. or Pinos it would seem) rises to 8,286 feet. The name may have changed from Noroeste to Abel during World War II when a military relay station by that name was located there. It is more likely that it was named for the county supervisor of this area in the late 1930's, early 1940's, Stanley Abel, who was instrumental in the creation of a road and the winter sports area on the mountain in 1939 – opening the mountain to year around access.

In July of 1940 the road from Maricopa to the top of Mt. Abel, dubbed *"The Highway to the Stars"*, was dedicated. The

BAKERSFIELD CALIFORNIAN reported that 2500 people had gathered in the cool mountain air for the opening of *"thirty miles of highway on which Kern county can speed to mountain freshness and all-year recreation."*

Following the barbecue of *"eight and one half beeves"*, the program was held in a huge natural amphitheatre on a platform *"bedecked with six flags"*. The newspaper reported:

> *"Stanley Abel, supervisor from the fourth district, outlined the history of the building of the 30-mile road in six years. Hal Kennedy, assistant county counsel of Los Angeles, lauded Kern County's officials for taking the lead in public recreation work, declaring that playgrounds such as Mount Abel are this country's strongest weapon against foreign rulers. He stated, 'While men in Europe fight in the air and on land and sea we come to the top of this mountain to give thanks for peace we have in the land we love'."*

James Cole remembered that he and his family from Taft attended the dedication of the new road and enjoyed the generous barbecue and a western band that played for the event.

County Supervisor, Stanley Abel

A unique feature left near the summit of Abel Mountain is what might be referred to as an *"arborglyph"*. A large cross carved on a huge Jeffrey pine tree there, possibly as a blessing to the mountain or could it indicate where worship services might have been held in an earlier time, or possibly to mark a burial.

Cross carved on a tree on Mt. Abel

Frazier Mountain was the mountain most *"used"* by man through time and was known by a series of names in the 1800's. It was first called *"Tosholol o"* by the early Chumash people and *"Kawitsatpea"* by those of another tribe. In the 1850's when the soldiers of Fort Tejon established a government lumber mill in the area of the present community of Frazier Park, the Mountain was called *"Pinery Mountain"*. By the 1860's, John Cuddy had acquired the property of the future Lake of the Woods and the mountain above it was called *"Cuddy Peak"*. But ever since the Frazier brothers found gold on the famous mountain in the 1870's, it has been known as *"Frazier Mountain"*. The stories that have come from Frazier Mountain are too numerous to tell but many are found in various chapters of this book, previous and those to come.

* * * *

In 1932 an event happened that impacted all the local mountain tops and is shared here as it offers another perspective to the mountain stories. The crash of an *"airship"*, or airplane as we now call them, was well covered in Southland area newspapers. The LOS ANGELES TIMES of January 30th, 1932 reported:

> *"Overdue many hours and apparently lost in the mountain and desert country between Bakersfield and Los Angeles late yesterday a tri-motored skyliner of Century Pacific Airlines with three women and five men aboard will at dawn today become*

the center of an intensive search by air and land. The ship, southbound from San Francisco disappeared on a flight that started from Kern County Airport at Bakersfield at 3:50 p.m. yesterday and was scheduled to end at Grand Central Air Terminal at Glendale an hour later."

It seems this was a commuter flight of sorts as the passengers were from Los Angeles, Pomona, Bakersfield, San Diego and San Francisco. The most notable on board was the Chief Deputy Sheriff of Los Angeles County, Frank Dewar, who it was said had been searching a ranch near Bakersfield – in the Buttonwillow area – for a *"band of notorious kidnappers and gangsters"*. Dewar was going to return to Los Angeles by automobile with other deputies but changed his mind at the last minute to travel on the *"ill-fated skyliner"*. Also among the *"lost sky voyagers"* was Hollywood starlet, Marie McSweeney, the daughter of a State traffic officer and his wife from Bakersfield. This plane had accommodations for 10 passengers and one pilot.

The article continued:
"The only clew in the disappearance of the ship was a report from the Frazier Mountain store, near Lebec, on the Ridge Route, (this makes it difficult to tell if this is the store at Frazier Mtn. Park or at Lebec) *that a plane was heard overhead about the time the skyliner should have passed on it way southward ... though at least four other transport planes traversed approximately the same route about the same time. Century-Pacific planes and those of other airlines and private operators are scheduled to take off at daybreak to comb the entire route from the air.*

Terrific winds and clouds were encountered over the skyway late yesterday by pilots of other air transports. It is believed that the Stinson ten-passenger cabin monoplane may not have pulled through safely the 6000 feet of fog reported above Bakersfield. If the pilot did not get above the top of the clouds he would have been buffeted by winds which were charted to have reached a maximum of 112 miles an hour at high altitudes. From accounts of other pilots who flew southward about the same time, piloting other ships from San Francisco, it was revealed that winds and clouds over the Ridge Route late yesterday were the worst that some of them had encountered. A 'flyer' landing in Burbank reported he was pushed by a sixty-mile-an-hour tail wind over the Ridge Route and that he had to make a landing at the emergency landing field in Antelope Valley."

With the advent of the new aviation industry, this landing strip had been put in, in Northern Los Angeles County – in the Neenach area, to aid pilots that needed to make a stop for any number of reasons. Also of interest is that the ill-fated plane had enough fuel to last three hours and forty minutes – 85 gallons. The flight from Bakersfield to Los Angeles was only an hour so a problem was confirmed when *"the time that the plane could have remained in the air* (indicating fuel available) *passed."* Prospective searchers also waited until morning hoping that by that time someone from the ship would have been able to reach a telephone.

The BAKERSFIELD CALIFORNIAN of January 30th, 1932 gave a description of the possible location of the crash. Excerpts from that article read:

> *"Searchers late today were concentrating their activities on an area north of Lebec, on both sides of the Ridge Route highway. Balked by fog in its efforts to cross the mountains to Los Angeles, the plane circled Frazier Mountain Park,* (the present Frazier Park community) *swung somewhere to the north of the General Petroleum pump station, midway between Lebec and Grapevine station in Tejon pass* (at the present entrance to Los Padres Estates). *A General Petroleum employee reported that sometime before 5 p.m. he had seen the airliner, flying at a safe altitude directly over the pump station and in a northerly direction. Authorities believe that the plane traveled southerly as far as Frazier mountain, was trapped in a dense fog and started back toward Kern County Airport."* It was later stated that if he turned around: *"he would have then had the terrific winds on the nose of his ship instead of riding them as speed aids coming south."*
>
> The Bakersfield newspaper reported:
> *"A great squadron of 35 airplanes, including three United States Army ships are battling rain, clouds and fog to find the air liner. The flyers report a ceiling of only 500 feet and rain falling which was changing to snow in the mountains. The planes are using an emergency landing field at Tejon* (this would be by the lake at Lebec) *for an operating base and a fleet of fuel trucks has been stationed at Grapevine Station. With darkness rapidly approaching, combined forces of 200 horsemen ... among them expert horsemen of Tejon Ranchos, hikers and aviators concentrated on the area. More than half a hundred deputy sheriffs and police officers of Kern and Los Angeles counties, and scores of unemployed men recruited here have joined in the hunt. The great posse is being served with piping hot meals by*

Century Pacific Airlines, owner of the missing ship. Dozens of maps of the mountainous territory in which the plane is believed to be disabled were dropped to searchers during the day."

Late that night, two white flares were seen in the hills west of Mojave but proved to be a power line downed by the storm. It was also reported that the area where the plane was last heard was the same in which a pilot and three passengers had died just a few months before during a night storm.

The next day the search was widened reaching from the Cuyama District, the Caliente country, and Cummings Valley near Tehachapi. The Bakersfield newspaper reported that the Tifft family at their ranch in Lockwood Valley saw the plane as it was turning north – though about the same time someone at the Lebec Hotel and an oil worker in Tejon Pass reported seeing it flying low and heading north

On February 3rd, the Los Angeles newspaper reported:
"In the wild Tehachapi region north of Los Angeles a veritable army of hunters, on the ground and in the skies, penetrated into a wilderness of snow and ice in search of the Century-Pacific air liner, missing since last Friday. The aerial force, upon which the searchers depend to locate the missing craft, will be augmented by a great fleet of other aircraft now held in readiness at many points between Los Angeles and San Francisco for the hunt. (It seems downed planes were not uncommon in those early days of flight.)

With many clews furnished, the most credible report was evidence of a wide swath on Frazier Mountain, a strip apparently sheered by a falling ship, and wreckage at the bottom of a canyon. The heavy fall of snow that has made the search doubly difficult prevented officers from definitely ascertaining the nature of the wreckage. A blizzard forced the party away from the scene."

Reports were coming in of a crash seen near Elizabeth Lake, Neenach, along Piru Creek, Lockwood Valley, on Grapevine Peak and near Tehachapi. Headquarters for the search were established at Sandberg's Lodge on the old Ridge Route, near the government weather station there, with authorities of Los Angeles, Kern and Ventura County involved. The weather did not clear for four days but when it did:

> *"for two hours the huge fleet of aircraft available for the quest were able to soar over the district. More than eighty flights were made out of Los Angeles, while countless flights were recorded in Bakersfield and other points where 200 planes are based."*

On February 4th the Bakersfield newspaper reported the mountains have been swept by storms continually until yesterday but many concentrated their search on Frazier Mountain and dog sleds were brought in. The newspaper reported:

> *"Blizzards swirled around the peaks blocking searching by air and snow is piled from six to twenty feet deep. Men on snowshoes and on horses broke trails in desperate efforts to find the ship and were rewarded only by frost bite and weariness."*

Later that same day a special edition of the BAKERSFIELD CALIFORNIAN was printed with the headline: *"EXTRA ... Lost Plane Found ... All Passengers Dead ... Report Liner Burned"*. It had taken the man who found the wreckage two hours to travel from the plane to Lebec – or to Fort Tejon as one newspaper reported – where the information was telephoned to Bakersfield and Los Angeles

On February 6th the LOS ANGELES TIMES reported the wreckage had been located on Tecuya Peak, one mountain north of Frazier Mountain. The newspaper read:

> *"The ship was found late Thursday by Paul Apodaca, a Tejon Indian rider* (cowboy), *near the head of Johnson's Canyon, close to the crest of Tecuya Ridge, three miles southwest of old Fort Tejon. An all-night vigil in sharp, biting winds was kept and at dawn the burned and mangled corpses were brought 2000 feet down from the mountains over precipitous trails on slushy and insecure footing. Investigation revealed that watches on the various bodies were stopped at approximately 4:20 o'clock, indicating that the crash occurred one-half hour after the ship left a Bakersfield airport."*

The article went on to describe the conditions, location and items found with each body and ended with:

> *"The search for the ship was one of the most dramatic in the West with hundreds of men tramping relentlessly through deep snow and foul weather for a week running down scores of false clews as to the whereabouts of the wreck and those on the ship."*

The Bakersfield newspaper reported that Mr. Apodaca found the plane while searching on foot with his three shepherd dogs though the paper also indicated that he was using the dogs as a dog sled team. This newspaper said the wreckage was located on the rim of a box canyon four miles west of Fort Tejon and that less than ten feet of altitude separated the pilot and passengers from safety. Mr. Apodaca received a $500 reward for his efforts.

The story didn't end with locating the airship. It seems Los Angeles and Kern County officials got into a bit of an altercation as to under whose authority the plane belonged. Even though the plane had taken off and was located in Kern County, because there was a Los Angeles County Sheriff on board, the latter wanted to be in charge of the wreckage. Guns were drawn and shots fired. Los Angeles County Sheriff's deputies held Kern officials at bay for some time until the disagreement was resolved and Kern officials were allowed to be in charge of the study of the crash.

One can only imagine the activity on, above and below the local mountain tops that week. The Frazier Mountain area has had more than it's share of airplane crashes since then as well.

In later years a Navy jet fighter crashed in the Tehachapi Mountains on Tejon Ranch. The LOS ANGELES TIMES of August 5, 1961 reported:

> *"The jet plane plummeted into a mountainside after its pilot had bailed out because of engine trouble. Lt. E. E. Luetschwager received minor injuries when he parachuted to the ground at Wheeler Ridge. The fire caused by the jet's crash is raging in El Paso Creek canyon* (near the Tejon Ranch old headquarters). *More than 100 firefighters were on the fire lines in the inaccessible terrain – some flown in by helicopter."*

XXI - LOOKOUT TOWER EXPERIENCES

In 1910, range and forest fires burned across this nation. Caused by humans, drought, railroads and lightning, three million acres burned in three days through Idaho and Montana alone. This disaster brought about the emphasis to control the problem. An effort to put roads, lookout towers and improved communication into the National Forests was begun.

The first lookout towers in the National Forests were erected about 1915. At first they were little more than platforms in the tops of large trees where you didn't want to be when the wind was blowing. These *"outlook trees"* soon became *"Lookout Towers"* built with a staircase and enclosed viewing area. Lookout stations or towers first served as fire observatories and a place of rescue. They included a structure built on the highest point of the mountain that served as the observatory. Some included living quarters in the tower but most provided a cabin on the ground nearby. The first lookout station or tower in the Los Padres forest was built on Frazier Mountain at 8,013 feet at some date between 1910 and 1917 as both dates have been found.

Upper right is the first lookout station on Frazier Mtn and to the lower left is the new and improved second lookout on Frazier Mtn – a tower – built in the 1920's

A second lookout tower was located in the south of the District at 6,935 feet on Thorn Point above Thorn Meadows from where the ocean and islands could be seen. This area was named for a U.S.G.S. Surveyor, William H. Thorn, who surveyed the forest boundary in 1904-1906.

The Thorn Point Lookout Tower – 1950. The cabin at the base of the tower was available for Forest Service employees, hikers and hunters. (Harry Thompson photo)

Herb Lemmer operated the Thorn Point Lookout for many years in the 1940's & 50's (Harry Thompson photo)

Local reporter, Grace Bradley Toenjes, wrote an article about the Thorn Point Lookout for the BAKERSFIELD CALIFORNIAN of July 12, 1970. In it Grace recorded some interesting information about how supplies were taken to the lookout tower. Mrs. Toenjes traveled along with Tom Cashman, the U.S. Forest Service fire prevention technician, who was responsible for purchasing and transporting the supplies to Thorn Point. Stationed at the tower was Ruth Albee, related to the owner of the MOUNTAIN ENTERPRISE. Ruth would call in her order for supplies by means of a field phone, Cashman would do the shopping and make the trip to Thorn Point once every six weeks.

To accomplish the trip Tom would first transport the mules, *"Carol"* and *"Red"*, to a Forest Service corral three and a half miles from the lookout. Early the next morning he would load a Forest Service truck with the supplies and mail for Ruth, put *"Teddy"* his palomino horse into a horse trailer, and in this case a horse for Grace as well, and drive to the Thorn Meadow corral. There he would load each of the mules with 150 to 175 pounds of supplies which included water and butane gas. Grace wrote:

> *"The journey took 1½ to 2 hours. A large portion of the path consists of switchbacks. Many peculiar trees may be seen, with one huge tree grown around an enormous boulder. When Thorn Point Lookout comes into view, 'Susie', Ruth Albee's German shepherd begins to sound the alarm. Ruth prepared lunch for us and Tom fixed any broken objects that needed his attention.*
>
> *Thorn Point Lookout was established in the 1930's. The structure was transported in pieces by helicopter and pack mules. An all-weather station shack, used during World War II for an airplane sighting point, is still standing and made useful by Ruth as a storage shed.*
>
> *Mrs. Albee is completely alone at Thorn Point except for Susie's present stay. There is no electricity though she has a butane powered refrigerator. Ruth claims she much prefers life this way. Indeed she has spent most of her life in the great outdoors. Before coming to Thorn Point, she previously spent four years in San Mateo County with the State Division of Forestry. An article appearing in the National Geographic magazine of May 1942, tells how Ruth, her former husband Bill, and their three children hiked 260 miles in the Yukon wilds. She also once spent seven years in Alaska and two of those years were in an Eskimo village.*

Presently Ruth takes a daily two hour hike, watches for smoke and sends weather reports to Ojai, Santa Barbara and Frazier Park. In her spare time she reads, knits, writes letters and makes baskets of pine needles. On a clear day Ruth can even see the trees on the Channel Islands off the coast of Santa Barbara

We made the return trip to the Chuchupate Ranger Station leaving Carol and Red in the Thorn Meadows corral for Cashman to retrieve the next day. Tom brings with him Ruth's mail and the trash to dispose of."

The forest was closed to public use during the World War II with military units using various locations for training and relaxation away from hot valley military bases. Following the bombing of Pearl Harbor in December of 1941, the lookout towers of the Los Padres Forest became an integral part of the war effort due to their strategic location to the newly constructed West Coast military installations. The towers were manned year around, twenty-four hours a day, by civilian members of the *"Aircraft Warning System"* with food, fuel and water parachuted in during the difficult winter months. It took real determination for these observers to stay on the lonely mountain peaks. The people accepting the challenge were retired couples, men who did not qualify for the service, women wanting to do their part while their men were overseas, miners, and often the forest service guards and their families. Locally, Ruby Hensley, a widow, accepted the call to serve in this capacity. Sometimes Ruby would take her children with her but they stayed with families in Frazier Park when school was in session. Ruby later became the postmaster of Frazier Park.

Geraldine Hensley at Frazier Mtn Lookout in the 1940's
(Hensley Family photo)

In March of 1942 ten posts were manned as military lookouts in the Los Padres Forest. By August of that year thirty-six had been established throughout this forest, strategically located along the California coast. Most of these lookout towers continued in operation until the threat of foreign invasion lessened. Observation posts were discontinued in June 1944. Because of flight patterns, so many planes flew over some of the lookouts that it was almost impossible to identify, record and radio them all in. The Frazier Mountain Tower was one such high reporting location with over 500 planes a month. Children of the AWS observers, as young as five, prided themselves on being able to identify the type of aircraft, sometimes by only the sound before they could even see it. In the 1940's and 50's there were as many as 8,000 towers in use nationwide affording the country a good deal of security when needed.

This poem by an observer, Grace Radonich, in the Eldorado area of the forest expressed the responsibility of these faithful workers well:

"The East wind whistles, we keep very mum
For nothing counts but the motor hum...
He's giving his all, so let's you and I
Help keep him safe up there in the sky...
Stifle that yawn, up with the chin,
Don't sleep on the job and our boys will win."

Curtis Newman recalled an intriguing spy story about this area of Frazier Mountain during WWII. Mr. Newman said:

> *"In the early 1940's an older, tall, thin woman with steel gray hair pitched her tent near the entrance to the Chuchupate Ranger Station – near where there is an old round trough today. She was very intelligent and spoke with a German accent. Her 'hobby' was photography and she had the most advanced of camera equipment. She would photograph birds, children, scenery and more. Military vehicles often passed her tent on their way up the mountain for training and to their electronic station on the top of Frazier Mt. and were no doubt photographed as well.*
>
> *Before the colder months of winter came on, the Forest Service got her to move her tent using the excuse that they felt it would be too cold for her to survive camping there much longer. She moved into Frazier Park just north of the rock houses on Los Padres Drive where she was arrested a short time later. It wasn't certain what she was arrested for but the local rumor was that she was a spy."*

Ronald McLane remembered that during World War II, two pilots from Minter Field near Bakersfield flew south over Frazier Mountain and somehow didn't clear the mountain. Just clipping it they were able to safely let their BT-13's (trainers) slide into a ravine. It was near the Frazier Mountain lookout tower so they were quickly detected. The men made it safely out but others were sent back to remove equipment from the planes, break the windshields so the sun wouldn't reflect on them, and spray the planes green so they wouldn't be noticed from the air. This was done so that if another plane went down in that area those doing an air search would know that that wreckage had already been located. Men were usually sent in to remove the wreckage when convenient, again so as to not throw off future searches.

A rare occurrence was recorded by two Aircraft Warning System observers still stationed at the Frazier Lookout on January 30, 1945. The following is what Norman Brice, an artist and illustrator, and his wife Myrtle, recorded of that night:

> *"2:00 A.M. - Line check. Blizzard increasing in violence, wind due east, 55 to 65 MPH, snowing, also fog very dense. Visibility 100 feet or less, weather very bad. Believe this to be worst storm of season.*
>
> *3:15 A.M. - Discovered very brilliant white light shining thru storm toward lookout, bearing 52 degrees NE at horizon level that is, at eye level. Country in this direction un-inhabited, no roads or buildings, elevation 8,000 feet. Was puzzled as to how any light no matter how strong could shine thru such dense fog and snow, as light appeared on high ridge about four miles NE of lookout.*
>
> *3:23 A.M. - Phoned Ranger Station, asked night operator Yvonne Tifft to awaken Jack Curran Assistant District Ranger. We discussed the possibility that light might be a white magnesium flare from a grounded plane that had made a forced landing and that it should be reported to the Army Filter board.*
>
> *3:25 A.M. - At this time, my wife who was off duty and sleeping down below in the AWS shelter, a separate building, came up in the tower to report additional lights showing thru the storm not visible to me. There new lights appeared much further down on the same ridge and much nearer the lookout approximately 2 1/2 miles due east and 1 1/2 miles south of the first light.*

3:35 A.M. - I now talked to Mr. Meyer the District Ranger who reported the above to Army Filter board for investigation when we were unable to determine a satisfactory reason for these mysterious lights.

3:50 A.M. - I made final check up from catwalk with binoculars. The first light having burned steadily for nearly an hour with equal intensity, never wavering or moving an inch from its first reported position, as I watched thru the glasses, disappeared and I reported it to Ranger Meyer. Ten minutes later the light or rather lights came back on in the same position just as before while other lights appeared on the ground in the snow. Now on all sides of the lookout beginning with two bright white lights about the size of very strong flash lights held waist high above the snow, one slightly behind the other so as it appeared to be two people on the road SW of the lookout wading thru the deep snow. When first seen these lights were 150 yards west of the lookout. We watched them from the catwalk preparing to hail them for identification before permitting them up in the tower. They disappeared within 30 yards of us.

Reported this to Ranger Meyer who remained on the phone advising us. I reported I was sure there were two people from perhaps a wrecked plane but could not understand their disappearance so close to the tower. It was then that a large pine tree about 30 yards began to light up even as I watched, first a high branch on the north side and then gradually the whole tree from top to bottom taking about 15 to 20 minutes to be completely covered on all sides. The lights appeared in long strings as the one took 40 or 50 foot lengths of wire and attached light globes the size of small hen's eggs at fairly regular intervals of a foot or so and flung them each string of light haphazardly every which way across and around the tree, much as one would light an outdoor Christmas tree.

Each light was separate and distinct and glowed with a strong white light and were so numerous it was impossible to count them. In this case a deep blue-green haze developed around the more light branches. The above tree was some 100 feet or so from observers on catwalk. High wind and snow did not affect lights which when once appeared burned steadily by the hour. On turning away from this we observed many lights coming on all around the lookout, some were single, separate, in the middle of open spaces on the ground, bare of everything but snow. Others were on tree trunks and thru the branches in-

numerable. All shown brilliantly thru the fog even at times when trees and other objects disappeared completely in a particularly heavy gust of wind and snow.

4:00 A.M. - I now reported to Ranger Meyer that lights were appearing on the catwalk within reach of my hand. First my wife noticed that some wooden uprights attached to the railing of the catwalk were glowing brilliantly near their ends. At this time the insulators (porcelain) on the radio antennae (vertical) suddenly glowed with an intense pure white light, these were only a foot away from the railing of the catwalk and were within easy reaching distance. There was no trace of a bluish-green haze around these. They were dazzling white and since the tower was in total darkness, the effect was most unusual. The numerous wires, radio, telephone and tower brace wires at all times remained invisible.

It was now that the 2"x4" cross pieces or top ends of uprights became brilliantly lighted. These cross bars (wood) 18 inches long had square sawn ends from each corner of which there are four to an end, a separate cone of fire about six inches long projected from each so there were now eight distinct cones of fire. These fluctuated at high speed and were of an intense blue light with a small white center and resembled in size, color and fluctuation the standard size plumber's or tinsmith's blow torch. These cones were white fire the size of a thimble at the small neck of the cone where attached and gradually faded to an intense bluish-green on the broad end of the cone. These were the only lights that appeared to flare in unusually heavy gusts of wind.

Many of the lights were within easy reach of the observer and permitted the closest inspection. Several times I held my gloved hand to their outer edges. I was under the impression that had I held up my hand, lights would have appeared on all five fingers. I had intended to place my bare hand in a number of the light cones, especially at their base, to see if there would be any feeling or sensation but did not do so because the intense cold quickly numbed my hand. The lights were not on all corners of the lookout and did not always seek the higher projections. None appeared on the lightning rods and none on the corners where lightning rods passed within a few inches. The telephone poles next to the lookout, having rods, did not show lights, however, our flag pole being of iron pipe showed a large brilliant white light on its top. This appeared to be of the intensity of a fifty-watt bulb light surrounded by a blue green haze the side of a basketball. This was also very steady in its intensity and glowed for hours.

I might add that about forty minutes after the first light was sighted, there were two vivid lightning flashes about a minute or so apart. All this time the storm, the worst we have experienced, was at its height, intensely cold, extremely high wind from due east, blinding snow fall, at times everything except the lights being blotted out. The dense fog and high wind did not seem to effect them in the least or lesson their brilliance. The cones of light on the catwalk flared out in all directions, seemingly unaffected by the heaviest gusts of wind.

It may be noted that the storm that produced this phenomena was one that with the exception of several brief periods of comparative calm, started from the northwest and completely covered all points of the compass with equal intensity until five days later, ending up where it began, in the northwest. The wind exceptionally high, gradually shifting from northwest to west, southwest to south to southeast, east to northeast, northeast to north, etc: snowing all the while. We observed the above lights from the cat walk for some two an a half hours after which time we retired indoors, first phoning Ranger Meyer that I believed I had solved the mystery be recalling an illustration I had once studied in my school geography showing strange lights on the masts and spars of sailing ships known as St. Elmo's Fire. How much longer the display lasted I do not know, as all our windows had been thickly iced over preventing further observation."

A *"St. Elmo's Fire"* is produced by static electricity creating startling flashes of light during unusual snowstorms and under certain conditions at sea. Such an electrical phenomenon has never again been recorded in this area so the account that Mr. & Mrs. Brice have left us is very appreciated. The snowstorm they experienced was one of the heavier snowfalls ever recorded in these mountains leaving deep snow all the way down Grapevine Canyon.

Another unusual mountain top experience of strange lights was recalled by former Frazier Park resident, Gene Weigel back in the early 1960's. It was a beautiful Fall day about dusk when Gene and his future wife, Nancy, had gone up on Scott Russell Road to Tecuya Ridge. Gene recalled:

"While there we noticed some lights reflecting up in the trees. The trees seemed to be turning an iridescent whitish green. When we looked for the source, the light seemed to be coming

> *from Black Bob or Salt Creek Canyon but it so flooded the area that we couldn't focus on it or even shield our eyes to see exactly where it was coming from. It was like a thousand carbon arch lights coming in waves, maybe two miles below. It was like looking into the sun. We decided it was best to leave."*

When Gene later shared the experience with a friend who lived at the old YMCA Camp near the *"Y"*, the friend said he had seen the same thing in San Emigdio Canyon some years later.

Back to the lookout towers, the couple known to longest serve as peacetime seasonal lookouts at the Frazier Mountain Tower were a retired couple, Charley and Hazel Upham from Cuyama. The Uphams thoroughly enjoyed their summer stays on top of Frazier Mountain with the magnificent view over into the Antelope Valley, the wildflowers blooming all summer and being able to watch fireworks from Bakersfield to Los Angeles on the Fourth of July. They began their mountaintop adventure in 1964 and continued on for sixteen years during which time Hazel was known to always have homemade pie ready for visitors to the lookout.

Hazel was the official clerk of the tower and gained notoriety in September of 1964 when she spotted a small column of smoke way over in the Angeles National Forest on the south slopes of Liebre Mountain some fifteen miles from her tower. She gave the men of the Los Angeles County Fire Department at the Quail Lake Station the exact location and they found a deserted campfire with a smoke column barely a foot in diameter that could have soon taken the entire hillside. The men of the Forest Service affectionately called her *"Hawkeye"* thereafter. Charley and Hazel would spend the summer months on the mountain and the winters at their ranch in Cuyama. They retired to a mobile home on Mt. Pinos Way in 1980.

In the 1960's the Frazier mountaintop also served as a repeater station for Union Oil, the Air National Guard, the FBI and television stations from Bakersfield and Santa Barbara.

The use of lookout towers was discontinued in the early 1990's because of improved communication systems, aerial reconnaissance and because the greatly increased populations in and around the forests seemed to locate and report fires as quickly as someone in a tower could.

Frazier Mtn Tower as photographed by Harry Thompson in 1950

When the Frazier Mountain tower burned in a fire in 1952, an old tower, built in 1936, was moved from Camuesa Peak in Santa Barbara County to the site and is still there today

XXII - FIRES IN THE FOREST

One of the primary purposes of the forest reserves was to control burning so that the cover of the land in the watersheds would not be destroyed. The most valuable resource in the forest is the water. Some one and a half million acre-feet of water flows from the local forest watershed into reservoirs and lakes within five miles of the forest boundary each year. Pyramid Lake, Tejon Lake (formerly Castac Lake), Buena Vista Lake and Lake Piru are now the major collecting basins of water in and near the Mt. Pinos District. When the trees, brush and undergrowth burn, the water runs too quickly off the mountains and hillsides causing a lack of moisture for future growth, erosion, silting in dams and reservoirs, as well as serious flooding to private land owners.

Fire management is critical for the protection of the watershed. The first government officers examining forest reserve lands during the late 1890's and early 1900's recorded that most of the area now a part of the Los Padres Forest had been burned over at some time during the preceding two or three decades. The earliest people used fire to clear away the brush to improve their hunting and food gathering. As the ranchos and homesteads were settled, the cattlemen and sheepherders used fire to clear brush as they left the mountains in the Fall so that when they returned the next summer there would be plenty of green grass for grazing. Farmers also burned the brush to clear fields in the foothills.

This indiscriminate burning did improve with the creation of the forest reserves but it was the casual visitor that became the next greatest threat. By the early 1900's the forests began to overflow with the new influx of people who had moved to the cities of Southern California and still wanted to experience the more primitive life of the generations before. The ever-increasing use of the gas-propelled vehicles brought more and more campers, picnickers and sportsmen. Notes in the rangers diaries of the day indicated that one of their daily activities was putting out the campfires left burning.

Well over a thousand fires were recorded in the Mt. Pinos District and the surrounding area between 1900 – 1960 though most of these were less than an acre. Many were caused by lightning but even more were caused by careless humans. The major fires to affect the Pinos/Frazier area in the past have been recorded by the Forest Service. Some are shown here in relation to various areas of the mountains as follows:

Alamo Mtn - 2000 acres - 1902
Alamo Mtn - 1160 acres - 1923
Gold Hills - 3340 acres - 1951

Tejon Pass (Foley's) - 300 acres - 1908
Tejon Pass (Foley's) - 11 acres - 1926
Tejon Pass - 55 acres - 1927
(Tejon Ranger Station lost)
Tejon Pass (Foley's) - 172 acres - 1928
Ridge Rt - 2816 acres - 1928
Caswell - 17 acres - 1936
(Gorman Post Road)

Lebec - 160 acres - 1907
Mesa Valley - 600 acres - 1911
Lebec - 1940 acres - 1912
Tejon Ranch - 800 acres - 1915
Grapevine - 1920 acres - 1920

Frazier Pk - 400 acres - 1930
Frazier Pk - 36 acres - 1935
Frazier Pk - 600 acres - 1951
Frazier Pk - 560 acres - 1954
Frazier Pk - 45 acres - 1956

Frazier Mtn - 640 acres - 1921
Frazier Mtn - 1650 acres - 1928
Frazier Mtn - 1240 acres - 1941
Chuchupate - 2370 acres - 1947
Chuchupate - 320 acres - 1948

Lockwood - 19 acres - 1919
Mutau Mtn - 1700 acres - 1940
Lockwood - 4130 acres - 1942
Mutau Mtn - 130 acres - 1948
Brown Mtn - 900 acres - 1957

San Emigdio - 1000 acres - 1908
Pleito Cyn - 1280 acres - 1919
Cuddy Val - 80 acres - 1919
San Emigdio - 280 acres - 1924
San Emigdio - 12,545 ac - 1927
Mil Potrero - 34 acres - 1934
Black Bob - 140 acres - 1940
Mil Potrero - 97 acres - 1956
Apache 212 acres - 1958

These records seem to be insignificant compared to the mega fires taking place as this book is being written. Considering the methods used to fight fires in the early years of the Forest, those firefighters of long ago did a commendable job of limiting the growth of a fire. Of interest, however, is that no significant fires have been recorded on Mt. Pinos – possibly due to the protective powers of the Native spirits that are believed to exist there.

Following the Alamo fire of 1902 the ranger (Don Cuddy?) wrote: *"Fire is all out and I am glad of it for I am tired out myself"*. Mrs. Cuddy also remembered her husband had to recruit two hundred miners from the Lockwood Borax Mines to fight that fire. She said the miners were willing workers (or ordered to fight the fire) as the fire was in an area where they obtained timber for fuel, mine shaft beams and lumber for buildings. Even the women of the area did their part to fight the fires by carrying food and water by horseback to the men on the line.

The BAKERSFIELD MORNING ECHO of August 1, 1907 reported on the fire northwest of Lebec as follows:

> *"Word was received in town* (Bakersfield) *late last night that a fierce fire has been raging in the San Emidio country since Sunday afternoon. The fire started in the O'Neill Canyon, about two miles west* (southwest) *of Fort Tejon, and took a westerly direction to the Tecuya, cleaning up everything in its way. A large force of men have been working continually in an effort to head off the flames and they expect to meet with success before the fire reaches the San Emidio ranch, but thousands of acres of wild feed have already been destroyed and at last reports the fire was far from being under control.*
>
> *The origin of the fire is unknown but it is more than likely that smoldering embers left by campers, of whom there are many in that section of the country, were carried into the dry grass by the heavy wind which prevails there at times. The fire would have to burn over a great amount of territory to reach the San Emidio ranch and as no word had been received at the office of the Land Company* (Kern County Land Company, the owner of the Ranch) *last night regarding the fire, it is hardly thought possible that the company's property there is in danger."*

A July 1930 issue of the Automobile Club's magazine TOURING TOPICS carried the wonderful interview with early ranger Jacinto Damien Reyes also mentioned in earlier chapters. He explained some of his experiences with fires as follows:

"Fire, of course, heads the list of nearly every forest ranger's adventures, and I regret to say that the fire record of my district, and the whole Santa Barbara Forest for that matter, has been disastrous.

I know the horrors of forest fires only too well. I've fought so many fires it would take a long time to even mention them all. I've seen fires when tongues of flame shot through the air like bolts of lightning. I've seen such bolts of flame leap right out of the main fire with a roar like thunder, shoot through the air and set fire to new tinder as much as a quarter of a mile away. When a fire fighting crew gets caught in that sort of stuff, there's nothing much to do but to run, and then try to check the flames at some more favorable point.

If you really want to see what a good fire is like, you should see it get into a stand of big juniper trees! Juniper trees can be as green as cienega grass, but they're all full of resin and inflammable oil. When the fire hits 'em they go as if they're soaked with gasoline. And, late in the summer when they get pretty dry they're about the same as gunpowder. If you're near one when the fire gets close to it, you'd better high tail for open ground. A dry juniper literally explodes in a hot fire, throws burning embers in all directions, and with the most terrific heat imaginable. They also make a dense black smoke, and that smoke seems to be largely gas that keeps on burning high in the air."

Photo from the Touring Topics article of July 1930

There were years when overworked forest officers toiled day and night from one fire to the next. On one such fire north of Ojai in 1917, which burned 30,000 acres, Reyes was credited with saving thirty-two trapped men from almost certain death. A newspaper pictured him with an axe in one hand and a machete in the other clearing a path through the brush for the fire-fighters with the caption: *"it was a feat of strength possible only for a woodsman of Reyes' physique."* Two other rangers reportedly herded 152 men over a cliff just ahead of rapidly advancing flames caused by very high searing winds. Some of the men had their clothing scorched and others badly torn in the mad scramble for safety. Other men were forced to take refuge in nearby creeks when the fire blast went over them.

J. D. Reyes at work

In 1921, Ranger J. D. Reyes spent thirty-five consecutive days on fires and had to go to Maricopa and raid the pool halls and saloons for more help. As the Automobile Club article continued, J.D. Reyes described one of those fires:

> *"I'm rather proud of the fact that in all the fire fighting I've done I've never yet lost a man. Of course, I've had quite a number of men pretty badly burned, and have been burned plenty myself. In the Big Pine fire of 1921, I sent in a rush call for 200 men. They arrived ... anything that could be recruited in a hurry. I had to dismiss about half of those men. Some didn't have proper shoes or clothing, and others didn't have the backbones, hearts, or lungs to stand such hard work in the combination of fire, dust, smoke, grime, ashes and altitude.*

After I'd sifted the men to those who were able to stand the torture, we fought that fire from the fourth of August until the seventh of September. We worked like tigers with very little sleep, insufficient food, and trying to keep alive on coffee. Men fighting forest fires always drink barrels of coffee...gallons of it every day.

But no man can keep going forever on coffee, and we were all getting pretty well worn down when a sudden change of wind trapped the whole gang of us in a canyon. The fire kept gaining on us until it looked as if we were all set for a date with the priest. There seemed to be just one desperate chance to escape, and that was to dash through the fire into the burned area. I gave orders for all the men to tie wet cloths over their faces. The water in our canteens was so hot by that time we couldn't drink it. Then I directed the crew to the one spot of the fire line that seemed to have the least fire, told them to follow me, and run for their lives. We all got through, although most of us were pretty badly singed, and we had several serious cases of burned feet.

The fire problem is still, and probably always will be the nightmare of every forest ranger's life. There are so many ways for fires to get started, and only one way of putting them out. Spontaneous combustion from smut in hay and grain crops causes a good many fires. Lightning causes some. Carelessness with fire by people in the forest causes most of them, and I'm convinced that pack rats are to blame for a lot of fires. I've seen several fires start in unoccupied cabins and around camp sites where nobody was camping That leads me to believe that pack rats start fires by getting matches, caching them in the nests, and later chewing them.

I also know of several fires that I believe were deliberately set. In 1928 a fellow set a fire trap down here in Cuyama Canyon about eight miles below my station. By rare good luck a hunter found it and reported it to me before it went off. The sportsman was poking around in the brush after a rabbit when he found a bundle of about sixty matches set heads up in a pile of dry grass, leaves, and twigs. Above the matches and fastened to a forked stick was a lens such as used in the head of a flash light. This contrivance was arranged so the sun would strike the lens and concentrate the rays on the match heads about one o'clock in the afternoon. The hunter found it about ten o'clock in the morning. We tested the lens on the matches and found it took about three seconds to set them off. It seems the person responsible wasn't a fire fiend, but was making a pasture for his stock."

William *"Bill"* DeLancey, a Lockwood Valley homesteader of the 1920's, has left us with this excellent description of an early day fire on Alamo Mtn. – possibly the 1923 fire. Bill writes:

"It takes only one hot day of climbing around on a stony mountain, fighting forest fires to wear a man down to nubbin. If he stays in his clothes for five days, stumbling down to the creek only to drink, eat, or sleep fitfully, he ends up dead on his feet. Merely breathing the acrid smoke is enough to do him in.

Every able bodied man from far and near becomes involved in fires, and our fighting equipment was primitive in the early 1920's. Firebreaks were made by gangs welding shovel, pick and axe, getting in their best licks around dawn, or late in the afternoon when the wind stood still.

One phase of a bad five-day fire on Alamo Mt. had its comic opera side, while other angles of it turned out exciting, and very dangerous. Every hour was downright tough physically.

The smoke plume of this fire was first noticed by someone at an outside picnic, attended by everybody in the Lockwood. Luckily, the food had been consumed and we'd started a ball game in the canyon of Center Creek. Bert Snedden, the cattleman, took a long look at the smoke, then issued his valuable judgment."

Lockwood Valley picnic – 1920's

"'That fire,' he said, 'is about eight miles from here. It's the north slope of Alamo Mt.'. With that he gathered his family into his automobile and sped away. He'd be putting together a big pack string ... and no time to lose. His ranch lay halfway to the fire, in the southeast corner of the valley, where Lockwood Creek made rapids in a gloomy canyon.

Leaving our vehicles at Snedden's and striking out on foot, we followed the rough creek bottom between nearly perpendicular walls. On the left soared Frazier Mt., and straight ahead, 3½ miles southeast, smoke from the Alamo enveloped the whole region. Snedden had worked fast. His packhorses overtook us, and hurried on."

Samuel Snedden leads pack horses to fire area

"At the junction of Lockwood Creek and the larger Piru Creek, we stared across the latter, up the side of Alamo Mt., at a most remarkable scene. The fire had cut a swath half way to the top of the steep, stony slope, and heading toward it moved a slow parade. Some forty teenage boys, herded from behind by Head Ranger Virgil DeLapp and another Ranger on horseback, picked their reluctant way upward over the rocks. The kids looked ready to drop in their tracks. But it was their costumes that caused us to hurriedly wade the cool, plunging Piru. We had to have a closer look.

When the single-file marchers took time out for a breather, Wes (Green – also from Lockwood) *and I caught up. If we, too, were breathless, it was from laughing. The boys wore white flannel trousers, white shoes, brilliant blazers, and straw hats! Los Angeles high school boys, they had been pulled from two buses headed north to a baseball game at Bakersfield."* (They no doubt were commandeered when their buses made a rest stop at Gorman or Lebec while traveling the old Ridge Route.)

Ranger DeLapp leads baseball team up mountain to fight the fire

"Not even their parents knew where they were, and already their clothes had taken a beating by catching on the brush along several miles of uphill trails. But the worst was about to come.

Wes and I had our instructions from DeLapp. 'Take twenty of these boys and go east along the mountain to where you see that isolated smoke over there about half-a-mile. A big, smoldering pine tree has rolled down into an unburned draw, and if it isn't kept under control it might fire up a whole new area. There's a small spring nearby. Carry water from it in your canteens. Clear the brush all around it, and make these boys work.'

This last was the hardest part of the assignment, because outright mutiny lay in every well-dressed young heart. We ourselves cringed visibly when they finally stepped off the trail into at least three inches of powdery black dust left behind by the consuming fire. That was the end ... the last good-bye to their finery.

The boys proved absolutely useless. They hid out wherever they could, and hated to spend one drop of water on the log. So little flowed from the spring that they could drink every lonesome trickle that worked up through the stones. The log wasn't burning much, so Wes and I managed to keep its flames soothed down.

It was there we came so close to becoming fire victims that our escape still seems like a miracle.

The spring lay in a sag, or bench (flat or level area) *on the mountainside, one of several such benches. While we were tending the log, a whisp of smoke seemed to come and go almost as I looked at it, rising from some bench lower down. At that point the unburned pinyons clung in close formation against the mountain, and just above them, a strip of tangled second-growth scrub mahogany. We hurried to the edge of the bench, saw that whisps were rising periodically from somewhere below, and forced our way straight down through the dense, head-high tangle. We would douse this little blaze with our canteen ... we believed.*

Suddenly we were trapped. From close below us a yellow flame jumped up the steep hill, straight at us. In our hasty retreat, we almost panicked. It was catching us fast, and as if by agreement we stopped, breathless, above a four-foot-wide opening. This blaze, luckily isolated, had traveled only a few rods. We faced it waiting, pressed back into the chaparral, then hurled ourselves down through the flame wall when it dimmed slightly at the opening."

deLancey and Green dive over the flames

"Falling deep into the hot ashes, we rolled and writhed, finally getting to our feet, blackened, hot all over, but not quite scorched. Our lungs hurt, I couldn't see through my glasses, and for some minutes we staggered around in an agonizing daze. The fire grew hotter, ran on up to our opening at the log, then died away. The school kids had fled to the creek bottom, where they were having a cool and noisy swim.

Now it was sunset, so we stumbled back to the main trail and down the mountain for supper. Downstream, a jack camp had been organized on the stony bench beside the Piru. All around were trees and greenery, and dreamy music from the tumbling trout stream. Along with some 60 other men, we slept among the rocks, and liked it. The forest fire seemed to have died out, but this was only an illusion.

Next morning we found out what keeps a Western forest fire going. It's the numerous little whirlwinds, or miniature cyclones, that carry sparks into the unburned timer.

By the light of a strawberry dawn, we stood on the mountain and looked carefully around us. Large sections of forest had been burned off the north slope, but nowhere could any smoke or fire be seen. The air stood deathly still.

Then the sun came up. This heated the deep ashes, and within minutes, we were anxiously watching four or five newly-hatched whirlwinds rising along the burned-over strips. The wind devils crossed them, stirring up small flames along the edges of the green, tinder - dry pinyons and pine trees.

Armed with shovels, we would rush in, throw dirt on the flames and look around for more. Men with axes would chop and clear, and for an hour the whole mountain seemed to be under control. Then suddenly it wasn't. 'Fire down there to the north-west!' someone would shout, and up would tower a long torch ... a blazing pinyon ... right in the middle of a thick and beautiful stand. Some whirlwind had tossed it, a red-hot tinder."

Men with shovels and axes, the only equipment available, fight the fire

"The Mexicans were by all odds the best fire fighters. A dozen of them, migrants to and from the crop lands of the San Joaquin, had been grabbed as they drove their trucks or trailers along the main highway. Leaving their families at the roadside, they worked uncomplainingly and efficiently at the job in hand.

All of us were thirsty, all the time. It turned extremely hot. But your thirst had to be fierce to hike down over those sharp rocks to the creek, then climb up again on the 45 degree grade. You know too that if the fire crossed the Piru and touched off Frazier Mt., the whole country would go right up in smoke. There was no time for comforts.

Along in the afternoon of the second day, Wes and I heard a rising murmur of voices, lifting along the fire line. The sound had a note of cheer. Then we saw a horseman emerge from some timber below us. He was leading two stout pack horses, laden with huge bidons of cool water. Moving slowly, the man doled out his burden to the grateful crews.

Somebody near us exclaimed, 'Why, that's old Tom Harris!' This news made me prick up my ears, and I waited with much interest for this distinguished 'water boy' to come up close. Here, I knew, was one of the almost legendary figures of the

Far West. He still worked his one-man gold mine on Frazier Mt., but I had never seen him.

When Tom Harris reached us on the fire line, we noticed that he wore two modest-sized pearl handled revolvers. As we drank water and visited briefly, Tom suddenly had the gun from his left holster in his hand, and stood pointing it down to the west.

'When I was up here real early yesterday morning,' he said, 'a black bear came running out ahead of the fire and went right down into that timber over there.' Then he put away his gleaming pointer, and soon was handing out water to more thirsty workers. That was our introduction to one of the most colorful men of his time. (There is more on Tom Harris in Chapter VII of this book.)

On the fifth day of this man-killing work, Wes and I, with three others, were given the dangerous assignment that stopped the fire for keeps. We'd notice a plane fly around overhead, and shortly thereafter Head Ranger DeLapp came riding our way. He led us down into the bottom near the camp beside the Piru.

There the canyon narrowed into a slot, with almost perpendicular slopes of densely growing pinyons, rising out of sight on both sides. We were spaced along the base of the Alamo side, and handed matches. On signal, we each touched off a backfire in the dry rats' nests and tinder under the pinyons.

Each of us had a tremendous boulder to run behind. Otherwise we would have cooked. With incredible fury and heat, flames leaped 50 feet at a time, consuming the mountain in a roaring furnace.

The risk of this strategy was in its heat setting fire to Frazier Mt., just across the stream at our backs. But the breeze held right for once. Even the noise seemed frightening, but soon the choking heat was all over. The whole beautiful mountain now stood naked.

All we had to do next was to walk 3 1/2 miles back up hill to the car at Snedden's."

On June 24, 1927, the LOS ANGELES TIMES reported on a fire burning in the San Emigdio area – whether that means San

Emigdio Mountain or San Emigdio Ranch is unclear. The article read:

> *"The San Emidio grass fire broke into the worst conflagration seen in Kern county in years when it went roaring out of control today and swept into the Santa Barbara National Forest with a flame belching on a five-mile front. It is estimated that the flames have burned over an area of 15,000 acres. Two hundred men, directed by national and State forest rangers and fire wardens, are blending all their efforts in keeping the fire from spreading. The front is eating steadily into the higher timber levels, aided by a stiff breeze that is carrying it in a southeasterly direction.*
>
> *Unless brought under control, the fire, believed to have been of incendiary origin, will be carried into the wooded area between Frazier Mountain Park and Lebec. Several homesteaders' cabins have been burned and their occupants forced to flee for their lives.*
>
> *Today the Ridge Route highway was choked with smoke from the conflagration, and hundreds of motorists stopped at the Tejon Pass Ranger Station to inquire as to the safety of the highway ahead. Officers at the ranger station declared that the highway is in no danger at present.*
>
> *State Forester Pratt today authorized the inspector and three rangers on duty at the fire to press into service sufficient men to bring it under control. Sixty men are on the fire line yesterday and the inspector informed him forty more will be needed. When it was found that it would be necessary to reimburse the fire fighters, Pratt authorized and expense up to $500* ($5 each!)."

Oldtimers remembered well the fire of 1928 which burned the north face of Frazier Mountain above the new little community of Frazier Mountain Park. It was said to have burned up and over the top of the mountain in only nine minutes. On July 14, The LOS ANGELES TIMES carried news of the 1928 fire as follows:

> *"Flames fanned by a west-by-northerly wind late last night were sweeping over Frazier Mountain in the Santa Barbara National Forest, and rangers leading nearly 200 fire fighters reported the fire as the most menacing of the season. Explosion of a gasoline stove in a cabin in the Frazier Mountain Park district, shortly after noon yesterday, sent sprays of liquid fire into surrounding brush and by midnight last night 1500 acres*

> *of timber and brush had been swept over, reports from the fire zone said.*
>
> *District Forest Supervisor Delapp, of the Tejon district, in charge of the fire fighters, reported the flames sweeping west toward the Ojai district, but expressed hope that additional men being rushed to the scene from Ventura county will be able to halt the flames progress in that direction. At a late hour only four cabins, including the one in which the fire started, had been destroyed, but forty others are reported menaced.*
>
> *Thirty men and women campers from Los Angeles, who were in the vicinity of the explosion, took up the burden of fighting the flames but soon were relieved of the work by rangers, and all of the former in an exhausted condition were taken from the zone. Campers about Frazier Mountain Park Lake, one report declared, were forced to flee for their lives. Another report is that there is a possibility of the flames surrounding a mountain settlement from which the campers have not all had opportunity to escape. Lebec Lodge* (Lebec), *on the Ridge Route, and about six miles from the fire, reported that some of the campers had arrived there on foot, leaving everything behind.*
>
> *Oil companies and county authorities of Kern county were reported rushing help and it was expected that 800 men with equipment would be on the grounds by early this morning."*

As cigarette smoking gained in popularity, a 1933 issue of CALIFORNIA HIGHWAYS AND PUBLIC WORKS they reported:

> *"Smoking has been prohibited in all National forests in California except at 'fag stations'* (a designated place to rest or have a cigarette) *established along trails and roads and at camps and places of habitation. A report states that 999 fires in 1932 were caused by lighted matches and burning tobacco being thrown into dry litter of the forest and dry grass and grain fields of the State."*

Fire fighting techniques and the delivering of men, tools and supplies improved greatly in the 1930's when mules were replaced with rugged trucks, tanker trucks and airplanes. The human-caused fires did reduce in the 1930's through a national effort to educate people on fire dangers. The Forest Service knew they need a symbol that the public could identify with the forests. The first animal to debut in fire prevention posters was the young deer *"Bambi"* recognized because of the movie of that name that depicted the fawn caught in a fire. Bambi was replaced by a bear in 1944 and when a young bear was actually rescued from a New Mexico forest fire in 1950, and then named *"Smokey"*, the public seemed to better recognize what the fires were doing to wildlife as well as the forest. *"Smokey Bear"* became the most powerful force in the United States in stopping forest fires. When the program about Smokey was taken to the schools, children promised to help Smokey Bear and as they grew to adults they seemed to remember that promise and the Forest Service estimated that forest fires were cut in half as a result. The Smokey Bear symbol soon became recognized as standing for fire prevention throughout the world.

Poster for the 50th Anniversary of the Smokey Bear effort

View of Frazier Mountain during a 1941 fire (Ridge Route Antiques photo)

Concern for the forests was not lost during World War II as in 1941 a *"Penny Pines"* program was developed as a cooperative effort between the Forest Service and private individuals and organizations for the reforestation of burn areas in the National Forests. The San Francisco Sportswoman's Association began the program in Northern California. A donation of $68 would allow the Forest Service to plant trees on approximately one acre of National Forest land and your name, or the name of your group, would be listed on a sign at the site. The pennies for the pines were primarily collected from school children and the program was begun in the schools locally in 1956.

Penny Pines sign with list of donors on Frazier Mtn

There are several Penny Pines Plantations in the Mt. Pinos Ranger District. One plantation is the San Emigdio plantation located at the junction of Cuddy Valley, Mill Potrero and Mt. Pinos Roads planted in 1962-63 with additional trees planted in 1973. The Frazier Mountain plantation is located two miles south of the Chuchupate Ranger Station. Most of the trees planted at these sites were Jeffery pine though some were Jeffery/Coulter crossbreed and a Monterey/Knobcone cross that were being experimented with. This is still an active Forest Service program though replacement cost is a now a good deal more than a penny.

Another early report of reforestation comes from a March of 1950 article to the BAKERSFIELD CALIFORNIAN by local resident, Grace Bradley. She wrote:

"It took a crew of seven men three and a half days to plant 12,000 two year old Jeffery pine trees on either side of the road leading from the Ranger Station to the Frazier Mountain Lookout. This is the territory in which a forest fire burned 3,000 acres in 1947. Funds for the trees were secured by the salvaging and selling of timber in the burnt area.

Al Weisgerber, district ranger states that the prospects for the grazing land of the district is very poor again this year since the rain precipitation is only 6.32 inches so far this year. This record dates back to July 1, 1949. To insure plenty of springs and good grass the amount of rainfall should average twice that amount."

In another brief news article, Mrs. Bradley wrote:
"To control soil erosion and reduce damage by future floods, the Forest Service broadcast three tons of mixed grass seed over the burnt sections of Frazier Park and Frazier Mountain where the 600 acre forest fires occurred in October 1954. The cost of the reseeding project was approximately $3,000 and was carried out by the use of a helicopter."

In the 1960's Mrs. Bradley wrote about another plantation:
"Two burns in the Los Padres National Forest caused by forest fires in 1956 have been reseeded with 38,000 Jeffery seedlings. The reseeding was done by the U. S. Forest Service from the Chuchupate Ranger Station. According to the District Ranger Robert Janes, the Mill Potrero fire, which threatened Camp Condor, burned 90 acres. The other fire on Frazier Mountain burned 40 acres.

Trees in the burned area as well as trees nearby were weakened by the tremendous heat and become a living target for insects ... especially the Ise beetle and the flat headed borer. One way the Forest Service combats this infestation is the utilization of the burnt logs for timber. Approximately one half million board feet of lumber was salvaged by the Ivory Pine Lumber Co. of Dinuba from these two areas. Following the logging and the spraying of smaller trees and brush, the slash is burned in preparation for planting. The seeding trees from two-year-old stock are planted by hand.

The year 1962 was the biggest year for the Forest Service activities of timber sales and tree planting in the 57 year history of the system in California. Some 350,000 board feet of lumber were sold in the Mt. Pinos district with hundreds of acres of successful planting of 65,000 one year-old Jeffery pines here."

Forest Service personnel plant trees in burn area – 1962
(Grace Bradley photo)

In a 1963 article to the BAKERSFIELD CALIFORNIAN, Grace Bradley wrote about the Penny Plantations:

> *"Seventy-five thousand, year-old Jeffery pine seedlings are being planted on the north slope of Frazier Mountain. Most of the trees will be planted in the burned area caused by the terrific forest fire of June 1947. The fires started in one of the lower canyons of what is now the Lake of the Woods subdivision, and raced up Frazier Mountain, spreading wide on its way to the top. By some peculiar quirk the fire circled the Chuchupate Camp grounds, leaving the camp intact.* (Possibly through the magical powers of the legendary Princess Chuchupate.) *The seedlings were grown in Placerville and cared for at the Chuchupate Ranger Station until planted. About 1000 trees are planted in each acre."*

After a planting in 1967 a Forest Service newsletter quipped:
"Now if we can convince the rabbits and ground squirrels that they really don't like the taste of pine trees."

View from Frazier Mountain, looking down towards Chuchupate Ranger Station, after the fires of 1947 & 48 (Grace Bradley photo)

Fire concerns were still serious in the 1950's as the District Forest Ranger, Al Weisgerber, reported that he only had a crew of seven men and district consisted of 231,000 acres. Among their obligations were the communities of Frazier Park and Lake of the Woods as these villages were located within the Mt. Pinos District. Weisgerber stated that the training and orders of the crew were to fight forest fires in preference to structural fires.

A former Forest Service employee, Jim Kane, remembered that in the 1950's the old crank telephone system was used in the Forest Service buildings. They were wood boxes on the wall with the hearing device that you held with one hand as you cranked the number you wanted to reach. One crank rang in the office (one ring), two cranks or rings was the cook house, three rings – the lookout tower, four rings – the bunk house and five rings or more – meant there was a fire and you had to grab your gear and report to the office immediately. Living in the bunkhouse meant you held your breath every time the rings got up to four to hear if there would be a fifth ring.

A majority of fires from the 1950's on were caused by lightning. A climatic feature in the Los Padres Forest is an absence of electric storms over most of its area except for the Mt. Pinos District where lighting caused fires are a common occurrence.

A fire in August of 1951 was one another of the most serious to have burned in and around Frazier Park. It is said to have started in a campground near or at the corner of Los Padres Drive and San Carlos Trail where a beautiful stand of pine trees, lost to this or an earlier fire, once stood. The BAKERSFIELD CALIFORNIA OF Monday, August 20th reported:

> *"More than 200 men battled today to quell a forest fire burning in Frazier Park which has already blackened 600 acres, destroyed at least three cabins and endangered 50 others. With fire lines already gouged out around the blaze, forest service officials expect to have the flames controlled by late today.*
>
> *The fire, believed to have been caused by a careless smoker, started about 3 p.m. yesterday, and within minutes was whipped into an inferno by light winds which swept the tinder-dry brush. Burning up a brush-covered ridge, the flames leaped to the Pine Flat area and swept into the northern fringe of the park, endangering more than 1000 campers.* (It must have been hunting season!)
>
> *Minutes after the fire was reported, 30 men, 2 bulldozers and 2 pumpers were sent southward by the Kern county fire department. Lost in the blaze were a 1942 Chevrolet pumper belonging to the county fire department and a pickup truck owned by the forest service.*
>
> *The pumper, driven by Robert Easton, had moved out in front of a flash fire to spray an endangered home when it bogged down in sand by the roadside. Both trucks were lost in the flames when the forest service vehicle moved in to save Easton's pumper. Easton, a bulldozer operator, narrowly escaped injury when his clothing burst into flames, but the county fire department employee bravely continued battling the fire.*
>
> *With thermometers standing at 100 plus, fire fighters yesterday touched off a giant backfire while 15 forest service pumpers patrolled the area. Forest service officials believe the backfire, fanned by a timely change in the wind's direction, broke the fire's back.*
>
> *Al Weisgerber, district ranger of the Los Padres Forest, is directing over-all operations from a base-camp set up at the Frazier Park School* (this would have been when the school was located in the building that now houses the Assembly of God

Church on Mt. Pinos Way in Frazier Park) *Bulldozers worked throughout the night before a fire line was finally drawn tight today.*

The Frazier Park area in 1947 was ravaged by flames which burned over almost the identical area now being consumed. In the previous fire, one of Southern California's finest stands of timber went up in flames."

After World War II air drops by old bomber planes became the most effective method of fighting fires in these rugged hills. Jim Kane remembered that in the mid-1970's one such tanker crashed into Tecuya Ridge because the load didn't release and the pilot could not pull up in time. Many such stories of the dangers of those flights could be told.

Photo of the 1951 fire looking up Walnut Trail
west of the Rock Houses in Frazier Park
(Weigel Family Photo)

XXIII - FLORA & TIMBER

A common growth important to preserving the watershed in the Mt. Pinos Ranger District are hundreds of species of high elevation wild flowers, especially apparent in the Gorman hills. The Frazier Mountain area often puts on some of the most spectacular floral displays in Southern California in the Spring and Summer of the year. Efforts to protect them from being picked have been minimal though phrases such as *"Enjoy, do not Destroy"*, *"If you must take the flowers with you, do it on film"* and *"Let it be said that they died with their roots on"* have helped raise this consciousness some. The deep roots of this groundcover protect the watershed and provide an amazing habitat for critters below ground.

The next step up from the ground plants and flowers are the shrubs or brush and the most common among these are scrub oak, mountain mahogany, wild lilac, manzanita, Fremontia, juniper, sage, yucca, wild rose and elderberry. Brush covers about 60 percent of the area. The primary woodland and coniferous trees range from the smaller live oak and pinon pines on up to the fragrant Jeffery pine, sugar pines, a few stately ponderosa pines and in surrounding areas the Coulter pine with it's huge and dangerous pinecones.

Charles F. Saunders has left us a pleasant description the beautiful *"Fremontia"* plant in his book THE SOUTHERN SIERRAS OF CALIFORNIA, which he wrote in 1923. The Fremontia bush is supposedly named for the famous explorer John C. Fremont who was an owner of the San Emigdio Ranch in the 1850's. The bush, with its golden yellow blooms, still covers our hills at the 5000-foot level and is especially prolific just west of Frazier Park. It is commonly known as *"flannel bush"* for the soft fuzzy leaves. Mr. Saunders wrote of his summer travels in the area:

> *"I came upon a Fremontian reminder truly vivid ... a hillside covered with little trees of the sort that California mountaineers call 'slippery elm', but to which Science, wishing to honor the discoverer, has given the name of Fremontia. The trees were still in abundant bloom, and it was as if an innumerable company were encamped there in tents of cloth of gold. I like to think of them there looking down on the ancient trail and blooming every summer to the glory of Fremont; for I think his must, indeed, have been a kindly heart, to have given thought,*

in the midst of pioneering hardships and crowding political perplexities, to the flowers of the wayside."

A "Femontia" bush west of Frazier Park

When the state mineralogist, Stephen Bower, researches the area in 1888, he records the yucca plant with its stately *"Lord's Candle"* as follows:

> *"The Spanish bayonet (yucca whipplei) grows larger in this section than elsewhere. The stocks are over 12 to 16 or 20 feet height and 4 or 5 inches in diameter. There are millions of them in this section sometimes 8 to 10 growing from one stock."*

The local San Emigdio Mountain forest regions are known to hold some of the largest surviving trees in existence. A Jeffery or yellow pine some twenty feet in diameter can still be seen along the Mil Potrero Hwy. It was named the *"Jim Whitener Tree"* after the Forest Service employee who discovered it in 1942. Mr. Whitener, a fire guard at the Apache Saddle Ranger Station, was out on horseback patrol, checking the Forest Service phone line that ran to his office when he discovered the tree.

Local writer, Grace Bradley later reported:

> *"The tree was found to be 151 feet tall, 19' 10" in circumference with a spread of 40 feet. District Ranger Thomas A. Neff thought this merited further investigation so he sent the measurements into headquarters in Washington D.C. and received the report that the tree was the largest Jeffery pine on record."*

Mrs. Bradley wrote that the tree stands near *"Torrence Meadows"*. A late 1800's map also indicates Torrance Meadow is near the Whitener Tree. Torrance in Spanish seems to indicate fast flowing water.

The Whitener tree – or more commonly called the *"Whitner Tree"* – is believed to be some 800 years old. It has been topped off at some time in its ancient history, a natural occurrence with this type of tree but is also said to have had its top snapped off in the 1857 earthquake that centered near there. It's excessive growth may be due to it's location above the confluence of the nearby mountain creeks.

Ranger Neff stands below the Whitener tree in July of 1956

The very tall Jim Whitener (6'4") stands beside the sign erected near the giant tree he is credited with discovering - 1952

In Pleito Canyon, near the Pleito campground, there once stood the largest big cone spruce (or Douglas fir) tree *"in the world"*. It was referred to as a *"champion tree"* for that species – rare for this section of the country. The District Ranger in 1950, Al Weisgerber, stated that *"having checked the tree with proper repositories of such knowledge, there is no larger tree of its kind on record."* It was measured at 24 feet in circumference and even though it too had been topped off, it stood at 116 feet high. According to a 1950 estimate, there was then enough lumber in the tree to build a seven-room home, or 15,000 board feet. The tree has since died, fallen and decayed. It has also been reported that this tree was near Antimony Peak.

To the south of Quail Lake, in the Angeles National Forest, is one of the largest oak trees still standing to be found measuring 22 1/2 feet in circumference and dated to be about 700 years old. And in Hungry Valley there is an oak tree located in the Oak Preserve called *"Grandmother Oak"*. It measures 20 feet 4 inches in circumference and is believed to be about 600 years old.

Students from Bakersfield College recently measured the "Grandmother Oak"

Also unique to the area is, or was, the *"world's largest grapevine"*. It appeared in the Davis Commercial Encyclopedia of the Pacific Southwest of 1914. It is located at an old ranch or farm off the road out past Pine Mountain Club in the southwest corner of Kern County. In 1954, Lester McDonald, wrote about the vine which he searched for and found on the Emerson Ranch in the Paleto Hills. He wrote:

> *"We found the old ranch house unoccupied but there was the vine. Not only was it there but it was still growing as tendrils*

branching out from the old growth gave proof of this. We counted sixteen stout piles (pillars of the vine) *supporting the thick roof-like mass which extends over a space roughly square in shape. Pacing it off, we estimated the vine covers at least forty feet on a side. Later we learned it had once measured 110 feet per side. Simple multiplication reveals that the vine once blanketed over 12,000 square feet.*

The enormous girth of the trunk is also difficult to believe without seeing it. Using a piece of rope we circled the largest section, and employing our known heights as a comparative figure, we found it be at least nine feet in circumference. The trunk is about twelve feet tall.

A few days after our trip of 'rediscovery' we secured the full story of the vine's genesis from Mrs. Josephine Bush, who resides in East Bakersfield. According to Mrs. Bush, her father Edward Simpson Emerson, came to Kern County in 1886 and settled near what is now called Paleto Springs. In 1890 the family moved to higher and better ground overlooking Cuyama Valley.

In those days it was a three-day roundtrip to Bakersfield by wagon. On one of those trips in 1892, Mr. Emerson stopped at the ranch of his friend, John White, west of the old Panama settlement where he was given some Madeira grapevine cuttings. On his return home these were planted by Mrs. Emerson and grew amazingly well at the 4000 foot elevation."

The area of Paleto Spring has been located on maps as being just northwest of Pine Mountain Club.

Lester McDonald by the unusual grapevine he rediscovered

Most of the timber operations in the entire Los Padres Forest had been on the slopes of Frazier, Pinos, Sawmill and Noroeste (Abel) Mountains. By the early 1900's all logging operations in the Forest Reserve were confined to the slopes of Mt. Pinos where a sawmill, located at the site of today's Mt. Pinos Campground, had for some time previously cut timber for mining interests and local settlers. Donald Cuddy remembered hearing his Grandpa Charlie Cuddy tell about the *"tugger"* located at *"Iris Point"* off to the southwest of the Mt. Pinos Campground. According Los Padres Forest Historian, William S. Brown:

> *"The entire cut of this mill between 1898 and 1904 was approximately 200,000 board feet. An older mill, located at the foot of Sawmill Mt., in the same general area, had confined its cutting for years mainly to big cone spruce* (or Big Cone Douglas Fir), *the lumber of which even in a section where sawn boards were scarce proved unsatisfactory to local settlers."*

The oldest mill was at the foot of Sawmill Mtn., at the top of San Emigdio Canyon, was thought to be established in the early 1850's by Joseph Gale with some of the lumber used in the building of Fort Tejon. A great-grandson of Gale, Charlie Cuddy, told family members that in his generation he used oxen to pull logs from Sawmill Mountain to Grouse Mountain nearby – for what purpose was not recalled. Also on Mt. Pinos, Charlie Cuddy remembered well the mill below the present McGill campground where the roads from Seymour and Mill Canyon met.

This photo, not from our area, would be an example of what
a mill at the base of Mt. Pinos might have looked like in the late 1800's

A mill located at the base of Mt. Pinos, possibly originally belonging to the Cuddy family, served the area from the late 1800's to the mid-1900's. The SOUTHERN CALIFORNIAN newspaper of March 14, 1875, published in Bakersfield, stated:

> *"the sawmill in San Emigdio Canyon is being moved to the other side of the mountain near the Cuddy place to the same location where lumber was sawed for the construction of government buildings at Fort Tejon".*

The equipment from the Joseph Gale mill was moved by his son-in-law, John F. Cuddy, probably to the site at the base of Mt. Pinos. This also confirms that lumber for the building of Fort Tejon also came from this location – at the base of Pinos.

Wm Brown wrote of a *"timber count"* done in the winter of 1905-06 on the Tejon Ranger District when J. D. Reyes led a field party during some unbearably cold winter weather. Brown writes:

> *"It was hard going even for the older foresters, since the party left their shack camp before daylight and returned after nightfall, generally regardless of weather. They laid off work on Sundays to wash their clothes and cut firewood for the following week. The also took Christmas Day off and feasted on turkey. Once one of the young foresters accidentally pushed Reyes' prize snow boots too close to a red hot stove with the results that the ranger later suffered frozen feet when the leather gave away. Reyes did not lay off work, however, but keenly remembers forty years later how he suffered until he was able to buy a pair of new boots from a miner. The result of this winter's 'timber cruise' showed a stand of sawtimber, mainly Jeffery pine, of twelve thousand feet per acre of an area of several thousand acres."*

The Sprague Family, who later lived on Tejon Ranch, has left a legacy of photographs from their days logging on Mt. Pinos in 1906.

Young Perry Sprague with logging tools – Mt. Pinos 1906
(Sprague Family photo)

Crew of lumberjacks on Mt. Pinos – 1906 (Sprague Family photo)

A *"donkey"* used to pull logs up Mt. Pinos – 1906 (Sprague Family photo)

Riding a log as it is pulled up – Mt. Pinos 1906 (Sprague Family photo)

Loaded wagon being moved to another mill site – 1906 (Sprague Family photo)

Perry Sprague taking a load of lumber to Bakersfield (Sprague Family photo)

The logging camp cook – Mt. Pinos, 1906 (Sprague Family photo)

An article in the May 15, 1927 issue of the LOS ANGELES TIMES reported:

> *"In the old days Mt. Pinos was the scene of logging operations. Two sawmills were kept busy cutting timbers to be used in the borax mines, which lie in the valley below, and the slashings went down the hill also, to be burned in the big cooking plants at the mines. The result of these lumbering operations has been to clear the sides of Mt. Pinos of underbrush and smaller trees, leaving the big monarchs of the hills thrusting up to heaven through a soft bed of needles and cones."*

In the 1930's, Roy Newman was still hauling timber from the upper sawmill down to Fife's General Store in Frazier to be sold to folks building homes in the area at that time.

In July of 1952 the local newspaper, THE FRAZIER MTN. BREEZE reported that the mill at the base of the east side of Mt. Pinos had burned. At this time the mill was owned and operated by Martin Obermire who also owned the Lumber and Hardware Store in Frazier Park. The article read:

> *"A fire, which lasted just nine minutes, burned to the ground the Mt. Pinos Lumber Mill and the home of Mr. and Mrs. Martin Obermire, owners of the mill. The fire which occurred at 1:30 a.m. on June 16 was supposedly caused by a short circuit precipitated by a cat which was found badly burned but still living.*
>
> *The Obermire trucks, machinery and tools were so badly damaged they had to be abandoned, and although no one was injured, the contents of the Obermire's home were completely destroyed and the family has moved to the bunkhouse.*
>
> *Quick action of the part of the Forest Service from Chuchupate Ranger Station, with assistance from the Kern County Fire Department, was all that saved the smaller buildings on the property and the tall timber close around the buildings.*
>
> *A saw mill has been purchased and hauled down from the Sequoias to replace the burned one and according to Mr. Obermire, would be operating in very short time. The Obermires expect to commence rebuilding their home at once in order to have it in readiness before the winter season which brings heavy snows to that area."*

Norman Ellis recalled working at the Obermire Mill before the fire. He said they would spend about three days on the mountain cutting and skidding logs which they would load on a truck with a winch to haul down to the mill at the base of Pinos – below the Snow Gate. At the mill they had a single blade saw that wasn't large enough to make a full slice of bark off any one side of the log so they would first slice off one half of a side, then insert dynamite to blast off the second half of the slice – interesting. The sawdust would fall into a wooden box on the back of an old jeep which they would then drive down hill from the mill where they dumped the sawdust among the trees below. The piles of sawdust are still visible there.

In 1955, local writer, Grace Bradley reported on two new lumber companies in the Los Padres Forest. It seems that the government had opened 50,000 acres to timber permits under a Salvage & Sanitation program to open growing space for the young trees. One of the lumber companies was the *"Ivory Pine Lumber Company"* and they had a five million board feet lumber contract. During the cutting season of the year, the logs were being taken from Grade Valley and Frazier Mountain and hauled to their mill in Dinuba, California. Logging trucks were running through Frazier Park day and night, averaging one load every hour – and that was when Mt. Pinos Way, then called Brand Blvd, was the only road through the community!

Unique to Ivory Pine Lumber Co. operation was that six stanchions were built at the head of Grade Valley and the timber brought seven to twelve miles from the woods where thirty men were cutting and loading the logs. The stanchions were placed so the trucks could back under the timber and by means of a lever, it was loaded onto the trucks by one man in four minutes time. Several miles of new road had to be made and several more miles had to be reconditioned before timber could be brought to the stanchions.

The second mill was established in the center of Cuddy Valley on the Tubbs Ranch. It seems that W. P. Payne and Alden Tubbs, Sr. – a Cuddy family descendent – had bought out the Obermire lumber interest, probably after the fire, and were calling their new company the Mt. Pinos Milling & Lumber Company. The *"latest model"* sawmill was constructed there in 1955 at a cost of $100,000. The company did their own logging with a crew of fifteen using chain saws and the mill with a crew of ten, produced 15,000 feet of rough cut lumber per day. Most of the logs were salvaged from diseased and partially burned trees. Logging was done at night during the height of the fire season because of the extreme danger for forest fires.

Still visible in the forest today, though rarely found anymore, are blazed trees. The lower branches would be stripped from a tall pine tree up some twenty to thirty feet so that it would be easily recognizable from quite a distance. A section of the bark was generally removed and some of the wood of the tree gouged out at eye level to indicate direction, to leave messages or for other unknown purposes. The practice of blazing trees was done from earliest time for a variety of reasons. A series of trees would be blazed to mark a trail or define someone's property or claim. In some cases the blaze work indicated something, or someone, has been buried below. These trees were also referred to as witness trees and since the 1800's they have been, and still are being used as bearing trees in surveys. Many of those limbed up were logged off as a pleasant source of an already trimmed tree.

A *"witness tree"* in San Emigdio Canyon - 1972

Blaze marks on the same tree in San Emigdio Canyon

Probably the oldest flora, plants or trees in the San Emigdio Mountains are found on Mt. Pinos. In the year 2000, Dahlia Grossman reported in the PINE MOUNTAIN PIONEER that a rare stand or grove of ancient limber pines is thriving on Mt. Pinos. While researching drought patterns in the Southern California area, a team of scientists documented at least one tree at the top of Pinos as being over 800 years old. The trees were spotted while doing a search for old trees by helicopter. Geologist Glen MacDonald of UCLA stated:

> *"Although only one tree in the stand was tested, it appears that it was only one of many limber pines on Mt. Pinos that are at least 500 and possibly up to 1,000 years old."*

The tree that was tested had a diameter of only two to three feet and stands only about 30 to 40 feet tall. Limber pines survive longer at the higher elevations where there is less oxygen to cause decay. MacDonald said that older limber pines have been found on the 11,000 foot-high peak of Mt. San Gorgonio near Palm Springs. Forest Service employee, John Kelly, said that the limber pines on Pinos are the western most grouping of this tree in the U.S. and are normally found just below an alpine forest.

Ancient *"Limber Pines"* at the top of Mt. Pinos
(Susan Sjoberg photo)

XXIV - HUNTING FOR SURVIVAL & SPORT

Before the arrival of the non-Indian element to these mountains the balance of nature had been undisturbed through time. Once herders and ranchers began to drive their sheep and cattle up to the lush green pastures in the higher elevations, the grizzly bear's and mountain lions found a generous new source of food, thus throwing off natures own wildlife management. Then came the indiscriminate hunting of the late 1800's and early 1900's. The grizzly bear is gone though black bears remain. Antelope have been reintroduced to the Antelope Valley and the Carrizo Plains with Big Horn sheep reintroduced to the mountains west of Pyramid Lake. Mountain lions and bobcats are still found but in reduced numbers. Never severely affected were the deer, fox, coyote, rabbits, skunks, raccoons and badgers (Tejon in Spanish).

Hunting was first done for the protection of early homesteaders and their livestock with professional hunters hired to rid the area of grizzlies, mountain lions and coyotes. Pelts as a source of income, and hunting as a recreational sport, further changed the status of wildlife until controls were instituted. One of the most devastating methods of clearing an area of wildlife was to introduce a heavy dose of strychnine poison to a carcass which would kill any number of animals that would be inclined to feed on the carrion.

Many accounts of the capture or the killing of the last of the grizzly bears have been told and written. One of the most detailed accounts appeared in COSMOPOLITAN MAGAZINE in July of 1890. It was written by Allan Kelly, a member of this hunting party. It seems the owner of the San Francisco Examiner had decided that a representative of the symbol on the state seal and flag should be in the San Francisco zoo. A hunting party was sent to the San Emigdio Mountains where grizzlies were still known to exist.

The hunt for a bear, to be called *"Old Monarch"*, began in June. Local *"mountain men"* were hired to assist in the task. A four sided *"log cabin"* trap twelve feet long, four feet wide and five feet high (inside measurement) was built with logs measuring from twelve to eighteen inches in diameter. The logs were fastened with stout oak pins and the trap tightly located between trees which happened to grow in an *"advantageous arrangement"*. The following are excerpts from what Mr. Kelly wrote:

> *"The door was made of four-inch plank weighing 200 pounds and was held in place by a rope running over a pulley and attached to a trigger projecting through the roof.*
>
> *Only three grizzlies came to Mount Pinos while we were there and they would not go near the trap, although it was baited temptingly with mutton, venison and honey.*
>
> *During the next three months we found trails of many bears, saw some grizzlies face to face and built several traps, leaving them in charge of local mountain men as we moved along.*
>
> *The grizzly's den was a rocky hollow covered with manzanita brush, near the top of the highest and most rugged ridge of the mountain, and from this almost inaccessible retreat he made regular marauding raids down through the timber belt to the grazing lands. A green flat near Castac lake* (at Lebec) *was strewn with the whitened bones of cattle that had been killed by bears and in an hour's tramp over any part of the mountain one would be certain to find the remains of from two to half a dozen of their victims. Frequently the trail was so fresh that great caution was necessary to avoid coming upon a grizzly suddenly in the dense brush.*
>
> *One day one of our men rode out to Gorman's store, ten miles away, to get some nails. Late in the afternoon while I was sawing and hammering on another trap, and making a great deal of noise, the grizzly came walking along a ridge within plain view and sat down, not in the least disturbed by my presence or noise."*

A bear trap located by Perry Sprague (Sprague Family photo)

After some five months a bear finally wandered into one of the many traps that had been built. For a full week the grizzly raged against the trap until he became exhausted. It was then time to fasten a chain to one of his fore-legs. Kelly writes:

> *"That job was begun at eight o'clock in the morning and finished at six o'clock that evening. A loop of chain was squeezed through the logs and laid on the floor of the trap but every time the bear stepped on it and it was pulled tight he would pull it off with his other paw. The feat was finally accomplished by letting the looped chain down between the roof logs so that when the bear stepped into it and it was drawn sharply upward, it caught him well up toward the shoulder.*
>
> *Having one leg well anchored, it was comparatively easy to introduce chains and ropes between the side logs and secure the other legs. The bear fought furiously. The next operation was gagging the bear so that he could not bite. The door of the trap was raised and a billet of wood was held where he could seize it which he promptly did. A cord made fast to the stick was quickly wound about his jaws, with turns around the stick on each side and passed back of his ears and around his neck like a bridle."*

A number of other chains were attached, and with a lot of muscle and struggle the bear was hauled out of the trap and bound to a rough sled. Mr. Kelly continues:

> *"Great difficulty was encountered in securing a team of horses that could be induced to haul the bear. The first two teams were so terrified that little progress could be made, but the third team was tractable and the trip down the mountain to the nearest wagon road was begun.*
>
> *The gag removed, the bear was released from the sled and chained to trees every night where he was fed and so long as the camp fire burned brightly he would lie still and watch it attentively, but when it burned low he would get up and restlessly pace to and fro and tug at his chains, stopping now and then to seize in his arms the tree to which he was anchored and test its strength by fiercely shaking it.*
>
> *Every morning the same old fight had to be fought before he could be tied to his sled. He became very expert in dodging ropes and seizing them when the loops fell over his legs, and strategic skill was required to lasso his paws and stretch him out.*

There was no trail down the mountain and therefore the journey was very uncomfortable for the captive, although all care possible was observed in hauling him over the rough places. He was pretty well worn out when, after four days, the wagon road was reached and he doubtless enjoyed a few days rest and quiet that were allowed him while a cage was being built for his further transportation. He made the remainder of the journey to San Francisco by wagon and railroad. The grizzly accepted the situation resignedly and behaved admirable during the whole trip. We became very good friends in a distant sort of way.

Close acquaintance with the grizzly inspired me with genuine respect for his character and admiration for his indomitable courage. Our acquaintance reached this stage of intimacy: that he would allow me to handle his chain and would take food from my hand. He knew my voice and when I called him by his name 'Monarch', he would look up at me not unkindly and, if I had nothing for him, lay his head upon his paws again and go to sleep; but if a stranger came near his cage he would assume a watchful attitude and utter low warning growls. If he regrets that he was captured I sympathize with him for I'm more than half sorry myself."

It seems that local resident, Tom Harris, was one of those who took part in the capture of Old Monarch as Lockwood Valley homesteader, Bill deLancey, later wrote of the incident:

"The miner, Tom Harris was one of the best known figures in these mountains. He was a man of medium size who trapped between logs, just above the Stauffer post office, (the south side of Mt. Pinos) *the last great grizzly bear captured in California. With the help of another man* (no doubt several other men), *he hog-tied 'Old Monarch', as the bear was long known thereafter, hauled him 400 miles northward to the Golden Gate Park Zoo at San Francisco. In Lockwood one of our local 'sights' was the small ravine where lay the rotting logs of Tom Harris' famous trap. This spot was widely known as Bear Trap Canyon and neighborhood old timers could relate the fantastic capture of the huge bear that was long the main attraction at the 'Frisco' Zoo. There Old Monarch fathered more little grizzlies, but is now long gone."*

While covering the hunting of bears the other *"last of the grizzlies"* story should not be forgotten. *"Old Club Foot"* was every bit the legend locally as *"Monarch"* was. It seems that in the mid-1800's a young bear was caught in a trap but managed to escape with a badly damaged foot – thus gaining the club foot name. As with all grizzlies, Club Foot had a habit of feasting on the local ranchers livestock. Through the years the bear was reported having been hunted and killed on most every mountain in the area.

* * * *

In the days before Sanctuaries and Reserves, these mountains were hunted, of course by the original indigenous people, and then by the early day market hunters, who would sell the meat in communities near and far. Local miners also used the great variety of wildlife as a food source. In August of 1907 a hunter by the name of Kaiser recorded this enjoyable and informative story of his experience, and that of his companions, in an article entitled, *"Tales of Camp Life on Frazier Mountain"* printed in the Bakersfield MORNING ECHO. He wrote:

> *"Frazier is a good deer hunting country and many are yet left in that region to entice the eager sportsmen. In fact the whole country on the borders of Kern and Ventura counties is fairly well covered with good deer signs and the skillful hunter should experience no difficulty in bagging a deer or two in a season. Doves are quite numerous as are quail and some tree squirrels. Phil Klipstein managed to be the champion deer hunter. He killed two bucks and proved to be the best meat provider in the camp. Four deer was the extent of our game bagging and they were amply sufficient for all purposes and enough to bring a few steaks along to town. The camp was well supplied with venison and the meals were devoured to the last crumb and steak every time. The rattlesnake signs in this section are very beautiful. We killed six, two of which were nearly six feet long."*

Some of the members of the hunting party of nine were *"Skinny"* Fawcett and the Klipstein brothers, Tom or *"Tup"*, Phil, and Henry – *"who dwell in the San Emedio hills on a big mountain ranch"* (located between Pine Mountain Club and Maricopa). The article continued:

"Ben Barret had a magnificent time, devoting his spare energy to picking foxtails from the feet of his pet dog, Joe, to riding the fiery mule, Sir Robert, up the steep mountain."

As to the location of their camp Kaiser wrote:
"From 'Camp Three Counties' one of the prettiest scenes in Kern county is the view of Castac lake from the upper end of the canyon or from the top of Frazier mountain. Castac is not always filled with water, but heavy snows of the past winter washed the creeks and rivulets full. On clear mornings several of the party saw the top of Mt. Whitney at a distance of about 200 miles away."

As he calls the camp *"Camp Three Counties"* it is assumed that they camped out on the eastern end of Frazier Mountain, near where Ventura, Los Angeles and Kern Counties then met. They travel to Gorman Station and Buckhorn Station. Few references have been found to the settlement of *"Buckhorn"* but an article in the LOS ANGELES TIMES of June 16, 1907, about the road from Los Angeles to Bakersfield puts Buckhorn in the approximate location of the present Frazier Park exit from the Interstate 5 highway.

Kaiser continues:
"The camp is full of lively spirit and many exciting as well as humorous experiences varying from the finding of a rattler with nine rattles under Red Farnum's pillow to the hot games of pedro and whist won generally by Phil and the writer. Then there are the endless camp jokes. Harry Byal, the popular barber, finds no end of amusement in ribbing up fun at our expense. The end of the second week in Camp Three Counties found everybody enjoying excellent health eating three and sometimes four meals a day, and sleeping the sleep of a true follower of Morpheus nightly. Sky Bill Crockett and Al Swofford, borax teamsters have been our guests to venison steaks and the former Mayor of Bakersfield, 'hiizzoner' Mac McDonald and Hilman Arms of Tejon have been partaken of the camp's hospitality." (Interesting how the news got around when someone was having a good time on the mountain. . . .)

It seems that their hunting trip was not limited to the four-legged animal as Kaiser wrote:
"Skinny spent much of the time cooing a mountain maid and who would fain have wooed and won a fair lass who lives at a happy canyon home between Rose Station and Lebec. Skinny called often to see his fair maid and used his horse up so badly in making the trip that he was compelled to give the poor beast

a week's rest after getting home. Henry too found a pair of bewitching eyes and a dainty ruddy faced blond maiden from Los Angeles who was spending the summer in the mountains. He took to the lass like a duck to water and despite the rival affections of his handsome brothers, and maybe one or two others, contrived to hold her captive to his wiles all the time he was in camp. Nevertheless the bunch greatly enjoyed the spooning in the Tejon Hills."

Mr. Kaiser goes on to write:
"One of the big features of the trip was a dance given at Ed Tibbet's house at Buckham Station (Buckhorn). *The dance was a signal success from every standpoint, Tom Stevens keeper of Tom O'Brien's ranch near Castac Lake was the main fiddler. He was assisted by C. L. Woods, a Frazier Mountain miner who has spent a great part of his 73 years in the wilds.* (Woods was the owner of the road stop in Lebec and had been the postmaster there.) *The partitions were taken out down stairs and quite a roomy floor was exposed. There were six ladies, including Mrs. Joe Barnes* (this would be Mary Cuddy Barnes), *Mrs. Ed Tibbett, Mrs. Gene Poole, Mrs. Srufflin, Miss Amelia Pettit and Miss Marguerite Sanderson, the last of Los Angeles* (no doubt the ruddy faced blond maiden spoken of above).

There were men galore, but it was a good time we all had and the dance went on until just about daylight next day. One who has attended a country dance will appreciate the immense fun that everybody had from the word go. Round dances lasted twenty to thirty minutes and quadrilles went longer. Bert Stratton, known in Bakersfield as 'the Pop' and who is at O'Brien's ranch for his health came along and looks improved." (The Tibbets or Tibbetts mentioned above were well known in Bakersfield and had a mine south of Neenach.)

* * * *

From Ranger J. D. Reyes we have this description of early hunting:
"During the hunting seasons we rangers usually have a busy time of it looking after the hunters. I've packed out a number of men ... some dead, some alive ... victims of accidental shootings, falls, or other mishaps. In 1919 a man was shot and killed by a hunter who mistook him for a wildcat. The deceased was wearing a gray sweater at the time and was down on the ground cracking and eating some pinon nuts near a spot where another hunter had set a trap for bobcats when he was shot.

We've had a good many cases of men being mistaken for deer and shot at, even though the law says that only a buck with horns is legal game. Some hunters with the buck ague (fever) *would probably see horns on my hat."*

Lockwood Valley homesteader, William deLancey, left many great descriptions of the wildlife and hunting in the Lockwood Valley area in his writings from the 1920's entitled HOMESTEADERS HEYDAY. He writes:

"Of beasts, there were plenty living around there, through it took me some time to learn that I was residing practically in a nest of wildcats. When I learned how to deal with them, I collected ten bobcat rugs right on or near my own quarter-section. The cats kept out of sight, for the most part, yet were very stupid critters about traps. They fed on the numerous jackrabbits, brush rabbits, and two kids of quail ... valley quail and the much larger California mountain quail. Also preying on the same game were coyotes and foxes. The foxes were the gray variety, plus a few of the smaller kit fox.

Wherever the deer live in the Far West, there also prowls the elusive mountain lion. This powerful cat keeps well clear of a man, so that I saw only two in my years of outdoor living. However, I had many reasons to become aware of them at close quarters, and one with its feet singed by a forest fire was shot by a neighbor while it ate a dead cow in his pasture. The deer in the hills around the valley were mainly Columbian blacktails a sub-species of the mule deer, of which there were also a few."

Painting of a stone house, similar to some found in the Mutah/Piru area, with mountain lion on the roof (Artist unknown)

deLancey continues with a mountain lion story:
"One great desire I had was to in someway bag a mountain lion. The 7½ foot cats were around and probably watching me frequently while I worked in the young orchard. Twice I came close to getting in shot at them, but nothing can fade away much slicker than a cougar. I saw an example of the great muscular power of these 100 to 125 pound cats. One day I noticed that the sage brush was ripped up, flattened and disheveled along a sort of path that vanished into a small, clump of pinions and scrub mahogany. Out of curiosity I followed it and found the carcass of a full grown steer that must have weighed 900 pounds. The kill looked fresh and was only slightly eaten but had some twigs and brush thrown over it.

Fred Smith over at the Borax mine once followed such a strange looking drag mark on the ground over by Bob Cuddy's place (in Cuddy Valley). *Over a knoll Fred looked up into the face of a snarling cougar with the carcass of a stolen hog. Fred said he tried to bring up his gun but out of fear, his gun just wagged around so that he couldn't do a thing but back down the hill."*

deLancey is mistaken for a mountain lion:
"I was digging a water line ditch at Stauffer. I was standing in the bottom of the ditch, bent forward, with the long handle of the hovel stuck out behind. From the farthest ridge top a hunter fired and I heard the bullet whistling over my head. Almost at once another bullet came by, behind me. I fell into the ditch and lay there until the coast seemed clear. Deer season had just opened the day my shovel turned into a panther's tail but I wouldn't have known what it looked like if it hadn't been for old 'Willow' Downer. That afternoon Downer drove up and discovered me and stopped his car with the query: 'DeLancey, did you see anything of a mountain lion up near this spring this morning? Two young fellows from L.A. are staying at my house, and they took shots at a lion they saw here. They said it disappeared, but they didn't come off the mountain to look around – afraid they'd get lost.'

'Wish they had', I told him."

Rennie Brown, a "professional hunter" with mountain lion he shot in the Ozena area (Brown Family Photo)

deLancey continues with another lion story:
"Wildcats are unlikely to attack a man, but one night I had one do the most surprising thing. I was driving to a dance at the Ralph's Ranch on the Ridge Route and had just crossed slowly through a little stony wash on the east side of Tifft's Flat (near where the present Adams Trail crosses Lockwood Valley Road). *As I let the clutch pedal fall back into high gear on the Model T pick-up truck – which had no top over the home-made seat, the flivver began to pick up speed very gradually.*

In the next 50 feet it would reach an open area in the sage brush, but at that point the sage hugged close against the wheel ruts – within a foot of them. I suddenly became aware of a moving shadow under my left elbow. Peering down at it, I saw that it was a tall, rangy wildcat, on the gallop, but staying close beside the vehicle.

As the truck came out into the opening the cat surged ahead, and then I saw the reason for its using the headlights ... a jackrabbit that was hopping about in their aimless way. Now the bobcat had him dead to rights, and opened up all his jets. As the rabbit disappeared into the bush the cat made a bound for it. I didn't see the kill, but it undoubtedly took place. Later I thought how one easy spring would have put that well-clawed beast on the back of my neck, without my even knowing he was coming."

deLancey's first deer:
"My stroll took me up a dry wash into a pretty ravine. A sudden clatter arose on my right. Two deer rushed along the bank above me. My 9 mm (millimeter) *Lugar pistol was out of my belt and into my hand. The first shot hit nothing but rocks, but at the second crack, the buck tumbled headlong off the hillside, rolling to the bottom in a limp heap. Almost unbelieving, I examined him and found that the bullet had broken the spine in his neck, making an instant kill.*

This was my first deer ever, and I was a little appalled. For the first time, I thought about the law, and felt sure the shots were so loud they must have brought out the gendarmes. My jackknife seemed inadequate to the strange job of cleaning, and camp was only a loud shout away, downhill.

But not daring to raise my voice on account of the lurking Rangers, I grabbed the animal by its antlers and dragged it down the wash, stooping low so the brush would hide us. Then I hustled to my neighbor's cabin where he was waiting expectantly after hearing the gunfire. He told me that there was almost no local worry about shooting deer out of season when homesteaders needed meat. All there were glad to get the fresh meat and that night we dined on a pan full of liver."

* * * *

"Once I accidentally shot a doe. After we tracked it for hours and dressed it, I bound its legs into the usual backpack we practiced there and hiked for home. For safety, considering the doe was illegal, we walked near the dense woods all the way. Suddenly I heard directly ahead on the trail a voice that to my conscience spelled Head Ranger Dunn, the predecessor of DeLapp. My companions said the doe was off my shoulders and spinning through the air in one fast, violent motion. It spun 10 feet into hiding under the ground-sweeping pinyon branches, while we four flattened like quail, face down in the low sage brush lining both sides of the path. I was all ears for an order to 'come out of there'. Incredibly, the two men rode on between us, passed, never breaking their conversation. I later found out the men were two of my neighbors. One was a fire guard for the Forest Service that year and wanted no part of officially 'seeing' his friends in a delicate situation."

* * * *

"My rifle shooting was not always as ragged as the uphill blast that wounded the doe on San Guillermo Peak. The fanciest shot I ever made with a rifle happened northwest of the peak, in the weird, almost forbidding depths of Cuyama Canyon, along the ancient Wagon Road trail. This washed-out track had once carried freight wagons up from the Coast to the borax and gold camps around the Lockwood. A geologically 'new' country, it was full of dismal, dead-end side canyons that must have been the last stand of the dinosaurs.

Del Greenleaf and I were hunting down there one afternoon, walking side by side when I heard a sound like corduroy pants on a running boy. My brother's 30-40 Krag, being tried out for the first time, jumped to my shoulder and was on the buck when he leaped into the open. His second jump was his last, dead with a shot to the heart. This was the biggest deer, with the widest antler, I ever killed. Probably it was a mule deer, though I didn't know enough then to look for the difference in color of the tail ... black on the tip, from the Columbian blacktail ... all black on the outside of the tail."

* * * *

"Deer hunters from the cities began to find the Lockwood country in gradually increasing numbers and occasionally would inquire about accommodations at my cabin. Always in need of cash I decided to open my seven room house as 'Lockwood Lodge'. My brother and I put a sign out by the road and during hunting season we were kept extremely busy cooking and guiding. After a couple of years I grew tired of the endless deer hunting stories.

One of these hunters was a lone fellow from L.A. who had never been deer hunting before but he came well equipped with the proverbial beginner's luck. I was at work in my orchard as he set out to hunt and he asked where to find a deer. Very hot, thirsty, dusty and tired I abruptly replied 'you see that circle of tall pines over south there, there's a low brush all around them but inside the circle it's perfectly clear. Right in the middle of that ring of trees is a nice buck. He's standing there right now.' 'Thanks' he said and started off to walk about two miles.

A couple of hours later he was back, lugging a nice young forked-horn, his first ever. 'How in the world!' he inquired, 'did you ever know that deer was standing right there in that spot??'

'I could see him', I said, and kept on discing."

As to fishing, deLancey made this comment:
"Occasionally our diet would be varied by fresh brook trout. Why I didn't go fishing more often I can't say for each time I went the luck was satisfactory. Lockwood Creek offered the best chance for an angler to take 'brookies'. I never caught fewer than two or three trout in the 10-inch class. Putting a scrap of fresh venison on a hook I once cast into a pool and it was whacked immediately by a 12-inch Eastern brook trout!"

Early residents of Lockwood Valley often wrote of the good fishing in streams there. Steel head trout were known to make their way from the Pacific Ocean to Lockwood by traveling east through the Santa Clara River, up Piru Creek and to the Lockwood Creek. Twelve thousand fish per mile were once recorded in Lockwood Creek.

* * * *

As these mountains continued to be a popular hunting location, the RIDGE ROUTE RAMBLER of September 1939 reported:
"The Labor Day week-end brought the largest crowd of campers, picnickers and hunters to the Mt. Pinos District for the season. All campgrounds were filled to overflowing for the three days. Although hunters were scattered everywhere in the district, there were no forest fires, or hunters shot or lost, and very few forest regulations violated. This was reported by Ranger Walter Puhn of Chuchupate Ranger Station."

Primitive wilderness areas were first designated for the purpose of wildlife preservation and management in 1922. When the Frazier Mountain area was set aside as a wildlife preserve in 1929, hunting was only allowed to the north of the Frazier Park community and on over to Mt. Pinos. Signs right through the center the little villages of Frazier Park and Lake of the Woods declared the area beyond, a wildlife preserve with no hunting. Curtis and Alma Newman remembered that everything to the south of Los Padres Drive and on out through the middle of Lake of the Woods was a part of the game refuge. There were small signs posted that indicated no hunting from there to over Frazier Mountain – though you could hunt on the north side of Los Padres Drive – right in the residential areas of the town and all the way on up to Mt. Pinos. In 1948, well over six thousand hunters were recorded in the Mt. Pinos District hunting for deer, bear, mountain lions, doves, quail and rabbit.

In the early 1950's the Los Angeles Gun Club put pressure on the Forest Service and the State Fish & Game Department to open the Frazier Mountain State Game refuge for hunting. Much to the dismay of the areas 400 to 500 local residents and property owners, who were not notified of the action until after the fact, the reserve was declared opened in January of 1952. The local newspaper of the day, the FRAZIER MOUNTAIN BREEZE carried an angry editorial that spoke for many of the residents:

> *"The fighting spirit of Frazier Park and Lake of the Woods residents has been aroused to white heat by the recent action of the California State Fish and Game Commission which opened the game refuge including a large section of the residential area of Frazier Park, without giving residents a fair opportunity of voicing their opinions on this, to them, a most vital issue.*
>
> *Perhaps we up here just don't understand how many muscle-bound, running-board 'sportsmen', strangers to us, need 'relaxation' from the shop and office, and how necessary it is, with only a few miles to the really wide open spaces, for them to find this 'relaxation' in OUR back yards. And, I'm sure we don't realize how anxious these 'sportsmen' are to 'preserve' the creatures whose cause they so nobly espouse, and whose necks they so dearly covet.*
>
> *What if a few tax-paying residents get shot, and all dare not even sit INSIDE their homes, much less venture out into their own back yards lest they be used as targets by these would-be hunters, many of them merely slap-happy gunsters. Or what matters that a thoughtless someone throw a match into the dry tinder and burns our whole countryside as happened during the hunting season last year when our entire village was in the gravest danger of being completely destroyed by flames which raged within feet of many residences. The huge circle of charred naked tree skeletons bear stark evidence of this wanton waste, it isn't imaginary.*
>
> *Preserving wild life is one thing, but to 'preserve' a FEW deer for the convenience of some gun-toting city pillager to satisfy his blood-thirsty lust for the 'sport' of draping a carcass over his car for his friends to ogle, and all this by endangering villagers on their own taxed property, and hazarding children at play on*

public school play grounds, or playing in their own back yards, just doesn't make sense to me.

Even if the members of this red-hatted horde which invades our peaceful mountainside every Fall remained sober and in their right minds the danger would be great enough, but they swarm into our area by the thousands without being given a sobriety test which leaves many of them in the mood to shoot at the first thing that moves and should they actually see a deer they probably wouldn't be possessed of the good judgment to realize that someone's home or child was in the line of fire. Sensible men wouldn't take a chance using high-powered rifles in so densely populated an area, or close to it; it will be the foolhardy that we will be forced to deal with."

The August newspaper announced:
"5000 Hunters Invade Frazier Park: ... As of Monday morning, at 8 o'clock in the morning, the deer taken out through the exit of Frazier Park numbered 280, according to checkers stationed on the road leading to the Park. About 5000 hunters were checked in over the opening weekend. Friday and Saturday nights brought a constant stream of cars into the 'hunters' paradise'. There were thirty-five men as regular and reserves patrolling the Frazier Mountain, Mount Pinos, Piru and Lockwood Valley areas. Seventy arrests had been made as of Sunday night."

In the February 1953 issue of the same newspaper, Ranger Weisgerber reviewed the 1952 year and reported: *"Deer hunters last season totaled approximately 20,000 and many thousands more hunters sought other game there. More than 2,600 persons came to gather pinon nuts."* He also reported that in 20 weekends 51,000 persons were in the Frazier Mountain area to participate in snow sports. Weisgerber had high praise for the conduct of the public pointing out that in the more than 100,000 visitors last year only 200 had to be admonished or cited.

In 1954, newspaper reporter, Grace Bradley, wrote for the BAKERSFIELD CALIFORNIAN:
"During the recent deer season approximately 8,000 hunters were checked through the stations maintained by the U.S. Forest Service during the first two weeks of the season. No check is made of the quail, pigeon or rabbit hunter nor of the secretive uranium hunters that invade the country."

In a 1956 Mrs. Bradley wrote:
"With the record number of 10,222 registered hunters coming into Frazier Park for the opening day of deer season, the small mountain town was abruptly brought into activity. The greatest number of hunters was checked in from 10 p.m. Friday night until 2 a.m. on Saturday. Four thousand were registered in one hour's time during that period. Registration was done at the checking station maintained by the U. S. Forestry Service which is located about two miles east of Frazier Park.

One hundred and fifty one deer had been validated through the various checking stations maintained throughout the district by 5 p.m. on Sunday afternoon. Also, one mountain lion from Alamo Mountain and one wild cat found in the Grade Valley area were brought in.

The Forest Service flew a patrol plane over the entire district both night and morning, keeping check on open fires as well as the condition of the established camps. The Chuchupate Camp on Frazier Mountain was filled to overflowing with 500 campers. One thousand hunters were allowed to camp in a dry camp still some four miles higher up the mountain than Chuchupate. Four deputies from Ventura County under the supervision of Guy Noel were on hand to help control the hunters and the Kern County deputy stationed at Frazier Park maintained order in that immediate area. The State Highway Patrol officers took care of the traffic snarls and 35 rangers were in the field of action.

Biologists were interested in the condition of the deer, the health and age. If the hunter had no objection the whole lower jaw was taken for further study. They reported the deer to be in the velvet and in fair condition. The average age was around 2 ½ years and the average weight around 80 pounds.

District Ranger Neff stated many vehicles were driven into such steep canyons that help was needed to get them out. Some of the vehicles are still there as the canyons are so steep and rugged the commercial tow cars refused to go in after them."

Hunter registration at Lake of the Woods – 1950's
(Grace Bradley photo)

Hunters check out as they leave the area
(Grace Bradley photo)

From deer to birds, Del Black, who grew up in Bakersfield in the 1940's, has shared this story of early bird-hunting. Del writes:

> *"Back then there were so many wild pigeons that they blackened the sky when a flight flew over. If I remember right, it was always around November when we would drive up to Mt. Pinos. We would fill the pick-up truck bed level with pigeons. I guess they got tired of getting shot at because one year, round about 1946/47 they just stopped coming over. As we cleaned the pigeons, we popped the craws out and saved the pinyon nuts they had fed on. We would then wash the nuts, soak them in salt water and roast them and have them at Christmas each year."* (Another interesting aspect of hunting!)

Also in the 1940's, Monte Bianchi remembered hunting pigeons between Frazier Mtn. and Mt. Pinos when waves and waves of the birds would fly over. He also said the meat was delicious because the pigeons were in the area feeding on pine nuts.

This forest has been and still is the habitat for numerous species of birds from the smallest of hummingbirds to the condor, the largest native bird on the North American Continent. The condors were largely inadvertently poisoned in the process of reducing the number of coyotes but shot from the sky for sport as well. In 1931, a condor sanctuary, closed to all forms of public use, was set aside in the Sespe Range, though the birds didn't know it and for their own reasons, continued to range where they would like. In the 1980's, when total extinction threatened and only eight of the birds remained, the surviving condors were captured, the last one taken from the wild in 1987. The birds were taken to zoos until their numbers could be increased through reproduction and released again. It remains to be seen as to how successful this experiment will be.

Author Mary Hunter Austin, left a wonderful description of the condor, which she refers to as a buzzard, when it was yet numerous through our mountains. Seeing an unusual amount of them in the Southern San Joaquin in the late 1800's, she made the following observations and wrote:

> *"Fifty-seven buzzards, one of each of the fifty seven fence post, sat solemnly. The vast valley was palpitatingly hot and through it all the buzzards sat with wings spread fanwise for air. There is no end to them and they smell to heaven. Their heads droop, and all their communication is a rare, horrid croak. That year the scavengers were as black as the plague all across the mesa and up the treeless, tumbled hills. On clear days they betook themselves to the upper air, where they hung*

motionless for hours, distinguished by the white patches under the wings. They must have what passes for good qualities among themselves, for they are social, not to say clannish.

There are three kinds of noises buzzards make ... it is impossible to call them notes ... raucous and elemental. There is a short croak of alarm, and the same syllable in a modified tone to serve all the purposes of ordinary conversation. The old birds make a kind of throaty chuckling to their young, but if they have any love song I have not heard it. The young yawp in the nest a little, with more breath than noise.

It is seldom one finds a buzzard's nest but by making a business of it one may come upon them in wide, quiet canons, or on the lookouts of lonely, table-topped mountains, three or four together, in the tops of stubby trees or on rotten cliffs well open to the sky for easy access. It is probable that the buzzard is gregarious, but it seems unlikely from the small number of young noted at any time that every female incubates each year. One never comes any nearer to the vulture's nest or nestlings than hearsay.

A ground animal once down may be days in dying yet the buzzards have all the time, and no beak is dropped or talon struck until the breath is wholly passed. It is doubtless the economy of nature to have the scavengers by to clean up the carrion. Once we saw two buzzards, five ravens, and a coyote feeding on the same carcass, and only the coyote seemed ashamed of the company. Nothing happens in the deep woods that all who live there do not know and from their aerial stations the buzzards watch it all."

Condor at its nest (Carl Kaford - 1941)

A Forest Service newsletter of April 1967, THE LOS PADRES GRAPEVINE, stated:

"The Los Padres Forest has a number of unique recreational opportunities that can only be found on this forest. For instance, it is the only forest in the entire United States in which you can get a chance to see the California Condor as it soars and glides on the wind currents created by the ocean and the mountain ranges."

Hunting and gathering has not been limited to that of birds and animals as people have flocked to these hills since earliest time to hunt for and to gather a harvest of pinyon and pine seeds, and numerous other plants and berries.

In the early Fall of 1924 the LOS ANGELES TIMES carried a short news item as follows:

"Much interest is being taken in the large crop of pine nuts or pinones on Frazier Mountain and Cuddy's Ranch, in the Frazier Mountains, near Lebec. They are just right to roast now and will soon be dropping from the burrs. They are very fine this year. Many people regard these later months to be the nicest time in the mountains. The air is delicious and bracing."

The RIDGE ROUTE RAMBLER of September 1939 reported that Mr. and Mrs. Art Ellis gave a pinon or pinyon roast in Robert Cuddy's back yard on Labor Day with many of the Cuddy family attending. Mrs. Ellis was Garnett Cuddy, the daughter of Robert and Lily Cuddy.

Pinon harvest at the Plush Ranch in Lockwood Valley
L-R: Sadie, little Louella, Ella and Lou Plush (Plush Family photo)

XXV - DOWN IN THE PIRU

In the *"backcountry"* of Ventura and Los Angeles Counties, to the south of Frazier Mountain and along the eastern border of the Los Padres National Forest, is the area known as Hungry Valley.

The earliest inhabitants of this valley area were *"Tataviam"* people which to the Kitanemuk people of Castac Lake meant *"the people of where the morning sun rises"*. The Chumash people from the West called them *"Alliklik"* which referred to them as being grunters or stammerers. Commonly used presently is Tataviam. The Tataviam took part in both Kitanemuk and Chumash society and trade upon occasion.

Summer campsites for the gathering and hunting done by these early people were once apparent throughout the Piru/Hungry Valley areas. Milling stones, earth ovens and stone lined pits have been found for preparing, roasting and the storing of food items. One of the major trails of the native people came up from the Santa Clara River Valley, Violin Canyon and the Piru Gorge and up to Hungry Valley. This route was then located and occasionally used by early Spanish explorers.

The first non-native use of Hungry Valley was the Mexican Land Grant of Rancho de Los Alamos y Agua Caliente (cottonwood trees & hot water) in 1843. In 1865, the boundaries of this land grant were somehow moved from Hungry Valley to the Antelope Valley and the rancho became a part of the great Tejon Ranch.

In the era of gold prospecting, hundreds of men came and went from the area and the surrounding mountains. Some did stay, however, to try their hand at farming and raising cattle, others homesteaded building a shack mostly for the purpose of having a place to come to for hunting.

The State Mineralogist, Stephen Bower, was researching the mining activity in the area in 1888 and recorded some of the early residents of the Valley. He wrote in his journal:

"July 26, 1888 – after leaving Henderson's on the Piru we crossed the mountains and lost the trail. About the middle of the afternoon we came to W. A. Smith's claim and found we were three or four miles from Castaic. (This could be the mine by that name that was at the southern base of Bear Mountain) *Being too late to return to camp we left for the mine with Smith and returned to Henderson's where we remained until morning.*

Henderson's ranch is on the site of a large Indian rancheria, the circular depression of their dwellings still being visible. The rancheria at Henderson's covers 30 to 40 acres. It would seem that there have been at least two rancherias. At least the remains, of two sweat houses are here. They are some 35 feet in diameter. Mr. H. gave me a fine pestle he plowed up. He says he has uncovered several pestles and mortars with his plow. Near Henderson's residence is a large granite block about 7' wide, 7' thick and 22' long, square, lying with two faces vertical, the top horizontal but pointing 35 degrees south. It is a monstrous block. (How interesting it would be to know how this was used and if it still exists)

We traveled back to our camp on Lockwood creek about 12 miles and I witnessed two mines as we went along."

It seems that early on, the area was originally called Honey Valley possibly because it was a valley where good amounts of honey were being produced by industrious bees but in the early 1900's it became known as Hungry Valley as dry farming was not producing well.

In 1915, a young man from Los Angeles, William J. Schmidt, Sr., began to buy out those early homesteaders until he had some 3000 acres. He then settled in the western part of Hungry Valley. It seems that Mr. Schmidt had grown tired of dealing with the public at the bar he ran down south so he was happy to get away to the remote location. During the summer months he would graze his cattle up in the mountains on Forest Service leases and in the Fall drive those cattle through the Antelope Valley to the railroad in Lancaster. Supplies were bought in the village of Gorman and it was there that the Schmidt daughter, Edna, eventually met and married, Lloyd Ralphs, Jr. of that settlement.

The Schmidt family arriving in Hungry Valley
(Schmidt Family photo)

Young William Schmidt and sister Lucille at home in Hungry Valley
(Schmidt Family photo)

Hungry Valley went through many changes in the 1920's and 30's. In the 1920's a small homestead boom occurred but most folks did not last to prove-up their claims. In the 1930's the State began building an alternate Ridge Route Road to the west of the original road opening Hungry Valley to the view of many travelers. People were known to hunt right from the edge of the road. In 1937 Hungry Valley's first and only thoroughbred horse ranch was established by the Kinsey family and visitors from throughout the country came to see the horses run.

With the Valley *"discovered"*, it soon became a popular destination for camping and hiking. Many of the old shacks and homesteads were broken into and floorboards removed to look for hidden treasure, though when none was found the boards were put to use as firewood until few buildings remained. In May of 1966 the MOUNTAIN ENTERPRISE carried an article that $3,000 worth of damage was done to the Sterling place. All the windows had been shot out, holes were shot in a stove and refrigerator and the chimney flue was blasted with a shotgun. The Sterlings had been in the Valley for 45 years. This form of recreation was controlled with the establishment of the Hungry Valley State Vehicular Recreation Area in 1978.

In southwestern Hungry Valley there is an area long referred to as *"The Piru"* because the Piru Creek runs along the base of the north slopes of Alamo and Black Mountains there. A number of mining stories have come out of the Piru but in more recent years this author was fortunate to make contact with Monte Bianchi who's family had a cabin in the Piru at the base of Black Mountain in the 1930's and 40's. From the remembrances of Mr. Bianchi we learn how his family found the area and gain some valuable insight into life in that area of these mountains at that time.

Monte's father, Julius Bianchi, was an avid hunter. When driving a *"Rio"* truck between Los Angeles and the oil fields of the Southern San Joaquin Valley in the 1920's he would often pull over to, as Monte says, *"glass a hillside"*. Of one such drive along the Old Ridge Route Road in 1928 Monte wrote:

> *"From an early age, my father had become an excellent deer hunter. He always carried a pair of binoculars, and once, while viewing the surrounding hills, his eyes focused on a good sized California black-tailed buck. Later when deer season opened that year my father parked his truck along the highway and headed for the area in which he earlier spotted the big buck."*

The area Julius was hiking to would have been from somewhere west of the old Ridge Route road, across the present Interstate 5 and into the Piru. Monte continues:

> *"Later that same morning, while glassing a hillside, my father saw movement. Moving to another location to get a better view,*

he was surprised to see a mule. Looking up the ridge, he saw a person swinging a pick. Curious as to what this person was doing, my father worked his way over to the ridge where the person was working. He found a tall, lean, one-eyed man dressed in black with a black hat. His mule stood nearby tied to a clump of sagebrush. Also nearby was a World War I, British Enfield Rifle. As my father approached the man dropped his pick, picked up his rifle and pointed it in my father's direction. After an exchange of words between the two, my father learned that the fellow was building a road by pick and shovel from where he lived along Piru Creek and was within about four miles of where the town of Gorman is now. (A roadbed still used to this day.)

To my father and to our family, this person was to become known as Jack. It took Jack about a year and a half to complete the road so a Model A could use it. A few years later, my father drove our family's 1936, four-door Ford over the road. He first drove out through the sagebrush, then across 'Cloud Burst' gully, up a small hill where Jack's road began. As we traveled the switchbacks, we could see many huge birds soaring on the updrafts. We called them 'buzzards' but they were the California Condors.

California quail, jack rabbits, rattlesnakes, king snakes, bobcats, deer and coyote passed in front of us on the many trips we eventually made on this road. As we reached the top of the hill the road descended down a steep grade that followed the ridgeline. At the bottom was a sand wash and it was here that all passengers would get out to lighten the load. Dad would get a running start as he headed for the wash. Two out of three crossings, the Ford would get stuck. I remember we had to angle across the wash, as that was where the exit was that Jack had made out of the wash.

Once out of the wash the road followed down a point of land and, after reaching the end of the point, it turned and headed across a flat valley. As we approached the Piru Creek, the road entered the creek at a point where Jack has removed most of the boulders. We would drive down the bank, enter the creek, providing the water was low, and gun the Ford up the far bank. The road then followed the valley to where it eventually ended at Jack's 'shack'.

As we approached Jack's shack, the road entered the creek again and we had to drive down the middle of the creek for about fifty to seventy yards. Jack's place was located on a piece of high ground where it could not be flooded by the Piru. The shack was built from poles and old rusted sheeting hauled in on top of his mule. Being a hermit and not of sound mind, Jack rarely, if ever, took a bath. I am sure he only changed pants and shirt when they rotted and fell off. He always wore an old black dress hat. In all the many times I saw him, he always had the same clothes on. The back of Jack's hands and neck were caked with black dirt. His face was almost as bad. He had only one eye as he had lost the other in an accident and he had a large tumor on the side of his neck the size of a half of grapefruit.

Jack's shack was nothing more than a makeshift lean-to. It had a small opening for the entry. Of all the times that my father and I had taken food to give to Jack, we never saw the opening closed. Inside, there was a small pot-bellied stove, a single bed that had a ragged blue and white striped cover with a couple of old, worn, World War I wool blankets on top. His bed was surrounded on three sides by stacks of newspapers and magazines that he had picked up in Gorman and packed in by mule. Outside, there were large stacks of wood that he had cut into firewood. He would talk very little, but he respected my mother and father. I feel this was because they would bring him food and clothing."

In 1933 Julius Bianchi, his wife, Christena, and three sons, Stanley, Steve and Monte were living in company housing at the General Petroleum Pumping Station at the mouth of Liebre Gulch only a few miles southeast of *"The Piru"*. Monte continues:

"After the road was completed, my father began to inquire about obtaining land on which to build a cabin. He found that he could get a sizeable piece of land if he were to file a claim, open a mine, and actively work it for eight years. As he began to look the area over, he remembered that while hunting a few years before, he had run across a spring at the foot of what was called 'Black Mountain'. He staked his claim with the help of a good friend that he had worked with at General Petroleum. That friend, Loi Moffett, was very knowledgeable about mining. He re-worked the old "Castaic Mine" (at the southern base of Bear Mountain) *and had several other holes in the mountains around the Lebec area. He helped my father find an area in which there was color. I can remember the piles of stones that they had brought from the Piru, stacked them up about two feet and then placed an empty Prince Albert tobacco can, with their written claim inside, and placed the can in the pile of stones.*

With a gold mine claim filed and a spring for fresh water, the plans to build a cabin were put in place.

The General Petroleum Company was going to tear down a water-cooling tower at the Liebre station. My father inquired about the water tower and he was told he could have the lumber from it if he tore it down. Along with his best friend, Roy Hamilton, my older brothers, Stan and Steve, and several other friends, they tore down the tower. They pulled every nail and stacked the lumber according to length and dimension. His boss at the GP Transportation office asked how he was going to haul the lumber to the site where my father planned to build the cabin. My father said that he hoped he could find a truck to rent or borrow. His boss said that since it didn't cost the company a dime to tear the water tower down, he was sure he could find a truck that the company was not using, but my father was to pay for all the gas used.

The truck was found and loaded and on an early Saturday morning, Dad, my brothers and Roy Hamilton, headed for Gorman. No one knows how my father got that truck to the place where the cabin was to be built. All I can say is that my father drove trucks for GP for twenty-six years and never had an accident. For those days, that was astonishing. You might say he was the best of the best of truck drivers. I believe it took three or four loads to get all the lumber to the building site. (There was a road from the community of Castaic to Hungry Valley that ran past the Liebre Pump Station. It was in use even before the Ridge Route road was built.)

With the lumber delivered, my father and brothers, along with two of my oldest brother's friends, Harvey and Dickey Hafferty, built the cabin and outhouse. They also built a tower that had a one hundred gallon empty gas drum on top, which became the shower. A spring of water was dug out to a depth of ten to twelve feet, and the sides were boarded to keep them from falling in. The well maintained a constant level of water of about three to four feet year round. They then built a waterway by nailing one of eight boards in a 'V'. The trough sections were about ten to twelve feet long. They erected poles in a cross fashion, placed each section in the crotch of the poles and ran them down the slight incline to the cabin. The water was siphoned from the well by a pipe into the trough. When we left the cabin to travel home we would pull in the siphon."

The Bianchi cabin with Black Mtn behind (Bianchi Family photo)

"After the cabin was finished, a corral, made of poles, was built to hold our two burros, 'Jack' and 'Jerry' and at times my brother's horse, 'Freckles'.

After the mine was open, my brothers would take the two burros and spend the weekends and most of the summer at the cabin mining and hauling the ore out on the burros. Stan, my oldest brother, had a Model A coupe. In the rumble seat, he had two large wooden boxes in which the ore would be placed. They would then haul it out to the Assay Office. The mine produced sufficiently to make the effort worthwhile. Eight years went by and the property belonged to my family.

My father purchased a 1927 or 28 Dodge truck with wood spoke wheels from GP in the late '30's. They took the top off and built a wood flatbed on the back. While working for GP my dad must have bought eight or nine of their old trucks that he would fix up and sell. My brother Steve and his friend Dickey Hafferty would drive the old Dodge all over the Valley as well as Hungry Valley. Sometimes Jack would ask them to drive him to Gorman. Since the truck only had room for two in the front, Jack would sit in back and hang on for dear life as they headed for Gorman. It did happen that they would have to stop once or twice to pick up Jack when he would fall off the flatbed. When my dad would take us out rabbit hunting he would tie us on the back so we wouldn't fall off. We would just shoot from the back of the truck.

My dad purchased an old buzz saw with a tilting table. He would jack up the rear end of the truck and would fix a belt to the tireless rim. The belt ran to a pulley on the saw. He would start the motor, put it in gear, and the large circular blade would turn. To get the right speed, he would pull the hand-operated throttle out. We would then cut wood for the winter. I'm sure Jack was given a lot of wood by my dad also."

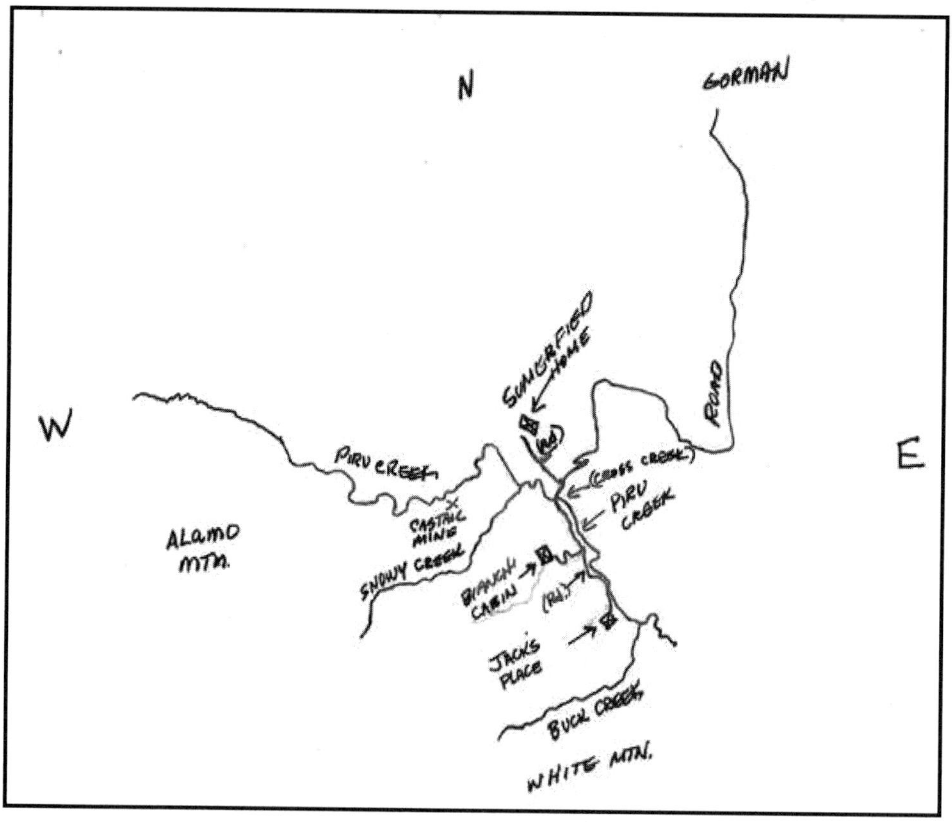

Map of Hungry Valley where the Bianchi family lived
(drawn by Monte Bianchi)

"On one trip to the cabin, my mother prepared a stew for the family. After dinner there was a fair amount left. She put the leftovers in a pot and my father jumped in his '29 Model A pickup and headed to Jack's shack. As we pulled in, we were met by Jack's three hounds, and of course, Jack, carrying his trusty World War One British Enfield. Dad told him we had some stew for him and gave him the pot. Dad got back into the

truck and told Jack we would be back for the pot later. Jack said no. He proceeded to get an old, rusty three pound coffee can, dumped in the stew and gave the pan back to us. As we left, Jack was sitting on an old wooden chair, spoon and can in hand. He would have a spoon full and then each dog would get a spoon full. This scene has left an everlasting image in my mind.

One of my father's very best friends, that he worked with and hunted with for over thirty years, had ridden his horse up the 'Buck Creek' trail hunting deer. It was dark by the time he hit the trail to Jack's shack. As he rode by Jack's there was no activity except for the dogs barking at him. About one hundred yards down the road, his horse shied up and almost threw him off. He managed to get his horse under control. Thinking it was a rattler, he turned on his flashlight and there was Jack, lying in the road, dead drunk, and passed out from red wine. How long he had been there, no one knows. Jack had a wine problem. Every time he would ride his mule into Gorman, he would come back with a gallon of wine.

We found out that Jack had a son who was a lawyer in New York and from time to time he would send a check to the general store at Gorman. One time my father and I stopped at the store and the owner asked my father if he would take some checks to Jack. There had to have been five or six he had received over the past year. He hadn't cashed any of them. Whenever we were at our cabin, Jack, aboard his mule, his rifle laid across his lap would show up to see who we were. Jack built a trail to his mine and later a road. It zigzagged back and forth to the top of the hill. It was one of the most perfect zigzags, switchback roads I have ever seen.

Our cabin was located halfway between Jack's shack and the Summerfield home. Bob Summerfield and his wife had a permanent home in the valley. Bob was a veteran of World War I and, while in combat, lost a leg. He was a tall, large man who had been an excellent prizefighter. The story goes that the champion of the world, at that time, was putting on exhibition fights in the rear areas for the troops. Bob's C.O. gave him permission to be one of the fighters to fight the champion at one of the exhibitions. Bob is said to have traveled all over France trying to fight the champ and he never would fight Bob. Bob returned to his company on the front lines and shortly thereafter lost his leg."

Roy Hamilton, Monte and Julius Bianchi and Bob Summerfield at the Bianchi place – August 1952 (Bianchi Family photo)

"My father thought we should have some shade trees like those that the Summerfield's had planted around their place. So my father planted some cottonwood trees. The spring supplied them with water and they grew rapidly. Once, when we had let the burros out to forge on their own, they helped themselves to peeling some of the bark off of those trees. My father wrapped burlap around the peeled trees, hoping that the trees would survive. All did.

My oldest brother would set traps to catch bobcats and coyotes. He would catch them, put them in a cage he had made, feed them and release them back into the wild. At one time, he had three bobcats and a coyote in his pen.

When I was twelve years old, I bagged my first deer, which was a black tail buck with a four by five rack. My dad and I hunted deer and quail around our cabin until 1953. About 1950, the game department began planting the Piru with Rainbow Trout. Fishing was very good and all the times we fished the Piru below our cabin and above the Summerfield home, we never saw another angler. The best fishing was done where Snowy Creek emptied into the Piru. During the summer, my mom, brothers and I would head for the creek each day for a dip. My brothers had arranged the boulders so that a nice deep pool was formed. In 90 to 100 degree temperatures, a dip in the Piru was something to look forward to."

Stan Bianchi with dad, Julian, bchind their cabin – with two bucks taken on Black Mtn – Dec 1941 (Bianchi Family photo)

Steve Bianchi cooling off in Piru Creek (Bianchi Family photo)

"Quail were abundant in areas along the creek. Mountain quail were abundant above our cabin in the draws. We also hunted doves on a ridge that ran along side of the cabin. I used to sit on the point over-looking the valley below with my older brother and we would shoot the doves as they bombed down the draw heading for the Piru for a drink.

In 1946 we moved to the State of Washington and my father sold the claim and the cabin. We moved back to Southern California in 1950 and continued to hunt and fish the Piru area but we never saw Jack again. On one hunting trip we were staying out in the open under a large oak tree at the Summerfield place. It was a beautiful night, clear with all the stars out. As we lay on our cots the acorns began to fall and I mean a lot of acorns. Boulders on Black Mountain and in the creek began to move and crash against each other. Then the ground move. It was the 1952 Tehachapi earthquake. A memorable event!

I have attempted to return to the site of our cabin a few years ago. I turned off at Gorman to see if I could find the road and all I found was off-road ATVs. As I drove into the backcountry on paved roads, we crossed the Piru and drove up Alamo Mountain. This was where my father would throw a packsaddle on our burro, Jerry, and hike from our cabin, up the Piru and on to Alamo Mountain to deer hunt. He would be gone for two to three days. When he returned, his clothes would be in shreds as there were no trails on the mountain. We used to hunt Hungry Valley for jackrabbits and quail.

I believe I found the road that would lead to our cabin, but the gate was locked as the area is suppose to be where the white-toed toad was breeding. Someday I would still like to return to the cabin site."

A footnote about Jack, it seems he had been a miner in the area for many years and was known by Forest Service personnel as *"One-Eyed Jack"*.

*   *   *   *

Another Hungry Valley story of interest, long talked about but now all but forgotten, was the crash of an airliner in 1946. LOST TREASURE magazine of October 2004 brought back some of those memories. In that article, Anthony Belli researched and interviewed Frank Sterling of the Sterling family mentioned earlier in this chapter. Belli wrote:

> *"Western Airlines Flight 23 vanished without a trace during a violent storm north of Los Angeles. The plane had received final clearance for landing at the Burbank Airport. The flight had originated in Alberta Canada on Tuesday, November 12th, 1946, made stops in Montana, Idaho, Salt Lake City and Las Vegas and was due to arrive at the Lockheed Air Terminal at Burbank with the eight remaining passengers and three crew members in the early morning hours of Wednesday, November 13th. Over the Mojave Desert the flight encountered severe weather. At 3:24 a.m. the pilot radioed Burbank that he was over Newhall at 9,000 feet and beginning his descent. The final clearance to land was acknowledged by the crew at 3:37 a.m..*
>
> *Three minutes later, at 3:40 a.m., 21 year-old Frank Sterling was awakened during what he thought was a fierce storm over his grandparent's ranch in Hungry Valley. He soon realized it was an airplane flying far too low. It was determined that Flight 23 vanished at 3:41 a.m.*
>
> *Shortly after sunrise an air search was begun but visibility was limited. The plane wasn't found until Friday morning, November 15th. It was found at the 5,900 foot elevation on the northern face of White Mountain* (just south of Hungry Valley)."

A DC-3 like the one that crashed on White Mountain in 1946
(Lost Treasure Magazine)

"A ground search was begun but the steep terrain and snow slowed the efforts. Rescuers finally arrived at the crash site on the afternoon of the 18th finding that the DC-3 had disintegrated and burned, killing all eleven persons on board. The Civil Aeronautics Board determined that the airliner had been blown off course between Palmdale and Newhall due to severe winds. It is thought that when the pilot radioed that he was over Newhall he was actually closer to the Lebec/Gorman area.

Unique to the flight was that one of the passengers was a diamond merchant and was supposed of have been carrying a leather valise containing $100,000 in cut diamonds. Mr. Sterling indicated that locals gathered at Holland's Summit, café and bar, reported hearing that the rescue crew may have found some of the diamonds. When Sterling's father, Francis, later hunted near the crash site he reported that much of the destroyed plane has been covered by a rock slide with only the tail section showing. A cross had been painted on the wreckage to signal other pilots that the wreckage had been searched."

Frank Sterling lives in Bakersfield and in a recent interview with this author he could add no more information to the story. Presently there is a Sterling Campground in Hungry Valley that marks the location of his grandparent's ranch where Frank operated a Hunt Club in the 1950's.

This author's husband, Jim Kane, also remembered the plane crash. He understood that on board were gamblers from Las Vegas and that when some co-workers from the Forest Service were sent up to remove the wreckage in the 1950's they found a silver dollar melted onto one of the seats. The crew went up the mountain with mules and brought down what they could so future air searches wouldn't spot these remains again.

XVI - SNOW & RESCUE

Except for the occasional three to four foot snowfall, snow, or white rain as early man called it, is always welcomed by the residents of the San Emigdio Mountains. It excites the heart and is one of the reasons most live here. Snow is one of our most important natural resources as it so slowly and evenly replenishes our local water sources.

Through all time, human beings and animals have found ways to enjoy a good snowfall. Various forms of winter recreation greatly increased in the local mountains after World War II. In 1939 Kern County did a considerable development for the purpose of winter sports play on their privately held Campo Alto Campground at the summit of Mt. Noroeste (Mt. Abel) where they built a lodge, parking and a rope tow. Some 5,000 people from warmer sections of the county satisfied their *"snow hunger"* there annually until most began to look for the better developed ski runs and resorts of the Sierras and elsewhere in Southern California. When the Abel Ski Resort closed the mountain top was returned to the care of the Forest Service.

Campo Alto Lodge on Mt. Abel

A 1949 Forest Service report indicated that there were no winter sports facilities operating in the area, yet 25,000 people came during the winter months and made their own ski runs and slides just by using the mountain sides.

In 1953 the Forest Service allowed a private concessionaire, Walter R. Pfeiffer, to develop a snow play area where the road then ended, at the Mt. Pinos Campground, reported to be *"the highest snow park in Southern California"*. There were three rope tows, one for beginners, intermediate and advanced skiers, plenty of sledding hills, a snack bar with a welcome *"warming house"* and first aid station. The concessionaire also established a shop at Lake of the Woods where skis, boots, pole sets, toboggans, snow scooters, snow saucers and tire chains could be rented – a business that has been owned and operated by the Gustafson family since the mid-1970's.

A 1959 newspaper article reported that Forest Service personnel, Highway Patrol officers, Kern County Rescue Squad and Civil Air Patrol were used to control the heavy winter-time traffic on the road to Mt. Pinos. The article also reported:

> *"Fourteen warming pits were established in the play areas for the convenience of the visitors. Here they may cook their meals or warm their icy hands and feet."*

By 1960 the road had been completed to the top of Mt. Pinos and the Chula Vista campground. A large parking area was installed, greatly expanding snow play to the summit. Newspaper articles indicated that as many as 35,000 snow enthusiasts were counted on Mt. Pinos during a single winter weekend. Another statistic located reported that in a two month period of time, from December of 1959 to February of 1960, 63,000 people visited Mt. Pinos. An article in the BAKERSFIELD CALIFORNIAN about that time read as follows:

> *"Spring may be here but winter sports drew throngs to the Mt. Pinos area during the weekend. District Ranger Jack Williams reports 10,000 visited the supervised snow area Saturday and Sunday. This is believed to be the largest crowd to enjoy winter sports at any one time on the Mt. Pinos site. The figure does not include the many persons who played along the Mt. Pinos Forest Highway. Williams said 800 cars passed into the play area during a half-hour period Sunday.*
>
> *The new supervised play area, the only one of its kind in Southern California, is in the experimental stage, Williams said. Future development of more safe play area is planned. Under a special use permit, Albert Myers has developed a play area at the end of the Mt. Pinos Forest Highway near the top of Mt.*

Pinos. The experimental project has four toboggan runs that are supervised and maintained in a safe condition by Myers. As this winter provided only four weekends of snow fun, the operation is still classed as in the experimental stage. A fee of 25 cents per person is made for using the toboggan runs. This grants permission to use the runs all day if desired." (Myers also ran a snow play area at Wrightwood)

Snow play activity at Chula Vista after the parking lot was opened - 1962
(Grace Bradley photo)

Traffic jam on the road to Mt. Pinos – 1962 (Grace Bradley photo)

Parking conditions at the Chula Vista parking lot – 1962
(Grace Bradley photo)

One day snowfalls in the three to six foot range have been common from Lebec to the top of Pinos, and continue to be so – but not as frequently in more recent years.

Cut made by new snow removal equipment on the road to Mt. Pinos in the 1960's
(Grace Bradley photo)

Snow play traffic on the road to LOWs – 1960's
(Grace Bradley photo)

One of many snow rescue stories comes to us from the January 1953 issue of the local newspaper the FRAZIER MOUNTAIN BREEZE. It read:

> *"Twenty-three Oxnard High School students received first aid in Frazier Park on Sunday, January 18, after have been lost in the Frazier Mountain area for almost 24 hours. The 14 girls and 9 boys who were lost were members of a group of 40 youths who were spending the weekend at the YMCA camp about 6 miles west of Frazier Park. The youngsters became confused at about 1 p.m. Saturday when a heavy fog rolled in upon them and were unable to find their way back to the camp.*
>
> *According to Al Weisgerber of the Forestry Department, the boys and girls were located at about 10:30 a.m. Sunday on Plato (Pleito?) Trail by search parties from the Kern County and Ventura County Sheriff's Departments and the Forestry Service. None from the group was seriously injured altho some suffered frostbitten hands and feet and all were cold and hungry. Snow from the recent snowstorms in the mountainous region still cover the terrain and temperatures drop to below freezing at night in the area which has an elevation of about 6000 feet."*

Another story of search and rescue from a January 1953 issue of the same newspaper read as follows:

> *"The body of Frank Arundell, 68, member of a pioneer Fillmore family missing since June 28 was found near his abandoned camp site in Fir Canyon in the Frazier Mountain area by members of the Fillmore Mounted Posse. Twenty-two men of the Posse hiked up the north slope of Alamo Mountain where they found the body. According to reports there seemed to have been no evidence of violence. The mountaineer's horse was found near the camp site apparently suffering no ill effects from its six month stay near its master."* (It's quite amazing no campers or hunters noticed the horse in six months time!)

Also in the early 1950's, area historian Grace Bradley wrote this story of survival. The Kabraris family from Inglewood drove up Mill Canyon on Mt. Pinos where Frank Kabraris decided to do some target shooting. Mrs. Bradley wrote that Mr. Kabraris said:

> *" 'One minute there was no snow and the next I was right in the middle of a blizzard. I couldn't see the car.' Oldtimers in these mountains recall storms like that do happen occasionally when the whole world seems blotted out in one vast swirling snowstorm. 'I waited a little bit and then started off toward the car ... or where I thought it was. I guessed wrong.'*
>
> *In the automobile the anxious young wife with a four month old baby and a two year old began honking the horn to let her husband know where the car was. 'I heard the honking but in that canyon the sound seemed to come from different places.' As dark approached Mrs. Kabraris and her brother-in-law drove to the Chuchupate Ranger Station to give the alarm. By midnight the rescue unit had a kitchen set up, stretchers ready and men spread out ready to begin the search at the first hit of daylight.*
>
> *High on the mountain Kabraris kept trudging through the falling snow. He was dressed in Levi's, a windbreaker jacket and had on low shoes. 'I knew if I stopped I'd freeze.' He had one match which he didn't dare use. The snow was coming down so hard he knew he couldn't light a fire. The one-in-a-million chance came. He stumbled across a plain ordinary old washtub that someone had left in a clearing maybe last summer, maybe years ago. He dug it up out of the snow and then collected twigs and branches. 'I propped up the washtub and built my fire underneath the tub. I held my breath until the twigs caught fire.'*

Kabraris built a roaring fire and only then did he dare rest for a while. Even so, he said, he didn't dare go to sleep for fear the fire would go out. He fed the fire steadily during the long night.

At daybreak the snowstorm lifted and Kabraris found himself able to see where he was going again. In about a half hour he walked up to the home of Wesley & Julia Cuddy Darling in middle of Cuddy Valley where he was taken in, warmed and fed. Darling notified the sheriff and the search was called off. Kabraris had walked across Mt. Pinos from the west side and along the ridge to the east."

From earliest time area residents (Indian and Anglo) have been called on to help look for neighbors or visitors who have gotten lost in these mountains and canyons. In March of 1962 the Mt. Pinos District Ranger, Jack Williams, put out the call for men to help rescue a man lost at night in Mill Canyon on Mt. Pinos, in a blinding blizzard that had come up without warning. The Upper Ojai Sheriff's Rescue Units responded to Lockwood's Deputy Sheriff Richard Alves' call and also men from the Ventura Sheriff's office. Men arrived at the Lockwood substation at daybreak driving their own vehicles with their own equipment. A base camp was established near where the man was last seen and three teams of men began the search. The base camp soon received word that the lost fellow was a nearby ranch house. This event was only one of many that made it apparent that a local Search & Rescue group was needed so that others didn't have to drive so far, lose time from work, etc. to get to our remote location. A local Sheriff's Rescue Unit was organized shortly after this event and was mostly comprised of men from the various law enforcement offices throughout the mountain.

As the need grew to assist the local law enforcement offices, a volunteer group was trained in rescue work and officially organized in 1962. Lockwood rancher Carl Hofmeister set aside one of his ranch buildings for a unit headquarters where equipment was stored. This first group of volunteers were Roger Thompson who worked for the Southern California Milling Company, Jerry Dent from the Richfield Oil Company, John Christensen a painting contractor, Otto Reynolds of the Ojai Oil Company, Arnold Sockwell a local ranch foreman, with Carl Hofmeister serving as the captain of the group.

Founded through the Kern County Sheriff's Department the group was first called the Frazier Mountain Search & Rescue Posse, then the Mt. Pinos Search & Rescue Posse and is presently known as the Southern Kern Search & Rescue Posse. Win Sanger, the first captain of the volunteer Kern County posse, recalled one of the first fundraisers locally. All the little communities of the mountain joined together for the common cause, to benefit the S & R. The event was held on top of Mt. Pinos and Charlie Cuddy did one of his famous deep pit barbecues. The organization has had many dedicated volunteers in its numbers through the years.

Southern Kern Search and Rescue Posse – 1976: L-R Lieutenant Ben Carson, Secretary-Treasurer Gary Eden, Captain Frank Capello, Training Officer Chuck Kinsman, Lieutenant Tom Moore, Sergeant-at-Arms Jim Taggart

The efforts of the local Search & Rescue group have been many, some successful and some not. The local editor of the MOUNTAIN ENTERPRISE in the 1970's, Fred Kiesner, gave this excellent description of one such rescue. In March of 1976 he described the event as follows:

> *"Stephen Barkley, an 11-year old Santa Monica youth, is alive today only because of the fantastic luck, and the dramatic rescue efforts of about fifty volunteers and local law enforcement and forest service personnel.*
>
> *The story began when young Barkley arrived at the snow play area high up on Mt. Pinos at about 7000 feet on Sunday, February 29. He was with a group of youths from the Santa Monica area, on a bus trip sponsored by the local park system. Sometime around three in the afternoon, the group was loaded in the bus, and they were set to leave when the supervisors found Stephen missing.*

They reported it to officials in the area but since this is not an uncommon occurrence on a weekend, with literally thousands of visitors to the mountain snowplay area, and often scores of bus groups, there was not a great deal of initial concern for the boy.

As details were being gathered and descriptions obtained the word spread among the 'snowbunnies' in the area that there was a boy missing. A man who was apparently a cross country skier, advised the officials that he had seen a boy fitting the description sliding in an area at least a mile west of the normal snow play area. He indicated that he thought it was strange that the boy would be that far away, and alone, but the boy did not appear to be in trouble, and did not ask for help.

Based upon this information, Deputy Zimmerman, Ranger Ron Baima, the man who had spotted the boy, and one of the bus group supervisors, along with another cross country backpacker, launched a search to the area where the boy had last been spotted.

About this time it was discovered that the boy had left his coat on the bus. The mountain was clouding over and snow flurries began to fall. There were forecasts that a bad storm might hit the area. Concern and tension began to mount.

Forest service and law enforcement personnel began to converge on the area and as darkness approached the local Southern Kern Search and Rescue Posse was mobilized and Sergeant Dave Merritt of the Kern County Sheriff's department arrived and took charge of the operation.

The bus was sent home to Santa Monica without the Barkley youth, and his parents were notified that he was missing. Two adult supervisors from the bus group stayed on the mountain to aid in the search.

In the meantime, the original small search party radioed that they thought they had found the tracks that might be the boy's leading off down the side of the mountain. There were thousands of other tracks in the area, so it was at best a long-shot, but it was the only clue to the boy's location.

Darkness was approaching, with wind and snow beginning and everyone that was out searching for the boy was called back in so that all could be accounted for and an organized search could be planned. There was a definite and real danger that others could be lost while searching for the boy in the moonless darkness, with high winds, sleet and snow. At times during the night, 'white-out' conditions existed on the mountain.

A command post was set up in the parking lot at the Chula Vista snowplay area and it was decided that a base camp would be set up for the search at the point where the possible tracks of the boy had been spotted."

Search command post at Chula Vista parking lot on Mt. Pinos
(Fred Kiesner photo)

"Ranger Bobby Holdridge and Kern County Deputy Rick Cox established the base camp and built a gigantic bonfire in hopes that the boy would see it and as a reference point for the two men as they began the search. When the team from the Search and Rescue Posse arrived one was assigned to stay at the camp and the rest began searching in pairs. They then formed an eight man team and with snowshoes, ropes and lights in hand began to follow the set of tracks that they thought might be the boy's.

The snow was often treacherous and at times they would fall into drifts with snow up to their waists. It was extremely hard going, agonizingly slow, but as the hours went by, it became more and more apparent that they were following a 'hot trail'.

At Chuchupate Ranger Station, District Ranger Dave Hammond and his people were coordinating efforts to organize additional searchers who were now arriving from the upper Ojai and Ventura areas of Ventura County. Close to midnight additional search teams arrive at the mountain top and are deployed.

An eight man team made their way to an area above Pine Mountain Club. A few minutes past 4 a.m. the radio at the command post crackled with the message that the search team had found the boy, and that he was alive. He, and they, had climbed down the mountain and halfway back up Sawmill Mountain. One of the searchers, Bill Langsfeld, had found him unconscious, under a bush, still clutching his red sled. A bonfire was built, and the rescuers began to thaw the boy out. He barely had a pulse, and his body was so stiff that it took nearly a half hour before could move his arms from over his head, the position they were in when he was found.

The main part of the rescue team stayed at the bonfire with the boy while Holdridge and Len Griffin made their way back up the mountain to join up with the Ojai and Venture Search teams. They arrived on the road to the Mt. Pinos Condor Lookout, about a mile above the parking lot command post, about seven in the morning ... in very bad condition. A fresh search team then followed Griffin & Holdridge's trail back to the rescuers to bring them food and to help bring them out.

Cloud cover prevented the use of a helicopter. Based upon the condition of the boy and six remaining members of the original rescue party, and the toughness of the climb out, the decision was made that the group would climb down the mountain towards Pine Mountain Club. The command post at the top of Pinos was dismantled and everyone scurried to PMC.

Finally, the pilot of the Los Angeles County Fire Department Rescue helicopter with a paramedic on board, decided to try to make it through a temporary opening in the clouds and fog. Through radio communication from the ground they found the group and were able to land. The boy was flown to the hospital in Valencia. He was in shock, unconscious, with a pulse of 40. He responded very well to treatment and will recover without any permanent damage to or loss of limbs.

Ground crews linked up with the rescue party and all enjoyed a hot cup of coffee. All converged on the Frazier Park Kern

> *County Fire Station where crews from the Ventura County Fire Department put on a big meal for all the volunteers. The rescuers represented three counties, six agencies, and three separate search and rescue posses. The boy's red sled was passed around and each rescuer signed it as a memento to be given to the lad."*

Writings about many more rescues, some successful, some not, some in the snow, some in good weather, can be found in the pages of the local newspapers. These mountains have centuries of stories and adventures to tell – if they could only talk. . . .

Another form of snow play - a sled dog team training at Chuchupate Ranger Station – 1960's (Grace Bradley photo)

Part Three

WATER

XXVII - 1800's EFFORTS

Without a doubt the most important natural resource of the San Emigdio Mountains is water. Located just 50 miles east of the Pacific Ocean, the area has long been blessed with a generous amount of rain and snow to replenish the mountain springs, ground water and streams. Before and since mankind, *"nature"* has continually rearranged these local water sources through excessive rainfall, devastating droughts and powerful earthquakes. The ever-changing locations of fault line *"sag ponds"* and mountain springs, gives proof to water captured and rearranged by the movement of the earth. Repeated flooding and drought have greatly changed the landscape as well.

Since the advent of early man, ways of moving water from one point to another have been studied and achieved. The first recorded man-made movement of water locally was in the 1850's, on the Tejon Indian Reservation east of Grapevine Canyon, when water was moved through ditches to irrigate the first crops planted there. When Thomas Baker settled in the future area of Baker's Field in the 1860's, he envisioned, and accomplished, the draining of the marshes along the Kern River to create farm lands and residential areas. He hired crews of Indians to build small dams and canals that extended as far south as Buena Vista Lake.

The next recorded channels were dug on the northern slopes of the San Emigdio Mountains in the 1870's for the purpose of carrying water from San Emigdio Creek to fields on the ranch at the mouth of that canyon. Throughout the San Emigdio and Tehachapi Mountains, miners and prospectors moved water by digging channels for long distances to enhance their mining operations. An article in an 1876 issue of a Los Angeles newspaper reported an effort to bring water from Elizabeth Lake to the mines in Hungry Valley – no small effort – though there is no further information that this was accomplished. The 1870's were years of extreme drought so Crain Lake and Quail Lake, the closest water sources to Hungry Valley, were no doubt dry at this time, as they often were, thus the attempt to bring water all the way from Elizabeth Lake.

(A side note: Crain Lake was at the east end of the present Quail Lake and the original Quail Lake was to the west of the present lake – both of the original lakes were sag ponds along the San Andreas Fault line.)

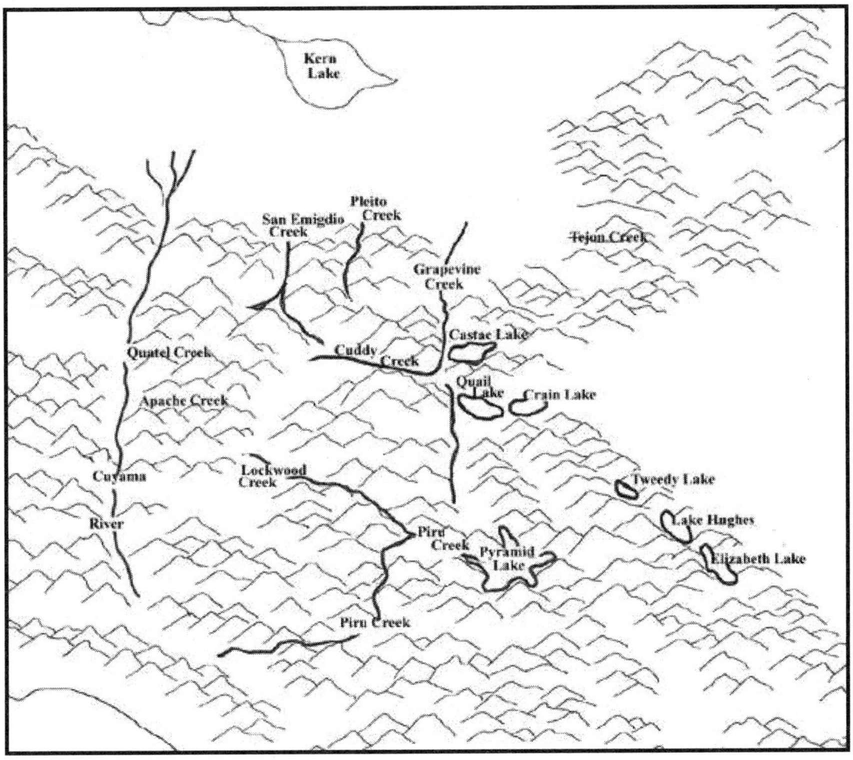

Natural water sources of the area

In the droughts of the 1880's and 1890's many irrigation canal schemes were proposed to the desperate homesteaders in Southern San Joaquin Valley. These water-racketeers would propose canals through impossible places never intending to dig them. The inexperienced farmers did not realize how ridiculous these plans were. Most homesteaders had no cash so they put up their land in lieu of money and soon lost those lands to the larger land holders who could buy them out. Because of the droughts, Tejon Ranch found it necessary to cut the fences so their cattle could have access to government land. Cowboys had the added duties of protecting water sources and pulling the dead cattle from the drying up water holes.

Water issues were of such major importance in the San Joaquin Valley that the problem was taken to court by two of the major land owners, Henry Miller of Miller & Lux, and Haggin & Tevis Ranch. Miller had so much land it was said he could drive his cattle from Bakersfield to San Francisco without leaving his own range lands – and he owned the water rights along with it. When Haggin & Tevis challenged Miller & Lux in court they fought for the smaller farmers as well but Miller won. Even the Governor considered it a devastating decision though Miller eventually set up a compromise to everyone's satisfaction.

By the 1890's the need for additional water in the agricultural areas of Southern California was becoming more apparent. Of great interest locally is an *"Engineer's Statement"* that J. B. Lippincott prepared for the newly created Antelope Valley Water Company in

1894. It seems he did an extensive study on the San Emigdio Mountain area as well as in the Antelope Valley. Lippincott writes:

"It is contemplated to divert the waters of Piru Creek and its tributaries and the waters of Cuddy Creek to the lands of the west end of the Antelope Valley in Los Angeles and Kern Counties, and the lands of the Rincon del Tejon in the southern limit of the San Joaquin Valley, also in Kern County."

The Antelope Valley Water Company's purpose was to *"file"* on all available government lands with water sources so that they could regulate the flow of the winter storm waters and store them in a series of reservoirs. The same company would then control the storage sites usage. Four *"Regulating Reservoir Site"* with dams were suggested – one where Lockwood Creek comes into Piru Creek, one on the Piru, possibly about where Pyramid Lake is today, one where Cuddy Creek flows into Castac Lake at Lebec and the last Crain Lake, which is fed by a number of streams in the West Antelope Valley. The dam at the Lockwood Reservoir was to be 125' high, at the Piru Reservoir – 120' high, at the Castac Reservoir there would be three dams 37', 52' and 79' high and at the Crain Reservoir three dams 30', 71' and 94' high.

Of these reservoir sites Lippincott wrote:

"Both the Crain and Castac lakes are reservoir sites that have few if any equals in the state of California. Both lie at the head of valleys that for fertility of soil and extent of area have few if any superiors in the State. Crain Lake lies on a summit at sufficient elevation in such a position as to completely command the entire area of the Antelope Valley. On the other hand Castac Lake is located in such a position as to completely command the lands in the southern portion of the San Joaquin Valley. The reservoirs would be located at the head of two of the largest and most fertile valleys in the State, commanding in each case many times more land than our water will serve, land that is almost barren without water and cannot be reached by any other supply."

The water was to be moved between the Crain and Castac reservoirs via *"the Gorman tunnel"*, as needed.

Of interest is that early in the report, Lippincott wrote:

"A rather crude record of rainfall has been kept by Mr. John Cuddy on Cuddy Creek for a period of about twelve years, and he reports an average rainfall of about 27 inches. He says that this

year's record low of nine inches is his minimum. Fort Tejon, at a lower elevation, records an annual precipitation of 18 inches from 1854-64. Other old inhabitants of the mountains, who are in the stock business where rain means grass and no rain means no feed, claim the rainfall of this region to reach 30 inches.

The prediction of runoff is impossible to determine exactly, owing to the varying soil and topography and the wide difference in the manner of precipitation whether rain or snow, violent storms or gentle showers and any prediction of runoff must be a matter of more or less speculation and at best only approximate.

The drainage basin of Piru Creek contains over two hundred square miles of area mostly in Ventura County. Much of it consists of drifts and polished rocks on the sides of precipitous mountains and canyons that create a frequent presence of high floods.

The drainage of Cuddy Creek of twenty-eight square miles is not included in this estimate as it has been reported upon and included in the estimate of available water supply for the Tejon project. In case it is not used in this way it can be utilized as a part of the Antelope Valley Water project. The waters are filed upon and held by the AVWCompany."

Elsewhere in his report Lippincott wrote more about the Tejon Ranch Project:

"Quite a strong movement is on foot for the colonization of the La Liebre Grant. It is proposed that the Valley land of this Grant shall be divided into small tracts and Eastern and Foreign colonists located thereon, that a town shall be built and railroad connections made with Newhall, which will place the Western portion of the Valley within 60 miles of Los Angeles."

The first *"Tejon Project"* mentioned above was to be around Castac Lake much as *"Tejon Mountain Village"* is currently being proposed. The second, was on the Liebre Grant – one of the four Mexican Land Grants that makes up Tejon Ranch and is located in the West Antelope Valley. This second colony suggested above would have been in the area similar to the present proposed site of the community of *"Centennial, California"*. Thus Tejon has attempted developments in these two areas for well over a century.

A letter of support was included within the report. It seems that the men of the Western Antelope Valley held a meeting at a Fourth of July celebration in 1894 and as a result the following letter was drawn up. Written from Fairmont, California on August 7th, 1894, it reads:

"Mr. J. B. Lippincott,
Engineer Antelope Valley Water Company,

Dear Sir:
At a mass meeting held at Lake Katrina, On July 4th last, a resolution was unanimously and most heartily voted to the effect that: 'It is the opinion of the resident land owners of the Valley and all others here assembled that it is absolutely necessary to the development of all interests here that abundant water for irrigation should be placed upon the land and to this end we pledge the hearty co-operation of all residents here assembled, with any one or with any company that shall undertake to furnish an adequate water supply.'

The plans of the Piru Creek Company were referred to of course, as that is the only one now planning to do this. This was a very large assemblage, some four hundred people living west of the Antelope hills were present, and more representative than any other ever held in this Valley. I was instructed to transmit the sentiment of the meeting to the Irrigation Company, which I now take pleasure in doing through you. There can be no doubt that when your company gets ready to go to work, it will receive every support that so beneficent an undertaking deserves.

You can command my services at any time and in any way that I can be of use.

Very truly yours,
A. R. Sprague,
Manager of Fairmont Orchard Co."
(The Sprague name was later well-known on Tejon Ranch)

The location of Lake Katrina has not been determined though it could have been a small reservoir in the Neenach area that held water run from the springs in the hills to the south. The reference to the Piru Creek Company would indicate that the people of that area (probably mostly miners in Hungry Valley) were also organized to see how the water could be put into reservoirs there. Obviously none of the water source changes were made but the Antelope Valley Agency still oversees the water distribution in that valley. At the same time Lippincott was studying the water sources in the Antelope Valley, similar studies were being made along the eastern slope of the Sierras as well.

XXVII – THE LOS ANGELES AQUEDUCT

The first manmade movement of water through the local mountains didn't take place until the Los Angeles Aqueduct was put through in the 1910's. It seems that the Aqueduct was the ingenious idea of one Fred Eaton who became the mayor of Los Angeles in 1898. Aware of the great runoff of water from the Sierra's into the Owens Valley in East-Central California, Eaton began devising a plan to acquire ownership to land and water rights there as early as the 1880's, and even laid out the route the water could take to move it southward. Eaton had decided that he would have Los Angeles build an aqueduct and then purchase the water from him.

Meanwhile Joseph Lippincott, a hydraulic engineer living in Los Angeles and a friend of Mr. Eaton, was doing the water study (reviewed in the previous chapter of the book) in the Antelope Valley. Following the Antelope Valley study, Lippincott was hired by the U.S. Reclamation Service to investigate the feasibility of initiating water reclamation projects in the West, and the Owens Valley was his new area of study. The government's purpose was to develop water resources in arid areas of the West to promote agricultural expansion and production by irrigation. Information was not located as to who urged the government to institute this program. In the summer of 1904, somehow Eaton & Lippincott are both *"vacationing"* in the Owens Valley and the Eastern Sierras – Lippincott to locate a dam on the river there for the United States Government, and Eaton to further research his ideas – though they no doubt already had plans to work together.

As a part of his plan Fred Eaton created the Los Angeles Bureau of Water Works & Supply and appointed his friend, William Mulholland, as the superintendent. Mulholland then went to the Owens Valley with Eaton and brought back his recommendations about the aqueduct project to the new Los Angeles Board of Water Commissioners.

> The INYO REGISTER of September 29, 1904 reported:
> *"Fred Eaton, ex-mayor of Los Angeles, and William Mulholland, who is connected with the water system of that city, arrived a few days ago and went up to the site of the proposed government dam on the Owens River."*

The person who took them around, the story continued, was Joseph Lippincott, the regional engineer for the Reclamation Service. Lippincott had already taken Eaton around the valley twice before.

Their actions were kept quite confidential fearing the increased cost of the acquisition of lands and water rights if the news got out about what their plan was. Meanwhile, the Owens Valley landowners were in favor of the Federal reclamation project and a dam for their farming needs so most thought that when Los Angeles speculators began to purchase land and water rights in the Owens Valley, that they too realized the value of the new agricultural possibilities.

Lippincott, Eaton and Mulholland review plans (LADWP photo)

A resident of the Owens Valley, the writer Mary Hunter Austin, was convinced that the valley had died when it sold its first water right to Los Angeles and that that city would never stop until it owned the whole river and all of the land. She traveled to Los Angeles to interview Mulholland and after meeting with her, he was reported to have said:

> *"By God, that woman is the only one who has brains enough to see where this is going."*

> In his book, CADILLAC DESERT, Marc Reisner writes:
> *"Senator Sylvester Smith, a former newspaper publisher from Bakersfield, reluctantly supported the plan to use water out of his district if the Owens Valley would have first rights to the water and any surplus water could not be used for irrigation in the San Fernando Valley, making investors there extremely wealthy. It*

was Smith who also suggested that it would be more valuable to the state and nation if it built up a great, strong, progressive city on America's weakly defended western flank instead of maintaining a little agrarian utopia in the high desert. This was a convincing theory."

Next a Los Angeles County bond measure to pay for the construction of an aqueduct passed by a ten to one margin in an election in June of 1907. With Federal approval needed for such a gigantic project, the environmentalist President, Theodore Roosevelt, agreed with the need to create another major city on the West Coast and was persuaded to withdraw all Federal water and land rights in the Owens Valley allowing for the plan to move water to Los Angeles to go forward. Mr. Mulholland, a self-taught engineer, was assigned as the Chief engineer for the construction of the project.

One hundred and thirty five thousand acres of land had to be bought for the protection of water rights for reservoirs and the aqueduct. This accomplished, Los Angeles investors owned 85 percent of all the property in Owens Valley. Supporters of the project argued that *"the greatest good for the greatest number"* would be achieved – President T. Roosevelt's motto.

In July of 1907, Joseph Lippincott resigned from the Reclamation Service and immediately went to work, at nearly double his government salary, as Wm Mulholland's assistant.

J. B. Lippincott and William Mulholland look over an intake valve somewhere along the aqueduct line (LADWP photo)

As the project got underway, the *"Elizabeth Tunnel"*, under Elizabeth Lake, was the first phase of construction begun in October of 1907. It was almost 27,000 feet in length and ten by twelve feet in diameter, mostly through solid granite. It was begun first because it was thought it would take five years to complete – though it was completed in a record time of forty months. It was thought that crews could dig an average of 16 feet of tunnel per day but crews reportedly dug more than 22 feet per day while constructing the five mile tunnel, finishing it twenty months earlier than the estimated five years. Elizabeth Lake is located almost above the center of the tunnel which is 250 feet beneath the surface of the ground below the lake. The tunnel was dug from both ends and electric locomotives were used to remove the debris. From the Los Angeles Department of Water & Power description of the work we read:

> *"The formation at the north half of the tunnel was very much broken and consisted mostly of decomposed granite. Much of the ground was very heavy, requiring close timbering and in numerous places the tunnel had to be re-timbered two or three times. Large flows of water were encountered and also swelling ground. The excavation of this portion of the tunnel was most difficult and called for courage, skill and persistence. At 1,117 feet from the North Portal, large fissure filled with sand and water was encountered which broke through the face of the tunnel and could not be passed from that side. This caused considerable delay. This running water and sand was finally overcome by driving overlapping steel rails in advance of the heading, and closely following with careful excavation and timbering. Mr. John Gray, superintendent for the north end, has accomplished a remarkable work in the driving of this half of the tunnel without further mishap."*

Crew at the north portal of the Elizabeth Tunnel (Bledsoe/LA DWP photo)

The DWR description of the construction continued with:
"The south half of the tunnel was ideal tunnel ground and require little or no timbering. The lining of the tunnel was started in May 1911. Rock crushing and mixing plants were erected at both portals."

A reservoir at Fairmont, north of Elizabeth Lake, was put in place at the north end of the Tunnel and as the water left the tunnel, it continued through two power plants in San Francisquito Canyon and on to the San Fernando Reservoir. The total distance of the entire aqueduct was to be 233 miles – all of which was gravity flow, with no pumping required. At the time it was the longest aqueduct in the Western Hemisphere.

This Alzola Family photo read: *"Fairmont Reservoir – where the Los Angeles Aqueduct from Owens Valley ends"*

In a 1913 publication, HERE ROAMED THE ANTELOPE, written by the students of the Antelope Valley High School in Lancaster, they wrote of one of the great construction projects in their area, and their era. This portion of their book reads:

"The Los Angeles aqueduct entered the Valley north of Neenach. Across the Valley it consisted of ten miles of nine foot steel syphon, skirting the foothills; five miles of covered concrete ditch, with four small siphons, and four tunnels; then the natural reservoir at Fairmont, and five miles of solid concrete tunnel extending under Elizabeth Lake. Since the first load went out of Lancaster, October 2nd, 1907, there has been constant hauling;

sometimes as many as fifteen teams going out a day, until the freighting from here was finished about two months ago. Millions of sacks of cement, as well as hay, machinery, grain, provisions, steel, portable houses, lumber, gypsum and even pebbles and sand, comprising the loads. The usual teams were of from twelve to sixteen mules, but one twenty-mule team hauled for a while, carrying five hundred and twenty-five tons of cement. At this time fifty-two carloads a month was the record. This vast amount of material was stored in the warehouse at Lancaster."

The Alzola Family's new Ford on the rim of the Fairmont Reservoir - 1930

Mark Reisner wrote:

"The aqueduct would traverse some of the most scissile, fractionated, fault-splintered topography in North America. The city of Los Angeles would build 120 miles of railroad track, 500 miles of roads and trails, 240 miles of telephone line, and 170 miles of power transmission line. The concrete making capacity of Los Angeles was not adequate for this one project so a huge concrete plant would have to be built near the limestone deposits in the Tehachapi Mountains. Since there was virtually no water along the entire route, steam power was out of the question and the whole job would be done with electricity; therefore two hydroelectric plants would be needed on the Owens River to run electric machinery that a few months earlier had not even been invented."

Workers came from all over the world to work at the high paying aqueduct jobs that would last for several years. The jobs not only paid well but provided food, shelter and medical care. Numerous workers lived in construction camps in the Owens Valley, near the communities of Tehachapi, Mojave, Rosamond, Lancaster, Fairmont and Neenach with some staying on and homesteading near those areas.

Fifty-seven construction camps with water, power and telephones were built. The existing railroad was extended north from Mojave and a nine-mile temporary track was laid to Jawbone Canyon where the Monolith Cement Plant was built to furnish the 1,500,000 cubic yards of concrete needed. The cement plant was built east of Tehachapi along with the new village of *"Aqueduct, California"*. Del Troy of the Tehachapi Heritage League described this community as follows:

> *"Streets were surveyed, sewer and domestic water systems were installed and an excellent artesian well supplied abundant water. Within a short time the city of Los Angeles had constructed 21 dwellings of one to six rooms each and six frame tent houses. Seven bunkhouses accommodated 130 bachelors. A kitchen and mess hall, as well as a hospital building had been constructed. A schoolhouse was built after the Aqueduct School District was formed on February 4th, 1909. When the post office was opened in 1910 the federal government changed the name of the town to 'Monolith' which was what the Southern Pacific Railroad was, by that time, calling its siding at that location. Presently (2007), the cement plant is still in operation but one would never know that a thriving town once existed on the south side of the road across from this plant."*

According to the Smotherman Family of Three Points, another though smaller construction camp was located at Neenach where the post office had been located for some time. They had a good source of water already being piped down from the springs in the mountains to the south to a man-made lake that had been created there. Workers and mules were housed here. On their time off the men would often go prospecting for gold in the hills south of Neenach and many would quit their jobs as soon as they found a nugget or two – only to have to return to work when their luck ran out. A number of local residents worked on the line or hauled freight.

One of the *"boom towns"* was Fairmont, a small settlement in the valley just north of Hughes and Elizabeth Lakes, near the reservoir being built there. During the construction of the Owens Valley/Los Angeles Aqueduct, Fairmont grew to about 500 people. A rock plant was opened there where a volcanic ash product, from the remains of an ancient volcano, was crushed with equal parts of cement for use in building the tunnel. A post office had been established at Fairmont in 1888 with the same name as a town in Illinois and continued to distribute mail until 1939. A well known resident and merchant of Fairmont in the early days was Harry Libbie who had a wonderful old general store there. It included everything from the usual jars of candy to Model T parts that hung high on the walls. There was a room alongside the store where Libbie, also Justice of the Peace, would hold court and where fist fights were known to break out during cattle rustling trials.

This road grader, located at a private residence in the Antelope Valley, was used on the building of the Aqueduct

Among the workers to settle in the Antelope Valley was the Harry Womersley and family. Mr. Womersley had come to America from Otley, Yorkshire, England in 1870 at the age of sixteen. After acquiring a wife, Maria, in Illinois, and through the years working his way across the country, he was hired by the contractor to build the twelve miles of the Los Angeles Aqueduct from Fairmont to Neenach. The family homesteaded west of Neenach near 300th Street.

Thanks to Harry Womersley's grandson, Richard Hardaway of Lebec, we have Harry's story of traveling to Fairmont to set up a work camp in 1909:

> *"We left Los Angeles on the 8th of January after loading all the tools and equipment on twelve wagons with six mules or horses on each wagon. When we reached the Newhall grade we had to put twelve head of stock on each load to get over the pass in going through the canyon. We crossed the river forty times* (as they traveled up San Francisquito Canyon). *Just when we were ready to leave the canyon it started to rain so we had to stopover one day. After it stopped raining we made the grade and in going*

into the Antelope Valley, before reaching Fairmont, we ran into snow. To reach the place we were going we had to put six mules on a plow and make a start as it was the last day on which we had to start work to save the contract. We were six days in going the ninety miles from Los Angeles to Fairmont. (!!)

After a good nights sleep, we got out the plow team and low fresnoes (scrapers) *and set them to grading. I started camp by putting up what tents we had so we could have a place to sleep and a large tent to cook and eat in until we could build bunk houses and arrange things so that we could take care of two hundred men and one hundred horses and mules.*

The third day we were here it started to snow again. We had to sleep in the tents. In the night I woke up feeling something cold in the bed. I lit a lantern and found that the snow on top of the tent was melting and was coming through the tent and running down into the bed. With no other place to go we lived through it. In the morning it was a sight to see the horses and mules as they had never been in or seen such snow before. The snow lasted three or four days. We built a blacksmith shop and shed for the stock and carpenters came out to build the bunk house. After about a week, we had a steam shovel come to Lancaster. The freighter wanted $500 to take it out to the camp but I said we could move it for half of that amount so I took two men to Lancaster and took the shovel down (apart). *We loaded it on wagons and rebuilt it at Fairmont for less than one half. When I got back to camp, they had the bunk house built for the foreman on the job and one bunk house for fifty men. They built a good cook house and dining room then a large amusement hall to play billiards."* (and so the little settlement at Fairmont grew)

Construction Camp at Fairmont (Bledsoe/LADWP photo)

Steel pipe being hauled by 52-mule team, though 20-mule teams were more commonly used in most areas (Bledsoe/LADWP photo)

In an undated article, Ann Gregg of the West Antelope Valley Historical Society wrote:

> *"During construction, hauling was by mule team, truck, and tractor from the nearest railroad site to the job site. Sixteen 20-mule teams hauled material from the railroad at Lancaster west to the pipeline at Fairmont. In 1912, Howard Brothers of Lancaster brought a fleet of white trucks with hard rubber tires. Land trains consisting of tracked vehicles with large steering rollers in the front were tried, and found not to be successful. Several of these machines can still be seen around the valley.*
>
> *There are twenty-three inverted siphons on the aqueduct. These siphons were made of curved plates that were made, rolled, and punched for rivets in the East. They were then shipped to Los Angeles where some lengths were riveted into short sections before going by rail to the nearest siding. The pipe varies in diameter from eight to ten feet and in the lowest section is 1 1/8 inch thick. The highest portions are made from concrete pipe which is buried.*
>
> *The longest siphon is across the Antelope Valley. In 1914, a cloudburst washed out the center of the Antelope Valley siphon. This caused a vacuum in the pipe resulting from the rapid outflow of water. This, in turn, caused the pipe to collapse. Most of the*

engineers thought the pipe would have to be taken apart and shipped back East for the plates to be re-rolled, and the pipe rebuilt. Chief Engineer Mulholland, however, had a much better idea. The break was repaired, and the water slowly let into the pipe. The pressure of the water was all that was needed to re-form the pipe. The same pipe is still in use today."

Mark Reisner wrote of the building of the aqueduct:
"The project was finished under budget and ahead of schedule and if you asked the men why, they would say it was because of Mulholland. He inspired all his workers with his loyalty and heroics. For six years he all but lived in the desert, patrolling the aqueduct route like a nervous father-to-be, giving advice, offering encouragement, sketching improvised solutions in the sand. He initiated a bonus system that shattered records for hard rock tunneling. He pitted them against the world's most illustrious tunnelers, the Swiss, who where digging the Loetchberg Tunnel at the same time (Reisner doesn't indicate who won). *He would eat with the men and complain louder than anyone about the food. To the city of Los Angeles he was honored more than by his men as to them he was Moses bringing manna to the desert."*

(A side note from Reisner: *"A man once trapped in the tunnel by a landslide was fed by rolling him hard-boiled eggs through a pipe."*)

Aqueduct workers pose for a picture

Hoisting machinery to put the pipeline in place (Bledsoe/LADWP photo)

Above ground pipeline

Underground pipeline being covered with concrete (Bledsoe/LADWP photo)

It should be remembered that much of the meager population of the Frazier Mountain area – Lockwood Valley, Hungry Valley, Gorman – got most of their supplies, mail and traveled from the railroad at Lancaster at this time. Therefore they would have seen and watched all the activity going on in that part of their world.

On November 5th, 1913, some 25,000 people gathered, with their picnic lunches, for the opening ceremonies of the Los Angeles Aqueduct. Excited citizens arrived on foot, on horseback, on a special train to the event that charged $1 round trip from Los Angeles, in automobiles, wagons and buggies. Pennants, a popular souvenir of the day, were selling for 10 cents and bottles of water were passed out. When Mulholland arrived a band played *"Hail to the Chief"*. Speeches were given with Mulholland giving credit for the project to Fred Eaton who dared to dream such an monumental effort. The raising of a United States flag gave the signal to open the spillway gates which took five of Mulholland's top assistants (Mackay, Van Norman, Reaburn, Hanson, Chaffee) to accomplish. As the water came rushing down the *"Aqueduct Falls"* and on into the San Fernando Valley the crowd rushed forward to dip their cups into the churning stream. Automobile horns beeped, hats were thrown in the air, handkerchiefs, pennants and flags waved. The sky was filled with bursting aerial bombs and rockets as horses reared in freight and the band played "Yankee Doodle Dandy".

"Aquduct Falls" to the east of the present Interstate 5

An upper segment was added to the *"Falls"* when the California Aqueduct was put in and the downhill water flow then became known as *"The Cascades"*. Ironically, by the time the aqueduct was completed, extraordinarily wet years followed and Los Angeles had plenty of water from its own resources – though the dry years followed as usual. The aqueduct had taken five years to complete with approximately five thousand men working in extreme heat and cold.

When the farmers of the Owens Valley began to feel the effects of the loss of water the *"Little Civil War in California"* began. A sign was erected north of Bishop that read: *"Los Angeles City Limits"*. The once lush green valleys of the Owens Valley became deserts and the lake had dried up by 1924. During the building of the aqueduct, and after it was completed, there were often attempts to destroy it with dynamite, causing much of the pipeline to be placed underground. Travelers known to be from Northern California were checked for dynamite if they traveled to Southern California. Men were hired who *"rode ditch"* every day of the week looking for leaks and sabotage though they more regularly encountered the dreaded rattlesnake.

One of the families from the area of Neenach that were involved with the aqueduct after it was completed, were the Andersons. James Anderson became a line rider or patrolman on the Aqueduct looking for needed maintenance and also to watch for those who would do it harm.

The portion Anderson checked was underground. Periodically the aqueduct would be shut down and the down time was used to check for needed repairs and damage inside the pipeline. Family members said Mr. Anderson would enter a manhole and walk the tunnel with a lantern to check it out. His wife, Julia, or daughter, Mattie, would help with this chore by walking the horses above ground from one opening to the next sometimes taking their turn at walking the damp, dark tunnel. Most often though, James would ride the surface to check for damage. His route was ten miles each way from his home at 259th and Avenue B.

Recent picture of the underground aqueduct pipeline

James Barnes settled in the West Antelope Valley about 1887 and when the Aqueduct came through he got a job working on the roads and his son, Pete, worked on the building of the aqueduct. Another of the Barnes sons, Roy, married Mattie Anderson and descendents of both families still live in the Valley.

When Chester & Zella Scott bought a homestead in the West Antelope Valley in 1915 they learned that a deal had been made with the local ranchers that they could draw water from the aqueduct for their livestock – no doubt in exchange for allowing the pipeline to be placed on their lands. Access valves were installed at various locations and the ranchers were permitted so much water per head of livestock. There was a trough with a float at these locations and as well they could fill a tank on a wagon or truck to haul to their cattle – a practice still honored today. It is doubtful if arrangements were made with farmers for the use of water from the aqueduct for farming purposes as dry field farming was still a viable method at that time.

From his book CADILLAC DESERT, Mark Reisner wrote:
"The irrigated acreage in the San Fernando Valley rose from three thousand acres in 1913 ... the year both the completion of the aqueduct and the annexation of the valley occurred ... to seventy-five thousand acres in 1918. The San Fernando Valley used three times as much aqueduct water as the city of Los Angeles itself, the vast part of it for irrigation. This news outraged the people of Owens Valley as their Valley turned to desert and the desert valley of San Fernando, owned by rich monopolists, bloomed. The San Fernando investors then began the biggest subdivision in the world. About the same time these same investors purchased the third-largest land empire in the history of the state ... Tejon Ranch."

One of the investment partners of Fred Eaton, the creator of the Los Angeles Aqueduct vision, was Harrison Gray Otis, who along with some other investors became an owner of Tejon Ranch in 1912. Otis was also the owner of the Los Angeles Times and ran many articles in support of the aqueduct in his newspaper.

With the opening of that first aqueduct Mulholland immediately began looking for a way to make use of the yet unused water rights from the Owens Valley and the Mono Basin to the north of Owens Valley. The *"Mono Extension"* was designed and worked on in the 1930's but World War II delayed the project. As a part of the *"Extension"*, it was decided that another reservoir should be added to the system and the San Francis Dam was built in San Francisquito Canyon.

The San Francis Dam, 205 foot high, was completed in March of 1926 – and then failed just two years later. The huge reservoir with eleven miles of shoreline emptied in a little more than one hour. A wall of water, initially 180 feet high, tore down through the canyon and through the Santa Clara River Valley, devastating the towns of Piru, Fillmore, and Santa Paula as it raced the 54 miles from the dam site to the ocean. The wall of water and debris was said to be still some 40 feet high when it reached the Pacific Ocean at Montalvo between Oxnard and Ventura some five hours later. Destroying everything in its way, between 400 to 600 people died. The catastrophe has been recorded as the worst man-made disaster in California history. Mulholland accepted the entire blame for the incident and the guilt left him a broken man.

View of the San Francis Dam and Reservoir in San Fransisquito Canyon

All that was left standing following the collapse of the St. Francis Dam

When actor and author, Will Rogers, went to the Owens Valley to do a film in the 1930's, he wrote:

> *"Ten years ago this was a wonderful valley, with one-quarter of a million acres of fruit and alfalfa. But Los Angeles had to have more water for its Chamber of Commerce to drink more toasts to its growth, more water to dilute its orange juice, and more water for its geraniums to delight the tourists, while all the giant cottonwoods here died. So now this valley is a valley of desolation."*

Norman L. Ross shared this observation, written by his father in the 1930's, as he described the San Fernando Valley before the Aqueduct:

> *"The valley floor was covered with sagebrush and cactus as far as the eye could see; peopled with jackrabbits, coyotes and rattlesnakes, nothing to say about the abundance of smaller animal and insect life. It was not until the advent of the Owens River Aqueduct that San Fernando Valley commenced to grow in earnest. The water brought wastes into rich orchards, enormous fields of alfalfa, beans, tomatoes and so forth. Taking the water from Owens Valley and bringing it to the San Fernando has transformed both of them within twenty years time. The first, once green for a length of some eighty miles is drying up rapidly, and the four main cities of that valley to the north have become small villages whose population dwindles from year to year. The opposite happened in the San Fernando Valley and today it is one of the richest valleys in the entire state."*

Work on the Mono Extension began again in 1953 and was completed in 1970. A second aqueduct was placed parallel to the first, though both pipelines come together and the water runs into the Lake Elizabeth Tunnel. These combined aqueducts provided seventy percent of Los Angeles' water with the other thirty percent from wells in the San Fernando Valley. This percentage changed when water was brought in from the Colorado River and later the California Aqueduct system.

In the early 1920's, Mulholland was already lobbying for the aqueduct from the Colorado River. This effort was temporarily defeated by wealthy Los Angeles investors in Mexico. When the first Colorado River aqueduct was completed the city was planning a second Colorado aqueduct, eyeing the Feather River 600 miles to the north and rivers as far away as Oregon and Washington. Between the arrival of Wm Mulholland in Los Angeles, and his death, the city grew from a town of fifteen thousand into the then most populous desert city on earth.

Inyo County and the City of Los Angeles signed an agreement in 1991 by which the Owens River and valley groundwater would begin to be reestablished – though the process is a slow one.

XXVIII – THE CALIFORNIA AQUEDUCT

In the mid-1900's the need for water in the southern portion of this state brought about the most gigantic water development program ever undertaken by man. With most of the State's water in Central and Northern California and a good deal of the State's agricultural lands and population in Southern California, the decision was made to move the water into a series of reservoirs. The effort was known as the *"California Aqueduct"* or the *"Feather River Project"*, as that river, north of Sacramento, was the source of the water. Plans were actually begun earlier in the century after it became apparent that the Owens/Mono Aqueduct and a Colorado River water project would not provide sufficient water for the future of Southern California.

In his book CADILLAC DESERT, Mark Reisner explains the shortage of water in the San Joaquin Valley as follows:

> *"By 1930 the San Joaquin Valley had exhausted their access at that time to a hundred centuries worth of groundwater – in a generation and a half. They did what any pressure group usually does; run to the politicians they ordinarily despise and beg for relief."*

The *"Great Depression"* and Second World War delayed plans until the 1950's. Such an immense project had never been attempted in the United States and there were those in both the Northern and Southern California that vehemently opposed it. The Feather River in Northern Sierras is the Sacramento River's main tributary. However, in the winter of 1955 California was hit by the most severe flooding since the monumental deluges of 1861-62. As houses floated toward San Francisco, the enormous rainfall helped convince those in Northern California that flood control in their area was needed.

The project was begun locally in 1955. The first newspaper article located about the *"Feather River Project"* locally was written by Frazier Park resident, Grace Bradley, who was also the area correspondent to the BAKERSFIELD CALIFORNIAN. In June of that year she wrote:

> *"The last of five exploratory test holes for the Feather River Project drilled in the Lebec area is nearing completion. This is the second contract let for this purpose. The drilling started in the Pastoria Canyon east of Grapevine Canyon and continued across that section of the Tehachapi Mountains to Quail Lake. The five holes*

ranged in depth from 300 feet to 1200 feet accomplishing 25 feet a day using two shifts."

Core drilling at the base of Pastoria Canyon
(Grace Bradley photo)

It seems the drilling was on-going as in early October of 1960 Mrs. Bradley wrote:

"Current drilling concerns the area where the proposed tunnels for the Feather River project will pass through the mountains. Eight holes are being drilled to gain the knowledge needed to make accurate bids for the waterway if the bond issue, coming up on the November ballot, passes. They are using a diamond drill so that the drilling is uniform but the ground is fairly well broken.

The test holes are being drilled for a dual purpose, first to ascertain the condition of the underground strata and secondly to locate a solid foundation for a pumping plant site.

Farmers have stood helplessly by and watched the water level dwindle thirty to sixty percent in five years. With the construction of the Feather River Project four million acre feet per year will be the maximum capacity of the aqueduct. Of this more than two million acre feet will be secured for the San Francisco Bay area, San Joaquin Valley, San Luis Obispo and Santa Barbara. The newly formed Wheeler Ridge-Maricopa Water District will receive adequate water from the project.

If the bond issue for the Feather River Project doesn't pass in this November election it will take another two to four years to formulate another plan or project.

Of the three tunnels, one will be 2,400 feet in length and three holes will be drilled. The second will be 2,800 feet and three holes will be drilled. The third tunnel is only 1,200 in length and will need only one hole drilled."

A proposition was placed on the ballot in the state-wide election of November 1960 to issue $1.75 billion in general obligation bonds to be paid off by the water users. California's North-South regional rivalry was a strong factor in the election. The proposition was narrowly approved when the voters of Southern California outnumbered those from Northern California. California Aqueduct historian, Mark Reisner, wrote of that election:

> *"When the votes came in, 48 of the 58 counties in the state had voted against the bonds but the populous counties in the artificial paradise of So Ca all went heavily for the project. It was, after all, early November, and they hadn't seen real rain since April!*
>
> *About seventy percent of the original works of the State Water Project were financed by the LA Metropolitan Water District's customers. Actually they paid for the project twice: through daily water rates and through an assessment of 12 cents on every $1,000 of property value in the service area, which they paid whether they got water or not."*

Much of the project was paid for by those who would be using the water. Thirty-two public water agencies were created along and near the Aqueduct and they began their payments in advance of receiving the valuable resource. Former Wheeler Ridge-Maricopa Water Storage District Superintendent, John Opheim, explained how this was done in the Southern San Joaquin Valley:

> *"The 'Kern County Water Agency' was formed and under it nine member districts had to pay in advance for the amount of water they expected to use and in turn an estimated amount of money was collected in advance from farmers and cities as well. Therefore the Aqueduct was built based on "user-pay", not on tax dollars. The Los Angeles Department of Water & Power was the largest purchaser and the Kern County Water Agency, with its nine member districts, the second largest using nearly 30% of all the water moving through the aqueduct. The Federal Government paid the State for the costs of reservoir construction in flood*

control areas. Power production was to bring millions every year to the Project as well."

Some of the local water districts established are:

- The Wheeler Ridge-Maricopa Water Storage District starts just past Taft and extends east to the Edmonston Plant in Pastoria Canyon, south half way up Grapevine Canyon and then to the north of Mettler (220,000 acres)

- The Castac Water Storage District (within Tejon Ranch) is from Grapevine Canyon to Castac Lake

- Arvin-Edison Water Storage District is to the east of WRMWSD and is basically agricultural

- To the northwest of WRMWSD is the West Kern Water Storage District which includes Taft, Fellows and the oil fields

- Kern Delta Water Storage District extends to the north of Bakersfield

- To the south and east of the Tehachapi Mountains, in the Antelope Valley and near Mojave, the East Kern Water Agency was created with borax processing a top industrial use of the water.

The Arvin-Edison water storage facility was begun shortly after the proposition to build the aqueduct passed. It was expected to distribute some 200,000 acre feet of water annually to lands that were previously obtaining their water supply from underground. The receding groundwater table had induced the intrusion of water with high boron concentrations causing the removal from production of substantial amounts of irrigated land. The Arvin-Edison District is one of the most highly productive agriculture areas of the state and in 1960 had produced crops at more than $40 million.

In April of 1961 Mrs. Bradley wrote:
"Preliminary exploration and core drilling for the largest pumping plant in the Feather River Project and also, the largest in the world is being carried out on the Tejon Ranch by the Dept of Water Resources." (This would have been in the area of Pastoria Canyon just east of Grapevine Canyon where the massive plant is now located.)

Two exploratory tunnels were dug in the Garlock fault zone. The first of these pilot tunnels was some 350 feet in length. The second was to be 450 feet long but work bogged down in muddy, decomposed granite 335 feet into the side of the mountain. The exploratory tunnels were to furnish information for contractors who would bid on the tunnel jobs.

One of the cores that were drilled to study underground stability (Grace Bradley photo)

The purpose of the aqueduct was to move surplus water from the Sacramento-San Joaquin Delta southward. One of the first structures was the Oroville Dam on the Feather River north of Sacramento. It was completed in 1967 and is the tallest dam in the United States at 770 feet high and is 6,920 feet long at its crest. Locally, the State Water Project was to establish five pumping plants, four reservoirs and three power plants from the Southern San Joaquin Valley to the community of Castaic.

In September of 1964, the local newspaper THE HILL NEWS carried a powerful editorial written by the owner of the newspaper, Grantly Vaughn, Sr. He indicated that the project was the subject of considerable conversation and doubt amongst the local *"lay engineers"*. Portions of it read:

> *"Frankly, the Feather River Project, comprehended only in its barest terms, is described only faintly by the over-worked, watered-down-by-over-use, Hollywoodian adjective, 'stupendous'. Another such adjective, 'enormous', applies to the numbers and amounts of money, men, machines, time, effort, thought, and planning involved in this thing. And in spite of all the tremendous obstacles and difficulties, and the probability that on its*

completion in the middle 1970's it will be out-moded, it will be finished. It will, in the considered judgment of a large segment of the engineering profession, on its physical aspect alone, have legitimate claim to being the Eighth Wonder of the World.

We here on the Hill will witness a little history in the making because the Tehachapi crossing, as it is known, has given definite notice now that it is to be reckoned with. It is the toughest nut to be cracked in the whole of the project. And this one little tunnel is only the beginning. Gad! A dissertation on why this crossing was chosen, in relation to other apparently more feasible routes, would be beating a dead horse. (It would be interesting to know more about what he knew here.)

The Tehachapi crossing is what will concern us most, and our 50-yard-line box-seat view is the least important thing about it. There will be men, with and without families, coming and going, some to stay. The resulting effect on the economic and social life on the Hill should not be overlooked or minimized. A community as shakily organized as ours could be easily overrun and taken advantage of by those big-time operators who exploit a situation for all it's worth and leave nothing but a irreparable mess behind them.

No doubt about it, the country won't ever look the same again. There will be tragedy and loss. Old things, familiar things, useful things will be condemned and disappear. Springs will dry up. Roads going in all directions, fences, barriers, and warnings. Power lines and poles! And the big question: DO WE GET ANY WATER OUT OF IT ALL?!?"

In 1965, long-time local resident, Max Schmeling, arrived to work on the project. He had been hired by Perini Construction out of Pittsburgh, Pennsylvania as a *"walker boss"* to oversee the excavating, drilling, blasting and timbering (with steel) of the tunnels. Max had twenty years of experience in this line of work that he had been doing in mines in the *"Gold Country"*. His line of work was very dangerous and he remembered one instance when a man was killed when he returned to the blasting area too soon after dynamite failed to fire on time.

Mr. Schmeling also remembered that shortly after beginning work the Engineer's Union went on strike shutting down the project for about six weeks before an agreement could be made with them. Max related:

"The strike really hurt a lot of people who had just moved to the mountain. Local merchants such as Vern & Jean's Market and

> *Howard Lenke's gas station in the Frazier Park area were so great to give credit to all these newcomers in town until work started up again."*

Four years later, when Mr. Schmeling's work on the tunnels was completed, he and his family continued to live in Frazier Park and he continued to do mining work in the San Emigdio Mountains and throughout Southern California.

In December 1966 the first issue of the new local newspaper, THE MOUNTAIN ENTERPRISE, carried an article about the Aqueduct. Editor Jess Hawley was knowledgeable as to this huge construction project as he was a soils engineer on the building of Interstate 5 that was going on at the same time. The article reported:

> *"The California Aqueduct originates at the Sacramento-San Joaquin Delta and terminates 444 miles to the south at Perris Reservoir in Riverside County. It is the main Aqueduct in the State Water Project, which will supply water to homes, farms and factories in areas where two-thirds of California's population live.*
>
> *The Tehachapi Pumping Plant will pump more water higher than any other pumping plant in the world ... and will do it in a single lift. Lifting power will be provided by four 78,000 horse power pumps. Tests have shown that the pumps, designed by Department of Water Resources engineers and consultants will give 91 percent efficiency.*
>
> *Construction work is progressing on the last of the four tunnels, the Carley V. Porter Tunnel. It is 4.8 miles long and 20 feet in diameter and will require nearly four years to dig. Work on the tunnel began last year. The tunnel was named in honor of the Compton assemblyman who coauthored the legislation which set in motion the State's huge water project. Delivery of water through the 12 mile Tehachapi crossing is scheduled to begin in 1971."*

The same newspaper informed the public that the State Department of Water Resources was taking bids for the construction of discharge lines and control valves for the Tehachapi Pumping Plant. The discharge lines were to be two steel-lined tunnels with a finished inside diameter of 12.5 feet for a length of 4,600 feet and 14 foot diameter for a length of 3,400 feet at an estimated cost of $23 million. The article indicated that the construction of the tunnel would require excavation of 200,000 cubic yards of rock and earth, concrete fill of 111,000 cubic yards and 7,500 tons of steel tunnel liner. The work was scheduled for completion in August on 1970.

A second bid was being let for the designing, manufacturing, installing and testing of fourteen 48 inch spherical valves, including hydraulic and electrical control systems at the Tehachapi Plant. These were to be completed by December of 1971 at an estimated cost of three million. The Tehachapi Plant was to lift water 1,926 feet from the San Joaquin Valley through the discharge lines and a series of four tunnels from which it would flow by gravity through the mountains of Tejon Ranch. The plant was to lift nearly 110 million gallons of water per hour.

Also in December of 1966, the MOUNTAIN ENTERPRISE reported:

> *"Granite Construction Company has established an office in Lebec. The company is excavating and lining with concrete, tunnels #1, 2 and 3 in the Tehachapi Crossing of the Feather River Project. They are also constructing a permanent asphalt access road that will connect with the various water resources' facilities in the state."*

Besides building roads to connect facilities throughout the state, twelve miles of roads were built though rough terrain on Tejon Ranch. This road entered Bear Trap Canyon at Lebec and came out at the Tehachapi/Edmonston Pumping Plant.

An undated article from the Los Angeles HERALD-EXAMINER read:

> *"Work on the world's largest man-made waterway, the 826 mile-long California State Water Project, has reached the Tehachapi Mountains and is spreading to Los Angeles County. When completed the water will flow like a river of white gold, diverting more than 2.5 million acre feet of northern California water to the Southland each year."*

The same article gave some interesting information on the tunnels in relation to the Garlock earthquake fault. A portion of the article reported:

> *"Because of earthquake danger, the aqueduct is being built over the Tehachapi mountain tops in a series of four tunnels rather than being put through a single 26 mile tunnel. One earthquake along the Garlock Fault could, in a split second, dam the flow of the buried aqueduct. The first three tunnels are simply called Tunnels 1, 2 and 3. There will be a space between No. 3 and the fourth, the Carley V. Porter Tunnel ... a scant 100 feet ... which is where the Garlock Fault crosses. If there should be an earthquake, No. 3 tunnel ... which will be built with a slight downward slope ... should lift up causing small damage. The state has initiated a sophisticated project to measure crustal strain. Not only do such measurements help in the design of*

dams and aqueducts, they also aid in predicting earthquake possibilities."

Richard Hardaway, long-time resident of Lebec, worked for the California Department of Water Resources from 1961-91. He was the construction supervisor on the tunnels and later as the supervisor on the building of Pyramid Dam. He said that the DWR crew would work a continuous rotation of two weeks early shift, two weeks afternoon shift and then two weeks graveyard to vary everyone's hours.

Bob Gunderson - DWR Engineer (rt), and Pete Turner - the contractor (lt), inspect a blast area (CA DWR photo)

"Car muckers" Pete Turner, Bill Hellman, Bob Gunderson, Phil Skaggs (CA DWR photo)

Dumping muck quartz (CA DWR photo)

Lake of the Woods resident, Martin Vurpillat, an air compressor operator on the project, left this interesting description of one of the tunnels:

> *"I worked on the five-mile Porter Tunnel through the Tejon Mountains which runs from the Bear Trap Canyon area to the cement plant in the West Antelope Valley on Highway 138. We experienced a great deal of trouble with water and also had several cave-ins. The ground was broken into pieces due to many years of earthquake action so we had to line the five miles with steel rings every foot of the tunnel. We tunneled through several obvious faults and found sea shells 300 feet under the surface."*

Loren Brown worked on the north end of the Porter tunnel for four years as a miner doing drilling and blasting to create a 50' in diameter bore. He said most of the time they were setting the steel liner plates. He and fellow worker, Floyd *"Tex"* Walter, worked on the aqueduct for about 7½ years from about 1965-72.

South portal of Tunnel #2 at the Pastoria Siphon at different phases of construction. (CA DWR photos)

Local resident, Chet Rogers, a heavy equipment operator, also worked on the tunnels. He began commuting to the area in 1966 working at the Wheeler Ridge pumping plant, then called *"Windy Gap"* pumping plant, and later to the Quail Lake project where he was a foreman. Chet had to commute until housing opened up in the mountain communities. By this time, due to the *"Feather River Project"*, it was very difficult to find housing locally. The Rogers family found a house to rent only because the fellow living in it came down with Valley Fever and had to quit his job – one of the many dangers of working on the aqueduct.

The local communities did have their struggles with the immediate growth that the Feather River Project brought. A new school had to be built in Frazier Park and the Lebec community struggled with a serious lack of water due to the growth in that community.

From the Antelope Valley side, Chet Rogers ran a portable cement batch plant located at the entrance to the tunnel. The cement was delivered to a small narrow gauge diesel locomotive that hauled it into the tunnel in cars that would continue to mix the cement and could rotate to dump as needed. The wet cement had to be kept under 55 degrees so an ice plant was also located at the batch plant and crushed ice added to the concrete instead of water in the hot summer months. Rogers stated: *"The cooler the concrete the stronger it became."*

Mr. Rogers recalled the interesting transformation of Crain Lake into the present version of Quail Lake. Working on the project, Rogers said that the old Ridge Route Road always ran about where it is today – in front of the Kinsey or Quail Lake Mansion, but at a much lower level. In order to create a higher roadbed so that the lake could be filled to capacity, both the road and the yard of the mansion needed to be raised. Trees in the yard were removed, the yard raised, the trees replanted at the new elevation and new fencing put up. The road was originally raised 38 feet but when it flooded, an additional 12 feet in height was added for a total of 50 feet above the level of the original road.

For many centuries the Quail Lake area was a popular settlement for the native people of this area, providing excellent hunting opportunities. The new enlarged Quail Lake now has three miles of shoreline – three times the size of the original lake – which had been previously known as Crain Lake. The original Quail Lake was to the west of the present lake.

The largest tunnel of the four Tehachapi Tunnels, The Carley Porter tunnel, was begun at both ends. The Dravo, Atkinson & Groves (Grovers) Company started in from the Antelope Valley to the south and the Perini Construction Company began at Bear Trap Canyon on the north where there was also a construction camp. When the two sections of tunnel didn't quite meet, adjustments had to be made.

A steel liner was used to line the tunnel and a steel pipe with fans was in place in the tunnel as they moved along to send in fresh air. Fourteen foot shafts run parallel on each side of the tunnel to move the water out to a "*penstock*" – a gate where it is discharged. The fellows tunneling would work ahead of a "*shield*", and as they opened an area the shield was pushed ahead with huge rams to where they were working. As the shield was moved ahead huge steel rings would be put into place behind the shield. The rings were a 14' circle the outer layer being of 4" thick steel with 4" of steel webbing under that and another 4" steel circle under that creating approximately a 12' finished tunnel. The circles were brought in, in five pieces that would be welded and bolted together in the tunnel to create the liner.

The soil at the south end of the Porter Tunnel was very unstable due to earthquake activity. Long time local resident Gene Weigel, his parents owned the Frazier Park market, worked on the tunnel from the south end. Gene recalled that about two and a half miles into the Porter Tunnel the workers ran into the Garloek Fault that runs through the Tehachapi Mountains. Gene said:

> *"This caused water and mud to run into the tunnel like a river. The 'muck' ran into the tunnel for approximately a mile and had to be dug out by hand. It took them a year and a half to move beyond this point. Also, there were a lot of water problems in the north end of that tunnel. They would sometimes have to freeze the soil to keep it solid".*

Man standing on "*shield*" that becomes the lining of the tunnel (CA DWR photo)

Machinery placing a 20' form in tunnel (CA DWR photo)

Gene Weigel explained the blasting process. Holes were drilled in the center of where they planned to go next, then another circle around that, another circle around that and so on. The crew would move back maybe 1500' from the blast zone and listen as best they could to the number of blasts to determine if it was a good round. The center holes would be blasted first, then the next row around the center and then the next row around the outside edge – all within seconds of each other. The fans in the air line in the tunnel would be reversed to blow the smoke and dust out. The head of the crew, the *"shifter"*, would then go in to check for *"misses"* and when the workers returned the air would still be yellowish and gassy.

All the blasted debris was dug out with a *"Conway Mucker"* that traveled on rails. It had a front bucket like a backhoe bucket that was on chains. They would ram it into the debris to fill then lift the bucket chains and dump the load on a conveyor belt that would move it some 50 feet out to the rail cars that removed it from the tunnel.

For the amount of dangerous work done on the tunnels, accidents were minimal though one death was recalled. The most serious accident, which was well publicized, was a cave-in just before the Christmas holiday in 1967. In the early morning hours of

December 21st, seventeen workers and a state inspector were trapped some 125 feet below ground. To further complicate things there had been one of those three foot snowfalls down to the 4,000 foot level in the area the day before. All available personnel working on the tunnels were sent to help with the rescue. The BAKERSFIELD CALIFORNIAN reported:

> *"The tunnel collapse occurred at 5 a.m. trapping the night shift crew. Workers who were able to communicate briefly with the trapped men this morning said none was injured in the collapse of thousands of tons of earth and rock. The men reported they are warm and comfortable in the tunnel, with plenty of air. The men are trapped approximately 1,400 feet inside the bore. Efforts are being made to establish telephone communications through a four inch steel air line to the trapped men and it is hoped later to supply food through the same line. The bore is 25 feet in diameter and is shored by massive steel forms. Sixty-four feet of steel reinforcement collapsed under the weight of the earth slide early today. Rescue crews hope to reach the men by midmorning tomorrow. Rescuers must 'muck' through all the collapsed earth and metal, scooping up the debris mechanically and hauling it away in a tunnel car."*

According to Gene Weigel, who was not among those trapped:

> *"The south end of the tunnel had completed more footage than the north end – because of the water problems in the north end – so it was decided that they would redo some of the panels in the south end for a better alignment. When they removed three of the steel panels, leaving 12 feet of ground 'untimbered' (or unsupported) the cave-in began. Once the earth starts to moving there is no stopping it. The trapped men were working ahead of where the panels were removed but they had plenty of room and air to await rescue in."*

The Bakersfield newspaper of 12/22/67 reported on the rescue:

> *"A small band of hardhat sandhogs dug their way to glory Thursday in the underground. They began digging cautiously lighted only by an endless row of yellow globes. They used hand tools so as not to cause further collapse in the 80 foot long pile of rubble and 'shoring up' as they went. At mid-evening, rescue crewmen were huddled with some of the wives of the workers around a small fire near the mouth of the tunnel. The temperature had dipped below freezing and the muddy ground was hardening. Sixteen sections of steel lining the shaft collapsed 125 feet below the surface and sealed the men behind more than 70 feet of rubble and buckled steel. Rescuers worked with the fear that the steel forms lining the tunnel for the 1,400 feet to the point of the break, believed to be weakened by the breaching 64 foot*

section, might in turn collapse. Or worse, that further collapse might occur within the 25 foot chamber which confined the trapped men.

The entrapped workers set at once to dig a small drift tunnel through which a man might crawl alongside the shattered tube. Crews mostly with pick and shovel pushed toward each other from each end, digging the drift tunnel paralleling the aqueduct tunnel. Two other rescue efforts were pushed at the same time. Earth bore specialists were rushed from Los Angeles with California Highway Patrol escort to bore the 125 feet into the shaft from above. Contact was made at the same time with outfits who were to race to the scene with a huge auger device to attempt a rescue by boring through the collapsed earth within the tunnel itself.

The least spectacular effort, which at first appeared least promising, paid off with the rescue of the trapped crew. The trapped men were reached 19 hours after the collapse. They were pulled to safety through the narrow drift tunnel paralleling the aqueduct bore and brought out of the tunnel at 12:25 a.m. to be greeted by wives and fellow workers."

Nighttime photo of men preparing to enter the tunnel (Bakersfield Californian photo)

At the end of the newspaper article mention was made that Governor Ronald Reagan and State Water Resources Department Chief, William Gianelli visited the site that evening – in the presence of more than forty media personnel. The rescued men were from Lebec, Frazier Park, Lake Hughes, Bakersfield and Lancaster. The Bakersfield newspaper reported that the men were given a paid vacation through January 1st.

The next issue of the weekly MOUNTAIN ENTERPRISE reported: *"Maintaining a sense of humor throughout the entire ordeal, the men had a pool going to guess how long it would take to gain their freedom. The thought of never being rescued was put completely out of their minds from the first. Asked if they saw the governor ... they said: 'no but that he would have gained a few votes if he had just come down and talked to us through the communications tube, but did not'. Hill residents trapped in the cave-in included George Straub, C. A. Berenek and Charles Schroeder of Frazier Park and Lloyd Borud of Lebec. Contrary to early reports the men didn't receive a weeks vacation and double pay following their experience but were back on the job a few days later ... minus a few who decided the work wasn't quite their type.*

As most Hill residents know, much of the tunneling is being done near the San Andreas fault (and the Garlock Fault) *and the ground is all fractured. The disaster was the second major cave-in involving the same crew in the past two months."*

The Aqueduct leaves Tejon Ranch and the Tehachapi Mountains via Oso Canyon and the *"Oso Pumping Plant"* on the north side of the West Antelope Valley. From there the canal splits with one canal, the *"East Branch"*, going to the *"Alamo Power Plant"*, first known as the *"Cottonwood Plant"*, where it is sent on through the Antelope Valley and to Silverwood Lake in the San Bernardino Mountains. The East Branch ends at Lake Perris in Riverside County which supplies water for San Bernardino, Los Angeles, Riverside and San Diego counties.

The Alamo Power Plant in the Antelope Valley (CA DWR photo)

Distance view of the Alamo Power Plant and Aqueduct
coming from Oso Canyon (CA DWR photo)

The water through the *"West Branch"*, travels to the Quail Lake *"Balancing Pool"* – not technically a reservoir, then through the *"Peace Valley Pipeline"* where it drops 650 feet to spin the turbines at the Warne Power Plant. The water then rests in the Pyramid Lake Reservoir before it drops down through the Angeles Tunnel and into the Castaic Power Plant where it runs powerful turbines and is then stored in the Castaic Lake Reservoir. The Castaic Dam is 425 feet high and 4,900 feet long and the reservoir is a major water source for Ventura, Los Angeles and Orange counties.

The MOUNTAIN ENTERPRISE of February 1967 reported on the purpose of the Hydro Power Plant between Pyramid and Castaic. It reads:

> *"A recent agreement between the Los Angeles Department of Water and Power and the State Department of Water Resources launched what will be not only the largest DWP hydro development, but also one of the biggest pumped-storage power projects in the United States. The $225 million power development will be on the California State Aqueduct between Pyramid Reservoir and the Castaic Reservoir about 20 miles from Los Angeles. It will provide an 'on peak' power capacity of 1,250,000 kilowatts.*
>
> *The power development will take advantage of a 1,063 foot drop in elevation on the West Branch of the Aqueduct after it crosses*

the Tehachapi Range. The power generated will be used by the DWP Power System customers, and also by the State to pump water on uphill portions of the Aqueduct.

The power plant will include six generating units, each of 200,000 kilowatts, and a pump-starting unit of 50,000 kilowatts, which can also be used for power generation. The 50,000 kilowatt unit will be installed in 1970 or 1971. The first two of the larger units are scheduled to go into operation in 1973 and 1974 to meet the growth of peak load demand on the DWP electric system.

Use of power reaches a peak in Los Angeles usually during periods of one to two hours a day in winter, and six to eight hours per day in summer. The Castaic Power Plant will operate, and water will be flowing down the West Branch of the State Aqueduct through the power plant, during these peaks. During off-peak periods, the water will be stored at the higher level of Pyramid Reservoir.

The Castaic Project will have an interesting 'pumped storage' feature ... one of the largest in the nation. The six principal generating units will be reversible as pumps so, if necessary, water can be pumped back uphill from Castaic Reservoir into storage in Pyramid Reservoir during off-peak periods and re-used to generate power during peak periods of use."

Costs of the 'West Branch' alone were:

Canal, pipeline and tunnels	$82,087,000
Oso Pumping Plant	15,236,000
Pyramid Power Plant	27,303,000
Pyramid Dam and Reservoir	32,268,000
Castaic Power Plant	24,163,000
Castaic Dam and Reservoir	103,442,000
Total	$284,499,000

Bids for the Castaic Dam and Reservoir were advertised in the same issue of the MOUNTAIN ENTERPRISE as follows:

"The job is to construct a zoned earthfill dam 335 feet high with a crest length of 5,200 feet. The embankment will require 42.5 million cubic yards of earth fill and 100,000 cubic yards of concrete. The dam will form a reservoir with a capacity of 350,000 acre feet and surface area of 2,630 acres. It will have a shoreline of 33.6 miles. The reservoir behind Castaic Dam will be the terminal reservoir for the West Branch of the California Aqueduct. Work under this contract is scheduled for completion in October 1970."

In 1967, Frazier Park resident, Gene Weigel, started working on the Tehachapi Tunnel and said he was fired three times in the first week. It seems you would get laid off, get extra lay-off pay and then get hired right away by someone else that needed workers, over and over. Gene said that this was called being *"tramped"*. He belonged to the Union and made $300-500 a week – very good wages then. They received living expense, travel expense and made $6-8 an hour back when the minimum wage was $2.50 an hour. Mr. Weigel also took advantage of the unemployment pay and sometimes would not take another job to go off for a while to do some prospecting, mining, hunting or fishing. He worked for Dravo, Atkinson & Groves on the north end of the Carley Porter Tunnel and sometimes for Green Construction, one of the contractors building the Interstate between the new Pyramid Lake area and Castaic. *"There was plenty of work on the mountain in those days"*.

Then in October of 1967, the State Department of Water Resources advertised for bids on the construction of two exploratory tunnels at the site of the Pyramid Dam. The unlined tunnels were to be approximately 2000 feet with six test chambers. The Pyramid Dam was built to be 400 feet high with a 1,000 foot crest length. The capacity of the lake was to be approximately 173,500 acre feet with twenty miles of very scenic and mountainous shoreline surrounding it. The lake was and is located in the Los Padres and the Angeles National Forests in northwestern Los Angeles County.

The Pyramid Lake Reservoir was named for the pyramid shaped mountain that was created with the building of Highway 99. The rock or mountain can still be seen just below the dam. There is one large pyramid shaped mountain top in the lake that now appears as an island, though it is not the Pyramid shaped mountain that many think the lake was named for. The old Highway 99 enters the lake at the boat ramps on the north end and exits the lake under the dam at the south end. Actual construction of the Pyramid Dam was not started until the portion of Highway 99 that would be affected by the dam, and buried under the lake, could be incorporated into the new Interstate highway being built to the east high above the lake.

> The HERALD-EXAMINER reported:
> *"Sixteen miles north of Castaic ... halfway to Gorman ... markers have been placed where Pyramid Dam and Reservoir will be built. The 27.8 million dollar project will obliterate a portion of Highway 99 and the road is being relocated. Markers have also been placed where the eight-mile-long Angeles tunnel will be built to connect Pyramid and Castaic Reservoirs. Power plants to be built at Castaic and Pyramid alone will generate more electrical energy than Hoover Dam.*

The flow of the mighty, man-made river will be regulated from a computerized master-control room in Sacramento. A panel, with a detailed layout of the aqueduct, will line one wall. By pushing a button, engineers will be able to stop the flow of water at key points in case of an emergency."

Work beginning on the dam with Pyramid Rock just to the south (Hardaway)

Blasting on hillside above the dam (Hardaway photo)

Aerial view of lake filling from above the dam – showing the portion of Highway 99 that is now underwater and Liebre Mtn in the distance (Hardaway photo)

Pyramid Dam spillway (Hardaway photo)

The William E. Warne Powerplant at Pyramid Lake was named for the second director of the State Dept of Water Resources. The plant was designed to recover part of the energy required to pump water over the Tehachapi Mountains at the Edmonston Pumping Plant. It safely creates nonpolluting hydroelectric energy and heat pumps transfer heat to and from the lake providing heating and cooling as needed. Most of the plant is built below ground, with earth piled up on three sides to provide insulation.

The power plant at Pyramid Lake in the snow

Ariel view of Pyramid Lake – 1987 – dam at upper right

Another bid in February of 1967 called for development of the Oso Pumping Plant site on the Kern-Los Angeles county line. The work was to include excavation of the plant bowl, construction of access roads and construction of a general drainage system. Required would be the excavation of 1.14 million cubic yards of rock and earth, 15 million gallons of water for compacting the embankment, 138,000 cubic yards of compacted embankment material, 20,500 tons of aggregate base material, 6,000 tons of asphalt concrete and 8,000 cubic yards of air blown mortar. Work was scheduled to be completed in December of 1967. In June of 1967 a $2,250,000 contract was awarded to Newport News Shipbuilding and Dry Dock Company of Newport News, Virginia for furnishing and installing the pumps at the Oso Plant.

In April of the same year the State Department of Water Resources awarded a $2,229,350 contract to Allis-Chalmers Manufacturing Company of San Francisco for furnishing and installing ten pumps at the Buena Vista Pumping Plant which was to be located 24 miles southwest of Bakersfield on the southwest side of Buena Vista Lake. Construction of the intake channels at this plant began in 1965. The Buena Vista Plant was to lift the water 204 feet enroute to the Tehachapi/Edmonston Plant.

The Buena Vista Pumping Plant (CA DWR photo)

Also in April of 1967, the bid was let for nine pumps at the Wheeler Ridge Pumping Plant, to be constructed 23 miles directly south of Bakersfield and to be completed in June of 1971, and in the same bid seven of the planned fourteen pumps at the Tehachapi Pumping Plant, each with a capacity of 315 cubic feet per second, to be completed in March of 1972.

> (A side note: Historically the Kern River flowed into Buena Vista Lake but now enters the California Aqueduct at an intertie before it reaches that lake.)

In August of 1967 the local newspaper announced that Yuba Industries of Benicia was awarded a contract for $2,047,609 to install six 66" and thirteen 90" pump discharge valves and the operating control systems for the Buena Vista and Wheeler Ridge Plants. An 18 million dollar contract was let in October of 1967 for the construction of 27 miles of concrete-lined canal, siphons, checks, overchutes, highway and bridges from the Buena Vista Plant to the Wheeler Ridge Pumping Plant.

In October of 1967 the bid was awarded to a Pennsylvania company for three 48" and six 66" pump discharge valves at the Wind Gap Pumping Plant. In an interview with John Opheim, the former superintendent of the Wheeler Ridge-Maricopa Water Storage District, he said that the gap in the hills was caused by the winds coming out of Grapevine Canyon. The ridge is possibly the result of it being a sand bar at the end of the ancient lake that once covered the valley. The soil of that ridge has long been removed by a large sand and gravel company. Mr. Opheim also indicated that the aqueduct was originally suppose to tunnel through the mountains at Grapevine Canyon but it was determined that there was or had been too much seismic activity in that canyon so new access agreement had to be made with the Ranch and the Edmonston Pumping Plant was placed east of Grapevine Canyon.

The Wind Gap (Chrisman) Pumping Plant at Wheeler Ridge looking to the south
The pumps push the water to a height of 518' for a distance of 1,963'. (CA DWR photo)

The 12 ½' discharge lines at the top of Wind Gap looking to the north. From here the water flows southeast by gravity to the Edmonston station. (CA DWR photo)

In February of 1967, bids were also let for the construction of an overlook at the Tehachapi/Edmonston Pumping Plant. The work included an observation building with restroom facilities and a lower vista overlook with benches and sun shelter, etc. for public access. It would seem that the State felt that an area was needed for the public to watch the building of this unusual plant.

In May of 1967 the bid was advertised for the construction of the actual Tehachapi Pumping Plant at an expected cost of $17 million. The job was to construct a *"U"* shaped plant designed to house fourteen pumps. The work was to require approximately 160,000 cubic yards of concrete and 4,000 tons of steel. In July of 1967 the MOUNTAIN ENTERPRISE the reported:

> *"The contract for the building of the Tehachapi Pumping Plant was awarded to the Atkinson Company of San Francisco in the amount of $19,638,790. The work will involve grading the site, doing drainage work building a steel superstructure, constructing seven 48" diameter pump discharge pipes in each wing and doing electrical and mechanical work. 180,000 cubic yards of concrete and 4,000 tons of structural steel will be used.*

A $12,000,000 contract for seven centrifugal pumps at this plant was also awarded to the Pennsylvania company in October of 1967.

The Tehachapi/Edmonston Plant is the largest pumping facility of the State Water Project. It consists of 14 motor-pump units, each standing over 65 feet high and weighing 420 tons. Seven units are located in each of the two wings that extend northward from the plant. The plant is a split facility, where the two sides can operate independently of each other. The aqueduct is 70 feet deep where it comes into the plant, at the forebay, to allow for smooth intake of water to the pumps. Trashracks keep debris out of the system. Each of the two main discharge lines contains 5.5 million gallons of water at all times. The building itself is an amazing six floors most of which are underground with the control room on the top floor.

> According to the BAKERSFIELD CALIFORNIAN:
> *"One of the pumps alone can lift 2,356 gallons of water every second up 1,923 feet to the top of the mountain. When the 14 pumps are installed and operating at capacity, they will together lift two million gallons of water a minute ... greater than any other pumping plant ever designed. An 80,000 horsepower electric motor is required to operate one pump. The motor is mounted atop the pump in each station and the motor and pump together tower as high as a six-story building. Power supplied to the plant is 230,000 volts and when pumping at the full rate, 830,000 kilowatts of power will be required."*

Upon leaving the surge tank, the water enters a 23.5 foot diameter line and flows ten miles by gravity across the Tehachapi Mountains through four tunnels. The tunnels are connected by siphons or cast-in-place pipe sections which provide worker access. At the Tehachapi afterbay in the West Antelope Valley, the water continues on to the bifurcation (split) of the Aqueduct into the East and West Branches.

Pipeline connecting the tunnels through Tejon Ranch (CA DWR photo)

The Tehachapi Plant and tunnel complex consists of the Pumping Plant, Tunnel #1, Siphon #1, Tunnel #2, Pastoria Siphon, Tehachapi Tunnel #3, the Carley V. Porter Tunnel and the Tehachapi Afterbay.

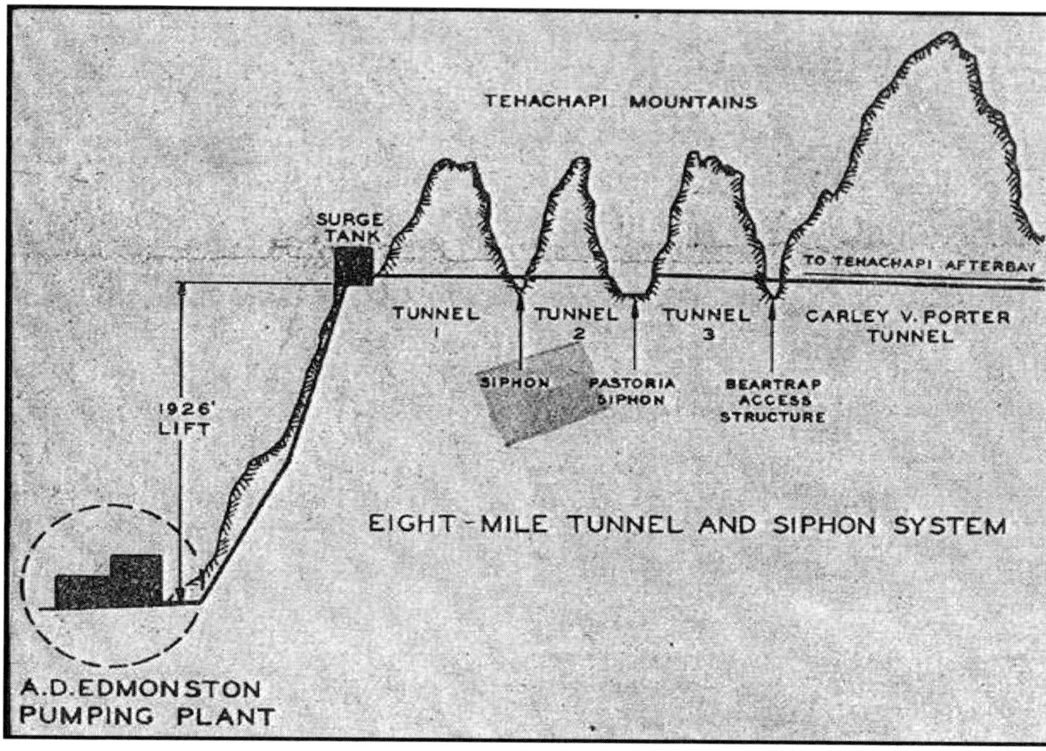

Tunnels and siphons through Tejon Ranch (CA DWR drawing)

In the fourth quarter of 1967 alone, about $66 million in construction contracts were put out for bid. The aqueduct resulted in about 25,000 new jobs in Kern County with some 75,000 persons involved in the *"support population"* for those workers and the supplies needed. As of the year 2000, the entire *"State Water Project"* includes 33 storage facilities, 24 pumping plants, and approximately 660 miles of canals and pipelines for a total cost of about $5.3 billion.

Big news in October of 1969 was that the miners of the Porter Tunnel had *"Holed Through"*. Lining the twenty foot diameter tunnel was being completed. This was to be followed by concreting the tunnel which was expected to take another eighteen months. The MOUNTAIN ENTERPRISE reported:

> *"The Porter Tunnel was named for Assemblyman Carley Porter* (Democrat from Los Angeles) *who helped author legislation for the Water Project. Mr. Porter was in Frazier Park a year ago August to view a concert directed by his son.*

As this phase of the Water Project ends, two more men have been added to the injured list this week. They are John Hicks and Wolfgang Braitsch, both injured in falls while working in the tunnel. Hicks was one of the men trapped for nearly two days before Christmas in 1967. Injuries now number 30 among the work crews in the tunnels but there have been no deaths reported. There will be a 'hole-through' party for all of the tunnel workers and their wives on Halloween night, October 31st, at the Castaways in Burbank."

The BAKERSFIELD CALIFORNIAN read:
"Champagne flowed freely yesterday as state dignitaries, dressed in suits, rubbed elbows with begrimed miners to celebrate the 'holing through' of a tunnel which will carry water through the Tehachapi Mountains to Southern California. Lt. Gov. Ed Reinecke flipped a switch at 11:10 a.m. to set off the blast which ripped through the remaining six feet of granite separating two mining teams working from opposite ends toward the middle of the five mile long tunnel.

Construction of the tunnel, one of four which will carry water through the rugged Tehachapis, has not been easy for the prime contractor, Dravo Corp. The tunnels lie over several earthquake faults, and in some cases the terrain shifted while digging was going on. The cave-in in December of 1967 set back construction work five months. Moreover, as the miners were digging through the hard granite, they often encountered surprise pools of underground water, slowing construction even more. In spite of the fact the tunnels are located over major earthquake faults, a DWR spokesman said the tunnels could withstand most tremors.

Nearly sixty state officials and newsmen made the journey to the 'holing through' spot three miles in the mountain and 900 feet underground, on two 'man tracks' which ran on a narrow-gauge, twisting track. Pools of water covered the tunnel floor and in many places the water dripped from the top of the tunnel wall.

The visitors got a taste of soft-rock mining after the explosion because the 'hole through' created the five mile long tunnel and ventilation fans were turned off to allow the change from two separate tunnels. While the fans were out of operation sulfur fumes (from the blast) *built up causing discomfort but no injuries.*

Though drilling of the tunnel is about complete, it still must be lined with concrete and reinforced. When all the work is finished about eighteen months from now, the tunnels will carry water at a rate of two million gallons per minute, or three billion gallons per day."

A 1970 issue of the BAKERSFIELD CALIFORNIAN reported:
"Nearly everything about the State Water Project is impressive ... it's size, capacity, feats of engineering and construction, capabilities and finally, cost ... three billion. From the Buena Vista Lake area near Taft the water will be lifted a total of 2,984 feet through four pumping plants and on through the Tehachapi Mountains ... one of the most ambitious lifting projects in the history of man.

Approximately 1,000 workers are still on the job from Buena Vista to Edmonston ... some employed by the Department of Water Resources and the rest by private contractors. The project has been responsible for contributing millions of dollars to the Kern County economy during the past five years in salaries, equipment and increased agricultural production. Recreation facilities at Buena Vista are expected to bring in added revenue."

By the time the Tehachapi plant and tunnels were dedicated, the plant was given its official name of the *"Edmonston Pumping Plant"*, after Arthur D. Edmonston, the State Engineer for the Division of Water Resources from 1950-55, who directed the early planning of the Central Valley Water Project,the predecessor to the California Aqueduct project.

View of the Edmonston Plant looking to the northeast (CA DWR photo)

View of the Edmonston Plant looking to the south (CA DWR photo)

This billboard was constructed at the Edmonston Plant
for the dedication in 1971 (CA DWR photo)

The Edmonston Plant was open for tours before and after the Dedication, which was held on October 7th, 1971. Governor Ronald Reagan pushed the button and after a second try, Northern California water finally reached the crest of the Tehachapi Mountains. A descendent of local pioneers, little Lori Wegis, presented flowers to the widow of A. D. Edmonston at the event and Caspar Weinberger, then the deputy director of the Office of Management and Budget, read a message from President Nixon who praised the project and all who had a part in it

Frazier Park resident, Gene Nelson, demonstrated the Westinghouse Main Unit starting motor at Edmonston (1971). Mr. Nelson worked as an electrician on the building and maintenance of the Edmonston, Oso and Warne plants. (Nelson Family photo)

In his book CADILLAC DESERT, Mark Reisner wrote:
"The A. D. Edmonston Pumping Plant, raises the water 1,926 feet ... the Eiffel Tower atop the Empire State Bldg ... a sizeable river of water running up hill. At their peak capacity, if it is ever reached, the Edmonston pumps will require six billion kilowatt-hours of electricity every year, the output of an eleven-hundred-megawatt power plant. Moving water in California requires more electrical energy than is used by several states. By the year 2000 it was estimated that it would cost at least $50 just to pump one average family's share over the Tehachapis, those same people would also be paying for water pumped sixteen hundred vertical feet from the Colorado River and water pumped from the ground."

In the Southern San Joaquin area of the Aqueduct there are four pumping plants:

- the Buena Vista Pumping Plant
- the John R. Teerink - Wheeler Ridge Pumping Plant
  (Teerink was the DWR Director in 1973-75)
- the Ira J. Chrisman - Wind Gap Pumping Plant
  (Chrisman was a member and later the chairman of the California Water Commission from 1960-76)
- the Arthur D. Edmonston - Tehachapi Pumping Plant

One more pumping plant, the Oso Pumping Plant, is located in the West Antelope Valley.

The four local reservoirs or lakes created are:
Buena Vista, Quail, Pyramid and Castaic.

The three local power plants are:

- the Alamo Power Plant near the Oso Pumping Plant
- Warne Power Plant at Pyramid Lake
- and the Castaic Power Plant at Castaic Lake

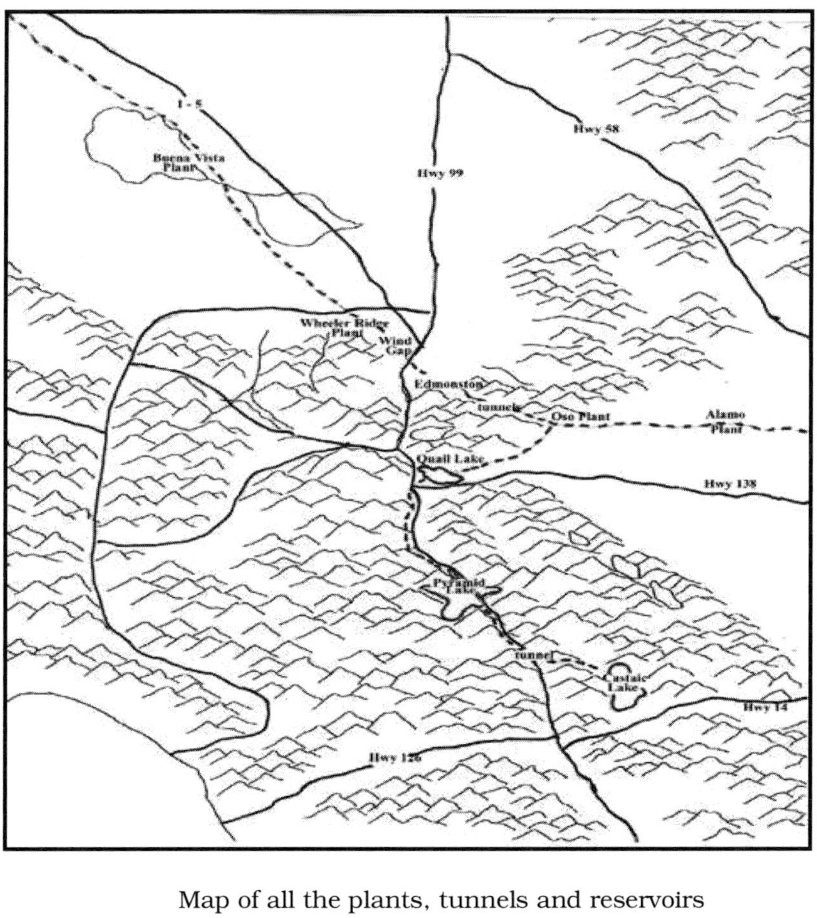

Map of all the plants, tunnels and reservoirs

In the early 1990's the largest Water Project Visitors Center in the State, Vista Del Lago, was opened at Pyramid Lake. It serves as the main place for the dissemination of information about the California Aqueduct.

The Vista del lago visitor center (CA DWR photo)

In 2001 the California State Water Project was recognized as one of the Twentieth Century's Greatest American Engineering Achievements. The only other engineering feat of the 1900's, in California, receiving the same award, was the Golden Gate Bridge.

Not only was all of the designing and building of the aqueduct, dams, tunnels and plants, going on but too the designing and building of the Water District facilities, training of personnel and the construction of the lines to their users. The demand for materials from water meters, valves and pipe of all diameters, to name some, was unprecedented. To meet the need a new fiberglass, reinforced plastic mortar pipe was developed and installed throughout California but failed within ten years. Over the years problems such as this have been resolved and the Aqueduct system is presently functioning quite well.

The amount of construction that was going on locally in the decade of the mid-1960's through the mid-1970's is almost more than the mind can conceive. Not only was there an interstate highway, an aqueduct, tunnels, a dam and reservoirs being built but at the same time so were the real estate developments of Pinon Pines, Pine Mountain Club and Los Padres Estates being planned and begun. A major portion of the cement for all of this building came from the new plant east of Gorman.

In looking back, other Twentieth Century man-made influences on the San Emigdio Mountain water resources have been the subdivisions of Frazier Park, Lake of the Woods, and Pine Mountain Club. The flow of water sources in these three communities were rechanneled to create ponds and improve the beauty of these mountain settlements as well as for fire safety – though nature removed the lake in Lake of the Woods during the rains in early 1962. The same is true for the proposed development of Tejon Mountain Village as *"Tejon Lake"* at Lebec no longer goes dry as it did for centuries past.

The careful study of this precious natural resource, water, will need to be kept foremost in all future considerations of growth and development in this mountain area.

EPILOGUE

As a tribute to those who settled in these mountains from earliest time and were blessed with abundant resources, the native people, the miners, the pioneers who came and invited others to follow, the men and women of the Forest Service who strive to protect it and those who created the communities, I dedicate this poem. B. K. Said wrote it for an event in the mid-1870's, to honored all Kern County Pioneers.

THE PIONEERS

So! In this, our Homeland
When the swelling human tide,
First touched its eastern limits,
And swept onward, far and wide,
Each succeeding human wave,
Driven by a feverish unrest,
Was forced ever, ever onward,
Toward the wondrous unknown West.

It surged through ancient forests,
Climbed many a mountain chain,
Swept on with resistless power
Over many a desert plain.
Sought out each lovely valley,
E'en those mighty forests felled,
Searched out the golden treasures
That the rock-ribbed mountains held.

Who! Are they in the forefront?
Who steadfast, fearless and brave
Press on with quenchless ardor,
In the face of the advancing wave,
Beset by countless dangers,
Facing death on every hand,
They search with tireless vigor,
For the treasures of every land.

The first! to see the beauties,
The first! to know the worth,
The first to take possession,
Of each virgin spot of earth.
They laid the deep foundations,
For the Nation of coming years,
They the vanguard of civilization,
For they were the Pioneers.

VOLUME IV
REFERENCES
(In addition to those listed in the text)

Black, Jack
BURIED TREASURES AND LOST MINES
OF SOUTHERN CALIFORNIA

Blakley, E. R. & Barnette, Karen
HISTORICAL OVERVIEW OF
LOS PADRES NATIONAL FOREST

Boyd, W. Harland
KERN COUNTY TALL TALES

Brown, William S.
HISTORY OF THE LOS PADRES NATIONAL FOREST

Campbell, Joyce
MOUNTAIN MEMORIES Articles

Clark, Howard D.
LOST MINES OF THE OLD WEST

Culbert, Virginia
SIX GENERATIONS IN CALIFORNIA

Dane, Edith
KERNLAND TALES Articles

Foote, H. S.
PEN PICTURES FROM
THE GARDEN OF THE WORLD

Gates, Paul W.
LAND POLICIES IN KERN COUNTY

Graham, W. J.
THE MYSTERY OF TEJON:
THE LOST PADRES MINE Article

Los Padres Interpretive Association
LOS PADRES NATIONAL FOREST
HISTORICAL OVERVIEW

Kahrl, Wm L.
WATER & POWER:
THE CONFLICT OVER LOS ANGELES
WATER SUPPLY IN THE OWENS VALLEY

Marmor, Jason
LEXINGTON:
VENTURA COUNTY'S FORGOTTEN MINING CAMP

Miller, Thelma B.
HISTORY OF KERN COUNTY

Newswanger, Stephen
LOS PADRES HISTORICAL TOUR GUIDEBOOK

Outland, Charles F.
MINES, MURDERS & GRIZZLIES

Powers, Bob
DESERT COUNTRY

Reisner, Marc
CADILLAC DESERT

Sproule, Wes
THE LOST MINE OF THE PADRES

Saunders, Charles Francis
THE SOUTHERN SIERRAS OF CALIFORNIA

Walton, John
WESTERN TIMES & WATER WARS:
STATE, CULTURE & REBELLION IN CALIFORNIA

INDEX

A

B

C

D

E

F

G

H

I

J

K

L

M

N

O

P

Q

R

S

T

U

V

W

X

Y

Z

ABOUT THE AUTHOR. . . .

After spending her first twenty-five years in the snows and lake country of Northern Minnesota, Bonnie Martin Ketterl and her first husband moved to California in 1965. When her husband was offered a teaching position at Cal State Bakersfield, when it opened in 1970, the family chose the cooler San Emigdio Mountains for their home.

Bonnie first worked locally for Tenneco, the developers of Pine Mountain Club, then for the realtors that sold the development and soon became the first recreation director for the Club. Next she went to work for the Tejon Ranch Company for five years as a secretary for the Engineering Division. Following that she went on to manage a local Savings & Loan Bank from 1980 – 90. Shortly after her marriage to James Kane in 1989 the newlyweds left the area for three years to live and work on the Navajo Indian Reservation in northeastern Arizona. Here Bonnie served as the administrator over the Lutheran Church sites and Jim managed the maintenance and mechanical needs of the facilities. While in Arizona Jim and Bonnie bought property on the Ute Indian Reservation in southwestern Colorado, so consequently the couple now live between a remote area of Colorado and the Frazier Mountain area of California.

Finding her love for history in college, Bonnie began collecting items of historic interest as soon as she moved to the Frazier Park area. She and her three sons, Jack, Jim and Joe have lived, worked, hiked and explored in and around most all of the local mountain communities. Bonnie has served on the founding boards of the Fort Tejon Historical Association, the Ridge Route Communities Museum & Historical Society and the Ridge Route Preservation Organization. The Ridge Route Communities Museum houses her entire collection of printed material, photos, slides, books and a number of items on display that she donated.

The author talking to a group in Mutah Flats – 1980's

P27 GEOLOGY OF LOST PADRE MINE
P42 NEENACH GOLD
P43 LOST PADRE MINE DESCRIPTION SUMMARY
P72 PS34 & ROMS
P93 LOCATION OF FRAZIER MINE